Acclaim for **Tom Horton**'s

AN ISLAND
OUT OF TIME

Also by Tom Horton

Tom Horton

AN ISLAND
OUT OF TIME

Tom Horton, environmental columnist for the
Baltimore Sun and author of five books about the
Chesapeake Bay, lives in Hebron, Maryland.

Chesapeake Bay

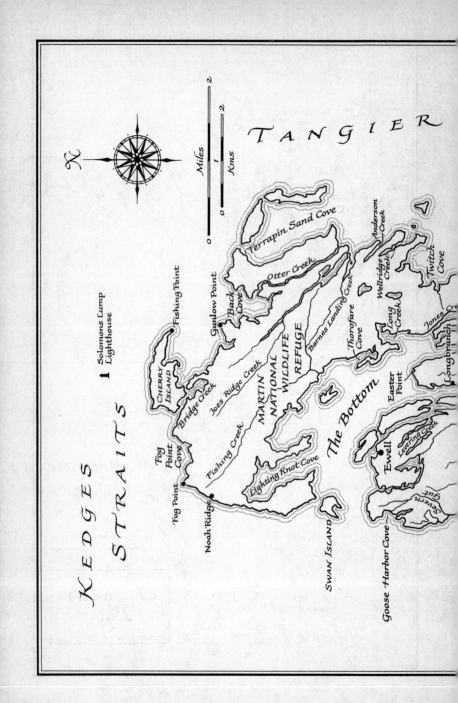

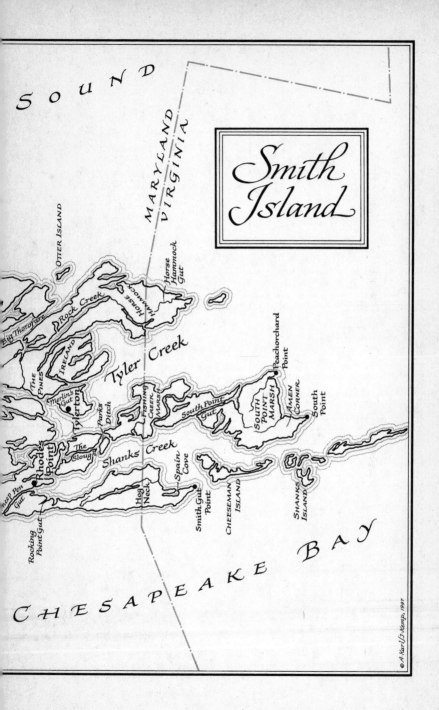

AN ISLAND
OUT OF TIME

A Memoir of Smith Island in the Chesapeake

Tom Horton

Vintage Departures

Vintage Books

A Division of Random House, Inc.   New York

FIRST VINTAGE DEPARTURES EDITION, JUNE 1997

Lyrics from the song "Dredgin' Is My Drudgery" (copyright, 1974,
Tom Wisner) quoted by permission of the author. Lyrics from
"I'm a Woman" by Jerry Leiber and Mike Stoller © 1961 Jerry
Leiber Music & Mike Stoller Music (Renewed). All rights reserved.
Used by permission of Leiber & Stoller Music Publishing.

Library of Congress Cataloging-in-Publication Data

Horton, Tom, 1945-
An island out of time : a memoir of Smith Island in the
Chesapeake / Tom Horton.
p.   cm. — (Vintage departures)
Originally published: New York : W.W. Norton, c1996.
ISBN 0-679-78105-6
1. Smith Island (Md. and Va.)—Social life and customs.
2. Smith Island (Md. and Va.)—Description and travel. I. Title.
[F187.C5H667 1997]
975.2'23—dc21 96-46869
CIP

Maps copyright © 1997 by Anita Karl and Jim Kemp

Random House Web address: http://www.randomhouse.com/

Printed in the United States of America

10 9 8 7 6 5 4 3 2 1

For Abigail and Tyler

Contents

CHURCH

ISLAND LIFE

YARNIN'

BOATS

JOURNALS

BETWEEN HOLLAND AND TANGIER

EPILOGUE

About This Book

THE LINES between fiction and non-fiction have become blurred, often controversially so. Therefore, a few words about how this book of non-fiction was done seem in order.

It is, above all, an attempt to faithfully represent Smith Island as the author experienced it, and as its people related it to him. There are no altered time sequences, scenarios drawn from other places, or conversations put down as I suppose they must have happened.

Sections written as if persons are speaking directly are based on my notes and tapes of actual conversations, and on published accounts. They have been edited and paraphrased for readability.

Some of these accounts are composites, i.e., based on multiple interviews and sources. There, I have used a generic name, such as "Pastors" or "An Old Lady," rather than a person's name. Those familiar with the island will readily identify actual individuals in some of these composite accounts, but they would be wrong to attribute every line to any one person.

In a few cases, an account was so nearly based on a single individual that I asked that person to review a draft, to see whether they would be comfortable putting their name on it, including a smattering of material inserted from interviews with others.

Acknowledgments

WITHOUT the patience and indulgence of Smith Islanders too numerous to list here, this book would not exist. For that, and the love and kindness they showed my family, I will always be in their debt.

Without the Chesapeake Bay Foundation, I could never have contemplated settling on Smith Island. I first met Don Baugh, their education director, in 1978, when the Foundation opened its Smith Island environmental education center and I came down to cover it for the Sun. One inveterate marsh mucker quickly recognized another, and we became fast friends.

On the occasion of my fortieth birthday in 1985, Baugh asked me what I wanted from the scant time left me. "Catch more fish, shoot more ducks, spend less time in offices," I said. The next year, he took me up on it, offering an education manager's position on the island—which brings me to my greatest acknowledgment.

My wife, Cheri, who has lived through five of these books now, had a different list of life priorities than a stepped-up harvest of fish and fowl, but consented to exile anyhow. Hang in there, babe. I know I promised the nineties would be your decade, but I didn't know the book would take this long.

Thanks also to my editor at W. W. Norton, Starling Lawrence, whose deft touch was exceeded only by his extraordinary forebearance with an author who kept promising much and delivering little. Also thanks to Lizzie Grossman, my agent, who believed in the book and braved aerial assault by the island's sea-gull hordes in coming down from Manhattan to scout the place.

INTRODUCTION

The Greatest Poets

THE DAWN comes up windy, shuddering the bedroom window. Senses kick in behind shut eyelids, divining the day's priorities from a puff of air. How hard is it blowing? From what direction? If it's southeast, better get out to the dock and drop the stern line on the skiff and let it swing, or it could swamp; and all my neighbors will likely be home early from work—easterlies make the crabs they seek bury out of reach in the bottom. Northwest? If it maintains from that direction, the tides won't make up high at all; forget any thoughts of taking the big workboat in shoal water tomorrow. Northeast? Sleep in. Cancel the pediatrician. The ten-mile run to Crisfield on the mainland would be just too rough and wet for a sick kid.

When you live and work on an island, you play these little chess games with Nature continuously. You become attuned, almost subliminally, to the winds and moon phases, to the ebb and flood of water and the lengthening and shortening of the days. And then you leave, one late-summer day, for the mainland, for the dream home you have bought, spacious and modern in a quiet, leafy suburb—good schools, neat playgrounds, near to major malls. Life there is so very much more convenient and predictable and controllable. Soon, you don't even notice the wind outside your bedroom window.

IN 1987 my wife, Cheri, and I decided to move to Smith Island, a fishing community of about five hundred souls in the middle of Chesapeake Bay. We rented our Baltimore row house for enough to cover the mortgage and took the two kids out of private schools. I would run environmental education trips for the Chesapeake Bay Foundation, which owned an old island house with twenty bunk beds. It meant a pay cut of about $35,000 a year from our mainland jobs (I a reporter, Cheri a social worker). Perhaps it seemed strange in Ronald Reagan's America of the eighties, with its emphasis on upward mobility of the most materialistic stripe; but in the midst of a prospering journalism career, I felt a need to shrink my prospects, narrow my horizons, and move on to smaller endeavors. As an environmental reporter I trekked through Amazonian rainforests, followed famine across Africa, and researched ozone destruction above Antarctica; but my roots were deep in less fabulous places.

A long time before I came to write about the overarching environmental issues of our day; well before I discovered Thoreau, John Muir, Aldo Leopold, and the other great naturalist-philosophers—before all that I just liked to muck around in the marshes of my native Chesapeake. I fished those soggy edges for striped bass, hunted the potholes for black duck, slogged through the clingiest black ooze this side of quicksand, and combed the wracklines for driftwood. I loved to hear the pock and slurp of waves in the marsh's honeycombed banks, to whiff the robust flatulence of its decaying organic matter, and watch sun and moon work filigrees of gold and silver on intricate braids of water and grass. To anyone who wondered how I trained as an environmental writer, the most meaningful answer was that I grew up liking to muck in the marsh.

John Steinbeck, in *The Log from the Sea of Cortez,** wrote of his expedition collecting marine life along the shores of the Gulf of California: *"It is advisable to look from the tide pool to the stars and then back to the tide pool again."* What he meant was that we can spend the next ten thousand years identifying individual creatures and dissecting them down to the level of the gene and the atom, and we may similarly roll back the curtains of heaven itself with our telescopes and spaceships; but the fullest wonder lies in comprehending nature's patterns, the wondrous webs of interdependence that entangle humankind in all creation, above and below. Smith Island, whose marshbound residents for about three centuries have paid serious attention to both God and crabs, and where the little white villages on clear, calm days float magically between sea and sky, seemed well stationed to observe tidepool and stars alike; and my kids were reaching marsh-mucking age.

SO IT WAS that in the spring of '87 we moved to the town of Tylerton, last stop on the ferry, unfrequented even by the tour boats to the island's other two communities. The population of 124 was mostly descended from English and Welsh colonists who came here beginning in the late 1600s. Half the town was named either Marshall or Bradshaw; also fourteen Tylers, thirteen Corbins; smatterings of Smiths, Marshes, Tulls, Evanses, and Lairds—and now, for the first time in history, four Hortons.

I took a house that had stood for 170 years, said to be the oldest on the island. It occupied a little peninsula of lawn—rare as emerald in those low-lying and salty environs. Huge old hackberry trees that shaded it bore every spring and fall a bonus crop of migrant warblers, orioles, tanagers, and vireos, glad for a rest on their way to and from the tropics. Every window and door had a view you would pay serious money for on the mainland, and there were thirty-six of them. That nearly half of these faced broadside to the North Pole would not strike us until our first winter.

*(New York: Viking Press, 1969).

My street, really just a path, had no name. With only sixty-seven houses and centuries of close acquaintance, islanders had never thought addresses too important. This gave United Parcel Service fits, and Federal Express and the *Baltimore Sun* circulation departments refused to deal with it at all. If you are not at a certifiable point on somebody's grid, in modern America you scarcely exist; so we made up our own addresses. As the mood struck, we resided on Water Street and Waterview Boulevard, Harbourview and Horton Pike. A friend once addressed me thus: "Tom Horton, His Own Way." Connie, our postmistress, took it all in stride. She knew where we all were.

We also resided "Up Above," as opposed to those Tylertonians who lived "Down Below," and this distinction was important. Assignments at PTA, Ladies Aid, and such were made on this basis, as in: "Up Above brings the meat dishes this time, and Down Below makes the desserts; all pitch in on the salads." Another island village was grouped into "Down the Field" and "Over the Hill." The whole island is nearly flat as a billiard table, and I once asked to be shown the "hill." Well, everyone knows sort of where it runs . . . maybe it has gotten wore down over all this time, people said.

Half a minute's walk either way along my street, or most any other in Tylerton, would land you in the water. It was a great part of what so charmed visitors when they first saw the island towns as the boat from the mainland neared the island—that they just ended, rather than bleeding off in the scattered jumble of strip development and suburbia that so uglifies much of the mainland. This abrupt edge between civilization and nature seemed less confining than you might think. The sun and moon rose at one end of my humble street and set at the other; and from where the pavement stopped the view stretched unimpeded, westward toward the mouth of the Potomac River; eastward across Tangier Sound and the vast prairies of salt marsh along Maryland's Eastern Shore. From my front door I could skip an oyster shell into the true Main Street of Tylerton, the channel of Tyler's Creek.

Everything entered and departed town this way: the ferry, the preacher making his Sunday rounds; crabs migrating, stingrays spawning; also sea ducks, black skimmers, diamondback terrapins, and the occasional shark. Between the channel edge and my front yard, egrets, herons, and gulls progged the shallow, submerged grass beds for soft crabs and minnows and grass shrimp. Here, the ancient territories of animals still overlapped, maintained some semblance of balance with the territory of humankind. One morning I watched a great blue heron battle a great black-backed gull two hours for a huge eel speared on the former's marlinspike bill. The eel proved the toughest customer, finally eluding both birds. Once an otter, the most secretive of marsh dwellers, loped onto my lawn and watched as I mowed grass.

One image is especially savory: Hand in hand, I walked Abby, six, down the lane back to the one-room school that served pre-K through sixth grade. Hot, early-autumn sunshine simmered down through the hackberries that had arched this path for centuries. Odors of steaming crab mingled with mown grass and the faint perfumes of salt and creosote that cling to older waterfronts. Overhead, Canada geese called, and in the shallows snowy egrets sipped minnows delicately. A lone crab, an escapee from the steaming pot, scuttled from under a building and preceded us down the path, dancing sidewise, seeking saltwater. It recalled Thomas Hardy's description of an English village so rural that "a butterfly might have wandered down the main street without interruption." Abby skipped along. So did I.

Tourists who take the half-day boat ride and seafood lunch special to Smith Island generally think the place unique, but ultimately dull and monotonous overall. There is in fact little variety in the vegetation of the tidal marsh that covers all but a few of the 8,000 acres here. Few plants on earth have evolved to tolerate salt, and the Chesapeake here—about halfway in miles and in salt content between the ocean at its mouth and its river-dominated headwaters—permits fewer species than flourish in even the meanest woodlot on the mainland. The marsh is amply compensated, however, because those few plants that can pass salt's stern muster grow like gangbusters in the nutrient-rich broth swishing hourly through their roots on the ebb and flood of the tides. The marsh may never draw aesthetic favor away from New England hillsides in autumn, but it is among the most productive of earth's natural systems, guilelessly surpassing all but the most energy- and labor-intensive applications of human agriculture. This is all well documented in the literature of ecology, and doctrine by now to generations of environmentalists. But there is more to marshiness than science—or even art and literature—has documented. Like so much about Smith Island, it does not shout its virtues, but yields them only to probing and observation.

A marsh-clad island is a place alive. It ripples sleekly beneath the wind's stroking, altering mood and texture with every caress and pummel. Its salty sameness stretches a perfect artist's linen beneath the sky, a playground for the romp of light, and exquisitely responsive to every shift of sun and season and weather. A thousand channels and cricks and guts rive the marsh, and through them the bay perfuses Smith Island like some great, amorphous jellyfish. And these watery thoroughfares, the main means of travel within the island, do something quite profound. They seldom run straight for long. They curve. I doubt George Santayana, the philosopher, ever went "gut running," an island sport that consists of racing one's skiff through the fantastic maze of loops and whorls and meanders the marshways make. But he would have understood the thrill. In his classic treatise on form in *The Sense of Beauty* (1896), Santayana wrote of the pleasure we take from the curved line: *"at every turn reawakening, with a variation, the sense of the previous position . . . such rhythms and harmonies are delightful."*

For one accustomed to the straight and the angle of mainland road travel, moving through the island's arteries is at first disorienting. Landmarks are sparse—three villages and half a dozen hammocks of trees spread across twenty square miles of low marsh and interior waters. Your angle of orientation changes continuously. Leaving Tylerton, one moment the town is holding reassuringly off one shoulder; the next it has hunkered down out of sight behind a hammock; then it reappears, broadside, all its homes in view and looking larger than life, only to begin contracting. The landforms seem conspiring to trick you—merging, hiding, elongating; from unexpected directions, *pouncing*.

Ultimately this physical and psychological to-and-fro becomes deeply stimulating, even sensuous. One contemplates the island's shape-shifting as you might slowly rotate a crystal, regarding familiar objects embedded within from an infinity of perspectives. Straight lines may never be proven inherently inferior, but from galaxies to the shells of whelks, it does seem the bent of the universe to orbit, oscillate, cycle and spiral, to meander and to turn.

Whorled and whirled may be the way of the world, and of Smith Island; but "flat" would be your first impression of the place. We had been there for months when I mentioned on an evening walk to Cheri how remarkably the lights of Tangier, half a dozen miles across the water, were twinkling in the clear air. What lights? she said. She had never seen them. It struck me then that she is five feet nine and I am six feet six. The additional elevation lent a whole different view. This flatness extended far beyond and below the visible island, radiating for miles in every direction along the most gentle of underwater slopes. What looked to be a limitless quantity of water surrounding us was in fact extraordinarily *thin*, ranging in depth from inches to a few feet. This shallowness fundamentally shaped island and islanders. Sunlight easily penetrates to the bottom in these skinny waters, growing lush meadows of aquatic vegetation that attract nearly every type of fish and fowl associated with the Chesapeake Bay.

Prominent among these is the savory blue crab, of which the bay yields more than 100 million pounds annually. Crabs must periodically shed their hard, spiny shells to grow; also, in the females' case, in order to mate. When soft, they are a delicacy and quite valuable. This molting and mating occurs each summer throughout the blue crab's range, from Texas to Long Island; but it is more concentrated and accessible than perhaps anywhere on earth in the grass beds within a twenty-mile radius of Smith Island. Islanders, who depend absolutely for their being on harvesting the soft crab, are connected to the grasses and the bay's essential shallowness as intimately as stalking herons or speckled trout cruising the submerged jungles for prey.

Here, within a day's drive of some 50 million moderns, exists a culture exquisitely attuned to its natural surroundings as only predators can be. "Left or right?" I asked an old neighbor lady one day as I fumbled to turn the burner on her gas stove to light it. "Turn it east, honey," she replied. I got similar instructions on a construction project. "Drive that nail more to nor'west." Even the phone exchange here, HA5, came from Hazel, the big hurricane that devastated the place back in the 1950s.

You could track the progress of crabbing just as accurately through the collections at the Methodist church as through any landing statistics kept by the state. In May, when the first big crab run hit Tyler's Creek, money put in the offering plate might go in a week from $200 to more than $2,000, on attendance of about forty persons.

Just as the elemental, chameleon marsh seemed at first glance monotonous, the fishing life of the islanders also struck outsiders as dreary and repetitious. In fact, every day demanded a complex assessment of tide and temperature, wind and changing season, and a dozen other considerations—many more felt than articulated—that would influence where to work, for how long, in what manner, and how much income there would be. It was physically hard, often uncertain to the point of overstress; but seldom uninteresting. Life on the mainland came to seem predictable by contrast. A shift in the breeze scarcely ever affects where one will sell insurance, or dictates how much paper can be shuffled by day's end.

STRICTLY speaking, you do not actually move to Smith Island. No post office by that name exists or ever has. One moves to Ewell, the "capital city" of about 250, or to Rhodes Point, at the end of the island's only true road, extending two miles across the marsh from Ewell; or one goes to Tylerton, the smallest and most isolated community, reachable from the other towns only by water.

Rhodes Point, they will tell you in Ewell, was called *Rogues* Point until a century or so ago for good reason, the implication being that some of the rogueishness lingers yet. Ewell, say the Tylertonians, is noiser (with maybe forty cars to Tylerton's couple), and is just a tad full of itself. As for Tylerton, well that is where the "holy rollers" still hold sway, where the Methodist religion, which is taken right seriously in all three towns, predominates most. Life there, feel people in Ewell and Rhodes Point, must be unbearably small town and dull. Over the centuries, things have gotten pretty well sorted out. I doubt you could muster a skiffload of islanders who have the slightest desire to move from the town where they live into one of the others.

Moving to Smith Island was not such a dislocation for me. I grew up on Maryland's Eastern Shore, close to the Chesapeake and its marsh islands. But Cheri was from Salt Lake City, and had never lived outside cities. As for Abigail, six, and Tyler, nine, they had grown up playing in Baltimore alleyways. The closest they usually got to water was the storm drain. How would they fit with the kids of crabbers and fishermen?

The enormity of it hit one steamy June day as I prepared for the family's arrival. The house was an oven. The church had asked that even our single down-stairs air conditioner be turned off: the pumps the crabbers used to keep water flowing over their catch needed all the available electricity. Clouds of biting insects swarmed outside. From under the kitchen, a rat, perhaps the only thing my wife hated more than bugs, was gnawing away. What had I done, committing my family to some personal dream of living on an island in the bay?

We were liberal, big-city Democrats. Tylerton was red-white-and-blue conservative. Cheri and the kids are Catholics, and Smith Island uniformly practiced a staunch and fundamentalist brand of Methodism. If you want to talk evolution, make sure you smile when you say it. The island has never opted for local government in its centuries of settlement. There are no jails, no police, no mayor, no town council. The church, to a greater extent than anywhere else in America, fills the role of government. If we didn't fit in, little Tylerton could become confining indeed.

The day before Cheri and the kids were to join me, a woman from down the street stopped by to chat. She came bearing the traditional Smith Island welcoming gift, an eight-layer cake. She said how glad everyone was to see our family moving in. Then she said something that I thought at the time was quaint—perhaps an island way of speaking—"It's so good to see your lights at night." It would be months later before I understood fully—and sorrowfully—what she meant.

That first summer on the island was instant paradise for Tyler. He was off fishing in a skiff with a couple islanders before he had unpacked all his bags. He roamed the town and adjoining marshes at will with the island kids. Lest this sound like stepping into a Huck Finn tale, I should add he also spent hours glued to the video games at the Tylerton store, and pestered us endlessly for a Nintendo like one of his compatriots had. Abby, shyer than her big brother, stuck closer to home; but it was not long before she was out on the dock with a buddy, enticing baitfish into a Mason jar filled with bread and dangled by a string into the water. "Minner, minner, come get your dinner," they sang, and fed their catch to the local cats.

Those first weeks were toughest for Cheri. I had my job, taking groups of schoolkids around the bay and marshes. The kids had playmates. "Mom, why can't you pick [crabs] like the other ladies?" Tyler asked. All Mom's skills as a clinical social worker seemed worthless here. She was welcomed, but she had landed on one of earth's greatest seafood plantations at high harvest season. The income crabs provide between May and September is the great bulk of the year's money for most islanders, and both men and women are feverishly devoted to catching and processing the crustaceans, rising early as 2:00 A.M. and going until 9:00 P.M., six days a week. Only their religion stops them every seventh day. The pace was so frantic, it seemed if the church hadn't stopped them, the people would have had to invent another reason to take a break, or risk burning out by the Fourth of July. It wasn't only the islanders who needed the rest, a waterman said. "The crabs need a break, too." And Monday morning was nearly always the best catch of the week.

Summer's bugs were vanishing before the frosts, the frenzy of crabbing season was slacking off, and Cheri's spirits were picking up. She was busy with PTA and helping out the Methodist ladies with church suppers. In a town the size of Tylerton, everyone's help is needed. We felt valued in a way rarely experienced on the mainland. If islands, by definition, isolate, then they also amplify their residents' sense of community. "It ain't much to look at, but we're close," a crabber said to me. Slowly but surely, we were forming bonds with people whose different cultural and educational backgrounds would, on the mainland, have segregated us surely as concrete barriers. Shortly after the *Exxon Valdez* had spewed oil across Alaska's Prince William Sound, I was leaving to cover the disaster for *Rolling Stone* magazine when Tyler came back from evening church. "They prayed for you tonight, Dad, that you come back all right." I had an insane urge to fax *Rolling Stone:* "Trust the staff there is praying for my success in this difficult endeavor."

With the Halloween Social approaching, Cheri was asked to bake a cake for the traditional cakewalk. This is played something like musical chairs. You plunk down a quarter and walk to music around a circle of numbered sections chalked on the wooden floor of the community hall. If the music stops and leaves you on the number that is drawn, you win the cake. Now cakes are treated on the island only slightly less seriously than crabs. You are offered eight-layer cake in Tylerton routinely as people on the mainland brew visitors a cup of instant coffee. No one expected Cheri to produce one of these masterpieces, but she felt less than three layers would be laughed at. The old kitchen floor tilted south to north, and so did her first efforts at a cake. She went next door to the kitchen where we housed the kids on educational tours; there she produced a cake that slanted east to west. By now there was nothing to do but make the icing as thick as possible, slap the layers together, and try to refrigerate the whole mess to a gluey integrity by showtime.

"You bring the cake, and for God's sake don't let it slide apart," she said as the time for the social arrived. I opened the refrigerator. One layer was in the back corner; another layer was in another corner; the third had begun to slide down the back of the refrigerator between the shelves. As it turned out, it was a blessing in disguise. At the social, we realized that the islanders, who could be incredibly gentle and sensitive, were the severest of cake critics. Each cake was cut in half and displayed before the circle formed for the cakewalk. "Nah, I wouldn't risk a quarter for that one," I heard as a gorgeous specimen was paraded around; and only a few people walked to the music. I kept thinking, what if we had brought a cake to the cakewalk and nobody walked? It would have been the ultimate humiliation—worse than wearing your oilskins tucked so they drain inside your hip boots.

My own work of motivating schoolkids to "Save the Bay" was going well. Few if any islanders thought of their community as an incredible educational tool; but on the final day of a field trip, I would play an ace that seldom failed, relying on the kids' inevitable fascination with Smith Island. On a large map that covered parts of six states, we would travel from the tiny island north to Cooperstown, New York; westward out across the Blue Ridge and Shenandoahs into West Virginia; and south almost into North Carolina. All that immense land, nearly a sixth of the eastern seaboard between Maine and Georgia, lay within the drainage basin, or *watershed*, of the Chesapeake Bay, I would tell them. What that meant was that everything humans in those 64,000 square miles did to pollute, from felling forests and farming destructively to flushing toilets and bombarding their lawns with chemicals—all of that was eventually carried by rainfall and forty-odd rivers downstream to the Chesapeake.

Ultimately, the most important grade for our civilization would be how well we achieved a long-term, stable accommodation between nature and human numbers that grew without limit. The Chesapeake was as good a final exam as anywhere on earth—a world-class resource, polluted big time, and now the object of unprecedented restoration efforts, even as population in its watershed burgeoned from 15 million to 18 million in the next few decades. Literally in the center of this struggle lay little Smith Island, some 500 souls totally dependent on a healthy natural environment, downstream from the other 15–18 million of us. If you go away from here remembering only one lesson, I would tell the kids, make it this: How responsibly you live back home helps determine whether this place survives. There were very few skulls and hearts that pitch did not penetrate.

WINTER hit hard and fast that first year on the island. The big nor'westers came screaming down Tangier Sound with nothing to impede them for thirty miles of open water and marsh before they slammed broadside into our uninsulated house, which had no central heat. We used to sit, huddled under blankets in the living room, watching the mainland weather mention "winds 6 to 12 knots, variable," while the house rocked in the grip of 30 knots and gusting. We began keeping items like salad oil in the refrigerator so they wouldn't freeze overnight.

If winters could be harsh, they always started well because of the Christmas holidays. Christmas is a big deal on Smith Island, and Christmas lights are an especially big deal. "You are going to put up lights," a neighbor told us, friendly but firm. It was the only time I can ever recall being *told* to do anything in this place where independence is valued nearly to the point of anarchy. I was never big on Christmas festivities, to Cheri's everlasting despair; but I managed a few cheap strings of lights, tucked into some cedar branches that I and the kids cut from the big heron rookery in a hammock out on the marsh. Everyone's lights looked great. They helped to disguise the fact that the town had been growing darker, and not just from the shortening days.

The "Save the Bay" house had been closed up for the winter. The few summer residents were gone until spring; and some of the older widows had left to live with children in Ewell or on the mainland until the weather warmed again. We went away the week after Christmas, returning in early January. One night, I walked outside. It was drizzly, a fog was rolling up Tangier Sound. Swans bayed like lost souls in the blackness down by Horse Hammock Point. The foghorn moaned out by the jetties above Ewell. All the Christmas lights were gone now. On my street, only three of seven houses had lights on. The other four were empty, or inhabited only by summer people—"gone dark," as the islanders said. A great wave of depression rolled over me as I thought about the neighbor who had welcomed me; how glad she was to see, finally, a house reversing the trend toward darkness.

Tylerton, you see, is dying, and perhaps the rest of Smith Island too. I do not even like to put those words down, but statistics compel it. In 1980 the Chesapeake Bay Foundation, my employer on the island, had done a census of the town, and there were 157 people. I updated it in 1987, and there were 124. By 1995, the year-round population was hovering around 80. The whole island, listed in the U.S. 1980 Census at around 675 (somewhat overstated, the preacher at the time thought), is closer to 400 today.

Old people are dying, ten in Tylerton alone within a recent five-year period; and only one baby was born on Tylerton (and five on the island) in that time. Teenage boys are still trying to make it on the water, although more than ever are eyeing jobs with the State Police, or as guards at the new maximum security prison on the Somerset County mainland. Teenage girls seem to have no such conflicts and are leaving. They feel there must be more to life than marriage to a waterman, than picking crabs and cooking and cleaning house and raising kids with limited access to shopping and night life.

Ten percent of Tylerton's population are bachelors. An island mother once interrupted my conversation about worrisome trends in seafood abundance in the bay. The Lord would take care of rockfish and oysters. What worried her was this: "Who's goin' to be left for my son to marry?"

I FELT more and more frustrated about Smith Island's future during our last few months on the island. Tylerton seemed at the point that even two or three more families' leaving could doom the place as a viable community. One day I got a new map of Smith Island and the bay for the education center: a LandSat image that showed the whole watershed from space in astounding detail. On it, you could cover Smith Island with your thumb; and among this thumbprint of marsh, smaller than grains of rice, were three slivers of white, signifying the precious high ground to which clung Ewell, Tylerton, and Rhodes Point.

They were so inconsequential, droplets in an ocean, and yet . . . I got out an old interview I had done years before with Russell Schweikart, the astronaut. Like others who had taken the dramatic step of leaving earth, his altered perspective of the planet had evoked deep emotions: "*. . . you realize that little blue and white thing is everything that means anything to you . . . all of history and music and poetry and art and war and death and birth and love, tears, joy, games, all of it is on that little spot out there that you can cover with your thumb. . . .*"

This book is a quest for the spirit of Smith Island, an attempt to give voice to a people whose eloquence lies simply in their three centuries of working and being here against all odds. A Chesapeake poet, the late Gilbert Byron, once called such fishermen "the greatest poets/who never wrote a line." Their lives are essayed in a fluid environment, inscribed on the hidden bottoms of grassy shallows and oyster beds. Each day, though they have been at it for centuries, the slate is wiped clean; and in a day my children may live to see, as global warming proceeds to raise the level of the oceans, the waters may close atop Smith Island, erasing all physical evidence that the poetry ever existed.

WHEN OUR FAMILY left Smith Island in 1989, the Bay Foundation held a pig roast for us and most of the town came. It was a fun day, long on eating, short on speeches. Many people seemed down, "out of heart," as they would put it. There had been five funerals in recent months, and in a place that close, even one death hits everyone hard. There were more summer people around than I had ever remembered. As more homes go dark, news of their relatively cheap prices is getting around as far away as New York. The "outsiders" who buy them have been, on the whole, nice people. A few single ladies from cities sought the place because they heard it was actually safe to walk anywhere at night and leave your door unlocked. All of them think Tylerton charming, and hope it doesn't ever change; but more and more you hear lawn mowers and power tools going on the Sabbath, and see people strolling in the streets, beers in hand, unmindful or uncaring of the local taboo on public drinking. Some holiday weekends now, for the first time in their long history, islanders wonder whether the place is theirs any more.

We had closed up the old house weeks before, when we put all our belongings on a 48-foot workboat and took them forty miles up Tangier Sound to the headwaters of the Wicomico River where our new home would be. At the pig roast, one of the new educators for the Bay Foundation came up and told me someone had left a light on in the house. It had been burning day and night now for some time. Did I want him to turn it off? I knew about the light, I said. I know you are preaching energy conservation to the groups that come, but please, let it burn a while longer.

Light and Dark—
A Matter of Balance

It was a dark and stormy night, which is more than a trite description when you are in the middle of Chesapeake Bay and your son is unable to breathe. Cheri reached me around 9:00 P.M. on the marine radio at Tangier Island, Virginia, about six miles south of Smith. Tyler was having another of his attacks, and for the first time she could not control it with our stock of inhalants, vaporizers, and steroids. I had better get home immediately to take him the twelve miles across the Sound to Crisfield's emergency room.

It was the worst fear we had about moving there—were we being irresponsible to take a severely asthmatic child to a place with no doctor and no nurse, and access to the nearest hospital nearly an hour distant, even with the state's Medevac helicopters (which, at any rate, might not fly on nights like this)? We both knew all the good reasons for moving the family to Smith Island would amount to so much self-indulgent smoke, weighed against our boy's death.

I had my 24-foot Grady White, a sturdy Fiberglas hull, streaking north from Tangier Island within a minute of the call. I seldom ran its big outboard at more than 4,000 rpm, but now I pushed it up to 5,500, its maximum, screaming along at nearly 40 mph into pitch darkness.

It was not the second leg of my route that night, the run with Tyler and Cheri to the emergency room in Crisfield, that concerned me. The E.R. even had a dock attached, to accommodate all the business that came by boat from Tangier and Smith. I had made that journey many times in the dark, once when my own bursitis got so painful that I took off, one-armed, at 3:00 A.M. on a February morning; other times it was students who broke limbs on field trips.

And there was the memorable occasion when Tyler, who could gorge with impunity whole hamburgers at a gulp, managed to stick a smallish marble halfway down his throat. I stretched him out on life preservers in the bottom of the open skiff I was using at the time, and headed east for the hospital. Halfway there, we passed Cheri coming west on the evening ferry. I hollered that her son was still breathing as we sped past, and Tyler waved wanly from the cushions.

The route from Tylerton to Crisfield was well marked its whole length by flashing navigation lights and reflective red and green markers that I could pick up half a mile off in my searchlight. But not so the several miles of marsh and water I must now first traverse to reach home. Many times I had enjoyed this run between Smith and Tangier precisely because it was so unmarked by any sign of human presence. It was where I once took a BBC film crew that was shooting a documentary on North America as it looked in pre-Columbian times. They could not have so much as a single Coast Guard navigation mark intrude on their filmed landscapes. On clear nights the absence of lights anywhere along the marsh made it a virtual planetarium for star watching.

But now the virgin wilderness I gloried in was merely dark, forbidding, and unfriendly. Racing north on a compass heading for Tyler's Creek, the quickest way into Tylerton, I realized I could not even think about risking that route. A low tide and the narrow, twisting channel, marked only sporadically by the casual wooden sticks of crabbers, would be nearly impossible for me to follow. I might easily hit a shoal, or even the low marsh, indivisible in the night drizzle from the water. At 40 mph, I would, at best, be stuck for hours.

Waves were beginning to break heavily over the Grady's bow, drenching me and wrenching the bow several degrees off course every time we pounded into a trough. "A noser," the islanders would call it. In such conditions in a small boat, especially in the harsh, closely spaced chop of Chesapeake Bay, you cannot operate a searchlight or marine radio, or adjust the knob on your depth finder, or even flick a bilge pump switch on without extreme effort. The boat's Fiberglas could take the ride, but I couldn't. I throttled back to 4,000.

My best option to the perilous back route required negotiating a fine line, navigating close enough to the eastern side of Smith Island to stay out of the fierce head seas, but staying far enough offshore to avoid running aground or hitting the marsh. For a ways I would be able, by watching my depth finder, to follow the bottom contours, which ran approximately in the direction I wanted to go; but about halfway up, these, I knew, would swing far off my course.

Meanwhile, I had reached the point I dreaded: where the last glimmer of Tangier's lights were gone, and Smith's were still several minutes away in the drizzled gloom. It was wet, cold, rough, and utterly dark. Intellectually, at such times, you know you are pretty much where you are supposed to be; emotionally, tossed like a chip in the wind and sea and black, you feel lost as hell. Then, well before I should have seen the lights of Smith, I saw a blinking red light.

It was the new microwave receiver tower for the telephone system in Ewell, so recently erected I was not even used to keying on it for direction. Instantly I knew where I was and made a minor course adjustment, pushing the throttle back up to 5,500. Within an hour, Tyler and Cheri were delivered to the emergency room and we all were breathing easier. Heading back to Tangier after midnight, a big moon broke through the clouds, and with a fair wind quartering off my stern I put the canvas top down and luxuriated in feeling like the only craft abroad on the whole Chesapeake. It can be so good, in this crowded world, to be alone, but a little light is always welcome.

The truth is, until that night, I had been bad-mouthing the new phone tower.

The only structure on the island higher than the church steeples, its lights marred the wilderness sanctity of my night canoe trips with schoolkids—a sign of human presence, always visible no matter how deeply into the trackless marsh we paddled. By contrast the islanders had welcomed it instinctively as a superior beacon; and now I could see why.

I began recalling the stories about the old days: how Paul's father, a fish netter, would sometimes not empty his nets until after dark, then run aground trying to negotiate the unmarked, unlit channels leading from the island to the fish buyers in Crisfield. Half a boatload of fish would spoil while the netters, bone-tired and dispirited, waited on the tide to float them off.

The longer I lived on the island, the more I came to appreciate the lights, and now, a few years removed to the mainland, I find they form some of my strongest memories—Little Thoroughfare, Easters Point, Cove Beacon, Puppy Hole, Outer Light, Inner Light—those were the red and white and green navigational flashers that marked the path from my house to the mainland, and I will be able to recite them, as well as the lesser markers in between, until the day I die.

Coming the other way, it was always a thrill and a comfort to sight the clusters of lights on Smith, to watch them twinkle in and out of the wavetops, blazing ever more steadily as you neared home. Nothing was prettier as evening fell than to climb to the tall, peaked roof of our house in Tylerton as the little, bright jewels of Wenona, Chance, Rumbley, Fairmount, Tangier, and other fishing towns began to sparkle on the blackening, velvety marshes of the Sound.

On the mainland, of course, we are jaded by lights, pounded senseless by the mercury-vapor greens, sodium reddish oranges, and grapey urban perfusions that dome off whole counties from the true night sky. Friends would often remark about our move to the island, how nice it must be to get back to nature, as if one had to choose, civilization or wilderness.

In fact, the more I thought about the lights, the more it seemed that the charm of the island was not so much its abundance of nature; rather, its juxtaposition of the human and the natural; and even more to the point, the fact that it had achieved a *balance* between them. We reel, desensitized, from too much light, but it is no black and lonesome wilderness most of us seek; rather, a pleasing accommodation of the light with the dark. You cannot fully appreciate either without the other.

OCCUPATIONS

The Essentials

We others, who have long lost the more subtle of the physical senses, have not
even proper terms to express an animal's intercommunications with his
surroundings . . . and have only the word "smell," for instance, to include the
whole range of delicate thrills which murmur in the nose of the animal night and
day, summoning, warning, inciting, repelling.

—*Kenneth Grahame, The Wind in the Willows*

Spring is always a thrill as it travels up the mid-Atlantic coast in April and
May. It fairly bursts upon the land, as if winter's skinflint sun, seeping feebly
into barren soil month after month, has finally reached some saturation point,
and the earth must explode in first forsythia, then shadbush and redbud, followed by azalea, iris, camelia, magnolia, and a thousand shades of new-minted
green.

On the island, meadows of *Spartina patens,* the fine, soft wild hay foraged
by the livestock of early settlers, flushes such a tender, refreshing green as to make
one wish to join the little wild goats who graze shoulder-deep in its succulent
waves. A wallpaper made from photographs of spring *patens* tossing softly in
the breeze, liberally applied to homes and offices, could reduce the national level
of stress overnight.

In the outlying salt marsh hummocks—Ireland, The Pines, Captain Dan's,
Hog Neck, Nordend—the tall, spreading hackberries leaf slowly, the better to
display their new ornamentation; for almost overnight they have been festooned
by arriving snowy egrets and blue herons and glossy ibis. Along the beach and
marsh fringes, gulls and terns, skimmers and pelicans and oyster catchers with
their Day-Glo orange beaks jockey for nesting position. Overhead, the ospreys
make easy meals of torporous eels, roused from their winter's rest in the mud
bottom and drifting near the warm surface.

The islanders slap gnats and hunt the delicate wild asparagus sprouting from
old ditch banks in the marsh. They paint their boats white and daub the bottoms with red anti-fouling paint; ready their nets, scrapes, pots, traps; and note
with approval that the "snowball bush," a prominent hydrangea behind Miss
Virginia Evans's house, is about to bloom—a sure sign that spring, so obviously

in the air and on the land, is also stirring beneath the surface of the Chesapeake waters.

Across 100 square miles of bay shallows, the bare, gray muds are blossoming into jungles of eelgrass, widgeon grass, and a dozen other varieties of submerged aquatic vegetation. Once, this occurred on a massively larger scale, before pollution from sewage, development, and agricultural runoff began to cloud the bay's water with excessive algae, beginning in the 1960s. This in turn blocked the light needed for the grasses' growth through perhaps 90 percent of their traditional areas. A decline like that in forests on the land would have riveted world attention, but it was years before scientists began seriously to investigate the great devegetation of the Chesapeake bottom. Only in parts of the bay remote from pollution, like Smith Island, did the grasses hang on in something approximating their old luxuriance.

To the islanders, this greening of the bay bottom is far more than a mere botanical phenomenon; for synchronized to the spring warming of the shallows, and abetted by the waning phase of the moon, a great wave has been building. It usually starts in April, down in the shallow coastal bays and sounds of the Carolinas, rolling up through the Chesapeake, cresting throughout Tangier Sound by mid-May, reaching nearly to New England before it is spent. It is called in these parts simply "the run," or "the rush," and a heady experience it is, welcome to the winter-weary islanders as a draught of cool springwater to a wanderer in the desert.

Like the reverse of last autumn's falling leaves, blue crabs by the millions are skirling up from their winter burial in the muddy bottoms, fusiform bodies in the sunny shallows glinting olive and ivory, tinged with crimson and cerulean on the claws. Among the first to arise are those immature females, "she crabs" or "maiden crabs," that did not quite make it to their final "shed" or molt before cold weather arrested them last December. Although the blue crab sheds its shell—the only way crustaceans can grow—some twenty times during its two- to three-year life, it is only on the final shed that the maiden crab becomes a "sook," capable of reproducing once before she dies. On becoming a sook her abdominal apron, or vaginal covering, changes dramatically, from a triangle to a shape that resembles nothing so much as the dome of the U.S. Capitol. The male, or jimmy crab is virtually identical to the female, except for a genital covering on its abdomen that is more slender and phallic-shaped. Environmental educators find it useful to teach that this "looks like the Washington Monument."

So it is that the May bay seethes with sooks-to-be that have only two things on their agenda, to molt and to mate. In nature, this leads to a courtship and consummation both sensuous and, well, *loving,* odd as that might seem for a creature whose Latin name is *Cancer,* and whose usual disposition defines sourness and feistiness. But envision the well-documented trysting that occurs between jimmy and sook (described exquisitely and in more detail in William Warner's classic on the Chesapeake crab, *Beautiful Swimmers*).*

Accompanied by tender gesturing of his big, hard claws, the male raises high on his swimmer fins and tiptoes through an animated courtship dance. The female finally signals her readiness by backing gently beneath him. For the next two days to a week, jimmy swims with sook cradled contentedly in his fierce-clawed embrace. As the hour of her terminal molt nears, the couple seeks the protective cover of aquatic vegetation. There, jimmy stands guard as sook performs the exhausting ordeal of leaving her old shell, literally shedding her virginity, emerging helpless, glistening, and silken soft.

And now, ever so gently, he helps her turn on her back. She opens the Capitol Dome, and he unhinges the Washington Monument, and face to face, pleopods to genital pores, hard body pressed against soft, they embrace amid the corridors of emerald eelgrass, waving to and fro with the tides. They may remain so for as long as twelve hours. In Warner's words, it is "a most affecting scene. You cannot possibly mistake these actions for anything other than lovemaking."

This only hints at May's promise throughout the vast, nurturing womb of the Chesapeake in which its islands bathe. It is a fecund and lusty time, marked by greening, nesting, mating; ripe to bursting with prospects for renewal. To whatever urges course through scores of the bay's creatures, the season seems to whisper: *Yes, you May*. Even as crabs sport in their grassy bowers, white perch and herring, shad and striped bass, are thrusting up the channels from the sea to spawn, jazzing dozens of Chesapeake rivers with their annual offerings of life. Oysters by the million are swelling with eggs and sperm, to be released in volcanic concert as water temperatures reach 72 degrees F.

Such activity underscores the fundamental sexuality of the bay. Science defines it as an *"estuary,"* meaning technically a semi-enclosed body of water, open to Atlantic tides at its mouth and receiving the flows of great rivers from as far off as West Virginia and New York. But the term's Latin root, *aestuare*, implies more, a heaving and surging, a boiling and a commotion where these floods of saltwater and sweet collide.

In and out, up and down; the tides daily gorge and suck, flood and drain every gut and slough and cranny of the estuary's 9,000-mile shoreline. Beneath this back-and-forth motion, a salty tongue of heavy ocean water licks constantly up-bay along the channel bottoms, injecting the whole place with the young of crabs and fish and oysters who have adapted to "ride" the salt wedge, penetrating the estuary well beyond their own feeble swimming capabilities.

To a geologic cadence, the entire bay enters and withdraws from its 4,000-square-mile recess in America's east coast, deflating with the Ice Ages and the

*(New York: Little, Brown & Company, 1994).

fall of world sea level; then, after a hundred thousand years of warming, swelling potently as the seas rise to flood the river valleys and form once again the estuary. Five times in the last million years it has come and gone thus, water making love to the land.

Just as essential as all the obvious spring sex, something subtle and delightful is occurring throughout the bay waters, and it has to do with smell. The bay is splendiferously odoriferous, the most sensuously perfumed of trysting places; a temple of olfactory delights, no less compelling for being largely without the realm of human perception. Our own sniffers, quite unremarkable in the animal world, still are able to discern thousands of compounds and detect some in dilutions as extreme as a single part per billion.

And even for us, the most gossamer tugs of scent can engage great trains of pleasurable recollection. One day on a dock on the Red Sea at Port Sudan, a tendril of fresh seabreeze and hot, creosoted docks, spiced alluringly with the rich, farty decay of marsh, transported me back to Smith Island at a speed greater than light. Whole subsets of our lives seem available only through odors: of the earth unzipped by spring plowing, fall leaves smoldering, and the smell of fresh-washed bluejeans; the sweetness of new-mown lawns, the July dust of a baseball diamond, the scent pooled in the hollow of a sleeping loved one's neck.

That is smell's way. It is our most ancient and evocative sense, an achievement first made by aquatic ancestors (we still need the watery medium of the nose's mucus membranes to smell). Something smelled does not dally around being filtered through the great, gray convolutions of higher thought in the neocortex, or new brain, whose development makes us human, and so logical that we scarcely trust our feelings. Odors, linked to older, more primitive parts of the brain, crash right over the transom of reason, grab us by the gut and the nerve endings, take us cascading down rivers of feeling more intense than anything flowing in through the eyes and ears.

And it is just so, and more, for the animals. A dog, surmises essayist Peter Steinhart, may get as much mental exercise from a summer breeze playing across its nose as a man gets at a Shakespeare play. The fabled capacity of west coast salmon to home in by smell on their natal streams from far out in the oceans only slightly surpasses Chesapeake river herring, whose spawning surges send a crackling vitality coursing through every vein of the bay's drainage.

Keener abilities than that exist in eels, which somehow navigate from their birthplace in the Sargasso Sea into creeks and rivers of the bay and the whole eastern American coastline. They can recognize certain scents when diluted to about three parts per *quintillion* in water—equivalent to adding less than an ounce to the entire volume of the Chesapeake Bay. Even the humble Chesapeake oyster, glued to one spot virtually all its life, has a brief and vital moment to smell the roses, so to speak. As a microscopic, free-floating larvae, it is able to sniff out suitable places to attach and grow its shell by homing on the odor of a good thick slime, whose presence signifies an abundance of waterborne nutrients.

And then there is the crab, jimmy and sook, for whom the smell of spring in the water is not only hedonic, but underpins a major part of the Smith Islanders' very being. You can see the results most any May morning aboard the little 40-foot ferries leaving the island for the mainland. They are crowded that time of year—upward of ten thousand passengers most days. A few are tourists bound for Crisfield, sunning themselves in the pleasant air; the rest are freshly shed soft-shell crabs, boxed in cardboard and softly agurgle on beds of cool sea grass, bound for salivating customers as far away as Tokyo. They will be sautéed in sweet butter and served plain or on toast, or crisply fried and sandwiched between slices of soft white bread with luscious slices of ripe tomato and a creamy slathering of mayonnaise. The lushest farms and forests on earth never produced sweeter fruit than the muddy shallows of this spare marsh island.

No one living can say how long ago it was that the islanders figured how to exploit the great spring rush of molting, loving crabs. Somehow, they learned what science even now has only sketchily proven in the laboratory: that she crabs approaching their final ecdysis exude a pheromone, or chemical sex attractant in their urine, so potent that a few molecules wafted on the tide are enough to excite acres of jimmy crabs. Dr. L. Eugene Cronin, a longtime leader in Chesapeake Bay's biological sciences, says he has examined thousands of adult female crabs from throughout the bay during several decades of research, and can only recall "two, maybe three that were not impregnated. The pheromones work, and they work with an efficiency that is almost unbelievable," he concludes.

Although science never has isolated a female attractant coming from the jimmies, no Smith Islander doubts one exists. Long before modern crab pots—rectangular wire mesh traps—were perfected in the 1940s, islanders would tie strings around jimmies' hind swimmer fin as the first run neared and stake them to poles along the channel of Tyler's Creek, says Bobby Marshall, a waterman from Tylerton. "There were poles and jimmies tied to 'em all up and down the channel through the towns. It wouldn't be long before every one had caught him a wife. Why I remember one jimmy, he caught seven wives just as fast as we could take 'em away and throw 'im back to get another. After the seventh, though, he acted like he didn't even want to look n'more. I guess we treated him dirty, didn't we?"

It is, of course, the "wives" that the crabbers seek, because at this time of year each one is guaranteed to be what is called a "rank peeler." "Rank" here means the sook-to-be is showing a bright reddish tinge, no larger than a fingernail clipping, along the edge of her rear swim fins. It signifies that she is within a day or hours of shedding, or peeling off her shell, and need only be held briefly in wooden trays through which seawater is pumped before her market value is transformed from a few cents as a hard crab to as much as a dollar and a half commanded by big spring softies.

Nowadays, the spring peeler run is cropped with industrial efficiency by a process known as "jimmy potting." The first spring I lived on the island, I innocently asked a top crabber whose family and mine were becoming good friends, could I have just a couple of his jimmies for my environmental education class. He looked as if I had asked for his firstborn as a blood sacrifice. Beginning in April, the island men begin to save every prime jimmy they can lay their hands on, even though they could sell them immediately for as much as $100 a bushel so early in the season. The jimmies will become live bait, inserted into a crab pot that at other times of year would hold dead fish or other food to attract its quarry.

In preparation, many crabbers painstakingly divest each jimmy of his claws. There is a precise way to do this, and even some watermen never get the hang of it. If it is done wrong, the crab bleeds to death. The claws are caught and clasped together, then extended and raised to a precise angle, at which point they seem to snap off at the crabs' equivalent of shoulder sockets with no effort at all. In fact, the technique convinces the crab to voluntarily give up his claws. It triggers a crustacean trait known as autotomy, the reflex separation of appendages at a joint, probably useful in surviving combat with other crabs. Most islanders swear that autotomized jimmies catch more wives. Just why is not known, but Chuck Foster, a friend whose education bridges the worlds of commercial crabbing and biology, speculates the stress results in an increased flow of pheromones.

Imagine then, a studly jimmy crab, confined in his underwater cell on a May evening redolent with the come-hither of peeler piss. The fragrance has him fairly trembling to be about his natural business. Frustration turns to joy as a rank peeler, seeking sookhood, enters the pot's opening, a narrowing funnel through which there is no return. Perhaps for a brief time there is bliss, changing at some point to sheer terror as more and more females crowd the pot—islanders say they have seen up to 190.

Perhaps it is with relief that he feels the crabber pull on the rope that attaches to a marker cork at the surface. The sooks are dumped in bushels, bound for the shedding trays, for New York, Boston, Baltimore, and Japan. Jimmy goes back into Tyler's Creek, and the whole process begins again. "It's not much of a story for women's lib, is it?" laughs an island wife; "all those women crawlin' after a male. It's disgustin'. It oughtta be the other way around."

A captive jimmy may last for the duration of the run, several days, if handled gently throughout his pot's many raisings and dumpings; but many succumb . . . to what? Perhaps the sheer psychic and emotional toll. Or if you prefer happy endings, perhaps they die of rapture. The surviving love slaves are dealt a final indignity. They get steamed and picked.

But their sacrifice scarcely goes unappreciated. April, the month preceding the first run, is along with March the most psychologically dreary time of the year for islanders. Oystering has long ended, and with it the last income many families will see until May. Yet boats must be outfitted and crab shanties put aright just the same. Once the run starts, it is too late, and not to be ready could put a family deep in the hole financially. By May, watermen are not only drained of money but beginning to question their very worth after weeks of relative idleness. What they will tell an interviewer then is often dramatically different from what they will say in September, coming off a good crab season, headed into oystering. Area news thus routinely has watermen in the same year lamenting the last days of Chesapeake Bay and later proclaiming the place is not nearly as bad off as the environmentalists say.

The collective sigh of relief and jubilance brought by the first big runs of May is tempered on the island by obligation. Even sinners usually send some of their profit the church's way, as the collection plate swells with folding money, from March's few hundreds of dollars weekly to May's thousands.

The run brings frantic work and long hours, but also creates the loveliest of scenes, with the local waters arrayed for the crabs' homecoming as beautifully as any meadow of wildflowers blooms on the mainland. Crab pots, of which an estimated 1 million are in use now throughout the Chesapeake, are marked by colored floats, "corks," attached by nylon cord. Most of the year they are set out in straight lines and dispersed throughout the 200-mile estuary. But in peeler potting every islander's pots are bunched chockablock, tightly concentrated in selected spots and along the edges of winding channels.

So it happens that, far as the eye can see, the channel of Tyler's Creek, snaking south toward Virginia, is brightly confettied, strewn with corks, striped and stippled and covered in a rainbow of colors, the only way each crabber can hope to make out which ones are his. Some May afternoons, when the water smooths and the slanting sun saturates the multi-hues of the corks, the creek looks as if it is carrying a tide of candy drops, spilled from the big spun sugar clouds afloat in the blue spring sky.

In the matings of crabs, and the mating of land and water that define and enable Smith Island, there is even better to come. Other, lesser runs of both male and female peelers will continue for months; but the most sublime congress of crabs and islanders awaits late summer. Mauve blossomings of sea lavender and the ruby blush of salicornia have begun to patch and dot the marsh with as much color as the stress of salt and flooding ever permit. In the translucent, olive shallows, the grasses have thinned enough to reveal "doublers"—jimmies and sooks, precopulatory or in the very act—scattered across the bottom in a last great effort to send every available breeder south to Virginia for the winter with packets of sperm. A female will combine these with her eggs in the succeeding summer to produce billions more little crabs.

Now is the time to shut down the rackety diesel in the big boat, to leave the pots and scrapes and larger crabbing gear at home; to take a simple long-handled dip net and your small skiff and go "nettin' on the Knoll." Actually there is the Knoll, the Gap, the Hill, Back 'o the Knoll . . . each nothing more than the subtlest of departures, measurable in inches, from the monotonous flatness of the grassy bottoms that stretch miles between Smith and Tangier. To the casual eye it is just broad miles of open water, edged on its western rim with sand slivers that separate bay from Sound by only a few yards in many places. To the island's soft crabbers, places like the Knoll loom as substantially as Mount Fuji to a Japanese.

The netter works in waters from a few feet to less than ten inches. He uses the circular steel bow of his long-handled dip net to shove along, standing in hang-10 surfer style on the bow-tip of his little flat-bottomed skiff, intent as any stalking heron on the doublers camouflaged amid the grass. The only sounds are the cries of gulls ar.d terns, and the liquid crush and burble of water beneath the skiff's bow as it is shoved rhythmically to and fro across the flat. Periodically the netter stabs the surface with barely a ripple, deftly scooping coupled crabs. In one fluid motion, he flips the loving pair high in the air, and as they separate, catches the female, who will soon turn soft, and valuable. The jimmy is let fall, to seek another wife.

Mullet and speckled trout swirl the calm surface, and cownose rays, broad as a man's back, glide companionably alongside the skiff. In the tawny, sunlit shallows, every blade of grass, every oyster and sponge and juvenile fish is visible, and once your gaze becomes attuned, the olive-backed crabs stand out like beacons despite their adaptive coloration. The effect of all this, moving beneath the skiff, becomes hypnotic, a meditation. You become absorbed in the minutiae of the underwater jungle, and with plucking, in effect, dollar bills from among its fruited groves; and then, to ease your back and shoulders, you lean back and look up at the limitless vault of sky, and out across the broad bay, and feel small as a gnat amid this serene grandeur of sky and sea; and there is a peace, a completeness, a connection that seems to run through you, from the worm-encrusted tunnels on the shell of an oyster below to the moon that pulls the tides through the oyster's gills.

Some days half the townsmen of Smith and Tangier meet like this out on the Knoll, seventy to a hundred skiffs strong. Elemental as runes, netter and net are the only verticals in a horizontal universe. As they shove and lean and brace and dip, the crabbers seem to be romancing their slender poles, waltzing with them languidly to the rhythms of tide and the blue crab; and to their every move the skiff follows like a thing alive. From a distance, the islanders perched on the bows are Chesapeake centaurs—half man, half skiff—silhouetted against the place where bay and sky merge in a luminous, silken monochrome, suspended in a dream between mud and heaven, between labor and beauty.

And so the soft-crab season, which began with a rush, glides to a finish. It is, say the islanders, the prettiest way they know to catch a crab.

Terrapin Men

IN RETROSPECT, it should not have surprised any of us when Dwight and Mary Ada's little girl gave the answer she did one day on a test in school. Name four of earth's precious natural resources, was the question. Gold, she wrote, and water and oil; also:

Turkles.

It was an answer that should never have been marked wrong. "Turkles," by which she meant *Malaclemys terrapin,* or diamondback terrapin, had been a much-welcomed addition to the Marshall family's winter income during the years we were their neighbors.

The terrapin, an aquatic reptile, is cosmopolitan throughout brackish and saltwater marshes from Canada to Mexico, and thrives especially well in Chesapeake Bay. Once, it was haute cuisine, its rich, subtly sweet meat praised by visitors to Maryland, from Lafayette to Oliver Wendell Holmes. A Baltimore mayoral candidate in 1938 used the slogan, only half-jokingly, of "a terrapin in every pot." In the first half of this century, a waterman supplying fancy restaurants might make a dollar for each inch of length, as measured on the three- to nine-inch underside of the creature's shell.

Predictably, terrapins in the bay region were hunted virtually into commercial extinction. Only a combination of the Great Depression and Prohibition brought about their de facto conservation. The former damped dining out, and the latter removed the Sherry and Madeira considered essential to their preparation and enjoyment. Having fallen from favor, the terrapin, which took a fearsome amount of preparation to elicit its diviner qualities, never regained widespread popularity. Though its population nowadays has rebounded nicely, most Chesapeake watermen scarcely consider catching them, or know how to.

Dwight, however, was a student of markets and master of harvest for an unusually wide range of seafood. He was probably better at seeking out the terrapin in its hidden winter lair than anyone on the bay.

Across the bay, up the Patuxent River, about an hour by boat from Smith Island, I had also come to know Willem Roosenburg, a young Ph.D. who was fast becoming the bay's other foremost terrapin expert. Summer after summer, patrolling miles of river shoreline day and night, Willem and his students had trapped and marked, with individually coded notches on their shells, more than five thousand terrapins. He was building a classic ecological study of a creature that can live for more than half a century and does not even reach sexual maturity until eight to thirteen years of age.

It could take decades, he said; but already he was documenting an arresting relationship between terrapins and the bay nesting beaches they returned to each summer, a bond as complex and intricate as that between returning salmon and their natal streams. Somehow, perhaps by olfaction, the female terrapins returned with astounding fidelity to the same places every June-through-August. At Smith, I once watched a flotilla of such terrapins pass for nearly half an hour, apparently paddling for a spawning beach. His work, Willem hoped, would lead to more protection of both terrapins and the undeveloped Chesapeake waterfronts to which they were bound.

It was with a sense of both fascination and trepidation that I had mentioned Willem to Dwight, and Dwight to Willem. Together, they knew most of what was known about the terrapin's annual life cycle. Each, predictably, was hungry to explore the other's knowledge—although for vastly different purposes. If the shepherd ever sat down with the wolf to discuss the behavior and whereabouts of the flocks, what might result?

That would have to wait. It was early January; Tangier Sound was thawing from an early-winter freeze-up. It looked like things might soon "get right for tarpinin' "; and when they did, Dwight promised, he'd show me how it was done. This brief, wintertime fishery was insignificant in the greater schemes of crabbing, oystering, and finfishing that typified Chesapeake harvests. But for that very reason it seemed a good avenue to understanding more about my neighbor, who seemed the most consummate waterman I'd met.

Winter terrapins represented an obscure window of opportunity; but the adaptability to exploit any of the Chesapeake's possibilities was key to successful survival among its inhabitants. The large and unpredictable swings in water temperatures, tides, salinity, and food supply that characterize such estuaries, where rivers mix with the ocean, all favored generalists and opportunists—the blue crab, the striped bass, the great blue heron; and watermen who could emulate them.

Dwight, like most modern watermen, was principally a crabber. There were men better in this or that technique among the many ways of taking crabs; and there certainly were bigger operators. Many "up the bayers," as he called those who operated from the mainland of more suburban counties to the north, had gone from fishing a hundred crab pots in the 1960s to more than a thousand. Sometimes they ran crews of three or four men on two separate boats. Despite such pressure, crab landings seemed to be holding their own; but fisheries experts, looking at what they called "catch per unit effort," were concerned by the rising amount of gear and man-hours needed merely to perpetuate the same level of catch.

"Up the bayers are never satisfied; all they understand is more pots overboard," Dwight would mutter; "they are the same ones that drove the rockfish down [overfishing led to a statewide moratorium in 1984], and now some are talking about crabbing twenty-four hours a day, seven days a week." Like all Smith Islanders, Dwight refused to work the water on Sundays, a church day, though state law allowed it. "I figure if I can't make it in six days, a seventh day won't be the answer. You need a rest. The crabs need a rest, too. No one ever said you're supposed to catch all of anything."

Dwight, too, fished more pots now than when he was younger, but never much more than 350, what he could handle alone, or with a single mate, usually one of his sons. The efficiency and zeal—joy, even—with which he extracted a living from the bay was at once marvelous and terrible to behold. No one, year in and out, ever got more out of a crab pot.

As early as February, blue-black poofs of thin smoke from the stove pipe of his tin-roofed shanty signaled the stirrings of his annual cycle of crabbing. Inside, he was stripping old nylon line from his pots, burning it for heat. He might also be painting up "corks," the Styrofoam floats tied as markers to the sunken crab pots. Most big-time watermen bought these new each year by the hundreds to replace ones damaged by weather and, increasingly, cut off by pleasure boats and tanker traffic. Dwight, nearing fifty, had never purchased one in his life, preferring to roam the Tangier Sound marshes on slow winter and spring days, picking up abandoned corks for recycling. He was one of Tylerton's two or three ranking "junkmen," scavengers who never threw anything away. He would stop and pry the lid from a discarded paint can, to see if it contained usable dregs. Even on the mainland, he seemed to spot dropped ballpoint pens and coins lying on the ground.

In March, well before the mid-Chesapeake warmed enough for crabbing, he piled dozens of wire mesh and iron-framed pots on his 36-foot diesel-powered workboat, *Miss Marshall,* for the first of several trips to the mainland. There, renting a flatbed truck, he reloaded them for hauling some forty-five miles across the narrow Delmarva Peninsula to the shallower, faster-warming seaside embayments that ran from Cape Charles, Virginia, up through Ocean City, Maryland. After running *Miss Marshall* a long day's journey down and out of the Chesapeake and up the ocean side of the peninsula, he spent three to four weeks pursuing early-swimming crabs, sleeping aboard in the small, heated cabin, often taking up and moving hundreds of pots every few days.

By mid-April, he moved the whole show back to the island, and began running each day ten to twenty miles west to set pots in the deep channels toward the Potomac River. Sometime in May, he switched again, holding back his best jimmy crabs, usually at a time when they were bringing huge prices, up to $100 a bushel. Set out as live bait in pots near the island, the jimmies exuded pheromones, attracting females about to shed their shells to mate.

Soft crabs are the island's most lucrative product from May through October. Most watermen simply catch them and ship them daily, taking what the markets offer. Dwight some years ago invested in a walk-in freezer, attached improbably to his rickety shanty that balances on a forest of poles over the shallows between his home and the channel of Tyler's Creek. Mary Ada cleans and wraps their just-shed crabs—freezing more of them or less, depending on Dwight's sense of the market. Many evenings while most crabbers are unwinding from a long day, lounging in the store or taking the breeze in a shanty, he is on the phone to state seafood officials or other contacts up and down the bay, sniffing the economic winds: Are the big soft-crab packers freezing a lot or selling fresh? Will the prices be higher later? One winter morning I saw him replacing rotten boards in his dock. Not long after lunch, I asked Mary Ada, "Where's Dwight?" "Oh, he just called from New York," she said; "he got restless and took the boat to Crisfield. He hitched a ride from there with the Overnight [a local trucking firm] to Fulton Fish Market . . . he just thought he'd check what they were buyin' and sellin'."

After summer soft crabbing, Dwight returned with his hard-crab pots to deeper water, and weeks of running westward at dawn toward the Potomac, delivering his catch in late afternoon back to Crisfield on the mainland, arriving back on the island around dark. This he continued, many years, until nearly Christmas.

In January, I began trying to get a date out of Dwight for going after terrapin. I was still in the mainland habit of making appointments in advance. The answer was always the same. We would go "accordin' ": accordin' to the tides, accordin' to the winds, accordin' to the cold—you need a good freeze before terrapins will bed down and hibernate. I was cooking pancakes for Abby and Tyler's breakfast one morning when Dwight appeared in the door. "About fifteen minutes?" he asked, nodding in the direction of his boat. It was going to be perfect for terrapins—tide ebbing, water clear, no breeze riffling the surface. You had to have all those conditions to see their "sign," where they had buried in the mud of shallow coves. We would be covering, he figured, thirty to eighty miles that day in *Miss Marshall,* dragging behind us a flat-bottomed, 16-foot skiff from which to gouge out terrapins with our long-handled crab nets.

Dwight on this day says he has "got a good lead" on where some might be, from a gill-netter out of Fairmount, up the Sound. The netter's been picking up some huge old cows (terrapin females; males are bulls) in his perch nets. Dwight has also secured a market that is willing to pay up to $4.75 apiece for terrapins, apparently to satisfy Asian tastes on the west coast. He has studied charts of the area, zeroing in on a large cove, protected from winter winds, with enough depth that low tides won't expose its bottom. These parameters, combined with a consistency of bottom he describes as "soft, but not real soft," are prime for hibernating terrapins. "I think we might make a day's work," he concludes.

The bay is so beautiful today, you cannot imagine work anyplace else would be as fulfilling. All around us, illuminated by the palest sun, there is perfect calm, as if the atmosphere is holding its breath, awaiting the big nor'wester forecast to pound the bay around nightfall. On the Sound, flights of old squaw startle up from our bow wake. Sky and water blend in a liquid, airy backdrop of blues and grays and silvers, a seamless environment in which all solid objects, from marsh islands to ducks and lighthouses, seem to float and loom, larger than life.

Dwight, hat and layers of outer clothing doffed in the warm cabin, smokes cigarillos and snacks from an assortment of goodies strewn across the dash— half a pie, a tin of cookies, thick slices of Mary Ada's eight-layer chocolate cake, salami, Cokes, and assorted packs of cheese crackers. His hair is thinning and graying, his shoulders slump, and he is packing a bit of a paunch he usually picks up after the frantic work of summer winds down. He yawns, and looks, in the act, very middle-aged, tired, a little soft.

A few minutes later, he is transformed. *Miss Marshall* is anchored in deeper water, and in the skiff, we begin probing the cove that indents the salt marsh for several acres. Feet planted on the very tip of the little boat's prow, pushing the bow-end of his long-handled net into the bottom, Dwight shoves in effortless zigzags and loops across the cove. He eyeballs the bottom with the intensity of a heron poised to strike. I am assigned to stand in the stern with the other net. Pay attention to the gray-green mud passing beneath us. I will "see" where terrapin have buried, he assures me. After several minutes, hardly breaking his rhythmic shoving, Dwight deftly scoops a bowling ball-sized mass of black mud and hibernating terrapin. Another follows, and another and another. We have discovered a major bed of the creatures. Dwight's every dip is followed by encouragement to me: "See? See their sign?"

Well, no, I don't. Dwight by now has about twenty-five terrapins and per-haps 100 pounds of mud slithering and sloshing around my ankles in the skiff bottom. Now he's got thirty. "See?" "See?" Yes, I fib, dipping blindly, gouging up impressive divots. At the end of that nine-foot handle, a net full of mud, even minus the two pounds or so of a big terrapin, is all I can lift. Dwight shoves and dips, shoves and dips. "See?" My shoulders are about to tear from their sock-ets. No, dammit, I don't see; but even a blind hog, they say, must root up some acorns, and finally I boat one, as Dwight passes the half century mark. Shove, dip; shove, dip; "See?" "See?"

I half expected this seeing terrapin sign to be harder than Dwight made it out. The summer before, we stood one night, in the light of a single, bare bulb, by one of his crab floats. Dwight was "fishing up," extracting those crabs that had shed and turned soft. He had a hundred or more packed densely into each of a dozen floats. It must take forever to go through the swirling, indistin-guishable mass of crustaceans several times a day, I thought. But at the first float, he reached in with a miniature, short-handled net and deftly extracted five soft-ies in less than a minute before moving to the next float.

How did he tell those, I asked. How did he know he wasn't missing some?

"They're the ones that look a little different," he said; "can't you see?" He might as well have pointed at the Maine woods: "Over there; see that pine tree? The green one."

Dwight read his natural surroundings as avidly as I might have gone through several newspapers before breakfast. Automatically as a dog extracts information from the breeze, he never walked down the dock extending from in front of his home without noticing what the crabs and minnows and bottom grasses were doing. He was always checking a few eel pots and crab pots he kept set around his shanty, just to test the waters.

The water's gotten heavier, he would say, referring to the infinitesimally denser feel of the cooling winter bay as it slapped across *Miss Marshall's* windshield; or, "The island sounds different now than it did when I was younger," meaning sea gulls now mewed and cried on winter nights, where the gabble and squawk of geese and ducks once predominated. He and a neighbor could engage in protracted discussions about the significance of a crab one had found "on top of the mud, lively enough to snap at me," at a time of year when it should have been buried; also how "the seaside seems to be breedin' a prettier jimmy crab than it did a few years back." Crabs from one place, they knew, had broad bodies and short points to their shells; from another, longer points. No detail was ever dismissed as useless information.

No one travels through the landscape more observant than the hungry hunter, Barry Lopez wrote in *Arctic Dreams;* and so it was with the very best watermen.

They are, I realized, the true, top predators in the bay's food web. Large, fierce creatures—the tigers and grizzlies and great white sharks—fascinate us with the scope of their appetites for prey, and range of territory. Perhaps this partly explains the claim bay watermen still lay to the public's imagination—the notion that the modern Chesapeake still can support such great, free-ranging beasts, emblematic of wildness and freedom, even as we have tamed the surrounding lands from Boston to Richmond past harboring anything more terrible than a coyote.

As a city newpaper's environmental reporter, who grew up tutored in hunting and fishing by watermen, I have spent much of my adult life alternately deploring and marveling at their ability to exploit nature. My terrapin sortie with Dwight is mostly a time to marvel. The skiff is literally filling with terrapins. Shoving and scooping and probing and balancing, he is a master of the long-handled dip net, using it to take both winter terrapin and late-summer soft crabs, astoundingly efficient with gear a fifteenth-century Chesapeake Indian would have recognized. Even to his erstwhile mate, the incentive of all this seafood coming aboard, nearly five-bucks-worth to a dip, becomes infectious. It eases the ache in your shoulders; makes you think like a predator.

During a lull, I mention to Dwight a new Doppler radar I have read about. It can be used from satellites to "see" up to several feet beneath the surface. It could revolutionize archeology, the article said. Imagine what it could do to lo-cate the bay's embedded treasuries of terrapin some winter. Dwight is intrigued, and reminded that he *must* find out more about where "that scientist feller up the Patuxent is tracking all those terrapin . . . what's his name?"

Ah, Willem. I had almost forgotten. I know what he would think about today's adventure. To the wildlife manager, terrapins are a species to be exploited with extreme care, because they do not readily replace themselves. Cows grow larger than bulls and make up most of the catches of terrapins large enough to fetch top dollar. It takes up to thirteen years for a cow to reach sexual maturity, at which point they usually measure more than six inches on their plastron, or undershell. Maryland's current six-inch-minimum size limit thus protects vir-tually no breeding females. They may reproduce for several more decades, but predation on their eggs by coons and foxes is so high, Willem estimates it takes three years of coming ashore and laying three annual clutches of a dozen or more eggs for a mature female to effectively replace herself. Put another way, Dwight's eventual take for today of about a hundred terrapins, netted within a few hours, will take any survivors a collective three terrapin-centuries to replace.

Now, the rising tide begins to obscure the bottom. The terrapins, all around our ankles and shins in the skiff, come to life, stretching necks and legs from their shells as the sun warms them. They are lovely; fleshy folds all striped and whorled and mottled in soft, creamy blacks and grays and blueish tones. Their dark, hard-shelled backs are not literally diamond-patterned; rather, an intri-cate arrangement of pentagons and hexagons. No two undershells are alike; col-ors range from cheddary orange through lemony and olive to amber, and each uniquely patterned. They seem at least as individual as humans.

It has been a satisfying performance for Dwight today—deducing this secret place, trekking up here and wresting several hundred dollars from the half-frozen bay at a time when the whole mid-Chesapeake is devoid of other watermen. In the warm afternoon light, the cove sparkles blue and the marsh stretches away all golden and shimmery. A lone goose honks from somewhere, and a flock of canvasback ducks bobs jauntily nearby. You fancy Dwight drawing himself erect there on the skiff's prow, mud-spattered and sweaty, dip net raised like a con-ductor's baton at symphony's end, as the ovation swells; but it is only wavelets lapping the marsh bank.

It does turn out, as we reboard *Miss Marshall,* that his virtuosity has not gone unnoticed. A marine policeman is busting across the river in his 140-horsepower Whaler. Dwight motions to me to pitch overboard a couple undersized oysters he'd dipped, then changes his mind: "If he's going to arrest me for two oysters, let 'im do it." We both know if the cop wants to be a hardass, and goes through every terrapin with a measure, he is going to find a few illegals, and a good pay-day will turn to dust.

Dwight exudes confidence, but just for good measure, he introduces me, before the Whaler's motor fully idles down: "This is Mr. Horton with the environmental group, the Chesapeake Bay Foundation, and he also puts articles in the *Baltimore Sun.*" The cop, a young man, seems more interested in Dwight. He wants to shake his hand. "I recognized your boat. I saw you win a docking contest with her fifteen years ago when I was a kid. I guess you and her's won about every docking championship up and down Chesapeake Bay."

"Am I that old?" Dwight grins back, relaxing. He says the coming summer may be his last hurrah in the fiercely competitive watermen's boat dockings that are a staple of seafood festivals around the bay. Many of the young watermen now are willing to invest up to $2,000 in hydraulic steering—not a lot less than he paid for his first boat when he started on his own. *Miss Marshall*'s mechanical steering and Velvetdrive transmission are getting less competitive in backing several tons of boat into a narrow slip under full throttle. Dwight loves the contests, and winning, as much as anyone, and might get hydraulic steering and a twin-disc transmission someday; but his old rig is simple and maintenance-free, and has served well for seventeen years. "Anything that works, I stay with," he says.

The policeman ignores our terrapins. He does want to make sure we know we are working around some private bottom here—oyster beds leased from the state by a big packing company that sits on the shore a few miles away. Dwight assures him he hasn't been into the man's oysters, and with a wave and a smile, the Whaler departs.

He's okay, just doing his job, Dwight declares; and of course he's right. Still, on some level it rankles—even I, who have written countless articles calling for tough enforcement of conservation laws, am struck by the feeling that here you are, in midwinter in one of the wildest, lonesomest spots on the mid-Atlantic seaboard, just trying to catch a few terrapins that you feel you've certainly earned; and even here you can't pass three hours without being checked and told to watch it, that some fat cat onshore has dibs on the very bottom of the bay. Private oyster leasing is often proposed as more efficient and encouraging of innovation than the bay's predominant "wild" harvest of the public shellfish beds; but today I can understand why watermen have fought through the centuries to keep the commons from being leased out.

THAT SEASON and the couple winters that followed, Dwight pursued terrapins with more diligence than any waterman on the Chesapeake. He would come back to this cove, on the hunch that more of the animals might be holed up in water just a bit too deep for the dip net; and using a small dredge behind the *Miss Marshall*, take hundreds in a single day. Some days he would spend half the morning cutting thick ice with the boat, then shoving it in slabs beneath the surrounding frozen surface, to free up enough water to net in. One day seemed particularly satisfying. On the way to Crisfield to visit Mary Ada, recovering from an operation, he was able to extract enough terrapins from a cove not far from the hospital to pay a good chunk of the medical bill—"Made a bank withdrawal, ye did," a neighbor joked.

At times, I felt the bay's terrapins could not stand more than a few hunters so zestful as Dwight. However, many of his runs produced no terrapins at all, or scarcely enough to cover his diesel bill. The market was small—a big catch of terrapins by just a few watermen could depress prices or even quell all demand for days, or weeks. And there were just not that many days of winter when conditions were right for serious forays.

Other reasons I thought motivated him to range for hours of running time, and dozens of miles in every direction from the island, returning on occasion well after dark. He went one better on the often-quoted lines from *Wind in the Willows*—nothing more fun than "simply messing about in boats"—nothing, perhaps, except making money while messing about; and better yet, making it on days when most of your competition was home by the fireside.

Frugal as he was with money, Dwight in those winters spent himself freely. There was nothing in terrapin hunting that would commend it to those who measure their labor on the basis of dollars-per-hour. What there was, though—Dwight often talked about it—was "the thrill of the chase."

DWIGHT MARSHALL, FORTY-NINE

✦ Of course I'm in the water business to make money, but there has got to be some fun to it too. A lot of this stuff, if it's not a little bit of a game to you, you'd better not do it. You take my going out in the marsh of a winter, pickin' up used corks for my pots. It saves me a little bit, but it's fun. Most watermen here make their own crab pots—buy the wire and put it together, and that saves money; but I buy mine made . . . I'd rather be diggin' ditches than set inside and bend wire.

I always liked to prospect. You can make a livin', and a lot of watermen do, by goin' where everybody else is goin' and day after day, just grind it out, grind it out. But I'd twice rather find a fifty-dollar bill than have somebody give it to me. My father and my uncle used to say the times when crabs was hardest to find was when they liked it best. "Time to go deep, to get out and get after it," they'd say. I've heard watermen say they wish it was always plentiful times, but where'd be the fun in that?

Sometimes I look at the map and dream about if I had the time and money to take my boat from Florida to Maine, just seein' what I could catch, up and down all that shoreline. A man from Maine told me last year that our blue crab, which, big ones, get to about 7 inches across the shell here, how they get 14 inches, some of 'em up there. I begged him to ship me one, frozen, just to have the chance to handle a 14-inch crab. Wouldn't be no fun* to do that.

My wife's father was one of the prospectors, which is why I always enjoyed working aboard his oyster dredge boat. It's never knowin' what you're going to find that keeps you going—it's excitin'; and of course if you always knew what you were going to find, a lot of days you'd never left the dock.

One winter Billy Smith and I were oystering over at St. Jerome's Creek on the western shore and we had been draggin' a chain—nowdays, of course, they got video finders, but then we drug chains, which would feel a certain way when you hit oysters. I had drug and drug and drug, and I was cold and tired and my arms were about to fall off, when I felt a little nub. It felt good, and I circled right around and, oh, man, just the way that chain ripped back across, I could tell, it was just the right roughness.

Well, I put the tongs down and came up with little strips of shell, which were the bills of oysters, and I knew I was on clare [clear] oysters. I caught forty bushels there by evening. Next day, I went there to my little marker buoy and caught ninety. Twenty-five was the limit, but if I didn't get 'em, somebody else'd get 'em; so I got 'em all—three hundred bushels before I quit. Findin' that little hill of oysters, or those crabs buried in the bottom that nobody else has got on, that's the thrill of the chase. You just need enough of those days to keep you going through all the rest. With oysterin' in the winter steady goin' down every year, it finally got to where there wasn't much chance for the thrills anymore, and that is why now I'd rather spend my winter piddlin', progging about, going after terrapin. ◆

It is a Saturday night in early March as Dwight relates this. The bay's top predator is kicked back, shoes off, in his big easy chair in the living room, a blaze in the fireplace kneading us to drowsiness. An open Bible, a copy of *National Fisherman,* and his reading glasses lie on the thick carpet. With the wind whipping up outside, I don't hear the single peal of the church bell, but Dwight pulls on his tennis shoes. "Come on if you want; walk over to church. I got to lead special prayer for a few minutes," he says, casually as some might go to the fridge for a snack. He is Tylerton's lay leader—has, in fact, served several terms. It is a major responsibility in a place that revolves around church as much as the island. Tonight's meeting is not part of the normal services, he explains: "It's the sort of thing we do when it's felt there is a need; we'll just gather and pray for the island, spiritually and physically—for help with the erosion, for the health of the bay and the seafood."

Dwight prosecuted such faith as resolutely as he pursued seafood. To the

*It would be fun. Islanders often use such "backward talk."

church, to the Lord, went 10 percent off the top from every bushel he harvested, from the biggest paydays down to a quarter from the $2.50 his kids got for helping make crab pots when they were little. Mary Ada told me about a time early in their marriage:

+ Things was tight that year. Dredgin' oysters with my dad, Dwight not only hadn't made any money, Dad had to give him $10 out of his own pocket so he could get home from up the bay. We were paying $20 a month rent in those days for a place with no inside bathroom; you'd tote water from the kitchen to the washer. Duke, our oldest, was an infant. There was few crabs that year and no money in the bank. We were down to our last dollar—I mean Dwight had exactly one dollar. Revivals were going on in the church, and he said, let's give it. If a dollar, one way or the other, was going to make him or break him, he was in the wrong business. I don't believe he ever had a year since where he ended up losing money. +

One might presume that Dwight was the driving force in the Marshall clan's prominence in seafood and community—if one didn't know Mary Ada. It was an extraordinary partnership. "To be a successful waterman, you got to be born to it," Dwight said once, adding: "your wife needs to be, too." His marriage after high school to the former Mary Ada Evans of Ewell was a union of thoroughbreds. Her father was among the island's elite oyster-dredging captains; also, with her mother, mainstays of church and community. Her brothers were excellent crab potters and businessmen.

Mary Ada could rise at 2:30 A.M. and pick 20 pounds of crabmeat and load it aboard the 7:00 A.M. ferry to Crisfield, then cook breakfast and get the kids off to school and clean the house and "cut and wrap" several hundred soft crabs for the freezer, before picking some more and rustling a several-course dinner for Dwight and four children. She could bake an eight-layer chocolate cake for a church supper, ice it, and have the cooking pans and bowls washed and put away—in twenty minutes, I have timed her—while licking the icing that is shiny and smooth as patent leather.

In addition to their all-out participation in the seafood business, she and Dwight also for several years ran the town's grocery store, carrying up to $18,000 in credit some winters when people's incomes faltered.

She was not shy about sharing her work ethic with the rest of the family. Indeed, many of their friends and neighbors joked—but only half-joked—that it was no wonder Dwight stayed out so much in pursuit of terrapins and such; he knew there was no such thing as laying around idle in Mary Ada's house. I called there once for Dwight, who had returned from an exhausting, fourteen- or fifteen-hour day on the water. Little Maria said, "Daddy has gone to lie down." "Well, rout 'im out, Maria," Mary Ada called from the kitchen. "He's been in the bed half an hour, and he's got to fix something in my picking shed any-how." Maria returned from the bedroom, grinning impishly. "Ma, he says tell you, go suck a egg."

But that was rare. Dwight believed equally with Mary Ada in the concept of "driving yourself" as the key to making their life work. "A lot of people that know how to crab don't make good crabbers," he would say; "you got to drive yourself when you don't feel like it, when you're tired, when you feel bad. When it's time to crab, you go, 'cause when they're gone, it won't make any differ-ence what you do."

By Tylerton standards, their family lived quite well. Mary Ada had a talent for decorating and always seemed to have one or more renovations going on, sometimes importing carpenters from the mainland. It was one of the ways, she said candidly, she kept from getting frustrated and depressed about all the things she could not do, the places she could not go, because of living on an is-land. With new vinyl siding, new bay window, new carpet, new bathroom, new porch, new yard plantings, their place would have fit into many an upscale sub-urb on the mainland. They had managed, at midlife, good credit, a healthier savings account than most of my mainland acquaintances, a fairly new car, good vacations, and a college education for their eldest son—this while paying for most of their health care out of pocket. When people asked me how much is-land watermen made, I pointed to Dwight and Mary Ada as examples of what was possible, though not typical. Virtually upper middle class, by mainland stan-dards, I said—but I didn't know anyone in any economic class on the main-land who worked as hard.

Mary Ada was as lively and effusive as Dwight was understated and taciturn. She had a flair with language, asking a visitor, "tarry awhile," and lamenting the town's population decline: "all the women that's still here has already laid their litter." She endeared herself to my wife early on, as she patted to a spot on the seat of a skiff between two island ladies and said, "That narrer little starn of yours'll slip right in here."

She ran her outfit like a general. Once she noticed Duke, her oldest, non-chalantly bringing a plastic bag downstairs. What is it? Why isn't your brother up yet? Was he drinkin' in Crisfield last night?

Duke mumbled and hustled out the front door, but Mary Ada intercepted him cutting around back to bury the evidence of the previous night's drunken barfing. Kevin, the younger brother, is now aroused and accused.

"Ye don't jump to conclusions none!" he fumed at Mary Ada.

"I don't know ye!" she shot back.

Another time she decided, after a family squabble at the supper table, that her children did not say often enough how much they loved their father. Well, Ma, Dad never says it to us either, they protested. That was true, she said, turn-ing to Dwight, and someday they'd all be gone and he'd regret it.

Well, shoot, Mary, my dad never said it to me either, but I knew he did, and that ought to be good enough for them, Dwight replied.

Well, it was not good enough, Mary Ada said. In Ewell, her family did it all the time. "And she made us all stay at that table until everyone hugged everybody and said they loved them," Duke recalled. "It was the hardest thing we ever did."

Then there is Mary Ada, standing before a Wednesday night prayer service in church, leading a discussion on prayer. She leaves off from First Thessalonians to talk about the call she got from her youngest boy, Jamie, in Japan. He was in the hospital with sores in his mouth, bad ones, and was asking for "special prayers" from the congregation back home: to "have the Lord touch my mouth." It was, she said, a testament to the whole town that one of its own had such faith in prayer and community.

"Of course," she said, eyes tearing, "as a mother, what I really craved to do was take my little boy [a Marine, 6 feet 4 inches and 200 pounds] in my arms and soothe those blisters with his head on my lap. . . ."

Sometimes, the family really did seem like the Waltons, transplanted from mountain to marsh; but Dwight and Mary Ada in those terrapin winters were under considerable pressures. Dwight probably found terrapin hunting a genuine respite. Earlier on, they were having to help financially as Duke struggled to establish himself in business on the mainland. Jamie, a bright student when he wished to be, was threatening to fail school in Crisfield. Kevin, the middle boy, was living at home in his early twenties, finding it harder than he had dreamed to get ahead as a waterman. He was an able waterman, and worked hard by most anyone's standards, but hadn't learned to "drive himself," Dwight would say. "And Dad'll drive himself into a heart attack," Kevin would retort (Dwight's father died of heart trouble, and an older brother had had two heart attacks).

Mary Ada wondered whether the bay could support a young man starting out any more. Indeed, Kevin's crab boat, a moderate one by current standards, had cost him $16,000, plus $3,500 for the engine, which was about what Dwight's entire first boat had cost. The little money he had gotten ahead his first winter of oystering, he spent on an appendix operation. The next summer crabbing, at the height of season he lost most of a week's work and paid $550 to repair damages to his prop and rudder from running aground; also one of the drains in his crab float stopped up, and dozens of prime peeler crabs escaped over the sides during the night. He was considering leaving the island to do carpentry work on the western shore.

Dwight, meanwhile, had been stiffed for $7,000 by a Baltimore seafood merchant. The one flaw in freezing and marketing his own soft crabs was that he often had to advance crabs to small dealers and wait for them to pay. The dealer, he was advised, had declared bankruptcy. He would probably never collect.

Virginia, where Dwight did a lot of his crabbing, was also turning the financial screws, raising license prices for out-of-state watermen to thousands of dollars in a patent attempt to preserve harvests exclusively for its own watermen. The Smith Islanders, Dwight thought, could hire a lawyer and prove that unconstitutional; but it would cost a fortune, even if they won. In the Maryland legislature, sportsmen were putting pressure on to make the striped bass, which Dwight hoped to begin netting in another winter, a recreation-only species. Mary Ada said she had never seen her husband so discouraged and disgusted.

One winter afternoon, after a cursory terrapin expedition near Crisfield, Dwight took *Miss Marshall* up and down the local waterways, progging for something new in his experience: land. He and Mary Ada were thinking the unthinkable, moving to the mainland. I had no doubt they would do fine there—better than ever; but for Tylerton, already battered by a steady decline in population, it would be a harsh blow, pulling a major pillar from supporting the place's economic, religious, and social life. Ultimately, it was waterfront that would determine whether he could make the leap, Dwight explained. Access to waterfront was critical—for his shanty, his crab-shedding floats, his crab pots, his boats; for his psyche. But even around the marshy, bug-infested, and somewhat seedy environs of Crisfield, waterfront was increasingly expensive, and guarded by zoning laws against any new proliferation of watermens' functional but rundown-looking operations.

The big crab-packing companies would, to be sure, rent you as many shedding floats as you wanted in their own complexes, where hundreds of tiers of floats were erected behind chain-link fence, the crab shedders' equivalent of urban high-rise housing projects. And university people in Maryland were pushing new, "closed-cycle" water circulation systems, where you could add salt to well water and shed soft-shell crabs in your garage on a mountaintop. All that appealed to Dwight about as much as a zoo cage to a wolf.

He never found a suitable place to relocate, for which I suspect he said a silent prayer of thanks. Within a few more winters, Jamie had graduated and joined the Marines. Duke had begun to distinguish himself as a young insurance agent for Nationwide on the Eastern Shore; he was building a new grocery store in Tylerton, not so much as an investment as to help keep the place a viable community. Kevin had moved out and taken up carpentering on the western shore, selling his shanty to a man from New Jersey who said he planned to move down any year and become a full-time crabber. Mary Ada had ripped out walls and reconfigured her dining room and living room.

She never dreamed, she said, when raising three boys, that not one would stay; "but not many are now. Henry's boy's gone to the Naval Academy. Charley and Francis had five and one's here; Fred's four, none left; Ruth and Waverly, four and two gone, Evelyn and James, five and all gone now. Kevin, I thought would be here 'til the last sea gull flies, but he just was not gettin' ahead. Jamie, he come home one day and said, 'Ma, I've got to go in my skiff to Ewell just to date, or talk to somebody my own age.' Winter was comin' on, and he signed up for the Marines."

DWIGHT WAS NOT doing much terrapining any more. Striped bass had come back to the point the state was allowing a modest winter gill net fishery, something Dwight said he had "always craved to try."

But that could change, of course; all "accordin': to the markets, to the seafood laws, to the bay." In a few places he was crabbing, Dwight said, he couldn't help but notice a lot of terrapin heads poking out of the water. They had to be bedding down somewhere, come winter, and he had a few ideas where that might be. And he had talked on the phone with Willem. The scientist had asked Dwight please not to bother his marked terrapins on the Patuxent, and invited him to come up and see his research project. Dwight had promised to take Willem out from Smith Island some winter day, to show him where the creatures hibernated. On a map, Dwight pointed to a few coves on the Patuxent. He would bet, if a man were to go there in wintertime, he'd find some terrapins.

WILLEM ROOSENBURG, THIRTY-SIX

On a July morning, Willem sits beneath a shade tree near the Patuxent River sorting and marking terrapins, and talking about a novel and fascinating twist his research is taking. He is beginning to think the Chesapeake's sandy edges, the beaches where its terrapins nest, may be divided into "male beaches" and "female beaches." It has to do with ESD, or environmental sex determination. This is believed ancestral in most turtles, as well as crocodiles and some snakes and fish; maybe in the dinosaurs. It means sex is not determined by X and Y chromosomes, as in humans; rather, by outside factors—in the case of turtles, the temperature of the sands in which the eggs incubate. It seems that what makes a Chesapeake terrapin a girl or a boy may be a surprisingly small variation in incubation temperature . . . 88°F gives you all females, while at 81°F, all males result. Such a narrow critical temperature range might have been why dinosaurs went extinct: a small lowering in global temperature resulted in not enough females.

Willem says it would be especially critical to identify those beaches of the bay whose solar orientation, or lower water table, causes higher, female-producing temperatures. Females are most critical to sustaining terrapin populations (as for the males, as in so many species, you don't need all that many for reproductive purposes).

Sounds good to me. Those beaches, I know, are also used by astonishing varieties of other creatures for nesting, from horseshoe crabs to black skimmers, pelicans, and terns. Protection is good. I do wonder whether we may go from there to identifying and protecting hibernation areas, and whether that won't someday remove another plank from the stage on which the predator-waterman performs his dance, that goes "accordin' to" the bay's ever-shifting opportunities.

Perhaps we can work it out, if we listen to both Dwight and Willem, who both have looked into a terrapin's eyes and seen something special. I saw it happen first with Dwight one afternoon in Tylerton. Kids came running down the street: come see, Dwight has landed with the biggest terrapin anybody ever caught. Dave, my photographer friend, was visiting, and we hurried down to photograph the giant. It was a female that probably exceeded fifty years, fat as a football. Dwight's whole skiff was acrawl with that day's haul. Dave begged to do a portrait of the old girl, and Dwight obligingly posed her for the camera. After several minutes of this he sighed and said, "Well, I was afraid of that, if I got to lookin' at one. It's caught my eye. I'll have to throw this one back"— an affection that did not extend to her greater family, which went off the next morning in bushel baskets, bound for the stewpots of urban Chinatowns.

As for Willem, the more one gets to know scientists, the more you realize that the best ones are characterized by dispassionate sorting of the evidence, energized by a deep passion for their subject. He has developed a profound respect for his creatures' intelligence, and the elegance of their evolutionary adaptations. He and his assistants not infrequently mention a terrapin "catching your eye," with the clear implication that something, more felt than measurable, passed between researcher and turtle.

Willem finishes sorting terrapins. It is almost time to hit the beach again to check nesting. Money has been short for the project this summer, and he's been supplementing grad student salaries by running traps up and down the river for a local crabber, taking half the profits. If he had another life to live, Willem reflects, he'd like to try it as a waterman. "If I've had any success, it's because I'm persistent. I like to catch things and I don't give up."

I almost expected him to begin talking about "the thrill of the chase."

Saildays

I drudged the same boat for 44 years, never was arested or found for small oysters or anything else, never was before a commissioner for ill treating crew, never had a man drowned . . . had the same cook for 25 years, and for the last 25 years did not sail on Sunday to forward business.

"A Few Things I Am Proud Of"—from the diary of Willie A. Evans, a Smith Island oyster captain of the late nineteenth and early twentieth centuries

DRUDGING

IN DEATH, Elmer Francis Evans lay as he had passed so many nights in life. The flowers in the Ewell Methodist Church were arranged around him in the shape of the old captain's "drudge [dredge] boat." Aboard her, he had sailed from home every fall to work the Chesapeake's oysters. Before the coffin closed, three other old dredger captains came together by the flowery funeral ship. These were men who could employ a ten-ton sailing vessel like a surgeon's scalpel. Collectively, they knew the invisible, subaqueous Chesapeake across thousands of square miles as well as a farmer knows the contours of his homeplace. No words passed, but the force of shared experience was almost palpable. It was the gathering of an elite remnant, the fading link to an era of intimate relationship with the wind and a mollusk and the bay bottom, that shaped the island for more than a century.

In the 1820s, the exhaustion of New England's commercial oyster beds set the stage for the industry that would shift Smith Island forever from a subsistence and barter economy, and define its culture for the next century and a half. The world discovered the Chesapeake oyster beds, perhaps the richest trove of the shellfish in the world. During the decades after the Civil War, the exploitation built to the fever pitch of a gold rush. More than a thousand sailcraft—four-masted schooners, sloops, pungies, and bugeyes—dragged heavy iron dredges ceaselessly across the "rocks," as the reeflike agglomerations of oysters were called, catching them by the hundreds of bushels a day.

In that heyday of sail, islands like Smith probably were less isolated than at any time in their history, including present times. In 1886, the oyster harvest peaked in Maryland at some 15 million bushels, an annual production of edible meat, it was calculated, equal to the yield from 160,000 head of prime steers. The oyster fleet at that point employed a fifth of everyone involved in fishing in America. Oyster captains ruled the waves, outgunning the struggling Maryland Oyster Navy's attempts to enforce even modest conservation. On the positive side, the oystermen of this era used their political clout, forcing Baltimore to construct the nation's most modern sewage treatment plant to protect bay water quality.

So intense was the oystering that it would eventually alter the physical shape of the bay's bottom, breaking apart the reefs in which oysters naturally grew, and upon which ships of early explorers grounded at low tide. "The oyster rocks was not always large as they are now," wrote Captain Benjamin F. Marsh, a Smith Island dredge boat owner, in a journal entry referring to around 1900; "dredging has spreaded them out." New studies, comparing old charts of the bay bottom to new bathymetric surveys, have found a dramatic flattening of original bottom contours. This made oysters more susceptible to silting over, and perhaps more vulnerable to the diseases that now plague them—though this latter is still speculative.

As harvests slid from the unsustainable peaks of the 1880s, never to return, oystermen sought an easy-to-build, cheaper alternative to their big sail dredge craft; also one that required fewer crew. What evolved was a beamy vessel, usually 38 to 55 feet long, bottom made with simple crosswise planking. It could be built by a good backyard carpenter, and hundreds were. They featured a single mast, rising some 60 feet above the deck, set forward nearly to the bow, and raked at a 75-degree angle back toward the center of the deck. A boom as long as the boat ran along the triangular sail's bottom edge, extending out over its stern. The acreage of such a mainsail, aided by a smaller jib in front, could power massive, toothed iron dredges through a hard, shelly oyster bottom in even light air. It also meant that the shallow-draft vessels, which had no stabilizing keel of lead, just a wooden centerboard that was raised and lowered through a slot in the bottom, could capsize if the captain was inattentive to the wind.

By the early 1900s, there were more than fifty on Smith Island alone. Today, the twenty or so of these vessels that remain in the world comprise North America's last fleet of working sailcraft. They have been adopted as the Maryland state boat, and are called "skipjacks." But that was a city word, islanders say. They always called them, simply, "drudge boats." Through the first sixty years of this century, there were few able-bodied island men who never worked a winter aboard one of the dredgers. They were economic mainstays, and more. Each boat and captain had a reputation, a personality, a whole lore that developed around their annual voyages. Masts rising higher than anything but the church steeples, they were sources of small-town pride—ambassadors of Smith Island that sallied forth every fall to ports from Baltimore to Solomons, Annapolis to

Wenona. Returning every December from weeks away, the sight of the dredgers' tall masts parading in through the bayside jetties meant merry Christmas to wives, girlfriends, and children. "Warn't no fair sight to see them comin' down the bay . . . like Santa Claus on his sleigh," the daughter of one captain recalled.

Even in abandonment, towed on high tide up some marsh gut to rot and die, the dredge boats were where island children grew up playing pirate, swinging gloriously out over the water on ropes from the tall masts.

The men who worked the dredgers have their memories, good and bad, but no illusions. It was hard, cold work, dawn to dark many days, in sleet and snow and cruel wind, culling piles of oysters on hands and knees on an open deck; leaping to reef and unreef the mammoth sail several times a day, as the winds or the captain's strategy changed. The windlasses used to raise the dredges before engine power was substituted could just wear a man out in a few years. Before rubberized gloves, "your hands would get so chafed, you'd have to pull your fingers apart some mornings to start culling," a dredger captain said.

A small cabin below decks, measuring perhaps 12 feet by 10 feet, heated with a small cookstove, housed captain and four to six crew for weeks at a time. "One time a woman said to me at the dock in Annapolis, 'It must be romantic,' " said a retired crewman. "Romantic? That it were, a'sleepin on a shelf with your face about six inches below a leaky deck; wakin' up of a cold mornin' with your hair froze by the frost of your breath to the side planks." "Like sleepin' in a coffin," recalled another islander, who found life aboard too claustrophobic to endure. Another remembers the horror of his first night aboard, being kept awake by the fierce gnawing of what had to be a large rat, reverberating throughout the below decks; then the real horror, when he realized it was not a rat, which could be trapped and drowned, but the captain, who had a habit of grinding his teeth all night.

Romantic? Certainly not from most oystermen's perspective; yet the dredge boats caught the public fancy and endured, long past the time when combustion engines or the farmed oysters of aquaculturists might have displaced them. It was courtesy of a Maryland law that to this day allows oysters to be dredged only under sail (except for a 1966 amendment allowing power on two "push days," Monday and Tuesday). And in enduring, the old boats, originally devised as cheap workhorses, came to be part of the Chesapeake scene, bounding the time between fall and spring as much as the turning and greening of leaves.

The skipjacks' season begins in mid-November. A song by my friend Tom Wisner, the Chesapeake singer and poet, called *"Dredgin' Is My Drudgery,"* says it like this:

> When the summer sun is restin'
> And the crabs are settlin' down
> Trees are turnin' rusty

> And the marsh is burned and brown
> Then I long to feel the timbers
> Of a vessel brought to life
> By restless winds and hardy men
> Who join me in my plight

The late autumn has always provided a rich overlap of all that is central to pleasant living on the Chesapeake—fresh, steamed blue crabs still to be had, and now, raw, salty oysters for an appetizer; striped bass are still biting, and goose season's open too; loons and swans yodel on the coves, coon dogs bay in the night woods; harvesters lumber across waterfront farms, shelling corn into glistening mounds; and the fresh sails and new-painted hulls of the dredge boats, waltzing out on the oyster rocks, put a fine, bright exclamation point on the whole affair.

Come March and the old boats look as if they have been in a war, decks and sides worn to bare wood, bilge pumps pissing a constant stream. And Tom's song continues:

> Come March I'm feelin' weary
> And I long to go ashore
> My knees are growin' heels and toes
> My back is bent and sore
> I've culled 2,000 bushels
> And I'm rusted to the bone
> Wind and water whistles
> Where my muscles used to roam

For Smith Island, the dredge boat era ended in 1972 when its last one, the *Ruby G. Ford*, was sold up the bay to a Tilghman Islander. This is her captain's story.

DANIEL HARRISON—SAILING MAN

✦ The *Ruby Ford*, they say, was the first of what they called skipjacks out of Somerset County. She was built just across Tangier Sound from here in Fairmount, in 1891, and was 45 foot in length and about 15 foot beam. She was nothing fancy, just a boat that was built to do a certain job, but she would sail. One day we beat up the bay into Annapolis against a big storm of wind, and it set the old-timers there to fightin'. They said we couldn't have brought her up against that wind, but we did.

She was my first dredge boat, but I already knew a little bit about sail. I grew up scraping for soft crabs that way. Nowadays, scrape boats got an engine and they pull two scrapes, which is similar to small dredges, and think they are doing something. When I started, we had a sail and we pulled three scrapes out of a 26-foot boat. You would have two out off the windward side, and a third off your stern, held to the leeward. You would have to tend to your tiller, and reef and unreef your sail as the wind would change, and then when the scrapes got full, you would pull that leeward one first, and that would make your boat head up and spill wind out of her sails; and when the sails was just a'shakin' and you had cut your speed, it was time to pull those two windward scrapes; and each one a' them three scrapes, all full of grass and crabs, weighed, oh, maybe 50–60 pounds, and you would dump them aboard; and then you would run back around to the stern and throw that leeward scrape out first, then back to the windward side and throw the next, and the next; and then you would cull through all the grass and sort your crabs, all the time watching to make sure you were on course and your speed was right to make a good lick. There was more to it than that, really, but that will give you the idea of it.

My wife's stepfather had the *Ruby,* and he had been after me and my brother, Edward, to crew aboard of her. He said if we would come, he would sell half of her for $300 and the other half, when he died, for $300 more. So that winter we went drudgin'. Now, I knew right away that I could do better sailing the boat and dredging it than the captain could, but o' course I never wanted to tell him that. But the time came when we had found this little hill of oysters up the bay, and buoyed her off, which is the way you set marks so you can study how to dredge a place.

It is on them little hills, some no moren' a lump, just a rise of maybe five or six feet off the bottom, that you find some of your nicest and thickest oysters. Many of 'em aren't on any chart, or anywhere near the big oyster rocks everybody knows about, but they're there. Some are no bigger than this living room—why, not half as big; but even a little place like that, you could make a good day's work, couple hundred bushels. Nowadays, captains can use these video finders to look for lumps, but we would do it by using a sounding pole, or dragging a chain and feeling for the vibrations, which can tell what kind of bottom you had.

To work a hill, you've got to know just when to drop your dredge, and exactly what angle to bring your dredges across it to do any good at all. You watch your dredges, how they look, every time they come up; mud in the back of 'em, and oysters in the front, and you're droppin' too soon; oysters in the back and mud in the front, and you're droppin' too late. The trick is to just skip your dredges, nick the surface down there, and come up with clare [clear] oysters in that dredge.

If you can't get to know in your head whether a hill is shaped flat on top, or round, or maybe even what I'd call sprangled off in jangles; if you can't see that in your mind same as a painting on the wall, then you'll just be the kind of dredger that grinds it out, workin' the flat bottom and the places everybody knows about.

Really, it's an art to it. You got to take account of which way the tide is running, and how to cramp your sails down, for you don't want much wind for dredging a hill, just light air, eight or nine miles would be a'plenty. Now, when it is blowing, that hill is twice harder to get at. Say this is the hill [and he places a big, white family Bible on the table between us]; look at me now! I'm showin' you something. Now, if the wind is moderate, you can sail right up to the edge here, drop your dredge, and drag right over like this. But if it is a'blowing, then you have to go way down this way, shoot her up, and shake your sails to spill wind. And, a'course the tide can change all that around another way.

Anyway, that first winter on *Ruby* we had this hill buoyed off on one particular day, and the captain tried four or five swipes across her, and I knew there was more oysters down there than we were catching, and Edward did too, and he said, Daniel, go back there and tell him to let you try it. Well, I went back there. The captain, he acted like it aggravated him a little bit, but down in the cabin he jumped, and I made a lick, and both dredges were full of the most oysters you ever saw in your life. The captain come up to see what we'd caught. He didn't have any teeth, and you could see his pipe just a'workin' in those old gums; and he went back down in the cabin and sat, and I dredged the rest of that day.

I think that was around 1936, and I was twenty-one then, and one of the youngest captains on the bay. Now there was lots of good dredgers around here. I wasn't the only one. Some just did it better than others, like anything else in life. After I got to dredgin' *Ruby,* the old captain got sick, he got cancer, and he would have to stay home. And I would carry him money. The way the money worked on a drudge boat was the first eight weeks, from November up to Christmas, a third of all you sold your oysters for came off the top, "the boat's share," we called it; it went for repairing the boat, rigging her up, grub; and then the rest was shared by the captain and the crew. Then after Christmas the boat's share went to a fourth. Anyway, when I carried the boat's part to the captain, he cried, and he told me, Dan, you can make me more money when I am home sick in bed than I could dredgin' her.

One reason we were successful is we always had good crews. Many a man on this island and on Tangier, too, can tell you about winters aboard the *Ruby Ford.* I think a lot would say it was hard, grindin' work, and that they'd sign on again today for the same money they made some of those winters nearly thirty years back.

Among our crew, we didn't allow drinking. There could be some some rough characters aboard of drudge boats, and you had to watch it. They tell here of the time in 1916, a crewman aboard a boat from this island tried to shoot the captain eight times. The gun never fired, but they could count the times the firing pin hit the shell. Then he struck the captain thirteen times in the head with the blunt end of a hatchet; beat his little boy up, too, and took all their money. They lived, but the captain was never the same, and he died here two years later.

Dredge boats didn't always have a good reputation, though the worst of it, shanghaiing men out of bars, workin' 'em till their toes froze and that sort of stuff, was before my time. But we never had anything but good relations. The *Ruby Ford* was known all across the bay. Drudgin', you got to know lots of different ports. One captain from the island even had a black church in Baltimore, where he'd go when he was layin' in there of a Sunday, and he was treated just like a member of the congregation. There was a store to Solomons where we always used to dock, and the owner gave us the key. He said any time I'm not there, help yourself to what you need; and Smith Island boats were always welcome there, even after he was dead and gone.

We had an arrangement, me and Edward. I sailed the boat and rigged her, and he was in charge of finding the oysters. There was a lot of good dredgers on the bay, but I think we had a team that was one of the best. You got to have a lot of ambition to make a good waterman, and I don't think many had more than Edward. I have heard him say to crew, when one would give him a look that said it must be time to quit, "You only get outta this life what you put inta it," and we'd keep on dredgin'. He never did want to stop. Used to be mornings a'dredgin' that we'd be sailin' out and it would come such a storm you knew it wasn't fit to be out. We'd start to see these, what we called 'em was *"black flaws,"* where the wind would come down so hard, where she'd pitch into the water it got right dark and flawy-like; and he would say, "Dan, what do you think we ought to do?" Well, I'd know he wasn't anxious to go, but he hated to be the one to say it.

Another time, we had got away from the rest of the crowd and we had found some oysters. We must have had 550 bushels on her. Her scuppers were so close to going under, a mouse could of drunk water out of 'em. Loaded like that you would cork the cabin door shut, so when she took waves across her deck, she wouldn't fill with water. About that time Johnny, who was dredging with us that year, he looked down the bay, and he could see further than any man I ever knew in my life—naked eye, we called it—and he saw the rest of the drudge boats comin'. It wouldn't be long before they'd be on those oysters, and that would wind it up for us making another day's work there. Well, Ed looked at me and said, "Dan, what are we going to do?" See, it hurt him to stop and let those other dredgers get some; and us nearly 'bout sunk. I said, "Ed, I guess we could shove them all overboard and catch 'em over again." He didn't lack for push, Edward didn't.

One time that's just what dredgers did have to do, shovel 'em back over.

Now, we made some good catches in our time—more'n 1,800 bushels in one week—which was the best we ever landed. But there were tough times, too, you needn't doubt it. In 1933 we got as little as 17 cents a bushel, for the best oysters in the bay. Sometimes in those days the packers—when you got to Crisfield, and the whole harbor'd be so full of dredge boats you could walk across it on their decks—wouldn't even want your oysters. Captains would take their catch and shovel it back out on a bar, and then catch it up again and take it back to Crisfield when finally there'd be a market.

They used to have this old mule on the dock that would walk ahead to work a derrick that would take your catch off, a bushel and a half at a time, in a big tub. Well, I guess the fellow [that] owned him thought the mule was about to die; so one time when the market was bad, he made a deal with one of the island captains: Take the mule and I'll buy your oysters. And that's just what he did. About halfway back to the island, the old mule he fell down on deck and busted his head, and they thought he was dead right there; but they stood 'im back up, and he made it. He lived on the island for about a month before he did die.

There was times so tight we would jack up two of the valves in the engine on the little push boats we carried on our stern for power when we weren't sailin'—run her on four cylinders to save gas, and gas was selling for ten cents a gallon at that time. One of the island captains sold a pint of his blood in Baltimore for money enough to make it back down the bay one winter. Things was all on a different scale back then. We never had the options that the youth got today, everything from food stamps to college education. When we were able to change from a wood stove down in the cabin to gas, we thought we were livin' right. Edward, after we'd been sleeping aboard, under the stern deck all those winters, somebody gave him a sleepin' bag. Why, he thought that was the greatest luxury in the world.

For all that, there's days that Edward and I both miss it. I remember nearly every spot I ever dredged on that bay bottom. Sometimes the few of us left that remembers, we still talk it over. Every spot had a name—Snake Rip, Great Rock, Chinese Muds, Hollaga Snooze, Terrapin Sand, Daddie Dare, Apes Hole—where most of 'em came from, I don't know who could tell you, but I know 'em just the same as looking in a book. Now I don't think I am exaggerating a bit, and I wasn't the only one could do this, but when I was drudgin', if you had brought an oyster to me off two thirds of the rocks in Chesapeake Bay, I'd tell you what rock it come off of. It's all the same oyster, but accordin' to where it grows, the shells got different colors, different shapes. Right here in Tangier Sound, there's a rock called Turkle Egg and one called Mud Rock, and they join each other, but each one's got different-lookin' oysters. We would even use different dredges, accordin' to what bottom we were working. We always carried three sets: your hard bottom dredge, your mud dredge, and your gummer—no teeth at all—which we'd use around stones and old petrified tree stumps on the bottom. Sometimes it was a matter of using one type of dredge to sort of break into the bottom, then switch to another type to finish up.

The last years we drudged, there wasn't as many boats left on the whole bay as there once was at Smith Island. It seemed like about the time they began to get scarce was when everybody started to take an interest in skipjacks. We ended up with this camera crew from CBS aboard. They made a film, *The Sailing Oystermen* [CBS 20th Century Series, 1965], and they had Walter Cronkite to narrate it. They told me they took over five miles of film. I guess it was an all right film, but they were in the way an awful lot is what I remember most. I didn't let on I didn't like it, because it was more or less doing a favor, but really, I thought we were going to get something out of it. I think we got about $70–$80 apiece, and they knocked us out of, oh, $1,500 dollars worth of oysters. But they were fine people, and I still get Christmas cards from some of 'em.

It was after a big storm on Christmas Eve that we sold the *Ruby Ford*. We had her tied up at Tilghman Island. By that time, dredgers would come home on weekends more. The boats tied above us come loose and rammed us, and pretty well wrecked the *Ruby* up—tore the mast clean out of her, and the yawl [push] boat lost. It was getting harder and harder to find crew, so many of 'em was beginning to go on their own in smaller boats with these new patent [hydraulic] tongs they had developed for catching oysters. My son decided he wanted to go on his own, and Edward's son decided he wanted to go. Edward needed an operation. I asked him, do you feel that bad? He said he did, and we talked about how we'd been gone so many winters of our life, away from our families. He said, are you ready to sell her? I said, are you? And that's how quick it was done. A man right there at Tilghman came down and said, put a price to her. We said, I think it was $2,000—we could've almost got that for junkin' her. And then she was gone. ✦

WHEN DREDGE BOATS DIE

It's been nearly twenty years since the *Ruby* left Smith Island, and Edward, Daniel's brother, said he's heard she's layed up in a boatyard at Tilghman Island for repairs and he'd like to see her one last time. On a cold, sunny January afternoon we are hunting down a weedy dirt lane past two boatyards. The *Ruby*'s nowhere to be seen, just the rotting hulk of an abandoned skipjack, one of several around Tilghman that appear in various stages of disuse or ill repair. Those oyster harvests that once were measured in the millions of bushels have in recent years been reckoned by the hundreds of thousands, and very soon, it will be the tens of thousands. Only a couple dozen skipjacks are still working. The end of all drudgin', their captains say, is in sight. They never thought it could happen. Diseases, overfishing, and pollution get the credit, and things now are almost beyond worth arguing over which of the three is most responsible.

A worker in one boatyard directs us back to the first yard we stopped in. The *Ruby Ford* is there in a corner, he assures us. Ed sees nothing but the old wreck we passed before, which can't be the *Ruby.* That boat's bowsprit's been chopped off. The sun has drawn and cracked her oaken bottom planks an inch apart in places, and she is cancerous with black gouts of rot deep in her sides. Then Ed recognizes her centerboard, 12 by 5 feet, two-inch oak banded with steel, which he and Daniel built. "Gee whiz, golleee." It is about as strong a language as I have heard him use.

With some effort, Ed manages to crawl up on deck, which still seems solid, and begins prowling about, reminiscing. Forward, where the big pine mast once was stepped, he falls to hands and knees and comes up with a corroded nickel. By the date, it is the same one the brothers put under the mast when it was replaced, decades ago. It was put there for luck, and it cheers Ed, who seems on the verge of tears. The boatyard owner tells us the present owner is waiting for a federal grant to reconstruct the vessel; but it is obvious to all of us that *Ruby,* in her ninety-ninth year, is beyond reconstruction. On the drive home, Edward is quiet. Once, he says, apropos of nothing, "She didn't have to die."

WHEN THE DREDGE BOATS die, the oysters will die, too. I had heard some of the older islanders say that before. It wasn't rational—if anything, elimination of this very efficient harvest technique is that much less pressure on the shellfish stocks. But it reflected a deep belief—perhaps a need—to connect watermen's work with the health of the bay. An unworked bottom, it was felt, would not long remain productive. On some level, I think they felt the need to make obeisance to those invisible, sustaining oyster rocks.

Back on the island that same winter, discouraged men returned weeks early from "patent tonging," taking oysters the modern way, with hydraulic tongs from power-driven vessels anchored over the beds. They had made dismal amounts of money. With disease rampant among the bay's shellfish, harvests were around 1 percent of their historic highs a century ago. Record numbers signed up that March to go "bagless dredging," a clumsy make-work program that is Maryland's seagoing equivalent of agriculture's paying farmers not to plant.

For two weeks, they would be paid to drag the local oyster bars with dredges from which the catching part, the chain mesh bag, has been removed. It is plowing, pure and simple, on the theory that turning over the shells will cleanse them of marine growth, better enabling larval oysters spawned in early summer to "set," or attach to the shell and grow.

Scientists say it is a plausible theory, but only if the cultivation is done within a few days of the larvae's setting time, which won't come until around June. Of course by then, watermen would be too consumed by crabbing to need the work. So they plow in March, back and forth, up and down the oyster "rocks," listening to personal stereos, gabbing on the marine radio, some steering with their feet for a change of pace. It is boring, and probably futile; but it is $125 a day at a time when alternatives are scarce. It is what oystering, the mainstay of their fathers and grandfathers, has come to.

Conservationist of the Year

ℐN THE *1920s,* if you had been one of the rare summer visitors come to see Maryland's only offshore inhabited island, you would have marveled at the timeless, yesteryear quality of the scene unfolding as the new, modern motor ferry, the *Island Belle,* chugged from Crisfield through miles of twisting creeks toward the tiny village of Ewell, its white frame houses and big trees, shading oyster-shell paths, the only departures from the horizontality of the boundless salt marsh.

Crossing "the Bottom," the roughly circular expanse of shallow water at the island's center, dozens of graceful little sailcraft would have been gliding across the luxuriant underwater grass beds there, dragging dredgelike devices called "scrapes" to capture the succulent soft crabs that hid there to shed their shells.

And you might have noticed, as the August sun waxed hot in midafternoon, driving the crab scrapers in, that one boat, sailed by a compact youth in suspenders, straw hat, and bib overalls, stayed out longer than the rest. That's the Harrison boy—Edward—the islanders would tell you. He's a worker, going to be a right smart crabber, they would add.

IF YOU REVISITED Smith Island twenty years later, in the 1940s, you would notice some changes as the faithful *Island Belle* wound her way into Ewell: the first paved road, a few autos; the crab scrape boats have doffed their sails for single-cylinder engines that resonate with a *pop, pop, pop* across the clear, grassy shallows. The ranks of the crab fleet are shockingly depleted. A disastrous and mysterious dip in the crab population has caused a virtual exodus of able-bodied Smith Island men to the shipyards in Baltimore, looking for jobs to sustain their families.

Only a few, hard-core crabbers have elected to stick it out. One of them is a powerful man in suspenders, straw hat, and bib overalls. Edward Harrison, the islanders will tell you, in good times or bad is among the best crabbers of the island.

ANOTHER twenty years have passed. Aboard the old *Island Belle* you now hear passengers complain of the time it takes to make the twelve-mile passage to

Ewell, and her bilge pumps seem to run constantly. The sixties have brought big changes to mainland America—Vietnam, campus unrest, Woodstock. On Smith Island, some changes also: they have now got phone service, and a few more cars; and the crabs have come back. The scrape boat fleet plying the grass flats under the hot August sun seems assurance that at least one corner of the earth is still comfortable with the way it always has been.

And, as if to underscore the point, among the crowd of crab boats you notice an older waterman, straw hat, bib overalls, and suspenders, looking as if he had stepped out of the 1920s. Don't let his looks deceive you, the islanders will say. There's probably never been a crabber able as Edward Harrison.

ITS 1990, nearly seventy years since your first trip here. As your modern, air-conditioned cruise boat draws near the new harborside restaurant and gift shop at Ewell, the captain tells you a developer is fighting environmentalists over one hundred luxury condos and a marina for the island. He probably doesn't bother to point out the rotting hulk of the *Island Belle* in a muddy corner of the town's harbor. So many tourists, second home owners, and waterfront investors are coming here nowadays, all drawn by the changelessness of the island, that they are inevitably changing the place—at least the land.

On the water, crab scraping proceeds as it has forever, it seems, though the grass beds have been reduced by pollution in recent years, and fishing pressure on the blue crab has soared, baywide, as lucrative fisheries for oysters and rockfish have dwindled away. All over the bay, scientists and legislators and citizens wonder whether the day of the bay waterman isn't nearly done.

Perhaps. But just now, look over there, waving to you: the old, stooped man in the little scrape boat, straw hat, bib overalls, and suspenders, getting in from work, as usual, later than all the other boats. That's Edward Harrison, anyone can tell you; and all over Tangier Sound they say he's caught more soft crabs than any man who ever lived. If summertime and soft-crab season ever came without Ed there in the Bottom in his old boat, the *Margaret H.,* "you'd wonder if the tide was gonna rise," people say.

NO RENNAISSANCE man, Ed has been focused intently as a great blue heron or a striped bass on the stalk and capture of seafood from age eleven. Whatever drives him is elemental, almost animal, an instinct that is not to be switched off or even damped as its possessor's remarkable physical abilities have declined in the last few years. In 1990, attempting to lift a catch that crabbers half his age would not have attempted, Ed went over the side of his craft and was swallowed whole by the mouth of his scrape, to be dragged along underwater, pinned in the meshes among crabs and sea grass by the forward speed of the boat. Only a chance encounter with his son, out in a skiff hunting crab pot corks washed up in the marsh, saved him from a gruesome death. Bruised and shaken, he was back out crabbing the next day.

The next year he suffered a serious stroke, from which most men would not have recovered enough to enjoy a quiet retirement. Against the advice of both the medical and island communities, he returned to crabbing. One afternoon shortly after that I saw him come in after a twelve-hour day, temperature in the mid-90s. Leaving his boat he could not climb up on the dock, but he got his upper body laid on it to where with some effort he rolled his legs out and slowly gained his feet. Crabbing is going to kill him, everyone on the island says. It would kill him not to crab, says Ed.

THAT KIND of glorious and terrible motivation in another place or circumstance might produce a musical prodigy, an architect of great buildings, or a political leader or captain of industry. But this is Smith Island; and if there is any place in the world where forces might combine to produce the best crabber the world has ever seen, it would be here. The blue crab, *Callinectes sapidus,* ranges from Canada to South America and is abundant from New Jersey to Texas; but more than half of our commercial catch comes from the 180-mile-long Chesapeake. And as for soft crabs—the stage the blue crab enters when it molts, or sheds its hard shell for a day or two in order to grow—the bay traditionally has accounted for more than 90 percent of the national catch.

And throughout the length and breadth of the Chesapeake, the heartland of crabdom, no place is more ideally situated for soft crabbing than Smith Island and the surrounding waters. The island lies between what are in effect two major highways for the dispersal of young crabs throughout the bay after they hatch each summer around its mouth near Norfolk. Deep channels running to the island's east and west allow the heavier saltwater of the ocean to flow constantly up the bay beneath the lighter, fresher water near the surface, and baby crabs hitch a ride on this free express. Abetting this, the rotation of the earth, or coriolis force, tends to sling the saltwater more toward the eastern side of the twenty-mile wide bay, where Smith lies. The waters around the island, across tens of thousands of acres, are shallow enough to let sunlight penetrate, growing vast meadows of submerged grasses. The salinity of the shallows here is about halfway between the ocean salt at bay's mouth and the freshwater of some forty rivers that also feed the bay. Grass and warmth, salt and sweet, the mixture is elixir to shedding crabs.

And that is half the reason so many soft crabs come from here. The other half is the presence of several hundred souls as fully devoted to the pursuit of crabs as Iowa is to growing corn. And it is here in this soft-crab center of the universe that Edward Harrison is the pole star, a constant throughout the memories of most living islanders, and for half of the 140 years that watermen have harvested crabs commercially from the Chesapeake Bay.

How good a crabber was he? I. T. Todd, a longtime major seafood packer in Crisfield who buys soft crabs from watermen all over the bay, says that into his late seventies, Ed remained "way above the average catcher. You only see a few people like him in your life." "Where Ed oughtta be, really, is in the *Guiness Book of World Records,*" says a neighbor and fellow waterman, Jennings Evans.

People in the seafood business are not famous for publicizing exact harvest data; so how adept any waterman is usually can be resolved only by anecdote. But from 1946 to 1972, a remarkable data-gathering effort launched by Dr. L. Eugene Cronin at the University of Maryland, in cooperation with Ed, tracked all soft crabs and peelers (crabs that will soon shed their shells) caught by Ed and several other crab scrapers in the Evans & Harrison Crab Company in Ewell.

Here are typical comparisons of Ed's catch with the others' daily average—and nearly all these men averaged better than the island as a whole:

1957
Company average—415 crabs/day
Ed H.—679/day

1961
Company average—349
Ed H.—1,153

1963 (a terrible year)
Company average—164
Ed H.—604

1969
Company average—688
Ed H.—1,215

There were always a few other top watermen on the island who were at least in Ed's league; but most simply have not lived as long, or been willing to put in the same hours, decade after decade. "I well remember all the days we'd be back in, cleaned up and headed in a skiff to baseball practice, and there, up a little gut, we'd see Ed still scraping," said Dallas Bradshaw, a waterman from Tylerton.

In addition to his will and wiles, Ed probably just had good genes; maybe good karma—he and his two sisters and a brother, Daniel, have lived all their lives within a two-minute walk of one another, and all remain married to spouses of more than fifty years. Daniel, no slouch at crabbing himself, still follows the water, and often the brothers spend the day scraping no more than a few yards apart. Long before crab scraping got to be the industry it is now, both brothers were known baywide for their uncanny ability to catch oysters with their sail dredge boat, the *Ruby G. Ford.*

Ed was always proud of being able to help Dr. Cronin study the crab. "Do you know he got up before the legislature in Annapolis and said he learned more about the crab business here than in any class he ever took in a university; and he called my name out in the Statehouse, who he went out with and all. You can't help but feel right good about that, coming from a man who went through college."

In fact it is only recently that scientists have begun fully to appreciate all those crabs that Ed voluntarily weighed and sexed and measured—some 300,000 in 25 years, resulting in 2,500 pages of data. As never before, Maryland and Virginia are trying to understand how much pressure the blue crab fishery can take before it cracks, as so many other commercial species of the Chesapeake have done in the last two decades. The demise of shad, rockfish, and oysters has caused more watermen to turn to crabbing. Catches of crabs, now running close to 100 million pounds per year, at first appear healthier than ever; but the scientists fear that just reflects a mammoth increase in the number of man-hours and crabbing gear being used to catch them.

If crabs were to fail, there would be little left for communities like Smith Island to catch. It would be a major economic blow to the whole region, as well as to the millions of recreational crabbers who catch an estimated 30 million pounds a year. In addition, the blue crab is more deeply embedded in the ecology and culture of the entire Chesapeake system than almost any other creature. It inhabits every niche from the deep channels to the marshes, and the ocean to the limits of tide, miles up the rivers. Blue crabs eat everything from worms and clams and periwinkles to fiddler crabs, plant matter, oysters and—in surprisingly large numbers—each other. And they are in turn food for eels, striped bass, cobia, red drum, sharks, rays, speckled trout, catfish, largemouth bass, loggerhead turtles, herons, egrets, diving ducks, and racoons, just to name a few. Any long-term changes in crab populations would have major consequences for the whole ecosystem.

That would include human society. Without crabfeasts, it is doubtful Maryland politics could survive a single summer; nor could family reunions, Rotarians' gatherings, and any number of other vital social functionings. And what would Crisfield, the port for Smith Island seafood, become without its annual Crab Derby, highlighted by a race among the hardshells and the crowning of Miss and Little Miss Crustacean?

Data like Ed's crab survey are invaluable in understanding complex and highly variable ecosystems like the Chesapeake estuary. From year to year, something as capricious as a shift in prevailing winds, blowing on the crabs' spawning grounds at bay's mouth, may dramatically affect survival of the young; so long-term data sets are vital to sort out what really is going on. If scientists someday develop sound conservation plans for the bay's crabs, the old waterman will have played a significant role.

It was partly for this that I told my employers at Smith Island, the Chesapeake Bay Foundation, they should nominate Ed as their Conservationist of the Year. The decision to do so was not without risk or controversy. The Foundation usually reserved this honor for someone who worked to preserve land, or fought to reduce pollution. It had grown to be one of the nation's largest regional conservation groups by aggressively fighting for stewardship of the bay's resources. Now they were proposing to celebrate a man who had devoted his life—with spectacular success—to catching as many of the bay's resources as he was able. I figured Ed personally had made possible more than 3 million soft-crab sandwiches for American restaurant goers (not to mention those being air-freighted to Japan in recent years). Some in the Foundation wondered how many conservationists like Ed the bay could stand.

We did it anyhow, and I think it was fitting, and not just because of all the crab data Ed compiled. By many measures that seem increasingly popular, the bay would be better off without watermen. There are millions of sportsmen who will pump far more into the economy to catch a few fish or crabs apiece than we get by allowing a few thousand individuals to catch tons and tons. As push comes to shove over the bay's dwindling natural resources, the argument goes, can we really justify watermen's interests against all the rest of us? Perhaps that way lies the most rational use of Chesapeake Bay; but certainly not the most interesting. I found I could talk to my groups of schoolkids about the importance of crabs and the grass beds they lived in for days, with less effect than I got by pulling up for about three minutes with the kids next to Edward out there scraping for a living. He didn't say much, but what he said was always so honest, so compelling. If I wrote the words here, they would seem bland; but imagine if you were able to go up to any large predator in nature and converse freely with it about how things were going in the great out of doors. That is what it was like.

There is more to it, of course, than just crabbers and their crabbing. It is the places that nurture them like the towns on Smith Island, where the culture still is balanced by nature, and the marshy fastness has preserved a unique sense of community. Much faster, and more irreversibly than we are losing our water quality on the Chesapeake, we are letting human diversity slip away. Only by the narrowest of definitions should a bay with sparkling clean water, plenty of crabs, and no Ed Harrisons or Smith Islands be considered a "quality" environment.

SCRAPING WITH ED

It's 3.15 A.M., Saturday, July 9, 1988; high harvest season in the soft-crab center of the universe. For miles around, sequestered among the dark, sea-grass jungles, millions of blue crabs are in the throes of a mass ecdysis. A freshening south-west breeze puffs scents of flatulent marsh and honeysuckle, creosote and salt, down the main channel of Ewell. Gravel crunches by the dockside, and Ed drifts from the dark, feet out to brake the old one-speed bike he rides 200 feet from his house to his scrape boat, the *Margaret H.*

Easily a third as wide, amidships, as its 28-foot length, she is only the sec-ond scraper Ed has owned in nearly seventy years. Flounder shape notwith-standing, an old-fashioned scrape boat like the *Margaret* is graceful, her lines bespeaking an era when such craft were still sailed. Modern renditions in Fiber-glas, built to similar dimensions, totally lack this charm. Recently, the *Margaret* was on the local railway, where island boats are pulled out annually to be de-barnacled, caulked, and painted. A worker noticed her heavy pine bottom planking was worn nearly through—worn from the inside, from so many sum-mers of Ed's ceaseless back-and-forth pacing, attending to his scrapes.

Stiffly, Ed lowers himself into the boat, bails a few scoops of water, and hooks up his bilge pump by clamping an exposed wire to a battery terminal poking from the engine box. His son-in-law and grandson trudge by, wordlessly, to their own boats. The *Margaret*'s six-cylinder Ford engine coughs, coughs, wheezes, catches, stutters, finally hums, and we're off down main street with the tide.

Eastward across the great marshes of the island's Tangier Sound side, search-lights stab the starry night as scrapers wend the maze of shallow guts that save miles over traveling the marked channels. From the north comes a sound of thunder, or maybe just Army, A-10 "Warthogs" on an early bombing run at Bloodsworth Island, their practice range ten miles up the Sound. The temper-ature promises to hit 97°F by early afternoon, but in the predawn damp it feels good to catch the warmth from the *Margaret*'s rudimentary muffler, fitted to a pipe that rises straight out of the engine.

Ed has joined the stream of watermen's palaver meandering across the CB and VHF radios every scraper carries, speakers mounted on posts in their open-air craft. *"Hayee, Morrris"; "Purty sky this maarnin' "; "Yeeah, [but] change a'-comin' "; "Ye needn't doubt that."* The thickly accented chat mingles and flows, soft and familiar as tide through the marsh. The soft-crab season began badly, but now the dam has broken, as if the stubborn crabs could not stay pent up in their hard shells a minute longer. Ed thinks he may have caught more yester-day than any day in the last sixty-five years. On the CB, spirits are high, and there is talk about the wives "goin' off" this weekend to shop the malls in Sal-isbury.

Winding through the black maze of marsh, Ed has been keeping visual and radio contact with a scraper ahead of him, and at some point it becomes ap-parent that the greatest soft crabber who ever lived can't really see where he's going. Such arrangements, older waterman following a younger before the dawn comes up, are not unknown. The year before, one elder missed his connection and struck out anyhow. He ran full speed into the bayside jetty, breaking his shoulder and nearly destroying his boat.

"Cataracts," Ed is saying; "they're givin' me the very devil, but the doctors don't want to cut em yet."

"I'm right ahead of ye, capn'," the CB crackles; and from another crabber: "Hang in there, Ed, you're tuffer'n Mike Tyson."

Island people, Ed says, always have watched out for him:

✦ My mother died in 1921, and my father got to where he couldn't work. I was the oldest of four kids, and two weeks into the fourth grade, when they pulled me out to work. The mothers of the island, they took up a collection, and they looked after us as good as their own children. Nobody could have been treated no better.

I always enjoyed studyin' on things. I'm seventy-eight now, and I still wonder, when I am a'goin' through these guts, how they come to windin' all around instead of straight like a ditch. I knew I would not ever have the chance for more schoolin', so I put my whole mind on studyin' the water. I loved to listen to the old people, hear the old captains talk, and they taught me like I was their own boys.

I pay attention to the wind and tides, and how they make the crabs move around. I study the bottom—you wouldn't believe all the changes I have seen to it. There has been very few nights in my life that I have gone off to sleep that I haven't settled in my mind where is goin' to be best the next mornin' for to crab or to drudge [oysters]. ✦

It's 4:30 A.M. when we emerge into Back Cove, on the island's northeastern shore. A pretty dawn is kindling in the eastern sky, while lightning forks and big thunderheads boil from around the Potomac River, some twenty miles due west. The low tide has encouraged most of the scrape fleet to seek deeper water a quarter mile offshore. Ed has chosen his starting spot apart from the rest, scarcely a boat length from the marsh bank. With a deft shrug and twist of his shoulders, he throws overboard two heavy, iron scrapes, attached by about 12 feet of sturdy rope to cleats a few feet forward of each corner of the *Margaret*'s stern.

Unlike a dredge, a scrape has no teeth. It slides across the bottom, breaking the sea grass off at its stem rather than uprooting it. The first thing outsiders always wonder, seeing miles of bay littered with mats of floating grass, is won't such intensive harvesting ruin the bottom? The bay has, in fact, lost grassy bottom habitat by the thousands of acres in recent decades; but pollution, from sewage and farm runoff, seems clearly the major culprit. One of the few areas where the grasses have held their ground is in the scraping areas around Smith Island. Ed says that "working" the bottom not only doesn't harm it, it is necessary to keep it productive. There is no science to back that up, but every bay waterman, whether crab scraper or oyster dredger, believes the virtues of a tended bottom as firmly as he believes anything. It seems almost a need to feel their work is needed by the bay, a notion as old as agriculture, as ancient, perhaps, as Adam and Eve in the Garden.

Ed slows the *Margaret* nearly to a crawl, until pale, chocolate burls trail from each scrape. Too slow, and the scrapes can fill with mud; too fast, and they will ride up over the grass. "You got to get a feel for it—some never do," Ed says. He has been arranging the cramped interior to receive the day's harvest, placing baskets, buckets, and tubs of water around the floor. Into one tub will go "green peelers." Placed in holding tanks back at Ed's shedding shanty, these will emerge soft in several days. "Rank" peelers, which will shed sooner, go to another tub. Buckrams, which have shed but are turning just a little too hard to market as soft crabs, go in a basket, destined for home consumption. A damp, avocado-colored bathroom carpet will keep them moist, without providing enough water to continue reforming their shell. Hard crabs and soft crabs of various grades and sizes, and anything else edible or marketable, will fill the remaining vessels.

Margaret's propeller has begun to churn heavy, black mud from the soft bottom. In fact, I would characterize our situation as being aground. Ed, unconcerned, flicks the throttle up a tad and plows ahead. For most of the day, we will work in water that is little more than knee-deep. Often the scrape frames are nearly out of the water, so that gulls, perching on them, gulping fat grass shrimp roiled to the surface, appear to be water-skiing. It is these extraordinarily fecund edges where land and water merge, and along similar edges where the shallows drop off into channels, that Ed is famous for working so profitably. It is one thing to know that these narrow seams are rich in crabs, and quite another to work them. It requires extraordinary skill and concentration to spend all day maneuvering a beamy, minimally responsive boat in water where a few inches are all the difference between floating and sticking, and where hidden stumps abound to wreck your propeller shaft and rip your scrape bags as if they were ricepaper; to follow a winding, invisible channel edge no wider than a single scrape's mouth—all the time working furiously, head down, to sort the crabs from the grass.

Several minutes have elapsed, and a fierce rain squall is bearing down when Ed idles the engine and strains on the rope to the starboard scrape. His forearms are thick and tight as logs, and save for the leathered skin, could belong to a strong, young man. With a full load of thick, wet grass, a scrape weighs upwards of 60 pounds, and pulled through the water behind a moving boat, it feels like considerably more. It is going to be worth the effort today, it looks like. The great, glistening rolls of black and green grass Ed dumps on the deck are studded with the creams and blues and olives of crabs. Green peelers and rank, hard males and soft females, primes and jumbos, they fly into their respective tubs and bushels like cards from a croupier. "Dollar bills," Ed pronounces, plucking a couple particularly large softies from the grass heap; and a little later, "Dinner!" as a fat flounder of about two pounds shows itself. He'll have it with a side of fried buckrams, which are sweeter and better even than soft crabs, he vows. He sets one tub against the *Margaret*'s tiller, as a sort of crude autopilot, and commences to heave with enthusiasm on the portside scrape. I do not believe he could have been much more excited the first time he hit a good scraping spot—perhaps this very spot—seven decades ago.

By 8:00 A.M. it is known that the storm has knocked out power to the whole island. The radio is jammed with scrapers calling to their wives to hustle to the shanties and start their gasoline-powered backup pumps. Without a steady flow of seawater across the shedding softshells, the heat will kill them, destroying in a few hours the hard labor of several days. Ed is unruffled. He still goes with the old-time arrangement that employs a full-time shantyman, who receives and tends the crabs brought in by Ed, his grandson, and his son-in-law.

Right now, he says, reaching into the first of two capacious red and white plastic coolers on the *Margaret*'s stern, it's snack time. Ella Marie, his wife, fueled him up around three this morning on eggs and bacon, chased with a bowl of cornflakes and a banana. "I don't wanta brag," he says, "but in fifty years there's not been a mornin', no matter how early I left, she hasn't been there with a good breakfast." Now, he pulls out an inch-thick scrapple and scrambled egg sandwich; also a fist-sized chunk of cheese and a hearty slice of eight-layer chocolate cake, all washed down with cloyingly sweet black coffee. Later, he will get to his main lunch, a stack of clam fritter sandwiches, more cheese, and a slice of Ella Marie's coconut cake that makes her chocolate seem like a warm-up event. Food, he says, "is somethin' I've never denied myself." Ed's "bail," as they call the meals watermen here pack on their boats, is legendary, as is his lifetime consumption of certain sweets. A local song about the sights of the island, sung to the tune of "Galway Bay," has immortalized him, out crabbing, thus: "Oh, you will see Nut Sundae in the Bottom. . . ." He never could get enough of those sundaes, he chuckles. It's what they have called him since he was a boy; and it stands out even in a nickname-crazy place that features Shug, Gadget, Spot, Tank, Stink, Nig, and Bullet. "I never craved the world," he says; "but a nut sundae's somethin' else."

Lick by lick, hour by hour, as the sun breaks out and the marsh shimmers in bright heat, the buckets and bushels have begun to take on the appearance of a fine day's catch. You sense that Ed is making almost constant adjustments and decisions as he works his scrapes ever closer into the nooks and crannies of the island. It is subtle stuff, not much more communicable, perhaps, than an animal's hunting. He seems almost to *feel* the boat's ever-changing relationship with the bottom and the shoreline and the rising tide; and it is easy to believe that, cataracts and all, he *sees* the bottom with a sixth sense you can never know. Ed, not much given to such fancy analysis, suggests that maybe it's more a matter of "patience."

◆ I'll tell you about patience. Now, you take my scrapes. You notice they got side panels laced into them, and there's very few others that do that anymore. It makes it harder to empty the grass. Well, it makes it harder for crabs to fall out, too, so I lace 'em up. And you measure the washboards [side decking] on this ole boat and see if you can find another on the island as wide. I had 'er built that way for a reason. In hot weather them crabs'd go down in the grass along the channel edges, and I'd aim to be there, draggin', just as soon as it was light enough to see. Sometimes you'd get more crabs in four, five licks than you could in a dozen on the flat bottom. Now, I knew if the other boats saw me a'breakin' all of them out of the grass, they'd be right in on top of me. So I'd just pile it up and pile it up on them big washboards while I worked down that edge. The other thing to it is, those panels and them washboards keep your crabs from gettin' into the floor of your boat. It kills me when that happens and I step on one by accident, 'cause I don't love to kill nothin' without it's made use of.

You got to have patience to stick with it just as hard when it's poor as when it's a glut. I have left home at two-thirty of a mornin' to run all the way to Hooper Straits to catch a few dozen crabs, old single-cylinder engine a'goin' *pop, pop, pop*. That was a run to make to catch half a bushel of crabs, but we wound up with a little bit of money, and the rest ended up with none. I have heard some of the younger ones, when crabbin's that poor, figure how they might spend more money a'goin' out that day than they are likely to make on the crabs they catch. Well, that's what they know, but here's somethin' too—when you're out there, you always catch more crabs than when you're not.

I guess it is a lot more work, the way I do, but I believe 50 percent of the people give up work too early, 'deed I do. Once you get used to it, why, it's a job to give it up. ◆

It's 11:30 now, the sixth day of a long, hot workweek. On the radio they're saying it will soon hit 100 degrees. "Comin' in, Ed?" comes the call from a neighbor on the CB. "I'm a'comin'," Ed answers as always; and as always he will scrape another hour or two. In the brutal noonday glare the old crabber is looking his age, struggling so to hoist aboard a particularly heavy load of grass that he must climb and teeter dangerously on the *Margaret*'s gunwales to manage it. Much of a scrape boat's distinctive look comes from its extraordinary lack of freeboard. Its deck, where the scrape is dumped, is little more than a foot from the water, minimizing the distance all that weight must be dead-lifted. But what the soft crabber saves in energy here, he pays for with his back. Culling through the grass, he must work in precisely that position that orthopedists are forever warning puts something like a ton of strain on the lumbar vertebrae. Don't even brush your teeth in that position, they say. Ed, who cannot ever remember having back trouble in the last two thirds of a century or so, should donate his spine to the Smithsonian, I tell him.

"I been blessed," he says, as we dock back at his shanty, a trim, barn red building on a corner where the two main channels through Ewell meet. He paid his house loan off nearly fifty years ago, and has owned the *Margaret* outright since the early 1950s. As for car payments, he never did learn to drive, one of his few regrets. His credit, Ed says, is good in any store in Crisfield or Salisbury, and barring catastrophe, he allows as how he could manage comfortably if he never again worked in his life.

Times weren't always so secure. There was the Monday morning years ago that he and six other scrapers shipped 49 boxes of soft crabs—6,000 to 10,000 crabs—and got so little for them in New York, they would have saved money if they had thrown them back and kept the shipping containers. Then there was the most dispiriting year of all, around the start of World War II, when even Ed couldn't catch enough to make gas money, and gas only ten cents a gallon. That was the only time in nearly seventy years on the water that he lost the will to crab, Ed says. He decided to head for the shipyards and a job in Baltimore; but Ella Marie was tougher. She would "just as liv starve" as see Baltimore, she told her husband. "I said, well, we'll starve it out together, and come August some crabs hit, and we made a fairly good season's work after all," he says.

The shanty is blissfully shady, cooled by the tide sliding, bottle green, beneath the floor planks, and by the aerated spray pumped from the channel across the shedding crabs. Wild goats graze listlessly on the simmering marsh behind, and a great blue heron stalks through the pilings under our feet. In one corner, Bunk, the shantyman, has piled "sea oars," the dried, black sea grass gathered from the marsh edges. Moistened, it is used to bed soft crabs in their shipping boxes. A radio tuned to a Baltimore station is reporting traffic jams on highways heading toward the Delmarva beaches.

Ed is preparing soft crabs for shipment now, dividing them into mediums, hotels, primes, jumbos, and whales, sliding them across the honey green wood of shallow, handmade sorting trays, about three feet by two. Even Ed doesn't know how old those trays are, or who made them. They have the look of old-growth Georgia pine, cut from trees that were old and tall when America was discovered. They are smooth as polished stone, wetted and sanded to a rare luster from the rude hands of scrapers and the silken bellies of a million dozen soft crabs. Those worn trays and rough hands seem to sum up the day—and much more. They are icons of a life and a culture, that in their marshy, crabby context approach the level of enduring art.

EPILOGUE

It is a hot July day in 1992, and the marvelous crabbing machine has finally run down. It is the first summer in seventy-one years he has not been out there, Ed says. He can see better now than he could for years, since they took the cataracts off in 1989. It was his legs that finally got him. They just got weak and trembly. From the waist up, he is rarin' to go.

For a while, after the stroke, he even lost his appetite, which made news all over the island. He is adjusting, he says, but it's hard, sitting on the bench at the gas dock and watching the scrapers land their crabs. He sold the *Margaret* to a boy just starting out, at an attractive price; but he couldn't make a go of it, and now Ed is wondering whether one of the marine museums might like to have her.

"I know ashore is where I ought to be," he says, "but in my head I want to be goin'. Oysterin' and crabbin's what I dream of most every night." He seems to nod off for just a bit, then, brightening, asks whether I have heard about the peeler crab.

"It was rank, four inches across the shell, shed out a jumbo for sure. I have got it in the live box [holding tank] on a scrape boat right now. I found it yesterday evenin', crawled into the grass in my yard to hide. In all my years that never happened.

"On the radio, they are sayin' the crabs have come lookin' for me."

Proggers

Every part of this soil is sacred . . . even the rocks thrill with memories of stirring events connected with the lives of my people, and the very dust . . . responds more lovingly to their footsteps than to yours.

> —*CHIEF SEALTH (SEATTLE)*, mourning his people's
> move to a reservation in a speech, June 7, 1866

Of course I worried when he didn't come home. He's old to be proggin' about on the hottest day of summer. He got caught in a tide pond. There wasn't a thing he could do but to sit 'til the tide rose again and floated his skiff.

    I said, "Dad, I wish it hadn't happened, but I know you'd rather been in that marsh than been in Glory."   —*AN ISLAND PROGGER'S DAUGHTER*

FULL CITIZENSHIP

FAR UP the island's bayshore, by an eroding marsh tump, the progger's lone figure stops and squats, to examine . . . what? The spoor of fox or coon, muskrat or mink, or black duck's sequestered nest? China teacup handle of a nineteenth-century sea captain's wife? Apothecary bottle tossed by an eighteenth-century British naval invader? Coin dropped from the blouse of a seventeenth-century pirate? Spear point chipped by a caribou hunter who hunkered here in wait five thousand years ago? Perhaps the progger has discovered a silken, just-shed soft crab, a baby terrapin, the bleached plastron of a giant sea turtle; or a feather, a shell, a piece of bone; a wave-polished root of ancient walnut; a naval telemetry buoy torn from its moorings by the last storm.

    Stop and squat by water's edge, like some shaman divining the future; to gaze and dream, in guileless propitiation of some inarticulable bond here between islander and island. The islanders just call it "progging about." "Progging" is spoken with a long "o," never mind the dictionary's "prag" (as in "frog"), or its relegation of the word to "obsolete." Here, "progging" remains a rich and active word, as: "My teenager don't love to progue around in the refrigerator none"; or, "What I wouldn't give to progue around in a big library."

Webster's defines progging: "to poke [as] at a hole or log; forage, prowl, wander about idly or aimlessly." Proggers here say that about covers it; except once you begin to follow them afield, such definitions pale—like calling passion "the expression of emotions," or art "the visual rendering of concepts." If a life, unexamined, is not worth living, then even the prettiest place, un-progged, remains mere window dressing, a husk of landscape, a geology that stops at the earth's surface.

Imagine how well, as a child, you knew your own backyard, or perhaps a path home from school, an alley where you hung out or a tree you climbed in. You knew it with an intimacy denied adults, who mostly just transit such places on the way to somewhere—and who, these days, might be reported to police if they loitered. But the child tarries, explores, discovers—*imagines*—in those places. And this is just a glimmer of how islanders may relate to their natural surroundings, in whose constant communion they play as children, and hunt and gather a living as adults.

And among them, a transcendent few are proggers, existences webbed wonderfully into this waterland. Their gleanings and discoveries continually enhance and reforge the bonds between human and natural communities here. The Native Americans who littered the island with arrowheads believed, as Chief Seattle: *"when the memory of my tribe shall have become a myth among the white men, these shores will swarm with their invisible dead."*

It is not hard to imagine that certain individuals might still be attuned to, tugged by the old spirits. In the same sense that all Americans are citizens, all who wrest a living from bay and marsh here are proggers. But a few here aspire to fuller citizenship than most will ever enjoy.

A true progger loves, above all, to roam the edges where land and water merge. By that standard, all of Chesapeake Bay is a happy hunting ground, a place that, if you wiped it clean of people and began all over again, would shortly reinvent proggers. So fantastically do land and water twine along the 180-mile length of the estuary that the actual shoreline is estimated to approach 9,000 miles. These marshy, shallow toils sponsor a share of the bay's fabulous biological productivity out of all proportion to their acreage of the total watershed, or their portion of the estuary's water volume.

The edges were the primary staging points for the region's human history— where native hunters and fishermen congregated seasonally for millennia, and Colonial planters grew and shipped wheat and tobacco; where schooners and steamboats called, and port cities arose. So deeply and promiscuously do Chesapeake waters penetrate the Maryland landscape that even today, the great bulk of the state's 5 million citizens reside close by tidewater. It is no accident that the state dog is the Chesapeake Bay retriever, the state fish the Chesapeake Bay striped bass, the state boat the Chesapeake Bay oyster skipjack; that the state fossil, the four-ribbed snail, was dug from the bay's Calvert Cliffs; also the University of Maryland's mascot is an estuarine habitué, the diamondback terrapin (Go Terps!) improbable as that may seem.

Even among so much proggable edginess, Smith Island stands out. It is more than surrounded by water, it is *perfused* by water, run through as no other bay landscape by hundreds, perhaps thousands of miles of marshy creeks—"guts," in local parlance—resembling nothing so much as a sea nettle, or jellyfish, pulsating rhythmically with the tides that swish through its every pore. Such tidal wetlands, because of their productivity and capacity to filter pollutants, are variously praised as the Chesapeake's "gills," or "lungs," or "kidneys." I don't think one can improve on "guts," the literal alimentary canals through which the marshes gorge on nutritious seawater and void a rich broth of detrital plant matter back into the estuarine food web. It is at any rate a vital organ, and a progger's paradise.

Proggers have a way of *being* in the landscape, perceiving it in ways conventional maps and charts never will, even in an age of satellite photography and laser-precision depth sounders.

Partly this is because the island is so horizontal as to largely defeat topography and bathymetry. From the tops of the marsh vegetation to the depths of its interior waterways is usually only a few feet. But this seeming sameness obscures several subtle yet profound distinctions: the intersections of upland and high marsh *(Spartina patens)* grade with every few inches loss of elevation into *patens–distichlis, distichlis, distichlis–juncus, juncus, juncus–alterniflora, alterniflora,* tidal creek bank, mudflat, submerged grass bed, oyster bar. Each of these regimes is a distinct world for a progger on the hunt for fur, molluscs, crustaceans, wild asparagus, flint points, or other quarry.

Just beneath the island's waters, for example, was a third dimension, as real and familiar here as land and sky in other places. One November night a hushed, cold calm fell over the island. A raging nor'wester had blown out after two days, having expressed great volumes of water from the whole bay and blocked the normal return of the flood tides from the ocean. The water around the island fell lower than I had ever seen it.

Boats that normally floated in their slips careened on their keels, straining at dock ropes. Perhaps 75 percent of the guts and sloughs and ponds lay drained, their muddy, grassy bottoms jet black. A full moon, as it ascended, magically silvered every crevice and drain and hollow that retained the thinnest skein of water. Across hundreds of acres of crabbing bottoms gleamed an intricate filigree of long curves and fantastic whorls, etched into the dark bottom by the propellers and scrapes of the soft crabbers—a summer's work, the signature of a culture, writ upon the bottom. It was a map with neither permanence nor significance to anyone but islanders, to whom it signified their very being.

Geographers in recent decades have coined the term "mental maps" in an attempt to get at the intimate and personal complexities of how people actually perceive themselves within a given geography. I imagine one might get a simple feel for such a map by walking through the same rural landscape, on successive days, first with a developer, then an agronomist, followed by trips with an ecologist, a hunter, and a city dweller. You might end up thinking you had seen five different places; and a sixth, at once richer and less knowable than all the others, might be revealed through the family who had owned the land and worked it and lived on it for generations.

Barry Lopez, in a brilliant essay in his book *Arctic Dreams*,* pushes these concepts further, positing a "country of the mind" for the northern landscape, encompassing all that is evident to the senses, as well as what is retained in human memory, oral tradition, and in both myth and real-time history.

This should not seem so radical. Vastly fuller connections among humans and animals and landscape exist today around the world in aboriginal peoples, and are well documented among Native Americans. Only in the last few ticks of human evolution have most of us disconnected from needing to know the land in supersensory ways. Road maps, airlines, and macadam cannot have bred these deeper connections, more felt than articulated, out of us so quickly.

And it follows that in today's world—when the natural integrity of so many of the places we grew up, the places where we settle, is continually shattered and rearranged—it leaves us literally dispirited, bereft of more than acres of open space or scenic overlooks and ecological function; leaves us also deprived of community, of places in which we can imagine.

Through the simple lens of the island proggers, themselves a kind of joyful intersection of human and other communities, it seemed one could still catch a glimpse of the complex country we have left behind and desperately need in some fashion to reinvent.

THE PROGGER

+ Here you are. I found you in the marsh last winter. I picked up this old cedar root and I thought, dast if it isn't shaped like Tom in that toboggan hat he wore when he was livin' here a few years ago. I showed it around and everybody says, yep, that's him.

You have asked me a lot of times how proggers see the island, and I don't guess I know how to answer. I don't like talking into that tape recorder. Proggers just go out to see what we can see, find what we can find. You might go mudlarkin'—that's picking up oysters in the shallows—or spargassin', hunting wild asparagus; tarpinin', that's finding where the diamondbacks have buried for the winter; or go gathering mussels, or pokeweed, or picking up

*(New York: Charles Scribner's Sons, 1986).

old corks to paint fresh and tie to your crab pots the next summer; maybe lookin' for old coins up to Hollands Island—now that's some fun.

Sometimes the best proggin' is when you leave out not knowin' what you are going to do. You always find something interestin'. Once I found a Navy pilot. I saw his jet going down and ran to it in my skiff. He was all right, and said he'd like to just float there until his people picked him up—he'd radioed for help. I stayed with him 'til the helicopter came, and I think he was glad for the company. I have found sharks' teeth four inches long, and oysters growin' fat and healthy in some little patches of reeds by the shore when all over Tangier Sound they were dyin' from diseases.

You never know what you'll pick up. Years back, some of the Holland Island Parkses were picking up redheads off the water after a night shoot, and one said, "Boys, I got a nice one"—he had grabbed the hair of a drowned man.

Proggers find soft crabs in winter when they aren't supposed to shed, and swans in the summer after they have all flown back north; and the first big trout of spring when the water's still too cold for 'em to be around. No one ever knew there was foxes livin' on Smith Island until a progger from Ewell caught the first one in his traps. It was in the 1970s, after the bay froze solid to the mainland. He has it, stuffed, in his bedroom.

Sometimes you can even beat the wild birds out of their dinner. One old captain from here was out goose hunting and saw a great old bald eagle fly by with a nice rockfish in his claws. He fired on him, just close enough to scare him into droppin' his fish. Come home that day with a goose and a rock for dinner. I found a wigeon one winter afloat with his breast pecked clear through by gulls. You could see his heart as it beat. He had some meat left, and we brought 'im home. It was in the fall one year that I came upon the biggest bird I've ever seen, a gannet. They're supposed to spend their lives out to sea; but he must've come up here chasin' rockfish. In his throat was lodged one of at least three pounds. It had choked him to death.

Hunting's what I love in winter. I can get invited all I want to farms on the mainland where there's more geese in the cornfields in a day than we see in a winter in the marsh; but it's here in the marshes I do most of my gunnin'. A goose comes to you more wary over water, and it's a whole lot prettier to set by the water's edge than in a pit dug in the middle of a field. I make my own decoys of wood. They're not "artistic" like the ones the carvers make for the shows, but they got a shape to 'em, and ride nice in the water, and they don't make the noise of the plastic ones.

I don't even know who owns the marsh where I hunt. I don't think anyone does know. It's that way with a lot of places here. They say on the county tax maps it is just down as "escaped lands." Escaped from what? I don't know. Escaped from belongin' to anybody, maybe. It's a good place to hunt.

I always enjoyed airheadin' [arrowhead hunting]. I have a couple thousand, but I've given thousands away. I traded a builder from the mainland six hundred arrowheads to do the foundation for my house. The bayside of the islands, right along the shores, are good places to find them. Some people can look all day and see none, but some's got almost a special finding sense, like the airheads are a'drawin' 'em. One time I told a fellow, anchor here, along a certain shore where I was pretty sure we'd find a few. Where he planted the anchor in the marsh, I stepped out and picked up a perfect point.

People wonder how there can be so many left, but Indians was comin' here for a long, long time. Some of my points, the experts have said, is ten thousand years old. I've noticed that where our hunting is good for ducks and geese, most of those places you could find arrowheads. I think what brought the Indians here was just what brought the first of our people here. This was a good place to survive. They weren't after money and stuff back then, just survival, plenty to eat.

There's Indian blood in many an islander. A boy I grew up with here has found more than five thousand Indian artifacts. He always said when something was troubling him, or he had a tough decision to make, there's spots he'd go to on the shore where he felt like he could get peaceful and work it out. A progger in Crisfield—he's good at finding arrowheads—he has a birthmark shaped just like one. My own family on my father's side goes back to Captain John Smith and Pocahontas. Historians has said they never was married nor had children, but that is what I've always heard.

I respect science and education, but those people got to respect some things we know, too. There is an old blue heron I pass that is always standing by the edge of the marsh as you come from the Bottom into North End. I have been seeing him there for twenty years or more. I showed him to a man who comes here to put identification bands on the legs of fish hawks and herons, and he asked how could I know it was the same bird, because it wasn't marked with a band. Well, of course, he hadn't been looking at that old bird for twenty years, you see. Sometimes I think if we listened too much to the biologists about the problems of the bay, we'd just give up here and now. What I believe is, everything goes in cycles.

I'll tell you a story about a jimmy crab you won't believe, but it happened. One summer, Dallas, one of our watermen that works for the Chesapeake Bay Foundation now, had twenty schoolkids he was a'ferryin' around on a field trip. He had tied a string to a jimmy crab and let him down in the water from a dock pole to catch him a wife. In the right time of year a jimmy will attract females who are hot to double up and mate.

Well, it wasn't long before Dal and the kids pulled him up, and sure enough, he had a wife. They took her away and let him back over. Fifteen times they done it, and every time a wife; and you got to figure that was one frustrated jimmy. Next time they pulled him up, he didn't have a thing in his big ole claw but a pair of stainless-steel scissors he had found in the mud and was wavin' around. Don't you think they wasn't long a'cuttin' 'im loose. Wouldn't you have?

A lot of stuff in this marsh, I can't tell you the right names of—wops, bye-bye bunkers, pennywinkles, blare-eyed herring—those are our names for them. Everything's named, every gut and p'int [point] and holler, though many people now has forgot the names, and no map tells 'em all. I'll give you just a very few, most no more'n a few minutes skiff ride from Tylerton:

Hucksters Gut, The Fig Trees, Sedgey Island, Hams Point, Dipper Crick, Shelly Point, Merlin's, Juggling's, Eagle Hammock, Hog Neck, Ireland, The Pines, Sheep Hammock, Sheep Hammock Holler, Parks Ditch, School Gut, Back Landing Marsh, The Wading Place.

Also: Tim'ses, Cooney Island, Store Ditch, Injun Crick, Pig Point, Devil's Bill Gut, The Spit, Kizzes, Nordend, Lighter Knot Cove, Nigh Point, Joes Ridge, Fowlers, Solomons Lumps, Twitch Cove, Terrapin Sand, Fogs Point, Spang Cove, Pitchcroft, The Mud Hill, Ghost Gut.

And them's just places you can see. There's all the underwater names, the scrapin' and tongin' and nipperin' places: The Bottom, The Knoll, The Holler, Back of the Knoll, Apes Hole, Deep Swash, Mud Rock, Mussel Hole.

Some, like Billy Lowe Gut, was dug by old man Bill Lowe so he could shove through the marsh and save him some time; Lions Gut, that was dug with spades and dynamited nearly half a mile by the Lions Club of Tylerton for a better route to the Sound side of the island.

I like to say the names. It feels good to do it. Each one is a place where a lot has happened. Sometimes it might've been the simplest thing, like where those poles are down the creek. I remember the time it was snowin' and Alice's father saw a woodpecker on one, and said, watch this, and nailed 'im right to that pole with a snowball.

I always loved to rat. Rattin' takes you everywhere in the island, through the guts, to the cowholes and the ditch banks where the old people lived. A progger in Crisfield, he's had a colostomy, varicose veins, and two new kneecaps, and he's still a'rattin', though there isn't the market for muskrat or other fur as there once was. We used to get high as $10.50 apiece for prime black muskrat hide, and about $8.50 for prime brown ones. The island was a good place for the black ones, and certain ridges would have more black ones than other places. Around Rhodes Point and Fishing Creek and Horse Hammock seemed like it was particularly good for 'em. Around the ditch banks in Ireland and The Pines you'd get mink, and otter was all over. One day I thought I had caught the world's biggest muskrat—it was ten times bigger than any I'd ever seen. I showed him all over until someone said it was a nutria, a South American beaver. They had turned some loose around the bay years before, and they were starting to spread.

I almost never went anywhere without Luke, the best dog I ever knew. I would come back from my traps and he would have two mink he caught on his own, each laid across the bow of the boat, ready to be skinned. Luke—his father was a famous thoroughbred retriever named Tidewater Lucas—could kill about anything that lived in the marsh. He would go after an otter, which will do in most dogs, and keep after him, sometimes for more than an hour. One time I had to wash the blood off Luke and a big otter to tell which one had survived. That otter, I believe, was around five feet and two or three inches long.

Luke never lost a duck all the years we went—even a king diver he'd go after and find. A rich man, a hunter, was down here once and offered me $1,100 for him, and I said, he's not for sale. He threw his checkbook on the table and said, write your price, but I said there was no price. That dog loved to eat steamed crabs and oysters—shell and all. Luke's last few years—he lived to fourteen—I got to where I didn't much like to even go a'huntin'. It hurt him so bad to take him out in the cold and wet, but it hurt him worse if I went without him.

As much as I liked to trap, it always pained me to use those leg-hold traps. I would try to set my traps so the animal would drown, 'cause they could suffer a long time if they didn't. All of us were glad when those traps that killed instantly come on the market.

Now, you have seen how I can take a skiff, with all these miles of guts, and run it full out through near 'bout anyplace on the island and always know where to turn and which fork will have water and which ones will run you on the mud; and I can do that for all these islands, going right on up—Smith, South Marsh, Bloodsworth. It is like they are mapped in my head. It is the same with my traps, which was set across acres and acres of marsh that appears all the same. I used to rat with my father-in-law. He grew up in these marshes, but he had to stick poles and attach red flags with clothespins, to navigate among his traps. But it was like I could lay there in bed and just see every one of mine, where each was at. I would do this with up to a hundred traps, and I really believe if I'd had five hundred it would of been the same.

I don't spend more'n a week or two a year away from this place. Sometimes, come a cold February, I just head for Florida, or Hawaii—give this place some time to warm up and come back to life. One thing I love to do on weekends is go up the road into Delaware and progue around in all those flea markets. You pick up a lot of interestin' stuff.

My house here is about 30 feet from the water. From my front yard you walk right out on my dock. From the dock across the channel, on the edge of a big grass flat, is the shanty where my family sheds soft crabs all summer.

You wanted to make a list of everything that's layin' around my waterfront. Here goes:

A couple skiffs, both about 16 foot, with 50-horse Mercs; my big boat and my boy's—one's sunk right now and we'd like to sell that. Some propane tanks for steamin' crabs, electric golf carts, an old Yugo—I don't think she runs; picnic table, grandkids' bikes, dock lumber and poles, goose decoys, an old-timey crab float we painted white so my wife could plant flowers in it; gas cans, lawn chairs, a fig bush, a mimosa tree, my flag pole, metal clam baskets, a shovin' pole.

What else? A couple more Mercs that don't run, for parts; my grandson's toy boat, an old millstone I found up to Hollands Island, and in the float is a big old garfish I caught—that's unusual, 'cause they are supposed to be way up the rivers in freshwater. Also, a buoy that says, "Maryland-Virginia Line." Also culling boards, wooden and stainless steel; anchor line, five-gallon buckets, batteries, the boom off a patent tong rig. Yeah, and a kitchen sink.

There's more—all the stuff we fish with: gill net, crab scrapes, crab pots, bank traps, dip nets. Just about all of it catches by means of marshes [meshes]. What you catch is accordin' to your gear, and accordin' to the size of your marshes—different marsh wire and nylon in your nets and pots and traps will collect different sizes and kinds of fish and crabs. There's so much life out there. If you ever tried to catch it all at once, why, it would bust everythin'.

There's more to it than just catching things and finding stuff. I wish I was a painter good as Reuben in Ewell, so I could set down some of what I've seen, like the sunrise one summer as I was a'scrapin' for soft crabs in the big holler behind Hollands Island, the way it lit up five red foxes standing on the shore; and I don't know whether you've ever noticed how pretty a soft crab is when it fluffs out just after it has first shed.

That reminds me of one of our men, gave up crabbin' during the war [WWII] to work in the ship repair yards in Baltimore. When we went up to visit, he had begun to catch peelers around the drydocks. He would put them in five-gallon paint cans full of water, to shed them out into soft crabs. Crabs is so interestin'. you know. They tell of John Evans, when he was alive, goin' on vacation with his wife to Hawaii, and slippin' away from the crowd. When they found him, he was down by the base of that Battleship Memorial, trying to check out a crab he saw go under a ledge.

If I had this life over again, I wouldn't want much different—try to be a better Christian. You know what Job says: Man's days on earth are few and full of sorrow. Life's but a vapor. I spent nearly twenty years around rich people and famous people. That's how long I guided for the big lodge that used to operate up to South Marsh Island. It had seventeen rooms and two cooks and one man just to clean and pick the fowl. It was the best of eating, and credit to buy anything you needed for the lodge at any store in Salisbury or Princess Anne. We fed the ducks as high as 1,500 pounds of corn a day. The owners was wealthy, and a lot of their guests was admirals and generals and cabinet secretaries, Olympic skeet shooters—very interesting men. But it was a lot of pressure on you to produce, and you'd see these men call down and say they was comin' in from New York, their gun was in Washington, they needed a spare gun sent over; they had to get back to the mainland no later than 2:00 A.M., had to be somewhere else by the next day. If that was being rich, it was too many problems for me.

I told my wife when I died, she ought to have me cremated, and my ashes scattered over the marsh. I know other men who say they'd like to be set adrift in a burnin' skiff on the ebb tide, like the Vikings. Some others say they'd like to be buried over on the bayside, where the sun sets and it's good proggin'. The wives say they want us planted right here in the churchyard, not someplace where they'd lay awake every storm, worried we'd be a'washin' out of the ground.

There is something I would crave to do before I died. I was lookin' at a globe of the world, and it struck me how many little coves and bays and ins and outs there are around the shorelines of the earth. Wouldn't that be fun to progue around in them, see what you could find? ✦

WOMEN'S WORK

Women's Work

Look in any of the region's libraries under Chesapeake Bay, and you will find hundreds, if not thousands of stories written about the watermen who harvest it. Remarkably little is there about the female side of their existence—and then it is often about the anomaly, the rare women who have captained a dredge boat, or become a full-time crabber or tonger themselves.

In traditional communities like Smith Island, the women themselves often abet this bias, deferring to their spouses when asked for an opinion. But you didn't need to spend much time on the island to realize the extent to which women held together home and community—and they were quite capable of letting the men know how they were holding up their better-publicized end of the bargain:

"Ye want us t'be friends, haul your little ass back up the bay and find some oysters and get some money comin' in here!" I overheard that sweet parting one cold Sunday evening, as an islander prepared to head north for another long week of work in the remaining part of the bay where disease had not devastated the shellfish. I have never since felt quite as pressured by mere writing deadlines.

But that was scarcely our prevalent impression of the island women. "A giant lap" was the way my kids saw it. They could not walk down the street without women greeting them, hugging them, insisting they come in for fresh-made cookies or cake.

Cheri was struck by how hard women worked, and by how much the richness of community life depended upon them. One day on the radio, she heard the old Peggy Lee song:

> I'm a woooooman . . .
> . . . ain't nothin' I can't do
> I can make a dress out of a feedbag
> And I can make a man out of you. . . .

It should, she felt, be the anthem of Smith Island women.

THE WOMEN PICK AND TALK

Crack! Whack! Crunch!

It is four in the morning, but the workday began nearly an hour ago for the women, wrestling 50-pound bushels of steamed crabs into the outbuilding at the edge of the marsh, where they sit and dismember the crustaceans around a vinyl-covered kitchen table, beneath a bare light bulb. A mild breeze pushes up Tyler's Creek and through the screen door. It is 82 degrees, cool as it's going to get on a late-summer day—a day that for many of the ladies won't slow down, except for perhaps a brief nap, until 9:00 P.M.

Whack! Whack! Rrrip!

The sounds of picking recall a recording a scientist from the Smithsonian once made, using hydrophones to listen to a crab attacking and eating its prey. So perhaps it's a fit way for a crab to end.

Unless you have picked a crab, armored and spined without, and chambered within by cartilage into more than a dozen tiny, sharp-edged nooks and crannies, you cannot appreciate the speed and skill with which the island pickers transform heaps of the bright orange, steamed hardshells into mounds of glistening white, succulent meat.

The tools of the trade are basic: a brick; also a stubby, stainless-steel knife, half of it blade, for slicing into the crab and flicking meat from its multiple compartments. The other half is a heavy handle, for cracking claws against the brick. The average Marylander, no stranger to crabfeasts from birth on, might through diligent application produce a pound or two of crabmeat in a few hours. I have seen an island lady produce 20 pounds in a morning, although that was, she conceded, when the crabs "was extry good" i.e., fat with meat.

Probably a few pounds an hour is more the average rate; and of course the meat is far freer of bits of shell and cartilage than an amateur could produce. Smith Island crabmeat is known throughout the bay region for its quality, and the ladies sell it for $8 a pound, about half the supermarket price. It is in enough demand that even when we lived there, pickers were usually doing us a considerable favor to save a pound or two from their regular customers—restaurants and middlemen on the mainland.

Around 4:30, there's a break so the ladies can rustle up breakfast for men heading out to crab, and pack their "bails" (lunches). Picking interrupts again to pack up crabmeat orders for shipment to Crisfield on the 7:00 A.M. ferry. Some of the shipments, with ice, weigh 30–40 pounds, and it is the women who cart them to the dock and load them aboard.

The day wears on, so hot even the "skeeter hawks" (dragonflies) stop hovering and just cling to the reeds. A child wanders into the picking room and demands to be fed. One picker has been monitoring her baby, asleep inside the adjacent house, with a loudspeaker device, and now hears squalling and leaves. A widow, eighty-two, drops by to pick a few pounds, in effect subcontracting to the shanty's owner, whose husband supplies the crabs.

The picking is a perfect complement to the island men's soft-crab fishery. In dragging nets through the grass beds for crabs that have either shed their shells or are about to, they incidentally catch a number of big hard crabs, which they bring home to their mates to steam and pick. Some supplement this bycatch further by setting a few crab pots in the marsh guts around town, which they can easily fish each evening after soft crabbing. The money the women can make with this cottage industry is several times what they could get from selling the hard crabs live to big mainland picking houses, or from picking for such places.

Picking in most of the outhouses, as they call the outbuildings, adjourns for lunch, for housecleaning, cake baking, and other chores. Several women head down to the church, which they must clean for a community supper they will prepare and serve, and also provide entertainment for, later in the week. A couple ladies go by on their way to "fish up" soft crabs that have shed in their sons' shanties. The sons are out crabbing, but if the newly molted crabs are not removed from the water in timely fashion, they will harden again to become virtually worthless.

One picker, during her "break" time, cleans, wraps, and freezes soft crabs. Her husband feels it gives him more control over the market than shipping everything fresh, daily, to mainland buyers. She fishes up, and hauls a huge tub of quivering softies into her shanty. Quiver they might, because her big scissors make short work of preparing them for the freezer. She thrusts both hands into the writhing mass of olive backs, creamy white bellies, and red- and blue-tinted claws, and sets to work:

Snip, goes a crabby face; *snip, snip* go its gills on either side; flipped with a deft twist of the wrist onto its back, *snip*, goes the creature's abdominal covering. *Snip, snip; flip, wrap, snip* . . . it's 3:30 in the afternoon, and except for twenty minutes to swallow a tuna sandwich on the run, the woman has not stopped since 3:00 A.M. She wears braces on her wrists. She has had operations on both for nerve damage, a result of so much repetitive motion. It is the crabs' final revenge.

In the relative cool of evening, picking resumes in the little outbuilding, while fresh crabs steam sweetly on a propane burner in an adjoining room. A picker's young grandchild plays on the floor, while another, a girl about ten, practices cracking out claw meat. One woman as she picks conferences chattily on her two-line phone with friends picking in their own outbuildings and kitchens on the island and in Crisfield. One of the pickers hums the lyrics of a song she has just finished for the upcoming watermen's annual banquet. It refers to troubles Maryland and Virginia crabbers are having over the state line that runs through Smith Island. It is, she says, "what Elvis would'a sung to his wife if he had to catch crabs for her to pick."

Oh well, a-bless'a my soul
What do I see
Virginia police boats comin' after me
I pull my scrapes
Right out'a the mud—I'm a wreck—I'm all shook up. . . .

Other offerings follow, based like the first on everyday experiences of the islanders—crabby reworkings of Sonny and Cher ("We Got Crabs, Babe"); Julio Iglesias and Willy Nelson ("To All the Crabs I've Caught Before"); and a bittersweet adaptation of Mary Chapin Carpenter's song, "Lucky," which captures the women's love-hate relationship with their lives within a crab culture that is both the charm and fate of this place.

A VISITOR, a lady just off the late ferry, well dressed, comes in to sit and talk. She lived here all her life, until a few years ago. Leaving seems to have agreed with her. She cracks a couple claws. The pickers trade stories back and forth, about women's lives on the island and off:

◆ Look, this is not the most glamorous job in the world. You stink, you're rotten, you take baths all the time. Whenever a tourist or somebody doin' a TV story on our "island way of life" sees me lookin' like some old workhorse, I hate it. Oh, I've dreamed of havin' a lady's job, where I'd dress up and go to an office—who wouldn't? This ain't no lady's job, but it's our job.

Dad got me a state job after high school, and I was good at it. It was secretarial. It was always my dream to be a secretary and have a beautiful business suit and high heels and a briefcase. But I didn't know how to live in a city. I married a crabber and got a picking knife and old clothes and a smelly job. Women here work very hard to look their nicest whenever there's an occasion—home perms, nice jewelry, dressy clothes, cosmetics. It's like we are saying, look, some old fishwife is not all we are.

I always wished I'd fulfilled my dream of a real job. I don't know if I'd been happier. Here, I feel like I could call on anyone—physically, financially, emotionally—and they'd do what they could. It's a feeling of love I can't really explain to you. It's all I've ever knowed.

Excepting postmaster and, if you had the education, schoolteacher, there is nothing else a woman can do here to make money like she can from picking the crabs her husband brings her. Picking, of course, is just the start of what we call women's work. No man ever pushed a grass cutter here, I don't think. That is women's work. Women can also be custodian at the schools, sexton at the church, clerk at the store or the gas dock, keep the graves tidy at the cemetery, waitress at a couple restaurants to Ewell in tourist season; monitor the sewer plant for the state, take in a few tourists—make a little money that way.

But mostly, we're unpaid. Women do the school PTA, and cook and clean and organize the entertainment for all the church and social events; also they keep the books for the church and the fire department.

There is many things women do not do. Grave digging is men's work, and keeping after repair of the water and sewer lines, which the men have not done very well lately. Women do not do carpenterin' or regular water work or make crab pots or drive boats, except skiffs.

Husbands and sons here—and sons includes bachelors, some of 'em middle-aged—are cooked for, washed for, accounts kept, bills paid, bails packed. Many a woman still lays out their husband's clothes for church and such occasions. The old women say, if the man's not rigged out proper, it'll reflect on the woman. Many women is very much consulted on financial decisions, even the buying of a new boat.

Housework is of course women's work. Cleaning and washing and ironing is as regular as breathing. And cooking, well that's central—can't you tell? Not many narrar starns [narrow sterns, i.e., small rear ends] among this crowd. You cook for your family; you cook for entertaining, you cook for weddings and funerals, you cook to raise money for the church and the fire department. Our men don't like TV dinners and they don't like microwave. What with ordering food on the ferries, keeping the freezers stocked, planning community dinners and your own too, you really have food on your mind the whole day.

But you could have lots worse on your mind. I do think most women here love to cook. They're good at it. It's one of the only places we can be creative. It's not low calorie. It's lots of butter, lots of fried, lots of sugar, lots of gravy, lots of meat. I do think more people here now are aware of things like cholesterol, and some really try to watch it, but I can't see it has made much difference in the way we eat and cook. I know women who have tried to change their families' diet, and next thing you know, their husband's slipping down the street to his mother's for some of that eight-layer cake, or hamburger with gravy and dumplings. One woman, her husband come home from oysterin' up the bay and she served him a plate with a little lean meat, no gravy or sauce, and a big salad. It was the talk of the store and the post office, and she never did it n'more.

A woman came here once to live, workin' on her degree [Ph.D.] in sociology, and she wrote a book about communities like ours.* She didn't call us Smith Island; she called us Crab Reef. Some of what she put in there was

Fisher Folk (Lexington, Ky.: University of Kentucky Press, 1986).

none of her business, but a lot of it was true. She talked about how men make the big decisions here, and you might have got the idea they run the place. But let me tell you, it is women who keep the place running. Lord knows, men here works hard; but it is the women that keep them together and light a fire under them. I think it comes from when most of the island's able-bodied men would go away all winter, oysterin'. That's faded out some now, but the women had got used to being the strong ones.

This kind of picking is not that old, though some has gone on for a long time. I remember cracking claws as a girl in the 1950s to a man's crab house at Rhodes Point, where my mother and other ladies would come and pick for what he paid them per pound—it weren't much. They would sit and pick and sing hymns, and you would hear all the gossip. I remember one young woman bragging about having a drink the night before, some cheap liquor called Four Roses; and an old woman snapped at her: "I know that drink, and it's a disgrace to the rose bush!"

Picking, each for ourselves, like we do nowadays, began about twenty-five years ago, just as something for a little extra money. Then it seemed like people got more and more for trying to keep up with the mainland—cars in Crisfield, trips off, adding onto the house; and nowadays, with the oysters dwindlin' all through the bay, it has got to where the men can't make it any more financially without a woman picking. A few on here now make more'n their husbands.

Truly, we have caught up to the mainland. We're just as busy and stressed and not spending enough time with our kids, same as anyone there, at least in the summers. It wasn't so long ago we would go swimming almost every day. One year some of us had those inflatable chairs and we'd float all over this crick. We'd take children and lunches to the bayside and get back around 2:00 P.M., in time to get the men's suppers. In the evenings, sometimes we'd go nettin' soft crabs when nettin' was good; and there'd be baseball and softball games, and a lot more visiting. We didn't have much extra then—we wasn't poor, but kids'd have two pair of shoes, one for Sunday, one pair for the week; and a trip to Ocean City was a big summer outing.

You get like a robot, and you never really see a lot of your neighbors, except when you are picking, until church on Sunday; and then everybody looks about half dead and just wants to get home and rest up for Monday.

It's a love-hate thing, pickin'. It's not a career I'd have chosen, but it gives you self-worth and independence, a way of helping out. No one wants to be dependent on a man all their life. Why, wouldn't I be in good heart if I had to go to my husband for every cent I spend?

I'm eighty-two. I guess I really ought to be in a rocking chair, crochetin'. Hah! I just pick a few pounds to help out when the crabs are runnin' heavy . . . I enjoy the company, and it's nice to be able to earn. I don't owe no one a cent, or need to borrow.

Some of these men, now, when they land home with a big load of crabs, well, they think they done something. The first thing they expect is a big dinner, and the next thing they expect . . . *(lots of eye rolling and laughing).*

Well, hey! We'll sing you part of a song we wrote. It goes to the tune of "Lucky," by Mary Chapin Carpenter.

> Well, I woke up this morning
> Stumbled outta my bed
> Poured myself some coffee just to clear my head
> My husband looked at me and said,
> You're a great wife
> While I'm sittin' there with my picking knife
> My eyes are about to pop outta my head
> He's just sitting there, while I'd like to get back in bed
>
> Oh, he feels lucky
> He feels lucky, yeah
> He brings his crabs he caught in the bay
> Mmmmm, he feels lucky today
>
> Now, eleven bushels later
> He's fishing pots on Nars [Narrows] Bar
> He gets home on the double
> With them sooks all full of tar
>
> (Three women each sing one of the next lines):
>
> My husband's in the corner trying to catch my eye
>
> My husband's right beside me with his hand upon my thigh
>
> My husband loves me a'picking, it's simple but it's true
> Husbands sometimes stray, but ours never do
>
> 'Cause they're so lucky (growwwwl)
> They feel lucky, yeah
> They've got a crab picker
> They're a winner either way
> Mmmmmmm, they feel lucky today. ◆

THE VISITOR SPEAKS:

✦ I'm fifty-three now; gone ten years, but I'll always be a Smith Islander. The first place I lived off, I did just the way I had always done here—work, come home, clean, bake, tend the yard. A neighbor came up and said, "If World War III breaks out, you'll be a survivor. You're so strong and self-reliant." Later, he hired me to a good manager's job.

At the time, that just floored me. Strong? Self-reliant? I was just doing like you always did over here. But now I think Smith Island women are so strong. I never thought it was hard living here until I moved away. Now I realize how hard we all worked. I have thought back sometimes and realized certain times when friends had got sick over here, that it might have been just stress. Late spring was always a hard time, when money was scarce between oysters and crabs, and the stores were not giving credit like they once did. Freeze-ups were the worst, though. You may not want to go off, but knowing you can is important. When you know you can't leave, even if you don't want to, that's bad.

I have to say I am contented now, but there was a closeness here that I'll never have again anywhere else. ✦

THE PICKERS RESPOND:

✦ A lot of islanders, men and women, have gone away to make something of themselves. We have had school superintendents and state officials, successful businessmen and a Naval Academy graduate. I've often thought over what I might have become if I had left. Dad wanted me to go to college so bad. He never could, though he had an exceptional mind. He had to make a living. His father taught himself to read, and he read the newspaper cover to cover when it came, about two days old, on the freight boat. I read everything now and have always thought I'd love to write.

Dad offered me a brand-new car if I'd just go to college. Why didn't I? Well, I fell in love. And maybe it sounds awful now to hear that a woman didn't finish high school and got married at fifteen or sixteen, but at the time, we didn't see it as entering a hard life. It was our expectation, and we was comfortable with it. I think now, more than thirty years later, if I'd left I'd had an easier life, but maybe not one any happier.

Women more and more are sitting here in the winters and saying, here it is, the best working years of our lives, and if we were on the mainland, at least we could get piddling jobs, earn something year-round.

I have heard some of the old people say education will be the death of the island. I don't think they mean education's bad; but once the young people have got options. . . . The teenage girls now, they look at us, and they look at the water business, and they head to the mainland. Here, a woman is either married or she's nothing. Some of the boys and younger men still want to stay. People are always going to eat crabs, and somebody's got to catch them, they say; and maybe the oysters'll come back. I think moving is scarier for the men here. They don't know nothin' but the water, and here's the water they know best. Women think they could get a job somehow, and they think a lot about their children's future. A lot more women here would move than men.

I took a year of college twenty years ago, but it was just a fallback. I was already engaged to a waterman and had no desire not to come back and live on the island forever. It wasn't that hard to make money on the water then, and there's a closeness here that you never could find off. Maybe the best word for what's special about it is "trust"—knowing what you can expect out of everyone. Even those you can't trust, you know that, too. ◆

Excerpt from song written and performed by the pickers.

UP THE BAY AGAIN

(to the tune of "On the Road Again"; "up the bay" refers to going north for oysters each winter)

> Up the bay again
> I just can't wait 'til he's up the bay again
> The life I love is going shopping with my friends
> I can't wait 'til he's up the bay again

> Up the bay again
> Every Monday we go up the highway with all my friends
> He can stay as long as he sends
> Money my way—yea, my way.

AN OLD WOMAN RECOLLECTS:

◆ This island has seen prettier days. Once there was white picket fences and flowers blooming all along in front of the homes; and some of the little paths were covered by oyster shells that shone in the moonlight. And fruit trees— there was plum, pear, apple, fig, peach; gardens, too. People kept their waterfront up. They would go over in the marshland every year and dig turf, and fill in with that behind their puncheons [bulkheads]. Then they would layer over that with oyster shells. Even if it was a rented place, it was kept filled in.

Tylerton alone had twenty-eight drudge boats, which were the pride of the community, and employed many a man and boy here. Their masts, and the church steeples, were the tallest things for as far as anyone could see. They say that oysterin' is done for in the Chesapeake. Every waterman now is nearly a full-time crabber; but in my day a hard crab was something you ate, not your living.

Soft crabs, which is king here now, was just getting to be a business when I was born, early in this century. I was a little girl when the families of some seafood dealers came here to visit from the Fulton Fish Market in New York, where our men had begun shipping soft crabs. One of the wives watched us cleaning some for dinner and said: "Oh, my, we've been eating them whole."

There was money to be made in oysters back then, if a captain was able and lived according to his means. My grandfather never crabbed. He was captain of a dredge boat until he retired in 1926, and he was about seventy-six at the time. He retired to Nevada because of asthma, and when he moved, he said he had saved about $60,000.

Every October, most of the island's men and older boys would leave for drudgin', and they would not return until just before Christmas. I guess that is why Thanksgiving to this day has never been a big holiday here. But we would make up for it with Christmas. It was like Santa Claus and your dad comin' all at once to see the drudge boats comin'. They'd anchor off Horse Hammock, at the island's southern end. I can see the drudgers now, in a long line, trudging miles up that long path through the marsh from Horse Hammock to the towns, and us kids all excited, running to meet them. One Christmas they were walking up, leaning into a blizzard o' snow, exhausted. One of the old captains said, "Hey, I've got a tune we can sing that will get us up the road faster"; and they all came up through the marsh and the snow a'singing, "Hi Oh, Hi Oh. King in the Guy Oh." He made that up, and it got 'em going. After Christmas, they would be gone again until March.

Drudgin' oysters is one reason women here are so strong. We had to run things without the men near 'bout forever. I scarcely remember winters being lonesome, though. Most people had large families, and it wasn't like you had time on your hands, not by the time you took care of your children, did your housework and sewing, tended your chickens. Most homes had one or two hogs, and you needn't think the women didn't know how to butcher 'em. We didn't have electricity here until a few years after the war [WWII], except for some Delcos. Just getting a supply of good water from the old sandy, shallow wells we had then took time.

We had a great social life. We had school plays and adult plays and Tom Thumb weddings. We had dinners, and bonfires and skating parties down at the big pond in the marsh—the "taking-up place," we called it. Women would make cakes and pies and auction them, and if it was any man's gal made one, he'd bid a whole lot more on it.

A sight I remember as a little girl was on Saturdays, the women of my grandmother's generation would have their housework and cooking for the weekend done, and they would set off a'visitin', walking together on the road through the marsh in these great, black- and white-checked ankle-length aprons they wore. The aprons had big pockets that served like a purse, and they would carry chewing tobacco, and little bottles of cordials that you still find along the shoreline now—"contains opium," they say on them. Some of them smoked corncob pipes around the house, but for visitin' they would take a clay pipe. I see tourists and Save the Bayers find pieces of those pipes and think they have got something from Indian times, but they don't know. Certain women's homes were known as great taking-up places—where the ladies would gather with their pipes and their tobacco and their cordials and have a grand old time, I'm certain.

Baseball was a great passion that has only faded away as the towns have gone down in numbers in recent times. Each town and all the other islands and little communities up and down the bay—Solomons, Reedville, Kinsale, Tangier—had teams then, and ours would travel half the day by boat sometimes to play a doubleheader. Smith Island teams even had their own band accompany 'em, a good band for a little island. If you didn't hear 'em playin', coming back through the marsh on the boat, you knew Smith Island had lost. Once, they lost a big game, and comin' in the Thoroughfare, the band was asked to strike up as the town came in sight. "Nary a toot," the band leader said. That is how we made our entertainment. I think TVs and VCRs has got the young people's attention now.

There were hard times. More babies and children died in those days, and women in childbirth sometimes. Many babies got born at home, or to the doctor's office in Ewell. Some got born aboard a boat, tryin' to make it to the hospital in Crisfield. They say of one woman here that she ought to put her birthplace as halfway between the outer and inner beacons to Crisfield. A man to Ewell was delivered on the engine box of his grandaddy's crab boat, right on the Maryland-Virginia line, his granpap throwin' gear overboard as they went, tryin' to make her go faster.

I had a daughter born going across the Sound. I had been in Crisfield a week, waiting to have her, and decided to return to the island when a friend got sick over there. The very next day they sent me back to Crisfield with a waterman who was makin' a regular crab run that evening. We had hardly left when the pains hit me. The captain come back to where I was layin'. My husband was with me. "Hang on fifteen minutes and we'll be there," he said. "That ain't what's goin' to happen," I told him. He was banging on the engine with a wrench when the baby come. We had brought sheets. We were by the inner beacon. I had no time to be scared. I was just hoping I'd be over it before we got to the dock, where I knew there'd be a crowd. In we came, baby a'bawlin'. It was harder on my husband, I believe.

In the Depression years there was no money at all around here. Men stayed gone, drudgin' for weeks and came home with 17 bucks. "Well, you got your eats free," the captain told one of 'em.

Women always did about everything but work the water, and they would do that too if it was necessary. One I know, in Depression times, when her husband was in the hospital, would put her five year old in the bottom of the skiff to play while she fished crab pots she would set up and down the marsh guts. Another lady, you might as well say she was a better crabber'n her husband, and he would shove the skiff while she dipped 'em.

I heard of some island children who would hide in the marsh and watch for terrapins to come up and nest, and dig their eggs out of the sand for something good to eat; but I never knew of anyone here actually going hungry, though plenty had very little money. Lord knows, if you could starve out here, we'd a managed to do it long before now.

I've known widow ladies in my mom's day was left when their husband died young with as little as $100, and small children to raise. They made it with the help of relatives and the community. People would put money in Christmas cards and birthday cards for the poor and widowed—some still do it. There would be meals sent over and gifts of food; men would drop by extra fish and ducks and geese, and that's how they'd make it. Many widows would remarry quick as they could. Nowadays it seems they don't as much. With Social Security and electric blankets, they'd as soon stay single now, they say.

I have written down some of the most important "firsts" for the island in this century:

1905—first phones, but only on the island; it was 1951 before we could talk to the mainland
1917—*Island Belle* started regular ferry service, once a day
1923—first automobile on here
1949—got electricity
1977—*Captain Jason* began first twice-a-day ferry service
1979—first sewage treatment plants
1994—got cable television

I think the environmentalists of today are doing good, trying to save the bay and all, because we depend on the water for our livelihood; but it's the life of our people that concerns me. There used to be so many more here.

Just in Tylerton I can remember as high as fifty girls and boys and maybe two hundred people; and now they are talking about closing down the school for lack of children.

There were four stores in this little town alone. Drummers [salesmen] would come to us then, every Wednesday, and get their orders, and send the goods over later on the *Island Belle*. The big store down by the waterfront would open at 7:00 A.M. and not close 'til 10:30 many nights. There was confectionery on one side, hardware, shoes, and oilskins in another part, groceries in another. There'd be dozens of people inside. One day I took a visitor in and this was the scene—I can see it so clear:

Old Hughes is cuttin' hair to one side; and in the back they are shucking oysters and picking wild ducks and saving the feathers in boxes for stuffing pillows and mattresses. Another corner, a man is repairing oyster tongs. People is buying groceries and kids are getting candy—the drummers'd give 'em a nickel each for sweets. Eggs was money then, and a girl is trading some for chocolate squares. A young couple is eatin' ice cream, and the old men sit around the big old pot-bellied stove, roasting hot dogs on long wires and telling yarns. You could see our whole lives in that old store, plain as if they was on the shelves.

To the outside world's way of thinking we were isolated, but it wasn't something we dwelled on. They tell of a drummer sailed over here with Captain Ham Bradshaw, one of our older men and one of the best Christian watermen ever lived. He did not sell much, and on the way back he was griping to Capn' Ham about how hard it was to get here. "Farewell, old Smith Island," he said, and he wondered aloud "if God almighty would be able to find this place come Judgment Day." Well, Capn' Ham was a man of few words, but that was too much for him. He said, "Listen here. God made Smith Island; and if anyone as green and dumb as a drummer can get here, don't you worry, God'll find it." The drummer told that one everywhere he went for years.

People in my day *believed* in the power of prayer. My grandpa got a letter from a friend who had got his dredge boat so hard aground on the western shore, he feared they would never budge it. Grandpa studied on it some, and he wrote his friend that on a certain Tuesday, get his crew ready with poles and ropes. Meantime, Grandpa wrote he would pray for their success three times a day. Well, it worked, and that captain wrote Grandpa that he wanted to make "your God my God"; and he moved here and began to run the mail, and he's buried today right to Ewell.

It is strange to think how, with all of today's labor-saving machinery, we seemed to have more leisure time in olden days. Always, there would be free time when oysterin' was over in the spring, and again before it began in the fall, and many afternoons and evenings spent visiting through the year. On

Sundays we was strictly forbid to do anything that was considered like work. Children could play outside, chasing each other, but not play with toys. There's families even today don't let the children use scissors to make paper cutouts on Sundays. My father said he got the worst lickin' of his life for going out in a sailboat on a Sunday when he was young. He said he couldn't ride his bike then, either. Even when you did sneak a ride on Sunday, you would feel sort of condemned.

Now, when soft crabbin' began to get big business here, that presented a real problem, because the crabs shedded their hard shells seven days a week, God or no God; and if they aren't fished up and packed in sea grass soon after they shed, they will turn hard again and be worthless. So they asked a very wise preacher who come here about what to do. He told how the Bible speaks of Jesus and some men helping a cow that had fell into the mire, and the Pharisees condemned him for doing it, and Jesus says, is it better to just let him stay there and die, or to save his life?

And so, the preacher told them that he thought they were supposed to take care of what they had rightly earned, and it was all right to fish up on a Sunday rather than harm your livelihood. Now, the extras, like sorting out the green crabs [not ready to shed], which could be done easy enough on Monday, he didn't think they should do that. So ever since I was little I have heard people say, if we have some emergency that arises on Sunday, like sewing a button on that fell off your only good shirt on the way to church— we say, well, that's got to be fixed, that's an ox in the mire, we say.

This island has weathered many a storm, but never one like the one that hit us on August 23, 1933. Things never did get back the way they was before that awful day. It was raining and blowin' hard enough to shake houses when we got up that morning. Nowadays they call such storms hurricanes. Back then we didn't even know a bad time was comin' 'til shortly before it hit. It was the tide that was the worst. By breakfast time it was in the kitchen floor. All over the island, people were taking up their rugs and carrying furniture upstairs. Some brought the chickens inside. Hogs had to do for themselves, and a lot drowned. By noon it was up to some of the first-floor window sills.

The men looked as worried as we'd ever seen them. We'd seen tides, but not like this one. Later on, they told us in the records at Baltimore, which go back to the 1840s, it was the highest water ever recorded—and it still is. Over on the ocean side of Maryland, the storm cut an inlet 50 feet wide and 8 foot deep clear through Assateague Island. It gave Ocean City a harbor in its back bay overnight, which made it into a big fishing resort.

I can still see Papa eating his supper that afternoon, all of us upstairs and him sitting on the top stair, watching the tide rise and rise. There wasn't even time to wash the dishes when we decided to join families moving up to the church, which is built on the highest land of the island. We got in skiffs, carrying food and babies, warm clothes and blankets. The boys and men, pushing and pulling the boats, had a hard time making way against the storm and waves. They were rolling right through town by then. By evening the church began to reel and rock and snap and crack, and the tide had started up the steps of the building. I think that was the scariest time, because there wasn't a higher place to get to. By dark the wind had calmed down, and the tide was ebbing—finally! People were praying and crying. Some had gone to sleep in the choir loft and on the benches, they were so exhausted.

The next morning was beautiful and clear, and we were glad to be alive. But oh, what a wreck our island was! Boats in the roadways, bridges gone, fallen trees, dead chickens, pigs, cats; toilets washed away. And every floor downstairs was covered with inches of inky black mud. All of the chairs and carpets were full of it. Wallpaper was coming down and stoves had floated away.

Some never did recover. Down below the main town of Tylerton was a family that always kept their ditches and ditch banks up wonderful; tide never came in on them, and they had a farm there, and sold greens and milk to the rest of us. That storm tore them up, and they never did go back down there. Another couple that had been thinking about moving, the storm decided them. It seemed like we never did get all of our high ground back. People left their ditches to run down, and did not plant as big a gardens after that, and began moving in from places like Longbranch to the main towns. If we had a tide like that nowadays, I am afraid it would just about wind this island up.

We did fear for the end of the island in 1941. It was of course a bad year for the whole country, but nothing compared to what happened to our crabs that summer. Men like Todd Marshall, one of the best crabbers there ever was, would go from first light 'til noon and have no more'n a dozen. One day all the talk was that Elmer Francis [Evans], a waterman to Ewell, and a good one too, had netted all day and did not catch a single peeler. That was nearly impossible. The *Island Belle,* which normal summers would be carrying hundreds of boxes of crabs to Crisfield, was carrying hundreds of crabs. Before long, it was carrying people's belongings. The men left first, for wartime jobs in Baltimore, and then they would send for their families. Armistead Gardens in East Baltimore was turning into Smith Island in exile. The young men was so depressed that one day when a recruiting officer come over here, several of 'em joined on the spot. The year after, crabbing was better, and we've not had a year like 1941 since. But crabs has done that before, and they'll do it again. The older men warn the young ones: you think it'll be good times forever, but it won't, they tell them.

There was very, very few that didn't come back after the war, though. I believe the women were more eager to get back than some of the husbands. Some saw the hand of the Lord in the way the war made those jobs just at the time of our greatest need for other work.

The war later on took most of our able men and boys off to the Army and the Navy. I remember how whenever a soldier was coming home on the ferry, they'd start ringing the big bell in the church, and that made you feel good. That church bell is older than the church. I can't say where it came from. It rang out for every occasion—meetings, funerals, fires, weddings, and religious services of course. It had two ropes, one to ring, one to toll. Ain't you never heard a bell toll? It is the mournfulest sound there ever was—just one hard gong, and then it stops, and then another. They would do that while they were carrying the body in. They have stopped it now.

It seems like since my grandparents' day the island people have got pulled inward, closer together, all living in the three towns instead of all over the marshes and hummocks. But it is like we aren't as together as we were back then, either. What I mean is this. The drudge boats, which had crews and was like little communities, is all gone, and each man's got his own boat and works alone, or maybe with one mate. Soft crabbin's the same. It started with lots of men going together and hiring one to run the shanty—there would be high as eight or nine in a company, and they would all share the profits at the end of the year. Back then, you needed to do it that way. The floats they shedded the crabs in were great ole big wooden pens that floated in the water, and it took a lot of labor to haul 'em and scrape 'em and keep 'em up. Now, with electric motors and pumps, you can put the crabs in tanks right in your shanty on the land, and each crabber's got his own separate little operation. It has gone like that, too, with fishing. The old pound nets used to take a whole bunch, together, to set up and fish; now it is more individual like.

And the preacher never used to travel by boat to all three towns' churches every Sunday, like now. He would preach every third Sunday in a different one of our island towns, and everybody from the other two communities would go there and spend the whole day in and around services. It would be a whole day for sharing our yarns and our concerns about the island and the water business, and catching up with relatives.

Nowadays, everybody's busier. Radios and telephones should have brought us closer; but TVs and VCRs and Walkmans has taken us out of sittin' around and talking to each other. I guess I've loved the modern conveniences as much as anyone, but I have to say, I think, back aways, we were more content. ✦

PARTY TIME

The women have put together an "extry special" Valentine's Day Social this winter, and so we have gathered in the basement of the church, all the married couples of Tylerton, focused intently on barbecued chicken, potato salad, corn pudding, hot, fresh rolls, crab balls, crab Norfolk, turkey, Jell-O mold, four kinds of cake.

And love.

Uplifting Love, Redeeming Love . . . a trio of the ladies, fresh from clearing away the supper dishes, presents a medley of hymns about love.

Next comes a short dissertation on the meanings of love, including this: "Love, men, is not bringing your wife an extra bushel of crabs to pick."

Next, an older lady reads her always-popular selection of jokes, poems, and homilies clipped from *Reader's Digest* and the *Grit*. Nanny and Romey, as we expected, get the longest-married couple award; and we sing "God Bless Smith Island (Land that we love; / With its waterfront, / And its little lanes . . .)."

Then, Janice, who at forty-five is about to celebrate her thirtieth wedding anniversary, stands and says she would like to talk about love and something that has always troubled her in the Bible. Lord knows she loves her husband and has always stood by him, and she wouldn't trade her life as island wife and mother for any other, even if she has been known to grumble about it once in a while.

But it has always rankled, she says, the part in Ephesians (5:21–24), where it says just as the church submits to Christ, so should wives to their husbands, in everything. She just can't believe women get dismissed that easily. "Why, lookit how after the Crucifixion, it was women went to the tomb to anoint Jesus' body, because the men was scared.

"If you knew how I have studied on that part about submitting, how I have searched my Bible for some way to better interpret that," she says; and tonight she wants to share what she has found. The wife, she says, was formed from man's side, not from his head or his foot. To her, that means woman is no doormat, no mere thought of man; rather, the Bible is talking about sharing.

She finds, in fact, the Bible commands the man to do much: "Men, I tell you the truth, I wouldn't want to be ye." And she goes on to make a compelling case for "mutual obligation . . . not submission, and not domination." The duties and responsibilities of a marriage, she concludes, are not split 90–10, or 60–40, or even 50–50: "it is 100–100, men."

And as the "amens" of assent still ring—strongest from the women, perhaps—the decks are cleared for a little different look at love, Smith Island's version of "The Newlywed Game." It is as risqué as anything in the televised version, and then some.

What do you call her when no one's listening? What's the thing she says most often in the bed? How would he/she be most likely to show you he loved you? What's the main things he expects when he comes home with a big load of crabs? The answers are remarkably unrestrained. Cheri and I, pressed into service as one of the game's couples, are blushing fiercely, furnishing new grist, no doubt, for the island gossip mill for years to come.

Our prize for competing is a pair of anatomically correct, his and her tooth-brushes, "something to remember him by all those times he goes off on writin' trips." In the hilarity, one lady says the speculation is that the two of us, tall at six feet six and five feet nine, "must look like two sets of oyster tongs together a'goin' at it."

And then we closed the evening with a hymn and prayer.

THE VALENTINE'S DAY experience, from Bible study to sexual innuendo and back again, was delightfully typical, we would find. Few communities in America are more devout in religion or more committed to traditional family values. In America in the 1990s, such notions somehow have become sadly caught up in the polarizing and exclusionary "cultural wars" waged by the religious and political right. But humor, more often than not directed at themselves, was one of the great graces of the island. They could be devilishly clever mimics, and loved to mock every social and physical nuance of one another. Vince, a young crabber, emulated my own peculiar walk with painful accuracy and played to appreciative crowds. Years later, when I called his family to check a fact, they kept hanging up to great laughter in the background: "It's only Vince. . . . Don't he sound just like Tom Horton."

Though a casual visitor might come away from Tylerton thinking the strongest curse used was "Blessed Assurance!" or "Oh, my blessed!", the language and humor could get substantially earthier. The flow of conversation might swing from one mode to another easily and unpredictably as changes in the breeze and the waves. And in both religion and ribaldry, many of the Christian ladies of the island took a back seat to no one.

Sometimes it would just be a frank comment, dropped into casual conversation unexpectedly, as a grenade might roll from your pocket while reaching for change in the grocery checkout. A prim and proper woman, entering her grandson's home, might remark offhandedly, "I saw your new [bikini] underwear a'dryin' on the line yesterday. I worry it won't cover your bag." Or a waterman calling a neighbor lady to inquire whether his wife is there and remarking on the phone: "Tell her my bag looks like a dried fig that swelled after the rain fell on it"—which condition is immediately and loudly transmitted to both wife and a roomful of other women.

One day, waiting outside the post office, where the ladies gather to talk, as the men do at the store, I heard, "Give you a pepper dumplin'," accompanied by much cackling. Knowing how the islanders love dumplings, and thinking it some new recipe, I listened closer. It was nothing you'd eat at the supper table. One of the women had just returned from having surgery that required her pubic area to be shaved, and an older woman was describing how it would look, and itch, when the hair began to regrow. Unfazed, the subject of attention, a redhead, retorted that she expected to have a "paprika dumpling," thank you.

SOME OF the finest sport was to be had during our main party season, the weeks of early winter, beginning with the Christmas holidays. Christmas on the island is a time of homecoming and religious pageantry; a time to celebrate the harvests—summer's crabs and autumn's oysters—and to gird up for the hard times between January and May, when incomes drop and boredom builds. It was a time for sleeping in, loafing, and gathering in one another's homes for ample meals, parlor games, and lively conversation, stimulated by nothing stronger than iced tea and black coffee. A typical such evening began at a neighbor's at 5:00 P.M. That meant, we had learned, that invitees expected to get down to serious eating by 5:03; nor was chatting encouraged until a goodly quantity of food had been consumed. One unforgettable meal, whose main courses alone included steak, fried soft crabs, clam fritters, ham and turkey, concluded with the host taking a slab of eight-layer cake and slathering it, edge to edge, with butter—"spread it half an inch thick if I dared," he said between bites.

The guest list at such affairs tended to be married couples only. Sometimes widows were asked, but never bachelors or widowers. However, in high party season, like this night, no one had to be lonesome. There was a shrimp supper at the Volunteer Fire Department, and several of the younger couples were gathering for their own dinner. At a bachelor's trailer, there was drinking, and a doubleheader video—*Porn in the U.S.A.*—followed by home videos of the island children's Christmas program.

At our soirée, the talk and laughter swirled through the room in multiple conversations; everyone, it seemed, listening and participating in them all. World affairs, politics, books read and movies seen, even the omnipresent water business—none of these intruded much upon the evening. Never have I seen people derive so much entertainment and hilarity simply from themselves. A few excerpts follow, no more than the listing of ingredients in a marvelous stew. You cannot imagine the full aroma when they are all mixed together and bubbling in the pot:

We heard you two across the yard havin' a big blow. You were so loud, how could we not.
(Mimicking the arguing couple, first the wife)
"I'm going to buy that car. I've picked crabs for it all summer."
And then we'd hear (the husband), a'mumblin' like he does. "I'm just sayin', we oughtta wait and see what oysterin's like."
"I picked for it, and I'm a'buyin' it."

The car buyer retorts:

Yeah, and eight years later that car's still a'runnin'; and don't think we didn't know what was going on when your trailer'd go dark for about an hour and then the bathroom light would come on."

(Considerable discussion follows on whether it really took an hour)

Why IS your husband headin' home? It's early yet.

Oh, he's airbound tonight, and he's worried about the smell if he goes in your downstairs bathroom.

Well, that's the champ. Tell him I got an upstairs one too, now.

(Husband, frozen between laughing crowd and the back door, like a deer in car headlights) Dear, what must I do?

Upstairs, honey.

Remember you and those others partyin' one night on the boat where K.... and W... had two barrels of tar'pins they'd caught to ship to Crisfield the next day? Oh, you was all puttin' oyster shells in hats and throwin' em up to shoot in the dark. You got caught short and ended up a'shittin' in a convenient barrel; and all next day them pair was out there tryin' to scrub it off the critters, a'waitin' for 'em to poke their little heads out so they could clean 'em up.

Milford and Bobby went shopping that one Christmas in the five and dime to Crisfield. Milford got Priscilla a combination eleven-dollar dish and no-stick cook set. It didn't stick none! And Bobby got me a wooden spoon. He took it down to old bachelor Haney, and he gift-wrapped it with stickers and stamps he peeled off whiskey bottles.

How's Kev and Beth doin'? Think they'll get married?

Well, here it is Saturday night and she's here alone, all dressed up, and he's went litin' [night gunning] for ducks.

Talk about dressed up! Remember Elwood and Allen in that skiff, comin' home from oysterin', all duded up to go gallin' [courting]? Here they come, flyin' through the marsh guts, Elwood standin' in the bow on a piece of wood to keep his new white and brown oxfords from gettin' wet, and lighting this big cigar; boy, he's gonna make a great impression landin' back in Tylerton; and just then Allen hits a mudflat, full tilt.

Whatever was you thinkin' goin out the jetties crabbin' in that high wind?

Oh, I'd a' never gone except I had my teenage boy aboard. I wanted him to think hard about what he was gettin' into. We hit those waves, and the boat was slammin' like the bottom would bust. I said, "Well, old boy, this is what your life's going to be like if you choose the water; always gettin' up earlier than you want to, always pushing yourself to go when it's not fit to go; worry about arthritis, about your boat, about your back." I just wanted him to know.

Remember Juney? Now there was a headliner. Sank his scrape boat on the way to tong in Hollands Straits, waded ashore with his ship's stove, and commences to fire it up right there on the beach to cook his breakfast and dry his clothes while he waits for help. Fell asleep and let that stove burn every stitch he had.

The first Christmas after we moved off the island, Cheri and I were invited to a party in Washington, D.C., that included several well-regarded names from the worlds of writing and national political affairs. It was quite pleasant, and large ideas and provocative worldviews permeated the conversation. Driving home, we were talking about how fortunate we were to be included in such a circle . . . and yet. I guess we were both thinking the same thing, when Cheri blurted out: "Compared to the islanders, they all seemed dead from the neck down."

MISS LIDDY MARSH DAY

By the time I moved to the island, Liddy Marsh was nearing eighty, hard of hearing, and burdened by the weight on her short, stout frame. She seldom ventured out, even to her beloved church, virtually across the street from her pretty, gingerbreaded cottage on the main path through Tylerton.

She took in sewing, as much a community service as a business, it seemed. "A good bowl of beans and some dumplings is the pay I need," she would tell customers.

I often saw women dropping by Liddy's; and a couple times I noticed watermen slow their pace as they passed, and look toward Liddy's door before striding or cycling away.

And then, before I hardly knew her, she was gone from us. It wasn't many months after the funeral, though, before I heard of plans to celebrate Liddy Marsh Day at the church, on a Sunday in September. It would be a sort of unity day for the island, with people gathering from all three towns.

This was more intriguing than you might imagine. Islanders had eschewed electing any local government leaders for more than three centuries. They seemed to have a deep aversion to elevating any one of their number to special status or privilege above the rest. There was even a little of that sentiment heard over Liddy's special day, but very much in the minority.

The old woman who sat closed up in that house had been something special, though to a non-native it was anything but obvious. They are like their marshes, these islanders, exhibiting little variety and flair compared to the cultivated and fertilized garden spots of the mainland; but woven together beneath the surface in complex and enduring fashion. And Liddy, as people stood to testify in church that day, was rooted in her community as few others.

• • •

A preacher recalled how he was greeted on his first visit years before:

Good to see you; let's go to Liddy's and have some prayer, his hosts told him, easily as in other places they might have said, let's go have some crabcakes.

Indeed, women who used to gather at Liddy's spoke of how "she would get that little fat fist poundin' when she got down to hard prayin'—she'd talk of 'feastin' on the word of the Lord.' "

Prayer, they said, flowed from Liddy as from a deep spring. An anchor, a safe harbor, a lighthouse, people described her—unassuming as a channel marker, and just as welcome a sight when you felt lost.

Watermen stood and told how Liddy once said she would sit by her front window and pray for whomever she saw go by. After that, when times were tough, they would deliberately walk by, feeling better just knowing that the old lady might see them and ask a blessing.

Her house when she died was only five homes down the path from where she was born, daughter of a dredge boat captain; but in that short space, and eighty years, she raised four sons and was twice widowed. As a young woman, she became "slain in the spirit" at a revival service, said an old lady, adding, "I've always prayed for it to happen to me, but it's not given to everyone."

She became, self-taught, a Bible scholar. "She remembered every word she ever read, and had the prettiest prayers and the knowin'est testimony in the church," an old friend said.

Women would gather at her home to study the Bible, and hear Liddy's interpretations; and they would go there individually with personal problems. "She'd stop, no matter what she was doing, and pray with you. She could go Genesis to Revelation and back again; and no word would ever leave that door," the women said.

Liddy's prayers could also hew to the island's pragmatic bent. A lady told this story:

"One night in a freeze-up she come over. My water had all stopped working. She said, 'Sis, c'mon, let's have us a prayer.' She had prayed to the Lord earlier and He had unfroze a spicket at her house—just one, that's all she asked for. Well, she prayed for me too, and my bath tub faucet opened up. Now that seems impossible, but it happened; and then later on we realized that water had been turned off at the outside main to the whole house! But you see, she talked to the Lord just as if He was always with her. 'He's helped me thread needles to begin sewin',' she would say."

In the church, in a beautiful tenor, a crabber breaks sponteously into a hymn Liddy used to sing. She began to sing it, others remembered, after a blind man, whose favorite it was, could no longer make it to church.

Others recall the terrible fire in the last winter of her life that destroyed Liddy's home. A winter storm had just blown itself out when the fire siren sounded that cold Sunday night. Had the wind still been raging, we could have lost half the town.

The paths of Tylerton are too narrow for a fire truck to navigate, and the diesel pump mounted on the town dock to suck water from the channel for fire-fighting would not start. We were reduced to small-caliber hoses, hooked to crabbers' air-cooled pumps. These hoses would not even reach the main channel. We had to take water from the shallows, and algae kept clogging the pumps' intakes.

We might as well have tried to piss on the blaze. It was a despairing night. Women, watching, wrung their hands over the handmade quilts inside, and Liddy's treasured old family Bible (which would later be found intact).

Liddy was not there. She was recuperating from illness with her son's family in Ewell. Many feared the news of her home would be a death blow. The man who volunteered to tell her said this is how it went:

"I said, 'Liddy, there's no good way to put this, but your home and all your earthly possessions, they're all gone.' A smile come over her face. She said, 'The Lord gave me this affliction so I was out of the house when it burnt.' I think she was more worried about how bad I felt, tellin' her. That was just how Liddy was."

AROUND the time of her funeral, I often heard it said of Liddy, simply: "she'll be missed." I had heard the same at the funeral of a crabber I met my first year on the island named Billy Smith. He was in his fifties, and had recently had to quit working because of a bad heart. My whole image of Billy was of a man sitting on the sidelines, pleasant enough to nod to in passing by, but a marginal part of community life.

He did make one lasting impression on me, drinking one night with some of his younger colleagues in a shanty on the channel. The talk turned to rock music, and to the band Def Leppard. Billy, swaying a bit in his seat, perked up: "Leppard . . . y'know, I think I used to ship [soft crabs] to him."

For years after Billy died, there would seldom be a month when someone didn't mention him. He was, it turned out, a superb hunter and trapper and fisherman, a progger who knew the marshes like a farmer knows his home fields. Generations of islanders had obviously had rich and formative experiences afield with the man.

I hope someday to be missed as islanders are missed. There is so much about relationship here that goes back so far and so deep, so much that is known so well it need not, or cannot be fully expressed. It is like the tide flowing through a deep channel, moving so uniformly and implacably, you can't tell its power except where a snag or a crab pot marker perturbs the smooth surface. An outsider cannot realize how integral to the community here an individual is until they are torn from it, and the stories come welling out.

Crabmeat

JANICE MARSHALL

◆ I am forty-nine and grew up next door to my husband, who I married when I was fifteen. He remembers when he was a boy going to see me at the doctor's office in Ewell when I was born. Our daughter and son and their families, including two grandchildren, live not much more than 150 feet away.

I have always been one for joking and laughing. If you didn't laugh at yourself, you'd go nuts in a place like this. Maybe I get it from Daddy. He moved up here from Tangier. He was poorer 'n Pern down there, and I think he figured it couldn't be worse up here. He was thirty-nine when he had his first heart attack, but he had a big family and he couldn't quit work. He was shafttonging oysters over to Point Lookout on the Potomac when he died. He was forty-four. What I remember is how much he liked to laugh. He would come home from working hard enough to kill a healthy man, come home a'laughin'.

There've been times when I felt stuck, living my life out here. I did study a few years ago and finish my high school diploma, and I recently learned to drive. But there's no place in the world like here. Your children grow up so free and you don't lock your home, and there's a closeness and a heritage I wouldn't trade. I try to have a moral character about me, and I wonder if I would have, if I'd grown up on the mainland.

A Smith Islander and a crab picker is what I am. Picking's not the career I would have chosen, but this is where my husband chose to be and it's where I am, and—I guess it sounds corny, but I just try to be the best daggone picker I can be.

But the last few years, the women here have been made to feel more like criminals and outlaws. Between us and the state it's been a war out here—all over crabmeat; but crabmeat's our existence.

It all started with the raids during the summer of 1992. It was a Wednesday morning, about 9:00 A.M., when the ferry landed us in Crisfield. I was up picking since three o'clock, and I decided to ride over with my crabmeat and go visit my son, who was in the hospital for minor surgery.

I got off with some packages and I kinda' noticed this marine police standing off a little ways, looking like he'd rather not be there; and this man comes up to me and says, "I'm from the state health department, what ye got in those boxes?"

Well, I told him—it was things I was returning to Sears. But about that time, the ferry captain, who weren't paying attention to what was going on, he throws me two boxes of fresh-picked crabmeat. One is 29 pounds, an order that has gone every week for years to an old lady in Princess Anne who splits it with her neighbors. The other, five pounds, was marked with big letters on the outside, "MA," for my mother who lives to Crisfield.

So the health inspector says he is going to take them both—look, that's a lot of crabs I picked to make up that 34 pounds. And I told him, and not very ladylike and not very Christian; I said, you see that big mud puddle by the dock? If I wasn't on my way to see my son in the hospital, you and me'd be down in it, a'rollin' and a'pitchin'. I even asked the marine policeman, would he arrest me if I was to push that inspector off the dock. He said if it looked deliberate, he might have to do something.

Meanwhile here comes Ma, and she wants her five pounds of crabmeat, and that inspector's explainin' to her how we have always gotten away over on the island with picking uninspected by the state regulators, and how she wouldn't even want that crabmeat if she knew how much bacteria might be in it. And Ma's hollerin—look, you; I don't care if it give me the squdders [trots] three weeks runnin', I want my crabmeat! Oh, he heard a parable that morning.

There was at least ten or fifteen boxes of crabmeat the size of mine on the boat, but I hollered to the captain and he took off from the dock before they could seize it, or they'd got the whole island's production.

That was a bad day, but no one could of dreamed what lay ahead. You see, in a way, the inspector was right. Our crab picking always was just something women did in their own homes. It was a way to make some money while you tended your home and your family. Even if we could of afforded it, there was no way we wanted to get into building picking houses like the big ones on the mainland, which is what the state's regulations want.

I still say we put out the best crabmeat in the world, and there has never been a case of anyone getting sick from Smith Island crabmeat. Why, pickers in Ewell have told me some of the finest restaurants in Maryland practically fight to get it, and even the Naval Academy officers club in Annapolis has served our "bootleg" crabmeat. Every politician ever come here, and that's plenty, has gone back totin' a few pounds of our crabmeat, any picker can tell you.

There was two more raids that summer. The state had took over from the county the seafood [safety and health] enforcement; and the commercial crab houses in Crisfield was having tough times, which made them complain even more'n usual about "unfair" competition from us bunch of wives and widows. On the island, there was a rumor a day, and panic in the streets.

"Boston in the channel" would come across the marine radio—the marine cops rides in those Boston Whalers—and some women would be running down the street to hide their crabmeat. We prayed in church for the Lord to help us understand. Sometimes He has plans that we can only see a part of. Some women began to land their crabmeat to Virginia, which is a longer trip then to Crisfield, and you got to use your own boat.

A bunch of tourists to North End got sick from bad crabmeat in a restaurant, they said—later it turned out it was bad eggs. Men came here to do an erosion study—so they said—but every time we steamed any crabs, we felt they were just a'lookin' at us. A newsman came and wrote about an anonymous woman "slipping out to her shanty . . . [where] she begins cracking claws. And breaking laws."

What'd we do about it? Mostly what we have done before when the government gets interested in us—we just waited for them to lose interest, waited for it to blow over. We even had some fun with it. At the annual watermens' banquet in October, we got up a song to the tune of "Jailhouse Rock," which I can sing you a few bars of:

> Crab pickers threw a party at the county jail
> They were there for bootleg crabmeat they had for sale
> The pickers started jumping and the joint began to swing
> You should have heard those crab-picking jailbirds sing. . . .

One of our women, Kaki Bradshaw, also wrote a poem about the big raid; and we did another skit to the tune of "Rudolph the Red-Nosed Reindeer": S—— the Red-Thumbed Picker. It cracked the crowd up.

But the fact of the matter was, it wasn't going to blow over this time. The state said the public was so concerned these days about seafood safety, all it would take was one outbreak of bad crabmeat and the whole industry on the bay would be ruined. They said they would help us get legal; but if we didn't, they were going to shut this island down.

It was near Christmas, the day they came to Tylerton, all the state health bureaucrats. The marine police brought 'em, like they usually do with visiting dignitaries. Somebody asked, why was it that people who came here to help us always seemed to come in police boats? The church basement was nearly full. I believe we had every woman who picked, or thought they might.

We began with a prayer, and then a lady from the health department began to talk about getting legal. For a while, it was like two different meetings going on. The pickers wanted to know: could they get back the crabmeat from those raids last summer? How did it compare when they tested it for bacteria? If they got legal, just how often would the department come and check on us? Had anyone ever got sick off our crabmeat? I brought a little dinger bell to keep order, and I used it a lot.

The lady from the state was very nice, but if you listened, she was saying, look, things can't ever be the same again. We had also invited the newspapers and the TVs. It was the first time, really, we had ever let it out public about our picking. Everybody knew about it, and it wasn't something we was ashamed of, but it was not ever something you spoke of outside the island. When I look back, I can see it clear—we crossed a line that day, and there was no going back.

We were going to need pressure steamers, and stainless-steel tables, and commercial refrigeration, and buildings with concrete floors and walls, and separate picking and packing rooms. It could cost $30,000 for Tylerton alone—maybe as high as $60–$70,000. We could apply for loans and grants. Our heads were just a'spinnin'. Other places had done it, they said; but other places aren't Smith Island, said we. Little did we know that day what the real cost would be.

They would give us a reprieve, the state lady said. We could pick the next summer, but we had to have a plan for going legal, and prove we were working on it and would meet all rules and regulations of the mainland by April of 1994. We broke up the meeting agreeable, which people from off [the island] often take to mean that everybody's agreed on something. We served all the visitors bootleg crab balls, bootleg crab Norfolk, and bootleg crabcakes, which they agreed was some of the best they had ever ate.

That was the most discouragin' winter and spring. People I'd known all my life began to get down on me. A few of us women decided that right or wrong, the state meant business. I didn't see how we could afford to do what they wanted; but I didn't see how I could afford to chance it, either—married to a waterman with heart problems and oysters in the bay hittin' the lowest catch in history that very winter. Lately, it takes picking as hard as some of us can go just to pay off our last year's taxes by August 15 [the filing extension deadline].

What we needed to do, to apply for some money and to get legal, was to form a co-operative, the state and university people who was advising us said. You might think a co-op would be just the thing for a close little community like this. We *are* close, but we are independent, too. Sometimes I think if it weren't for ten miles of water all around us, we might just fly apart.

Maybe we should of been warned. Romey, one of our oldest men, had some old newspapers—all yellow and crumblin'—that told about the last time Smith Island tried a co-op. It was in 1949, and it was with oysters, which was our big livelihood then. The situation with oyster rules and regulations had made outlaws out of our watermen, who just couldn't make a living without dredging on bottom that was off limits to them. One day, a police captain chased a bunch of them into town—it wasn't the first time—and a crowd formed on the dock and things got ugly. It was the first time in his life he'd ever been called an s.o.b. by a woman, the officer said; and he told islanders he would talk to the state about leasing them some oyster bottom, where they could form a co-op and dredge legal for a change.

It was the greatest mess even getting permission. It was a big test case for the bay, whether oysters could be farmed instead of wild-harvested. Smith Island would be the test of it, the newspapers said. Watermen from the mainland carried their case against us all the way to the state Court of Appeals, which in 1950 give us the go-ahead. The co-op started in 1951, and things looked good, accordin' to the articles and the headlines:

1952 Smith Island Oystermen Triple Incomes Since Taking Leases
1953 Smith Island Oystermen See Continuing Prosperity
1954 Smith Island Oystermen See Best Year Ever

Then, in 1955:
Co-operative Oyster Farm Venture in Bay Folding Up

The articles all said it was lack of funding to manage the leased bottom right; but that's not what did it, Romey said. He said there wasn't enough marine police in the world to watch that leased bottom. He said—and he put himself right with the rest—that there was such stealing from one another and selfishness and taking the little oysters before they was legal size that it caused the co-op to collapse. He felt maybe there is just something in us against putting a lot of rules and regulations on ourselves.

With me somehow being the one to try and organize a crab-picking co-op, people began to think I was meaner'n Hitler, that I was trying to set myself up for some big profit. Ma, she joked about it. Ain't you the boss tippet* now, she said.

A few was willin' to join; some didn't know what to do, and some felt like they'd just hang back and wait to see if they could get by without it. There were times I felt like I didn't have a friend in the world. It surprised me to see such a lack of community interest.

I mean, if it was just me, I'd a' gone back to school and become a nurse. It would be easier on my body and my mind. But I felt like a co-op was best

---

*Tippet—a risqué way of saying queen bee; tippet is a local name for the genital area of a female crab.

for the community. I guess that had been more and more on my mind. It is no secret our population's dwindlin' away here. I think a lot of us could see it comin' even ten years ago, but for a long time, if you brought it up, people would just shut you off. They didn't want to hear it. I see us lose great people like Miss Liddy, who died recently and was a spiritual leader of this place; and we're so few there is no one to replace them.

A few years ago I went up the bay to an island which for hundreds of years was a community just like ours, until erosion drove the people off; and now the island is just a'washin', and soon it'll be gone. There were graves from their old cemeteries washing right in the bay, little baby graves, some of 'em; and I thought, they grieved just like we grieved. This was where their homes were, and their stores and ballfields—all gone under the bay now. Was that the fate we were going to have?

I look out my kitchen window down to Back Landing marsh every day, and that bay's a lot closer than when I was a girl. The old man in Crisfield that we sell crabs to—they say he was the last baby born on that vanished island. I've just got a little grandson, and a lot of us wonder, will they say someday that he was the last baby born on Tylerton? And my son just married a woman from off, and they are going to try to make it here. She is learning to pick, and she's got the speed already, she just needs to work on her technique. I have told her, if she doesn't pick, they can't even think about staying. So I have had the future of the community on my mind.

You would not believe what I went through for the next two years. I am not even in the habit of making long-distance phone calls, and here I was dealing with the health department, natural resources department, environment department, the county, two universities, the FHA, architects, soil tests, business plans, grant applications, news reporters.

They said we needed a permit to discharge five gallons a day of water from the steamer to the waters of Chesapeake Bay. Five gallons! Couldn't we put it through the town sewer plant? No, it couldn't handle it. Couldn't handle it? Sally, she monitors the plant for the state, has to flush her own toilet four or five times in a row just to get enough flow going through there to monitor—and it couldn't handle five gallons?

Why is your building design for the picking house so odd-shaped, they want to know. Because it's marsh all around and high ground is scarce, I told 'em. The federal engineers said there weren't the soils anywhere out here good enough to build anything on. Maybe not, but we been here about three hundred years now.

We don't see any parking places in your design, they say. We got no streets big enough for cars, I write back. How do you get around, they want to know. Walk, ride bikes; some of us has golf carts, we tell them. Oh, then you'll need a parking lot—with spaces for golf carts, they decide.

If you're going to have men trained to help with the steaming equipment, they write, you'll have to redesign your whole operation for a men's bathroom, or where will they wash their hands.

They'll wash 'em in the Chesapeake Bay, which is always close by, I say; and I felt like telling 'em when they sent their man down to inspect us, he could just pee out in the marsh, not in our bathroom.

I guess maybe the crab waste was the single most aggravating thing. We have always just thrown it overboard—right back where it came from, we figure. Even the Save the Bayers [Chesapeake Bay Foundation] in their environmental education center here do that after the schoolkids they bring down eat the crabs they catch. On the busiest picking day of the year, the whole island makes maybe 150 bushels of crab waste, and it is dumped a bushel or two at a time at dozens of different spots, where the tides take it off fast, if the minners and the eels and the crabs don't eat it up first. Save the Bay has even monitored our dumping places with an oxygen meter, and can't find it makes any difference. The bay, you know, is near twenty miles wide at this point.

Well, it is not permitted on the mainland, so it can't be permitted on the island, the environmental department said. The secretary of that department wrote a very high-sounding letter in the *Baltimore Sun,* where he said how even the smallest amounts of pollution were very important to control to keep the Chesapeake Bay clean. I just wished he was so bold when it came to some of those big industries and sewage plants around Baltimore, which his department seems to be much more understanding of their problems in cleaning up.

Maybe you can landfill the crab waste, the state said. But we got no ground high enough.

Compost it, they said. But high ground was still a problem, and we'd have to pay to import wood shavings for the compost.

Burn it, they said. But the county, which in all of this has been on the side of the big crab companies on the mainland, said it was afraid the only incinerator on the island wouldn't handle crab waste and our regular garbage.

So now it looks like we will have to buy a special machine to grind the crab shells. Then we would pay the ferry to take them to Crisfield. Then pay to truck them to a farm, and pay to have them landfilled. It could end up costing us $10,000 a year, and maybe high as $20,000.

Oh, the costs! It seemed everything just kept getting bigger and bigger, what we had to do. For the most part, it wasn't like the state was against us. A lot of people, in and out of the government, were really working to help us out. It is just that everything is designed for the mainland, where every year there is more people moving in. Out here, we're struggling to keep those we got left from moving out.

I wonder if people has ever really thought about what it is they want from us. I got friends who love to visit this place, and they say they could never live here, but don't you ever move, because we love to have a place to come that's so different. While all this crab thing is going on, I read that the state has just given a $300,000 grant to build a visitors' center and museum on Smith Island. Well, I think that's a good thing, but it seems like it's easier to get money to preserve us in a museum than to keep us a'livin' here. Everybody says, oh, you're so unique; but the laws all say we can't do things different. I wish they would make up their minds.

I don't laugh as much these days, but sometimes I just can't help myself. One day I was standing in the church after services, readin' folks the latest letter from the health department about the requirements for legal picking. I saw Miss Margaret, who's eighty-some and still picks a little, a'lookin' interested, so I added a sentence at the end: "absolutely, under no circumstances are women over eighty allowed to pick or even own a crab knife." Well, she caught like gas at that one.

Then, just a month before pickin' was to begin in the spring of 1994, we got the death blow. The health secretary said that as far as he could see, most of the pickers—we still had just five signed on to the co-op—had done nothing to work toward getting legal, and he was not going to give us any more time. They said the fines for getting caught illegal the first time could be $1,000 and ninety days.

I was to the point of panic and tears. I had worked so hard, for so long. Every day I'd get out all my boxes of files and permits and wait for the phone to ring for my daily assignments. I wanted to tell the state that a year might seem a long time to get a project accomplished to them, but it can go by here without much happening. It did put some fear into the other pickers. Practically overnight our co-op membership went from five to seventeen.

Then in June I got a call from the health secretary himself. He explained how he was out on a limb if he let us keep picking, uninspected, and there would be any problem with bad crabmeat. It could take years for Maryland crabmeat to get its markets back, he said.

He asked me what would I do if he gave us another extension. Would I come back again, and ask for even more time? I said yes, I imagine that's just what I'd do, if it came to that; beg and cry and plead. It's not just crabmeat; it's people's lives. Well, he got to laughing at that, and we had a nice conversation, and he said he would let us have the summer to pick again, if we seemed to be making real progress.

In July, I went to a press conference with some of the other pickers. It was to announce that the Smith Island Crabmeat Co-operative, Inc., was the recipient of mostly grants, and a small loan, totaling $170,000. The rest of the costs—the project was up to $194,000 by now—would be covered by private donors, including Frank Perdue, who lives in this area and loaned us $10,000. Construction is to begin later this year.

It still doesn't seem real. Nobody's real enthusiastic about it. It will mean a lot of changes, like going to pick in a building back of town instead of each in her own kitchen or outhouse. And it still may all just collapse before construction starts. I think about the old oyster co-op, and I wonder if it will really work, or will people just use the co-op as a cover to pick the way they always did. I don't know what will happen.

Has it been worth it? I have thought a lot about that. Right now I have to say: No, it has not. I've lost my relationships. We're still friends, but we're not as close, some of us. Maybe I'll feel different a few years from now. I know the state never will understand what they've put us through here. ✦

Born to Longbranch

WHEN I FIRST met Mabel, the author of this diary, she was in her seventies, living at the other end of our little street in a neat, modest house that had seen better days. Her life then revolved around her church and caring for Paul, her husband, who was crippled by strokes; but she always had time to chat with a visitor.

I assumed that like so many islanders, she had not strayed far from where she was born, but on remarking how far back her family must go in Tylerton was rebuffed: "Oh, honey, I'm not from here; I was born to Longbranch." And from the way she said it, you felt the place must have been pretty special, and a long ways off. It would turn out that dozens of islanders traced their heritage to Longbranch. Even the homes they were living in often had begun life in Longbranch.

Where was it? If you looked out Mabel's second-story front window, even on a hazy day, there it was, perhaps half a mile distant; a cluster of old cedars in the marsh near where the channel forks one way to Ewell and the other way to Crisfield. With perhaps a dozen homes, it had been the most prominent of a string of settlements—Johntown, Hootenville, The Pines (or Middletown, as Mabel called it)—connected by wooden footbridges and oyster-shell paths.

Nothing of these hamlets remains, except in the Arcadian memories of the old people:

> We would walk in from Long Branch to get fresh milk from a farm in Tylerton that had cows; and going back, we would stop at the footbridge to rest, wash off an oyster shell from the water's edge, and drink that fresh milk from it.

> Long Branch had lots of big shade trees, and iris and lilies, and every kind of fruit tree—peaches, cherries, apples, figs, plums . . . it was the most beautiful town in America, we felt.

> Rainy days, Dad would load me on his boat to take me into school at Tylerton, and on the way he'd stop at every little gut to fish his eel pots.

Paul died not long after we moved from the island, and Mabel went soon after that. At her funeral, a friend told me about Mabel's trip abroad to see her daughter, who had become executive secretary to a prominent U.S. official in Switzerland. When she returned, Mabel said she'd especially loved touring the little Alpine villages that dotted the Swiss countryside—didn't remind her of a thing as much as that walk long ago through the little places between Tylerton and Longbranch.

The following passages are excerpts from more than two hundred hand-written pages in five notebooks, reflecting the life of an island girl in those days.

1930–31   Volume I   Looking Back

◆I was born to Longbranch, which is by Tylerton, on April 3, 1915. There were not many people on Longbranch. It was about 30 head, but we all had very good times together.

When I was three, my cousin Audrey stayed the night. It was very cold. When we went to bed, she slept in a overcoat and cap. The next morning her overcoat was white all over.

When I was eight, I had a glorious time. I went to school and was in the third grade and was mean. One day grandma came to my house and told Momma to let me stay with her a little while. One day I went home and while going up the lane I saw Mabre and she was laughing and started to tell me something but Grandma told her not to.

I was walking around the house and heard a baby cry and it scared me. When I came in Mamma was in bed and lots of people was there. She told me to come and look. But I was so bashful. So Audrey pushed me and I looked and it was a baby. His name was Georgie Caroll Marsh, and he was the cutest thing.

But one night about twelve, something sad happened. My only brother he died. It broke my heart. My other two sisters and my brother were all dead and then I was left alone.

When I was nine, my mother would commence to take me to Drumpoint [Tylerton] of Saturday nights. A lot of our relatives has moved or died. My parents moved to Middle Town, which was just three houses. It was melancholy from Longbranch, but I got used to it. Every evening we would go over to Drumpoint and go swimming, or have a picnic up in the woods, or go down to the school house and play dodge ball or go and play Hide and Hope.

After we got warm and tired we would go to the Club and get a snowball or ice cream. We would crab of days, and I would make about $2.50 or $3 a week.

Our house was very large. It was five rooms upstairs with a garrett; three rooms down stairs and a hall. It was painted yellow, red roof and green shutters and a large front porch. My friends and I would play games there and jump rope. I had a playhouse up the stairs and we would visit each other, and play with our big dollies and have tea parties.

I had two chickens. The rooster was named Denie. He was very smart. but mamma killed him for her Christmas dinner.

I got for Christmas: a small cedar chest, a coat, hat, dress, gloves, manicure set, shoe trees and a toilet set.

I am 15. One Saturday night I went over to the Club and got some ice cream. Then, Doris, Lillian and myself went to Capt. Johnny's store and got some candy. Then we went walking around the graveyard. Romey was with Lillian, Woodland with Doris and Robley with me. We had a swell time.

July and August [*1930*]. Methodist Camp Meeting at Ewell lasts all week and is great. On Wednesday night, my mother and I stayed all night in the tent. Anna H. stayed all night with me. We sat under [inside] the tabernacle and talked. It was cool, and a sawdust floor. Every night boys and girls would stay out there and talk in the dark and they would sing pretty songs.

On Saturday night I was with Emery, sweetheart of all my dreams, who lives to Ewell. We got something at Capt. Bob's store and sat on Audrey's steps and talked, then we kissed each other good night.

One day Doris and myself decided to go to Rhodes Point. We were crabbing and had on our crabbing clothes. But we went and got Marguerite E. and Marie J. and all four of us went swimming. On Saturday night, Lillian and Doris stayed all night with me. We came home and played the victrola and danced and then we went to bed, but we didn't go to sleep.

March [*1931*]. One night we went to carry Miss Bessie some ice cream and cake. I was going by Edison's house and he thumped on the window and we looked. All the boys were in there, and only one sober. They were kicking up the greatest time. They tore up the house if they could have tore up a piece of the carpet. They all never left until 1 A.M. I was glad when they did.

Easter Sunday I went to church in the morning. They had a sacrament, but none of the girls took it. In the evening it was raining, so I stayed home. I think it is the lonesomest time on Sunday with raining. It makes you think of by gone days and your old lovers of long ago.

On Thursday night I had my [16th] birthday party. Romey brought me a box of powder. Winfield powder and ruff; Edison, $2 pair of stockings; Adrien a silk pillow; Nannie a silk petticoat; Anna hair shampoo; Lillian powder and toothpaste; Doris, box of powder.

Edison has got my initials on the back of his boat. He is the sweet heart of all my dreams now. I guess I will change when I grow up. Right now at the present I am going with lots of boys but I do not love none. The only one I care for is Edison.

I am sixteen and they say that at that age you get rum mad over love. I do lots of embroidery piece of quilts, and lots of house duties that take my mind a lot. I have done lots of things for my cedar chest. I like to work. If I ever get married I will have it all ready. I don't have a cedar chest, but my father is going to give me one for Christmas.

My life continues in volume 2.

1931–32   Volume II

June 21, 1931, Saturday night. Late that evening Anna and myself went swimming. Then I dressed up and went to Drumpoint. All us girls went up on Nannie's porch. John Callis asked me to go and get a drink, so I went and asked Lillian to go with us, cause I couldn't go by myself. So we went to the Club. Lill ordered ice cream and me and him ordered cocolas.

So him and I came home. Just as we were opposite our house he said— Every time I come over this bridge I like it more and more, no wonder— look at the sweet girl I got beside me. Then he kissed me good night and left.

Sunday night, John Callis took me in the church, the first time I ever did it. He was going to leave Monday. He is from Gwynns Island, Va. He got one of my pictures and my gold ring. I got his handkerchief and it smelled just like him. That's the reason I don't wash it.

He can sing too. In the parlor he was singing to me, a song called "I was made for you and you were made for me." Oh, boy, John Callis is really the sweet heart of all my dreams.

We all have a good time in the summer, but we have better times in the winter—parties and sports games. In the summer it isn't anything but swimming and croquet and tennis. During the days in summer, I craft some, but I don't have to do it. I do all of the house work first. I embroidery patch anything. Read and write. In the afternoon if I don't have any work to do I lay down and rest, then sometimes I go to the store for my mother and grandmother. Then after I eat my supper I dress up and go to Drumpoint and walk and eat and drink. Then Saturdays and Sundays I have my feller. Oh, Boy. I have a swell time.

August. Tuesday night stayed to Audrey's. She had a nice breakfast—fried head, coffee, fruit, pears, potatoes, breakfast bacon and hamburg. It was all good.

Friday I went crabbing and I caught 40 peelers, and Saturday I caught 54. I made one dollar and seven cents.

September. Pauline had her 19th birthday party. I carried her a box of powder and a pair of stockings. We played games—Snubb in the Well, Soldier Fashion, Kiss, Flat Iron on the Wall and lots more.

October. Wednesday night, our revival meetings had commenced. Anna and myself went. Preacher Romans preached. Nobody was converted. Thursday night, we went to the meetings again. Friday we had a long meeting, and lots of girls, and myself went down and got converted. Sunday morning they had experience meeting and all of us girls spoke.

All the men are away dredging now. Agnes had a quilting, so while Mamma was there, Anna, Mabre, Mary, Stella and myself stayed. Mary made chocolate candy with nuts in it and Clara made chocolate with peanut butter and coconut.

The next night some of us had a greens supper. There are only a few boys around, so they came and we played Blind Man's Bluff, Heavy, Heavy; Pleased or Displeased, Clap in Clap out, and Poor Puss.

January 5th, Tuesday night. I got an invitation to go to a goose supper. I took my bath and wore a chiffon dress. All the boys had gone away but four. We played Dollar Dollar, Handkerchief, Blind Man's Bluff, Cheyenne, and Chase the Quaker. We ate at midnight. We danced. I stayed all night with Laura and we never got home until one the next day.

1932   Volume III

March 6, 1932. Sunday morning it was raining and blowing a hurricane. By evening the tide was in the yard and was coming in the porch. Great white waves was in the yard and we were scared to death. Shingles was coming off the roof and we had to stop the chicken house up. Monday morning was calm as anything.

July 23, Saturday night. For two weeks we took some Fresh Air children. I took one, her name was Helen Kevel, 101 Washington St., New York. They all had a grand time here.

August 1. Calvin M. carried a crowd to Ewell to see and hear the four greatest evangelists in the world, a Mr. Mcarkale [sic] and wife, child and niece. In church, the woman played a piano and accordian and the son played a ukelele, and the man a coronette and banjo and the son and niece coronettes. They played and sang wonderful.

[Letter to Mr. Richard Day, 909 Cheapside, Dept. W101 Cincinnati, Ohio]:

If I had $3,500 I would get my skin clear, then I would get plenty of clothes. Then I would open up a business. If I couldn't open businesses, I would get married.

1932–33   Volume IV

October, 1932. Went to the Rhodes Point revival meetings. I am a Christian and that way is the only way to live in this world of sin. I went over there every night. I give my testimony whenever I have the chance. I caused John B. to get religion.

October 7. Emma Brown died from child birth. the baby lived until Saturday morning and then died too.

Emery asked me would I have a light for him Sunday night [a light left on in the parlor, inviting him to come in]. I said yes. He came by. He makes me laugh. I played the victrola and he layed down on the sofa and I sat by him. He said "Dagone, I got to go away with papa dredging Friday, ain't that bad."

October 31. Monday night, which is Halloween, I was masked in a blue suit, my father's suit and a black derby and a funny mask on with whiskers. My mother had father's white suit on and mask, quite funny; it had a large nose and a long mouth and some whiskers and she had on a large straw hat. Going over the bridge to Drumpoint cousin Mary fell in a hole in the marsh. We all went into the store, two by two and they liked to died laughing.

Christmas season, 1932. Papa came home from dredging Dec 9, a Friday. We were so glad to see him.

Dec. 25. Went to Sunday school. Sunday night the annual pageant. Us girls were angels. First we sang a Christmas song with all of our new dresses on. We sang another piece and spoke; then we were in a tableaux.

Tuesday I got an invitation to a midnight goose supper at Miss Julia Marsh's.

Wednesday, we were sitting in Aunt Mary's kitchen when we heard a knock on the kitchen door and Ronald and Robley came in. They asked mother to have a supper for them. They would bring over a chicken, greens, sweet potatoes and small potatoes. I told them who all they should invite. Ronald said, "Good Lord, we would have to bring over a chicken coop."

Another midnight supper at cousin Manda's. We had two tables playing rook. It was twelve when the first table ate. We had four black ducks, potatoes, dumplings, gravy, plenty pickles, turnips, and cake and peaches for dessert.

During these cold days and nights where I have to stay in the house I quilt. I work on a nine diamond and I have finished a four diamond. If I get tired I piece on my strip quilts. I have two sizes, one large and one smaller. I embroidery, make "yo yo" pillows and a lot of fancy work. I enjoy it. Feb. 10 I went over to Longbranch and Audrey was piecing up a Save All.

March 18. Emery wanted to see me. He said he had cooked for his father sometimes when dredgin. He said when his father and the rest was in the cabin and he was working on the winders [cranking up the dredges] he would sing "She's So Nice." He said that's all he could get on his mind.

1933–34   Volume 5

July. Momma has got up a play for the Longbranch people called the Corn Fed Baby. She carried it to Rhodes Point and Ewell also.

September 16, 1933. It was blowing and raining, also tide up very high. We couldn't go to the meeting. We all did make it to church Sunday morning.

March 1934. We have night schools now. Both married and single goes. Our studies are English and Arithmetic, which includes spelling and reading.

Almost every Saturday now Paul brings me two five cent bars of pure chocolate candy. He is very thoughtful.

1934–36   Volume 6

The house that we still owned to Longbranch was to be moved to Drum Point. So a man came and two boys came, and Papa had to get some men from here to help them. We had to have three meals for them. One at five, 12 and 6 that evening. Momma had scalded her foot and couldn't work, and I had to do all the cooking. I hated to get up so soon. Five a.m. was really early. The house went over. Then we had them rebuild and made different like we chose.

January 19, 1935. Well diary, I think I like Paul very much now. He don't drink, or smoke. I guess he would be good to his wife. I think we suit well and he is very ambitious. I like Paul better than any boys yet.

Jan 21, 1935. Monday night. We had a butter bean supper to Longbranch. We played Blind Man's Bluff, Bingo, Going to Jerusalem, Jacob Laughed at Me, and Honk.

We got home at 2 a.m. Lillian B. and me stayed with Mabre. We told jokes and laughed and laughed. I fell asleep and Mabre and Lil went down to the kitchen looking for some smut, but they couldnt find none, so Mabre found some lip stick and put some on my nose and cheeks. They laughed until about 5. When we got up it was eleven.

January 23, Thursday. Lots of ice around. The radio said it is the coldest time in 35 years.

Friday. The mail boat hasn't gone to Crisfield today. Everything is froze and everything is isolated. It is so cold I am not going anywhere.

Sunday. Evything is frozen over. The ice cutter and the mail boat has gone up to Ewell. Some Tangier people walked by with the mail and they kept on walking to Tangier [six miles of open water to the south].

One of them said Mrs. Essie Evans was dead and they have brought her home. She died of childbirth. They tried to cut through the ice for the *Island Belle* to take her to Crisfield, but they couldn't. This is a very sad time. All froze up and no doctor. But we trust to the Lord that he will keep us well.

Sunday evening. Lots of people came out of church when an aeroplane came circling over. The man threw a paper, and it said, if in want of food and doctor, walk on the ice, so we walked on the ice. Later another aeroplane came to Ewell and the man brought the mail.

Tuesday, Feb 4. The goods is getting down at the stores. They haven't no flour, meat and butter. We had an ice cream party to Lydia's.

Thursday. The ice cutter came into Horse Hammock [the southeastern tip of the island] and brought the dredgers home. They walked up the marsh to the towns. Two strange men came along and took pictures and asked about the sick and needy.

Friday. Everything when I got up was covered with snow. This is a very bad blizzard. The snow is on the floor upstairs and down. I ate my breakfast at 11 a.m. They said a state policeman was trying to cross the ice from Crisfield and lost his life.

Sunday, Feb 16, 1936. There wasn't any Sunday school. The men had to clear the Back Landing field for the aeroplane. The ice cutter is to Horse Hammock with Red Cross food.

Feb 19. The mail boat has just come. Before this she hadn't been here since Jan 29. Miss Lee is dead and the boat brought her casket.

Feb 25. It is beautiful and lots warmer now.

August. I got my wave. I got it to the Modern in Crisfield. It was curls all over. It cost me $2.95. Paul got Capt. Will to ask for me. While Paul and myself were in the parlor Uncle Will came and asked mom.

August 22. He gave me a yellow diamond ring.

October 3, 1936. Saturday, my wedding day, a beautiful morning. Everything was done. I made a pineapple cake. I ate my supper and took my bath. I played the piano, then I layed down and read and then I dressed. I had on my blue dress and I had a bridal spray of orange blosoms across my hair. My bouquet was white petunias and green foliage. Paul was dressed in his navy blue serge and white shirt and tie and blue hat. Stella played the piano awhile, then we all started for Ewell in Romey's boat.

When we got to the parsonage, nobody was there. Glennon switched on the lights and pulled down the curtains. Then they all showed up. It was short, and we soon come down home and all went in the Club. All of the girls and boys threw rice on us. We got ice cream and cocola. We went home, then we went to bed. Mom wasn't home. Papa was away with Capt. Ed Smith getting wood.

Monday. We slept until ten, ate our breakfast and galled awhile. In the evening we went and heard a baseball game up to his home. Monday nite we went up there awhile to get some of his clothes. We went over to Stella's awhile to visit, and had a old time.

March. The doctor told me I was pregnant. We are having the prettiest weather, everybody is working in their garden. All of the trees are budding and blossoming. Everything is all aglow with Spring.

Oct. 3, 1937. Sunday night I had pains all night. Monday morning Mama took me to the hospital in Crisfield. After they examined me, they decided to operate the next day. Taking the ether was terrible, and coming-to was bad. By Saturday, blood poisoning had set in. By Tuesday I was much better. I was overjoyed to go home, although I felt sad to think I had gone through so much for nothing.

Back to the hospital. It was a rough ride across the Sound. My baby was born at 10.30 Friday morning, October 7, 1937, a boy weighing 9 pounds and 10 ounces. Paul wants me to name him after his daddy, so I pleased him. So we call him Johnnie Carroll, also Snooks.

December 1938. We visit friends and go to suppers. We drop by the Club and the stores, and the church services are nice. The Christmas night pageant will be coming up soon. One of the men said tonight: We ain't much to look at here, but we're close. ◆

POSTSCRIPT:

Mabel's home, the one that was moved from Longbranch to Tylerton, down to the last brick in the chimney, is now owned by eight outsiders, including me. We use it for a weekend place and call it the Drumpoint Club.

FREEDOM

What They Came For

In the winter of 1977–78, Chesapeake Bay froze solid across much of its 4,400-square-mile surface; nothing like it had been seen since the 1930s, when a crew of oystermen returning home walked twelve miles to Smith Island from the mainland. All boat traffic ceased. The barge bringing heating oil and diesel for the island's generators lay stalled just offshore, gripped by foot-thick ice. Coast Guard cruisers stout enough to break such ice drew far too much water to navigate the island's shallow entrance channels.

The governor of Maryland mobilized the National Guard. Helicopters ferried sick islanders off, and kept the towns supplied with essentials. "Tiny island struggles to survive deep freeze"—it was the kind of news that touched a chord in mainland America, and before it was over, the response had overwhelmed the need. "It got to be embarrassin'," said Charlie, who ran the general store in Ewell. Some days the vital foodstuffs the TV would show coming off the choppers were mostly pet food, as people's freezers already were well stocked. Some islanders took advantage of the ice-up to hunt wild ducks crowded into the few remaining patches of open water. A brisk under-the-counter trade in out-of-season fowl developed, and the hunters' only wish was for an end to the prying surveillance of helicopter traffic and small planes carrying photographers.

The freeze-up news that shocked the island did not come out until the ice had broken up, and only small bergs still gleamed like great swans passing down the sparkling blue bay. An old islander returned from visiting relatives out of state to find his home in Ewell burglarized. A large safe was missing, along with tens of thousands of dollars in cash and negotiable securities. The house had been left unlocked, as was the custom. If the crime had occurred any other time, people could have blamed it on outsiders, and taken comfort in that; but this time no one could have come or gone because of the ice. It was clearly their own that had done it. People shook their heads and said they would buy door locks. A trust had been broken in a place that for three centuries had foresworn government, police, and jails. It was, everyone said, the first time in memory that a crime of this magnitude had occurred.

State troopers arrived to investigate. They set up a table in the firehouse, and announced they would be "available" throughout one day and night for confidential testimony from anyone having information on the crime. Around 11:00 P.M., several of us reporters went by to debrief the investigators. We found them alone, disconsolately killing a bottle of Scotch whiskey. Virtually no one had come forward.

Perhaps, I suggested, this was just too new to the islanders. It was, after all, the first major crime here in a long, long time. One of the troopers, descended from an island family, stared at me. I hope you all are not writing that, he said. This island has a list of major crimes to its credit as long as my arm. I was stunned. What was this long list of crimes that no one all week had thought worth mentioning?

Try attempted murder of a federal official, the trooper said; also aggravated assault, shooting at an aircraft, attempting to ram and sink a state boat, arson, and destruction of federal property . . . of course, he said, leaning back and grinning wryly, these crimes were all related to hunting waterfowl, and might not be counted as misdeeds by the islanders.

It is a hard thing to place hunting in context here. The images of shooting and lawlessness clash with the great gentleness and honesty that characterized so many of our friends and neighbors. The pursuit of waterfowl and other natural resources seemed to occupy a separate compartment from the conventions that bound the rest of islanders' existence.

For millennia, surely as the tributaries of Chesapeake Bay gather rainfall from the slopes of six states, great torrents of waterfowl have funneled autumnally from across a third of the globe, down into the fecund marshes that edge and stipple Tangier Sound. From Siberia and Alaska's north slope, borne on wings big as angels', come the tundra swans, baying like hounds on high; from the Canadian prairies in Alberta, Manitoba, and Saskatchewan, flocks of redheads and canvasbacks, pintails, widgeon, gadwall, baldpate, and a dozen other species wing bayward; and the Canada geese gather from across the tundra of Quebec and Labrador.

Once I told an old islander how mysterious it was to me that people had ever moved to such a buggy and remote place as Smith. It was not as if the mainland was crowded, centuries ago. He had no doubt: "They come for what was here and for what come here." What was here was fish and crabs and oysters. "What come here" was in large part one of the globe's great congregations of migrating waterfowl.

The decline of North American waterfowl from habitat destruction and overhunting has been a constant theme throughout the last half of this century; so it may come as a surprise that the numbers of swans, geese, and ducks that winter on the Chesapeake have remained fairly steady during the last fifty years—about 1 million birds. But the overall trend has masked a striking decline in diversity. One species in particular, the Canada goose, has adapted handsomely to feeding on land, in corn fields, as the underwater grass beds and marshes that were their natural habitat have succumbed to pollution from human development and agriculture. Even as the wild goose's numbers soared, more than twenty-five varieties of duck were declining. Some, like the redhead and the canvasback, deep-diving bottom feeders that scarcely could walk to feed in fields, have fallen to only a few percent of historical populations on the bay.

Beginning in 1918, and waxing increasingly serious since the 1950s, federal and state governments have regulated waterfowl hunting to stem the decline. The remote marshes of the Chesapeake, and particularly islands like Smith and its neighbor, Tangier in Virginia, have drawn at least their share of attention. More than in most parts of America, the island peoples have continued to see the nature that surrounds them as a storehouse—their storehouse. A waterman told me this story that illustrates the sharply divergent views of nature held by island and mainland:

◆ After Dad died, I had a trap set up in Jugglin's Gut to catch the swimmer crabs, the ones that would come to the surface and move with the flood tide. It would catch about a bushel a day, and it made a little income for my mom. I was a'scrapin' for soft crabs in the Bottom one day when Dave come by and said the police captain is down there taking up your swimmer trap.

I went there and found him—and this guy, I had met with him in the bar when I was younger, and we drunk together and everything and was, you know, good friends. He said swimmer traps was illegal and he had orders to get her. I told him how my mom had no income and this trap was $40–$50 a week to her. He said it was the law. I said it was for Mom.

Well, I got mad. I never get mad, but I got mad, and I said to him, I'm a'goin' home—I was in my scrape boat—and I'm goin' to get my skiff and my shotgun, and I'll head you off before you ever clear this island, and shoot you in the waterline and sink you in the big Thoroughfare; now you can suit yourself.

Now look, I had it on my mind that was what I would do. I loaded up with magnums and took off. On the way, I went by the trap and he had put her back in place, all tied up just the way she was before, and I never did have no more trouble. ◆

The man who told me this was one of the finest-natured and most gracious human beings I had ever met. Once, eating supper in his kitchen, I had asked his wife why she never followed up on a music scholarship offered her as a Tangier Island girl. Oh, it was her dream, she said, but one day, here came the Smith Island baseball team down to Tangier for a game, and she saw number 14 in his uniform, "and that wound me up for a musical career"—and the way she looked at old number 14, you knew she had no regrets.

Her brother, eating with us, smiled warmly at his brother-in-law and recalled: Oh, yeah; switch hitter, second base, arm like a rifle—I wrote my high school paper on you; we had to write on the topic: My Hero. You still are my hero, y'know. Blushing, the old waterman touched his brother-in-law's arm and said: I appreciate that—you have always been special to me, too.

All three of them just beamed at one another. It was a touching scene, and typical of the man and his family. So I had some difficulty recognizing him as the same man described by a game warden who encountered him years before in checking out island hunters on suspicion of illegal waterfowling—"without a doubt, the toughest, most belligerent confrontation I had in my career."

WHATEVER the right and the wrong of it, Smith Island's contacts with the outside world until very recent times have frequently involved fractiousness and subterfuge. Journalists, scientists, salesmen, and sportsmen—tales abound of such visitors who, having gained the confidence of island families, turned out to be game wardens. Perhaps the cruelest blow struck by "the guvment" in living memory was the acquisition, almost overnight, of half of the island into the national wildlife refuge system. In 1954 the estate of Glen L. Martin, a wealthy industrialist and aviation pioneer (Martin Marietta sprang from his original enterprise), donated to the U.S. Fish and Wildlife Service thousands of acres that the late Mr. Martin had owned as his private hunting preserve. By 1960, the service had secured adjoining parcels, and had proclaimed nearly eight square miles of island closed to all outside intrusion. Only the navigable channels of creeks on the new "guvment land" would remain open to watermen going to and from the scraping and tonging grounds.

For a nation attempting to preserve key habitat for its dwindling waterfowl populations, Martin Refuge was an acquisition as strategic as the Panama Canal to shipping. For the islanders, it was as depressing and dramatic as erecting the wall across Berlin. The refuge these days is home to one of the largest nesting populations of great blue herons on the east coast of America, and it is a blessed sanctuary for the beleaguered black duck, which flourishes in the isolation of Martin Refuge as in few other spots in the region. Still, another memory of Martin Refuge is hard to put out of mind. It was on a cold, bright December day that I encountered Allen, an islander, anxiously pacing the banks of a little marsh gut that divided refuge land from the rest of the island. Allen is a "progger," one of those watermen who, even after a week of hard labor oystering or crabbing, can think of no place better to relax than in exploring the marshes. Proggers clearly are the spiritual heirs of the Native Americans who originally used these islands as hunting grounds.

Allen this day had shot a goose, and the goose, badly crippled, had glided just inside the refuge to die. There was pain and consternation in Allen's eyes. He did not mind taking life, but he hated to waste it. There was nothing for miles around us but the marsh; nothing apparent to separate government land from the rest. Surely you can go in there to get one goose, I said. No, I can't risk it, Allen replied. His family had stalked these marshes since the 1600s, knew the territory as well as the herons. He is not an articulate man. Asking him whether he loved the marsh was, I came to suspect, like asking you whether you loved your arm—a subject past needing conscious thought. I knew it was a hard thing for him to look at half the island and accept that it was closed. His dog, Luke, whined and growled, not understanding.

At the time, it seemed to me there must be a way to accommodate ducks and islanders. Perhaps some concept of native rights as practiced with Alaskan Indian tribes might loosen the refuge boundaries without so much harm to wildlife. But bad blood runs deep between government and the island, going back to the very origins of the nation. During the American Revolution, the Colonial government of Maryland pursued a cruel policy of attempting to depopulate Smith Island, to nullify its suspected use as a haven for pirates and Tory sympathizers. In the War of 1812, with warships on the Chesapeake, the island again was caught between nations, with resulting destruction of its fishing boats, homes, and livelihoods on the water. The Civil War saw both Union and Confederacy suspect Smith Island, astraddle the line between Maryland and Virginia, of harboring and aiding the other side. In the first hours after John Wilkes Booth shot Lincoln, when his direction of escape was still unknown, there were calls for a federal blockade of Smith Island, on the theory that its shallow, lonely creeks and forest hammocks would make an ideal hiding place for the assassin.

In modern days the Maryland State Police staged an air and sea assault on what they believed to be a major transshipment center for drugs based on the island. After wrecking a man's home, the law enforcers were able to produce less than an ounce of marijuana. More than once, I saw islanders charged with violations of the natural resources laws taken off, handcuffed, by a contingent of police for arraignment, as if after living and working in the same place for a dozen generations, they were likely to flee. The son of one of our neighbors was involved in a tragic nighttime boating accident, after which his best friend, another teenager, was found drowned. On the day of the funeral he was preparing to be a pallbearer when the police showed up, insisting that they needed to question him. Frequently in dealings with the island, the police had their share of legitimate gripes—they had been fired upon more than once—but they did little to repair damage that went centuries deep. It was common on the mainland to hear islanders described as suspicious; but in fact, the remoteness and mystery of the island has seemed more often to fuel suspicions that whatever smoke seems to be rising from out there in the bay must indicate a fire.

For the most part, the islanders seemed surprisingly trusting and open. But that stopped when it came to one activity, duck trapping. Trapping, which has been illegal for decades, is a method of taking wild ducks that was imported from England with the original island settlers. It consists of training the fowl to follow a trail of bait into a wire mesh trap, entering through a collapsible funnel that permits entry but no exit. Simple in principle, it is an art to do it well, and requires the stealth of a ghost to avoid being caught, since even the sight of a trap in the marsh is illegal.

I lived next door to a trapper for two years, and I knew he was a trapper, yet I never saw anything to alert me to his activities. Twice I was told that if I really wanted to write about trapping, I should have talked to so-and-so. Each time, so-and-so had been dead about six months to a year. I prowled the marshes by canoe and kayak, and came to know them intimately, I thought; but the only trace of trapping I ever came across was a wide plank set just below the lowest level of the tide to bridge a deep marsh gut. To someone who knew it was there, it would afford quick access or escape, while a pursuing lawman would be in over his head if he tried to follow.

An islander whose family I knew as intimately as any lay on his deathbed with lung cancer that in another day or so would begin to distort his thoughts beyond coherent conversation. He seemed in a talking mood this night, though, and I told him I had heard that back in the old days, as a young man, he had done some trapping. Would he tell me how it was then? The recollections seemed to act like a tonic. He roused up off the pillow and recounted every detail with a gleam in his eye, down to the motion of the wrist used to reach into the trap and economically snap each duck's neck. He told me how the old-timers would painstakingly surround their trapping marsh with a spool of cotton worked down in the base of the reeds. If broken, it would give evidence that someone had you under surveillance. That marsh, he said, was our store. Once, he said, he was caught, and spent a day in prison for each duck, of which he had twenty-six.

He began to tire and have trouble talking. As it happened, it would be our last conversation. When was it that the glory days of trapping had ended for him, I wanted to know. Well, he said, settling his wasted frame back against the pillows, he would likely have to put it on hold this coming winter.

OLD PAUL MARSHALL, who lived down at the end of my street, where it tails off into the marsh, remembers all the hunting and trapping lore of the island, and can recount every run-in between gunners and the law in some detail, perhaps because he was so often a central figure. He recites the story of the refuge that took half his island like a distasteful litany. He thinks the newer generations of islander won't even know enough about how good it once was to roam that marsh to keep the old outrage kindled.

He is crippled now with strokes and diabetes, this man who they say could crawl up on a black duck, the wariest of the waterfowl, through the thickest stand of waterbush. He was a man who loved to roam and progue, to hunt and trap and fish; and later in life he began to draw and carve and paint waterfowl and other birdlife with a marvelous delicacy and eye for detail, before his right hand became useless. Once I asked him, sitting there inside his gloomy house, all gnarled up, what he would wish for if he could have any one wish. "My health back," "to carve," "the strength to progue those marshes again"—or so I was ready to write when his considered answer came: "to get the damn guvment offn' our marsh."

Once I loaded Paul into a wheelchair I wedged between the bow and mid-ships of a skiff and went up to look at the government refuge. Old pictures showed an elaborate boathouse and living quarters there; but now there were only steel-reinforced concrete piers and a solid steel building with no windows, its single entrance heavily bolted. It looked like a wartime bunker, I remarked. Well, it damn well should, Paul replied, because people had attacked it with fire and hacksaws and guns to protest the federal presence. Once I mentioned our conversation to a federal game warden, who rolled his eyes: "Paul said that, did he? Well, Paul should know."

In his devotion to hunting, and his clashes with the law, Paul was not the average Smith Islander, many of whom have hunted but little, or prefer to spend their leisure time anywhere but back outside on the marsh and water. Yet he and the other duck trappers and gunners of the island, by their being out there, by their stalking the dark and frozen and blowy seasons, bore a witness that was on some level important to all. The islanders would tell you these men satisfied the community's taste for wild duck and goose. I would add that the ducks tasted to them like freedom. More than anything, perhaps, that was "what they come here for."

Hunters

PAUL MARSHALL

IT WAS PAUL who first brought me to Smith Island in the mid-1970s—he brought me the last few hundred yards, anyhow. I'd run my new boat that day nearly one hundred miles down the bay. Near the island my outboard motor expired. Paul, out prowling the marsh, found me hunched over the engine, a creation that ultimately convinced its maker, the Chrysler Motors Corporation, that it should stick to cars.

I guess a lot of people down here know how to fix outboards, I said. That they do, Paul replied, but they wouldn't touch a damn Chrysler. He took me in ignominious tow behind his little skiff, pleased as punch to show off to the villagers what new flotsam he had turned up. I didn't know it, but I was the evening's entertainment.

For the next few hours, I sweated over the dead Chrysler as a steady flow of watermen came by to watch. They didn't know much about outboards, but they all wanted to tell me Chryslers "weren't no damn good." "Now if she was a Merc [Mercury], Haney could do something with 'er," they would say. Haney seemed to be the local outboard mechanic. Could someone steer me to him? Wouldn't do you no good; he wouldn't fool with no Chrysler. Finally, I decided the problem was in the carburetor. Island stores, surprisingly, did not stock so much as sparkplugs for outboards. The Saturday ferry had left. I could take the motor to Crisfield on the Monday ferry; of course then I would have to figure how to get it to the closest Chrysler place, about thirty miles further up the highway; and chances were I'd miss the last ferry back across to my boat on the island. I was probably looking at Tuesday before I could get going, Paul agreed. Of course, he added, there's plenty of Chrysler parts right here.

What did he mean—the anti-Chrysler capital of the world stocked with spare parts? C'mon, Paul said, and we headed for the marsh back of the town harbor. Lots of the islanders, he explained, had once bought Chryslers. But they didn't hold up, he said; and you couldn't get service, so now they are all a'layin' in the marsh. I know where there is one, same horsepower, and nearabout the same year as your'n.

Paul, I would learn, found about anything he needed in that marsh—food, sport, lumber, materials for his carving; and probably just being out there alone, under the big Chesapeake sky, nourished something in him as much as anything he ever brought home for the pot. By his own admission he was never much of a waterman. He was a middleman, buying crabs from others and selling them to the mainland. He never made more than a modest living from the water. His career as a decoy carver, had it lasted a few years longer, might have brought him considerable wealth from the growing national craze for collecting wooden waterfowl as art objects; but strokes began to cripple him by his mid-sixties.

It had to hurt him more than he could say not to be able to get out and go. Some days he would get one of us to push his wheelchair out to the edge of the town and sit there in the spring sun and gaze and chat about old times with passers-by. I don't think he had a romantic bone in him, and he was inarticulate of whatever poetry he found in nature; but I thought of Paul as the freest spirit of anyone I knew on the island. If there is such a thing as reincarnation, and any justice at all in the world, his soul is lodged now in the plumed breast of a great blue heron, shuffling his spindly shanks through the muck and grass beds to scare up minnows and soft crabs, poking his long beak into every nook and cranny of the marshy edge.

Not long after his family had to move him off the island into a nursing home, doctors had to amputate a leg because of diabetes; and with that, it seemed like Paul just gave up. Toward the very end, a friend who came in his room was distressed to see him propped up, eyes unfocused, shirt buttoned crooked, seemingly oblivious that his roommate had lost bladder control and urine was running across the floor. He looked, she said, just pitiful, like a little old bird, head cocked to one side, waiting to die.

I told her about a moment during my last interview with Paul, and we agreed that was how we wanted to remember the old reprobate. He had been reminiscing for two hours straight about the old days, bitching as usual about the "guvment" ruining everything, and it had been a long interview and he was getting tired. I had the feeling this would be the last time I'd see him, though neither of us wanted to admit that. Just as I turned off the tape and began gathering my equipment to go, Paul rallied and said, "Did I ever tell you what my dream was?" Frankly, I never associated this hardscrabble old islander with dreams.

"My dream," he said, "is I always thought I'd like to been at Custer's last stand; and I'd like to been with the Indians. From what I read about that deal, Custer was told that, look, you win one more big Indian battle, then you'll make President. Well, damn if he didn't do well. Yeeahh, by Christ, I'd like to been there with the Indians. They told him, we don't want to fight; all we want to do is hunt. But Custer wouldn't let 'em alone. And damn if they let him alone. They killed every one of them guvment bastards."

PAUL LIKED to talk about the hunting life, nearly synonymous with his life:

◆ You might as well say I have been in this same spot all of my life. The shed out back where I carve now, that was the site of the school where my wife and I went through the primary grades together. When we got married, we moved into it for our house. Then when her dad died, they moved this house on a scow from Longbranch, which was a little town out in the marsh that is all gone now. That was fifty years ago, and I guess when they bury me down the street in the churchyard it will be about the furthest I have ever moved. But I never felt closed in because two steps, and you were on the marsh, and your skiff was not far from the door.

This was always a fowlin' place—ducks and geese and swan. That is how people here made it—there was never no money here until recent—they made it on what was here in the water and what come here in season. Every bed around home when I was a youngster used to be a feather bed. It took 40 pounds to make a feather bed and 5 pounds to make a pillow. It took two geese to make a pound, and eight black ducks, and maybe ten pintail or bald-pate. It was a lot of ducks, and everybody here had feather beds. It was cold in those bedrooms in the winter, but you sink down about six inches in them feathers, and they'd throw five or six quilts over top of you, and you were all right.

Wintertime, it seemed like everybody in town was always pickin'. My grandfather, he would not stop with a goose 'til he had picked 'em clean down over the edge of their bills. The old store here of a night, there would be men settin' and talkin' and big piles of fowl just heaped up everywhere, and people pickin'. Now I remember when the guvment first began to put those metal bands on the legs of ducks to follow their migrations. It was a new thing, and old Capn' Woods, pickin' through a big pile, come across one and held it up for everyone to see: "Why, would you look at what the damned game wardens is a'doin' now to torment a poor duck," he said. Huh, and him just wrung their necks!

In my teens we was paid no more'n ten cents to pick a goose, and five cents a pair of ducks. They named Merle next door John L. Lewis for the labor boss, because in the store one night he up and said, "Nothin' doin for less'n thirty-five cents," and he stuck to it, and I think he finally got the price up some, but not that much.

We had live geese around town all year. Standin' geese, they were called, and people used to train them to honk the wild ones down into gun range. They would get to be regular pets, eat right out of your hand, some would. People had names for their favorites, like Bob, or Nig. One used to follow you to the store and back like a dog. I knew of a goose in Crisfield that lived for twenty-seven years.

I always loved to hunt. My dad, when I was a teenager, would get me and another couple boys and head down the creek aboard his boat, and we'd catch a mess of oysters, shuck 'em, and stew 'em up in the cabin for when we come in from hunting. Boy, that was the life.

Some have said that Dad and me, huntin', used to be top guns on this island. They mighta had that right. I'm not gonna talk about that, but I've done a lot of it, by God. I used not to go unless I'd carry 150 rounds of ammunition. This would seem like a bad thing, I guess, if everybody was doin' it, but they weren't. I would say at no one time could you have went out and found more than five people a'huntin' from Tylerton. The game wardens thought everybody out here was huntin' but they was hundreds lived here that never fired a gun.

It was that way, too, with the big guns. I'm one of the last ones ever used 'em. How big was they? Big enough they had names. They could be ten foot long or more, and weigh, my God, as much as a man. Their bore [barrel diameter] was two inches, some an inch and a half. My dad's was called the Chiseltine, I think [probably originally Cheseldine], and before him, it come from over the Potomac, and before that from England, they said.

Now, a big gun was mounted in a skiff not much longer than the gun, and there was just room enough for the gunner to lay flat alongside of it in the bottom; if you layed overtop her, when she went off, she'd kick you overboard. We loaded Dad's with a pound and a quarter of shot, and a quarter pound of powder. When you aimed 'er, you used two little hand paddles—maybe they was 18 inches long—you stuck out either side to point the skiff; and when you slapped that trigger, look out, 'cause she'd take her way a'-kickin' back towards the stern.

I have heard it said that there was more than a hundred of the big guns on the bay at one time. I know Smith Island had twenty of 'em. And people thought you could destroy the world with them, but it wasn't true. I've known three of 'em, firin' together on a flock of brant, to kill 108 one time, but that's the onliest time I ever heard of it; and I did hear tell of Romey's father that he killed sixty-seven pintails with one shot. But those were the shots of a lifetime. My grandfather used to be one of the best punt gunners [big gunners] ever lived—he could kill as many in the daylight as most people could sneakin' up on the fowl of a night—and twelve geese is the most he ever killed in a shot. I myself never got more'n ten geese that way.

People only remember the big kills, but let me tell you how it was. Of course they didn't have motors in them old-time skiffs, so wherever they went, they went shovin'. Shovin' with a pole against the bottom is how people used to go everywhere in and among these islands; shove to church, shove to school, shove to visit. They would think nothin' of shovin' all night long;

shove from Terrapin Sands clear down to Shanks's Creek, miles and miles; shove six miles to Shanks's Island and back to Tylerton just to gather some wild 'spar'gas [asparagus]. Now people wouldn't shove 20 feet. They'd have three or four poles and paddles in a gunnin' skiff. One about ten foot, that'd be what you'd cover distance with; then one about six feet and one about four feet. Then for deep water and for closin' in on fowl, you'd have your hand paddles.

A lot of things had to come together just right to kill much with them big guns. I remember when it looked like conditions was going to get just right, Dad would come home and get his supper right quick and go upstairs and get his binoculars and heist the window so's he could count the geese down Shanks's and see if there was a shot or not. And then two or three would get together and go shovin' down on 'em.

Sometimes they would be out there all night a'waitin' for the tide or the wind or the moon to get the way they wanted. They would go ashore on the marsh and cover up in sea oars [masses of dried eelgrass washed ashore] to keep warm, and go to sleep while they waited. The best times to shoot was that halflight you would get between sunset and dark. You would come from the night, from the east, so the fowl was a'lookin' at dark, but you could see 'em against the west, to aim. You could do the same thing under the risin' or the settin' of the moon. Sometimes you could do right well if you got directly under the moon. You couldn't have no angle to it [the moon] or she'd paint you white and shine on your sides; but if she was right overhead all the glow and gloss would be cut right off, and you could kill some fowl.

Now, gettin' close enough to shoot just as the fowl flew would've killed most people. You would be down in that little skiff, a'workin' them hand paddles, slow so you didn't close on 'em too fast, but fast enough to get up on 'em, and they'd all the time be swimmin'. My grandfather Bradshaw, they said he could make a swan fly using a hand paddle. Now let me tell you something, a swan can swim. He's got seven-inch feet, you spread them out, and to go fast enough to make a swan fly, that was something.

Many a night I remember standin' on the road in Tylerton and hearin' the big guns go off—*boom, boom, boom*—out there somewhere and we knew they'd soon be comin' with fowl. But many a time they didn't, too. My grandfather used to cuss the damn baldpates. They're a lazy duck; they swim around and pick up what grass floats to the top for food. A redhead duck now will pull it up from the bottom, but a baldpate won't. Well, they had a habit of whistlin' just about the time you got up on some geese nearby 'em for a shot, and you wouldn't get nary a thing.

One night a bunch of gunners left out of here about dark, tide a'fallin', and skiffed up on the biggest bunch of ducks and geese they ever did want to see. Closer and closer they got, 'til one of 'em sang out, "Throw it inta 'em!" Well, they let 'em have it. Huh. Weren't nothin' but clumps of turf broke off of the marsh and layin' there in the shoal water.

Romey's father, Oscar, the one killed all those pintails, he got confused out there one time just before daybreak and like to shot another hunter with his big gun. The fellow was a'huntin' out of a sink box, which is a rig where you are hidden in the middle part, which is below the water with just a little rail sticking up around the sides, and your decoys are spread out all around. Well, Oscar's eyes weren't as good as they used to be. He heard this goose off in the dark, and he began to skiff down on him when he run smack into this big crowd of fowl, which was the decoys around the hunter, who was a'lyin' in the midst of 'em. Oscar cut loose right into the middle of 'em, and when the smoke cleared, here's this feller raised up and saying, "What the hell are you doing? You get away from me or I'll start shootin' back."

There's only two big guns left here now. Some was stole, some was sold. It's been thirty-five years since my grandfather's was shot. I remember it. A lone swan pitched over across by Rhodes Point and my brother skiffed over there; and that swan was a long way away, but he got it, in broad daylight. Now I have got to where I can't do nothin', but I still think a lot about how you could improve on big gunnin'. I'd like to try nailin' mirrors to the side of a skiff and them fowl would see themselves and think it wasn't nothin' comin' up on 'em but another flock of geese.

I read once about how in West Virginia they still make moonshine, and if the feds find it they'll burn their stills and woods down; but still they make it. They ain't no real money in it. They just got a taste for the stuff. Well, maybe that's a little like it has been with us and duck trapping. I've done it, and I tell you, it's fun.

Maybe you knew Franklin, one of my uncle William's seven kids. Now that was a trappin' family. The last day anybody saw Franklin alive he was in the store, a'fixin' to run down and check his traps. He had a bad heart— seems like it run in that family—and had been told by the doctors that walkin' the marsh would kill him. All the women were sayin', "Don't go, Franklin," "Franklin, there's no need to go." Well, of course he didn't have to trap, but he loved it, and ya might's well say he needed to. He was out on the marsh when a man we all knew flew in to visit in his seaplane, and she looked from a distance just like the game warden's. It scared Franklin so bad his heart gave out, him a'bendin' right over his trap. Weren't the worst way to die, I can tell ye. The warden did get his brother, Russell, another time, and it wasn't long after that Russell had his heart attack.

This is all in modern times, when they wan't enough ducks, really, to more'n fool with; but for hundreds of years it was part of our livin'. When I was young, a man might still leave out oystering up to Holland's Island of a Monday winter mornin' with his tongs and seven bushels of corn for his traps. You would spend 'til Wednesday evenin' up in the marsh, tonging, trappin' ducks and maybe rats [muskrats] too. You had to be back home to ship your ducks for Thursday market in Crisfield, which was not a market like something out in the open, but everyone knew to come there for wild duck on that day.

Trapped ducks fetched a big premium, 'cause you knew they was corn-fed, and guaranteed not to have shot in the meat to crack your teeth. Ain't nothin' in the world better'n a corn-fed black duck, though a pintail's good too, and I like a goose just about as well as anything. Swan, now they're extry good, same as roast beef, and not strong like some people claim. When trappin' was big, George Bradshaw, "Black Duck George," we used to call 'im, would take our ducks and geese to Crisfield and sell 'em. It was all illegal, but George was a slick'un. One day, the game wardens decided they was goin' to get him. An undercover state man come up to George comin' out of the store in Crisfield, and said he was told that he heard that George could get him a nice pair of black ducks. He had the money right in his hand. George didn't bat an eye. He said, well, if the man would mind his purchases for a few minutes, he thought he could do the man some good. George took the money and soon as he got outta sight, took off for the island. By'n by, the guvment man figured he'd been had. He still had George's box. He looked inside, and it was the pair of black ducks he had bought.

It was always a war, though, with trappin'. The guvment fifty, sixty years ago had a big old wooden workboat called the *Loon*. They would run her down Tyler's Crick, anchor there, and go ashore and rob all our traps. I guess we coulda' lived with it, but they took to paradin' that *Loon* right back up through town, down the channel by all our shanties with the traps a'settin' on top of her cabin with the live ducks still in 'em. That was just a'throwin' it in our face. Well, one day she come through the channel and from every shanty the men opened up on her with shotguns—killed every damn duck in them traps. The next day they had the state troopers out here. They never found out nothin', and they never pulled that trick again.

Two things I never felt bad over—poachin' oysters or takin' waterfowl—and I never will. Whenever you make a law that applies to everywhere, it *can't* apply over here. We got no industry and no farmland—just our marsh and the water, and nobody takes care of us but ourselves. The game wardens wouldn't believe this, but there've been times, freeze-ups, when we sent to Crisfield for corn and fed thousands of starving redheads right off the stern of our boats; but now, if I wanted to kill a mess of 'em for supper, why, I'd shoot if the warden was comin' right up the creek.

I know I talk a lot about the [refuge] land up above us, and some here laughs at how I go on. Well, my day is gone, and talk is all I can do, but I'm a'talkin' for those comin' up now that never will know what a beautiful thing we once had there. I hope it is like the civil rights movement, that it never will go away. By Christ, that was a fowlin' marsh if ever they was one, ducks thick as hair. Ohhh, the guts and little creeks and the tide ponds where it was just right for trappin'.

And now the federal guvment has had it for twenty-five years and they have brought in foxes that eat the ducks and they have taken away our land, reduced us to the villages same as Indians on a reservation. I see the aim of federal guvment clear: to make life as miserable for the common man as they can.

I blame the people here for not keeping the land within the island. Once they had left off living up there on the north part, and moved into the towns, it went to a rich man in Baltimore for $7,000. Glenn Martin was his name, and I wish now I'd never heard of him. Me and my brother, Ullie, worked for him five years after the war [WWII]. He would come down in his yacht, she was 108 foot long, and he would bring two hundred bushels of corn at a time to bait the fowl.

And we would handle it, we were everything—put the corn out, guide the hunters, build the blinds, ferry water, cook—all for $50 a week; my God, we didn't know how to deal with rich people.

He was in the war industry, you know, and he would bring a stream of admirals and generals and high officials down to kill ducks, and only two there was in all those years that wouldn't shoot over their legal limit of fowl. That was Albert M. Day and his aide, and of course he couldn't shoot over because he was a big man in the department [Interior] that set the rules; but I bet you put 'em out by theirselves and they'd shoot over the limit same as anyone else.

Ullie and me always wanted just a little piece of land up there, but you think Martin'd give it to us? Naaahh, the rich bastard. After he died and went to California to get buried, his estate settled some sort of tax deal with the feds and that ruin't our chances forever.

Of course, they decided they needed a man down here permanent to watch over their property. The job went to our other brother, Stanley. Ullie never spoke to Stanley after that long as he lived, and when Stanley died, Ullie wouldn't go to his funeral. I never blamed nobody for takin' that job, 'cause God knows, if the guvment's big enough to win two wars over both oceans, they're big enough to put a man on Smith Island; but Ullie would blame Stanley for everything in the world.

The truth of it was, we both applied for the job ourselves, and Ullie wanted it especially bad; but of course both of us had, you know, records with the game wardens, and that hurt our chances. But that's what set Ullie against his brother—wasn't no matter of principle or hunting. Ullie come over home one day before he died, and he tried to talk about it—he knowed he'd been wrong—we had a talk, and he didn't say much about Stanley, but I knowed that's what was on his mind; but now he's dead.

So now you see they got those big fancy signs up all over that marsh sayin' "Glen L. Martin Bird [Wildlife] Refuge," like they done somethin' great, and I wonder, why can't they just leave us alone? If Smith Island was to sink tomorrow, what impact would it have on this nation? I think we could do just fine without the guvment here. But you look at how they've pestered us all these years over our game; I'm not sure they could do without us. ✦

LAST HUNTS

RICHARD TYLER SMITH (HIS SON TALKING):

✦ It was a day for gunnin', windy and snow blowin' all around, and I got Dad set up in the blind. He was gettin' on in years, and when two mallards come by, I had it all figured out: I shot his side first, and then I shot mine. He said, what'd you shoot my side for? I said, I didn't think you were gonna shoot. He said, you better believe I'll shoot.

Seven geese flew by, and we got six out of the air. An hour hadn't gone by when we had sixteen geese, and I went out to take the decoys up. He didn't want to go. I told him, Dad, we got a'plenty. I only want one or two for myself; you can have the rest. He said, look, boy, I'm gettin' old and I might never have such an opportunity again, and the way it would turn out, he was right; he would never kill another goose after that day. But I'd already unloaded both guns and set 'em outside in the marsh.

I was just gettin' in the boat when must have been three hundred geese flew right into the decoys. There I sat, right among the decoys and the live geese, and I saw his great ole big arm feelin' outn' the blind for a gun. He got hold of mine, which took a different shell than his. He jammed a load into her anyhow and opened fire.

When the geese flared up, they was so close they knocked the paddle outn' my hand. Dad's gun jammed after that first shot, but he had killed one more—goose had a hole in 'im biggern' an apple. Dad didn't want to quit. ✦

EDWARD HARRISON

✦ It was hard winter, channel in front of the gas dock froze except for one airhole, and a whole bunch of redheads and canvasbacks were feedin' there. I told the fellows settin' in the oilhouse, boy, I'd love to have a mess of them for supper, and they said, well, why don't you go get your gun and shoot us some?

I walked home and got my gun, threw three shells inta 'er, and leaned it against a pole to sight. Well, I throwed it up there to shoot, and I couldn't shoot. All the boys in the oilhouse was a'watchin' but I couldn't kill them to save my life.

I knowed they were hungry, tryin' to get somethin' to eat—they were feedin' on them little minners around the pilings of the dock. I had to walk away. Another man said, let me have the gun, and I said, nope, I ain't gonna do it.

Another'n said, you lost your nerve, and I said, I can't help it. If you were starvin' trying to get something to eat like that, you wouldn't want to be bothered. I walked on up to the house and my gun's been on the rack since. I used to be crazy about hunting, but you get older, you like to see things live. ◆

THE HELICOPTER

PAUL MARSHALL

◆ It was a Sunday late in February, and my God, they wan't no redheads in Tyler's Creek—ten thousand if they was a'one. My boy and me and a neighbor had gone to a blind just below the end of Tylerton. We was just putting shells in our guns when Dickie looked up: "there he comes."

It was a helicopter—one of them big State Police jobs they use to medevac people to the hospital when they are too sick to use the ferry. How he come to be there on a Sabbath afternoon, dad-blamed if I know, the bastards.

They was a'comin' down on us like a dive bomber when we piled into our skiff and run for home. The door was slid back and that game warden was half hangin' out. I couldn't tell if he was a'goin' to jump in on us, or was they gonna try to squash us.

I stuck a long shovin' pole straight up at 'im, us a'windin' up the creek channel all this time. I said, if he tries to cut our heads off, he'll have to run over this paddle first.

Folks in town had heard the racket, and they could see the helicopter, and this long pole stuck up in the air, both a'comin' up the creek. We hit the marsh at the south'ard end of town and scattered, every man for hisself. It was too wet there for 'im to land, and the helicopter headed up for the ballfield to pitch in there. But that one warden jumped right out and took after us.

Well, Dickie, he made for the church and climbed right to the steeple where those owls nest, and there he hid. Some folks said later it wasn't right to go inta the church like that; but Dick's right religious and maybe he felt entitled.

My boy and me had the shotguns. I throwed his overboard. He slung mine underneath a house. He slung it so hard it come on out the other side. Well, we give 'em the slip when they barged into that house where a man and his wife was a'livin', and her nine months pregnant and them like to knockin' down the door, guns drawn.

I shucked off my jacket, 'cause it had canvasback ducks painted on the back and I figured they might identify that, and I began to tell people what those bastards had done, barging in on a pregnant woman and all. We got a crowd formed up to the ballfield around that helicopter and some commenced to throwin' Coke bottles and rocks at it.

Now about this time here come the warden, and he said can he have a boat to get something he dropped outn' his helicopter into the creek—I think it was a camera. Well, he mighta thought I was the one in that skiff, but he couldn't prove it. I told him, ain't nobody gonna let you have a damn thing, and if you don't get away from here, we'll bury you.

They was beat, and they had to admit it. They left, and we never saw no more of 'em that winter. That was 1980, and I guess they'll talk about us comin' up the creek for a long time. Kaki, Dallas's wife, even wrote a little poem about it. ✦

KAKI BRADSHAW'S ODE TO THE WHIRLY BIRD (1980):

> *One Monday evening three men took a run*
> *Down to Back Landing to have some fun,*
> *And the first thing you knew over gut and crick*
> *Came a helicopter chasing old Paul and Dick*
> *They looked all over for gun and for barrel*
> *Saying where in the Dickens is old Johnny Carroll.*
> *They went up and down and tried to search*
> *For poor old Dickie who had hid in the Church*
> *So Dickie, Johnnie and Paul, don't say a word*
> *Or you'll be chased by a whirly bird.*
> *And don't try to go on a genuine caper*
> *Or you'll be needing White Cloud toilet paper.*

The Warden's Story

LIEUTENANT MIKE HOWARD, MARYLAND NATURAL
RESOURCES POLICE

✦ My grandmother on one side is from Smith Island. They say my great-grandfather, from Virginia, was a duck trapper and had his share of problems with the law. The bay's marsh islands have always been special places to me. I fished and crabbed there, and when I was single, instead of going home and sleeping in bed I would be on a boat just drifting in the creeks. Being out there on a full moon, listening to the sound of the waves breaking; the peacefulness of sunrise on a cold morning—it's a good way to live. I expect if you talked to some of those I've arrested, they would tell you the same.

When I was a little boy, I would go with my grandparents every Saturday morning to meet the "duck truck." Even then, which was in the 1960s, it was coming regularly with waterfowl from off the islands. It was $3 to $4 a pair for ducks, and Grandmother always said she did not want a duck that was full of shot. Trapped ducks brought a premium. I didn't understand then why it had to be so secretive, why the duck truck only pulled up when no other vehicles were around.

Now that I have been working with the Natural Resources Police for fifteen years, I can see how heavy the pressure on waterfowl was all along the Atlantic flyway. With the habitat destruction that's gone on, you could never allow the kind of hunting old-timers like Paul Marshall dreamed of. He thought if he could just run that refuge [Martin] on Smith Island his way, feed the ducks plenty of corn, he would have it all back like it used to be. And he would have got plenty of fowl that way, but just because the feed was concentrating them. There wouldn't have been any more ducks in the world, but you could not tell him that.

All over the Chesapeake there is a history of illegal shooting of waterfowl that runs through most of this century; but trapping, it seemed, was special to Smith Island and the mainland marshes around it—came over from England, I suppose, and it is something that goes back centuries and for all I know thousands of years.

There is an art to it, the way you play the level of the tide and the weather fronts and the phase of the moon, get all those right; then how you set your trap—certain ways of placing the funnel that leads 'em into the big wire cage will get you teal, but almost no black ducks, for example. And in recent decades, with all the law cracking down, they have had to do it all after dark. The best trappers are like ghosts. It's an art, trapping. It's an art to trap the trappers, too.

We tried for five or six years over on the island. We would find a handful of cracked corn in a pond with a dozen ducks or two, but never any traps and no evidence that anybody had even been there. And it seemed like every time we'd leave Crisfield on a patrol, before we started our engine the folks on the islands would know we were headed there. Then one year we got a break.

Up a little gut that runs into a pond back of the heron rookery near Tylerton, we found a duck trap hidden in the bushes. It wasn't set or anything, but I decided to set up surveillance.

I would leave after dark, sometimes late as 2:00 A.M., from a little landing way up the Pocomoke River, maybe thirty to forty miles from Smith Island. I had a 16-foot Whaler with a 115 horsepower outboard, which would cruise at 40, and I would come down the river, through the cut at Fox Island and across the Sound and up from Virginia, carrying a canoe aboard to paddle the last leg. Any motor will make suds—you know, little bubbles—that will linger a long time up in the edges of the marsh, and a smart trapper will see those and take alarm. And I'd always go when there was some tide up in the marsh, so I wouldn't leave any visible footprints.

Well, this went on every night for maybe two weeks, and sometimes it was pretty nasty weather crossing fifteen miles of open water in such a small rig, but the trap was a live one. He had maybe fifty to sixty ducks on bait in that pond, and we knew he wouldn't feed 'em forever. Soon he was going to have to make his move.

I contacted some federal agents I had worked with on waterfowl violations, and they said they were quite familiar with that pond. Four or five of them had staked it out in the past, and thought nobody knew they were there. Then, one night, two boats roared through the creek nearby and several high-powered rifles fired from it into the bushes where the federal boys were laying hid. The FBI investigated but never found anything. But the feds told me they thought it was a set-up and they would pass on this one.

My bosses were getting worried, too, and there was a lot of skepticism, questions about all the overtime I was putting in, the danger, whether we had the manpower to pull this off. We also knew enough about the man we suspected was the trapper to make us pretty cautious. He had shot a man with a pistol several times on the dock at Crisfield, which was ruled self-defense. And he had another favorite weapon, an *Uzi* machine gun, the kind that fits right under your armpit so you can carry it almost like a handgun. He was said to usually be armed, and I know for a fact that he almost never went without a buttoned jacket in Crisfield, even on hot summer days.

Years before, we were told on good authority, he was the one who went into the rookeries and shot dozens of mating great blue herons and egrets and tacked them on channel markers heading from the island to Crisfield, just to show some visiting federal game officials what he thought of them. I don't think in most of this he was really a typical island trapper.

Anyhow, there was a lot of pressure to cut our losses when I made the night surveillance for about the tenth night in a row. A moon was up and I could hear ducks cackling on the pond, and the trap was set in the water. And I noticed suds in the reeds like a boat had been through recently. It seemed like now or never.

I went back to Crisfield and rounded up a crew. It was 2:00 A.M. by the time me and a partner canoed back into the pond. We left two other officers down the creek in radio contact. We sunk the canoe so you couldn't see it. The marsh grass was only about 18 inches high where we had to hide. It was a little like trying to surprise someone in a huge, open field, out on that marsh that just stretches away to everywhere.

We were down almost on our bellies, and the tide was coming up in the marsh. The little fiddler crabs were crawling all in between our hands and biting on our fingers. The mosquitos were terrific. But we dared not move a muscle or make a sound. It began to rain. We hadn't brought any rain gear. We stayed like that until 5:00 A.M., about an hour until dawn, when we heard an outboard starting. It came closer and closer. The crabs and mosquitos were fierce. We were drenched. Our radios had gotten too wet to contact our help down the creek. Then the motor went away. Not a duck had gone in the trap either, and it seemed that a lot of work was going down the drain. But ten minutes later, we heard him coming back.

The motor stopped and you could hear a pole being put in the water to shove the skiff. He was up on the bow, you could see against the starlight, pushing with that pole, looking everything over. He was probably 50 feet away when he stuck the pole down, tied the skiff, and came straight for us.

When he got to the trap and grabbed it, he was no more than six feet away. Given his reputation with guns, I wanted him to have both hands full of trap when we showed ourselves. He saw me then, and I took a step backward. "Freeze," I said, and he froze. "You really scared me," he said. "You ain't going to shoot me, are you?"

I told him we were going to charge him with trapping and because he was a resident of the island he would be released on his own recognizance, and I said, let's go over and look at your boat, and he gave me a strange look. When we did, there on the bow, all laid out neat were seven black ducks with their necks wrung, pretty as you want. He must have had another trap, and lucky for us, because now we had a really strong case.

We had expected the worst, but he seemed pretty relieved we weren't going to shoot him; and then he got almost teary-eyed and began to talk about how this same pond had been trapped by his father and his father-in-law, and on back three generations, and how this was the end of it all.

We got him to court on the mainland, and of course he was found guilty and fined, I think, about $1,200. The judge said that he hoped this would break him of such habits, and the trapper looked at him and right there in court said: "I'm not going to promise you that, because that's my heritage."

If that was a win for our side, we had our frustrations too—like the time I flew over one afternoon in a State Police Medevac helicopter and surprised a few gunners out shooting redhead ducks.

We were coming in from the north, just routine surveillance, when I looked down and said, man, I can't believe this. There they are two months after season, sitting in a blind. Let's get 'em. The pilot, he was a Vietnam veteran, and he put her into a nose dive. We finally ran them ashore and I had the bay door open and was ready to jump, but one of them kept poking a pole up at me.

Finally, I jumped down—the 'copter was five or six feet off the ground— and ran after two of them. I heard the door to a house slam and stopped there to ask two or three people standing outside whether they had seen anyone. I think one of them I talked to was a woman. I don't even remember if she was pregnant, but later on when we got back to the mainland, there were these calls to the State Police complaining we had kicked in the door, guns drawn, and caused a woman to go into premature labor . . . none of that ever happened, but that is the way the story went.

Finally, I met up with this angry old man, who was Paul Marshall, but at the time I couldn't identify him as one of the gunners. Well, he was going to kill us and he was going to do this and he was going to do that—he had a crowd of fifty or so people all whipped up.

About that time the co-pilot came up and said we have got to get out of here. They are throwing bottles and rocks and if they hit the tail rotor, we're all dead. It is not worth it for a damn duck. The pilot had put his pistol on his lap. He was in a sweat, and he was adamant that if we stayed, we were dead men. I was more used to these things than they were, but I had to bite my tongue and go. It was the last time the State Police ever would permit one of their helicopters to be used for waterfowl surveillance.

That was not my last go-round with Paul. I think it was the very next winter when I shot up from Virginia in the Whaler and surprised him in the blind shooting redheads just before sunset. He got to his skiff and lost us for a minute, but then I saw the last light of day pick up the wake he'd left, and I knew where he was headed.

I said, he will not get to town ahead of me this time, and I took a shorter route and got out in the marsh between him and the houses in Tylerton. Well, he staked his skiff and got out in the marsh too, and we were staring at each other across about 500 yards, and we both started for the town, which was to our north.

Paul would walk 50 feet and I would walk 50 feet. He would speed up and I would speed up. It was freezing weather, and we had on heavy gear, hip boots and all, and he was carrying his shotgun, which of course I respected a great deal. It was half a mile to town, and now he began to walk faster. I kept pace.

He almost made it. He hit the bushes on that ditch outside of town at a dead run, breathing hard. I stopped shouting at him to stop and saved my breath for running. He looked back to see if I was gaining and that's when he hit an old sewing machine—you know how the islanders throw about anything out in the marsh when they're done with it. Down he went, and his gun flew out in front of him. He was terribly flushed and panting and cussing and I was afraid he'd have a stroke or a heart attack. I said, just leave the gun alone, and of course he grabbed for it and I put my foot on it.

Now about that time my partner caught up with us, and he was still new at this and didn't know any better, and he said something to Paul along the lines of, didn't he realize that it was important to conserve our waterfowl so that our grandchildren would be able to enjoy them, something like that. It was the wrong thing to tell old Paul:

"F... my grandchildren!" he said. "I am going to kill redheads and hang one from every telephone pole on this island, and I am going to save one pole for the first f...ing game warden that gets in my way!"

That has been ten years ago, and Paul has been dead nearly five years now. The trapper we caught that night has moved off of the island, and I have heard he teaches a class in environmental studies at the Vo-Tech in Crisfield.

Smith Island at this time is frankly not a high priority for us. The big waterfowl violations seem to be elsewhere nowadays. The generation that is in there now is more concerned in trying to make ends meet. The oysters are gone; you aren't allowed to catch rockfish any more, and although crabbing has been excellent, there is an awful lot of pressure on the crabs—too much to sustain, I'm afraid.

Probably there aren't twenty people on the island who pick up a gun every year now. ◆

Islander and Lawman

YVONNE HARRISON

✦ My husband, Mike, is manager of the federal refuge land here on the island. My dad, Stanley, was the first man on the island to ever hold that job.
He knew in 1959 when he began there would be a lot of resentment, and
some of the worst from his own brothers, which were Paul and Ullie Marshall.

Capn' Johnny Marshall was their father, you see, and when he remarried
Miss Margie—she was a Bradshaw—Stanley was young enough she was like
his mother, and she raised him gentle. Paul and Ullie were older, and they
never did accept Miss Margie's teachings.

Dad was a crab potter, and he had a lot of health problems, and he knew
he would need security for his family, and security just isn't to be found on
the water.

Many a time he tried to talk to Ullie, and Ullie let 'im die without ever
talking. But Dad taught us to love his brothers just the same, and we all went
to visit Ullie before he died, so he knew we forgave him.

And Uncle Paul, well, I hope he rests in Glory now, but he was a bird.
He probably knew a thing or two about how the federal building come to
be burnt up there on the refuge years ago. We went to the nursing home to
see him in his final days. I said, "Uncle Paul, I brought clam chowder." "Oh,
you hain't," he said. He was so tickled.

Mike: I'll tell you how it was I came to take the job after Stanley. I would
work the dredge boat with my dad, Daniel, and my uncle Edward, every winter. I worked the deck and I cooked, and looking up from that cabin stove
at Dad a'standin' out there behind the wheel, I'd see the wrinkles growing
on his face. One day I'll never forget, crossing the bay in a wet snow, goin'
to Solomons, and I watched a ball of snow gathering in the hollow of his
neck under his chin, and he never moved, and the ball growin' bigger and
bigger, and him sob wet [drenched] all down his front when we landed.

What finally decided me that I wanted something else was the week Dad
and I were oystering and made the biggest week's work I ever saw—$1,600—
and of that I brought home $60 after breakdowns and other expenses. I just

felt no matter how busy I was, no matter how much I did, if I took any time off it was against my family, not for 'em. I didn't know how normal people lived. This job was a Godsend. I love it and I think I'm good at it.

Now, there's no joy in doing law enforcement in your own country. There's been so many years here of grabbin' what they wanted when they could get it; that's hard to change. I get threats—one's goin' to burn me out; another'll say, there's ways of takin' care of me, things like that.

I don't let it bother me, but I'm careful not to put myself in situations where there wouldn't be room for anyone to back out. Sometimes I think attitudes are changing; but then again, it seems like it passes generation to generation in some families, like a cancer. Just the other morning there was a hot conversation in the post office about how they ought to do away with all law enforcement, and only a few spoke up against it.

Now, the refuge is half the island, and that is my territory. Of course, you couldn't be from here and not know who's trappin' and who's gunnin' out of season on the other half, down in Tylerton. I think I do my job as good as anyone could, but I've also got to live here, so let's say just don't ask about some of the goings-on down there in Tylerton. ✦

Cats

It HAS BEEN years, whole generations in their time since the holocaust, but there are still cats of the island who remember. They scatter at my approach or watch from beneath the crab shanties balefully, ears laid close to the skull and muscles tensed. I still don't like to look them in the eyes. They were just being cats. I was just defending my family.

For the record, I like cats; grew up with dozens of them, cried when they died, and devoutly hoped there was a cat heaven to receive their furry souls. For all that, I guess I never liked cats as much as the islanders, who support a feline population several times the size of their own.

The dogs here, even big ones, mind their manners around the cats. They are hopelessly outnumbered and they seem to know it. "Cats in heat tonight," is perhaps the most ubiquitous entry I find on reviewing my monthly journals. They are as much a part of the island milieu as sea gulls and foghorns. It was not uncommon to see a dozen, or even thirty, waiting for the daily handouts at the back doors of island homes. The rest of the time, no basket of bait or sack of garbage or catch of fish could be left unattended for a minute. Downy, new-born kittens consistently outcompeted my education raps to schoolkids. A cabin door left cracked on my boats was always an open invitation to spray urine. You met cats on the marsh, cats on the tideflats, cats in your compost bin and on your porch roof. At some point I began to think of them as vermin.

One morning at sunrise I stared, unbelieving, down our long dock to the boat we kept moored along the main channel through Tylerton. A fishing rod left aboard was jerking furiously, arced over the far gunwale almost to the breaking point. Somehow a huge fish had leaped and taken the baited hook reeled in nearly to the rod tip. I rushed to retrieve . . . what? A trophy bluefish, or a big striper, maybe a ray, or perhaps even a small shark. But no: hooked solidly through its lower jaw, pissing and hissing and scratching, a large tabby dangled, half in the water.

Theories ran the gamut as to why the island had so many cats. Some of the largest concentrations seemed to reside with older bachelor watermen—"the only soft pussy they'll ever stroke," the local ladies would sometimes joke. Naming cats was great sport. Chuck Berry, so called on account of "he is a old black cat," was so loved by his owner that even when his kidney condition grew obviously terminal, the man borrowed $100 one day to charter the island ferry in a vain dash to the vet for Chuck. Personally, I always liked Roy Orbison. He was a handsome tom with huge, dark patches around his eyes. One of Roy's kin, a low-slung, stocky animal, was called Little Jimmy Smith, for his remarkable resemblance, I was assured, to "Little Jimmy Smith over to Rhodes Point . . . he's got little short legs and this belly almost drags the ground." Little Jimmy, the islander, must have been a specimen, because once I began describing Little Jimmy, the cat, to an islander from Ewell, and before I even got to his name, the man said, "Hey, that sounds like Little Jimmy Smith to Rhodes Point." Another was named for an islander with an allegedly similar misshapen ear. Was it possible, I once wondered, that for every islander there was a companion cat.

Perhaps the charm of cats was also that fawning over them was an acceptable lapse in the overwhelming pragmatism that kept outward displays of affection to a minimum among even the most loving families in these hardworking communities. Two times in her life, a neighbor told me, she knew beyond any doubt how deeply her taciturn husband loved her. After she returned from a long stay in the mainland hospital, he blurted: "I am gladder to have you back than to have a new roundstern [a design of bay workboat now outdated, but in high regard at the time]." Another was the time he said, "You look purty as a goose."

Also, cats acknowledge no masters, and that surely touched a chord in the independent islanders. And in a place where children had become scarce, cats bred with abandon, welcome waves of new and adorable life washing over the island, regular as the tides. Never mind the appalling sights every winter of mewing, staggering, crusty-eyed kittens, born too late to make it through the cold weather. Sporadic attempts by the Bay Foundation to institute population controls ranged from moral suasion to bringing in vet students to provide free neutering and spaying. Routinely and politely, we were rebuffed. Somerset County officials on the mainland had long ago ducked the whole issue of burgeoning island cat populations by making sure their pet-control ordinance applied to dogs only. This was not so smart as they thought, since one way islanders periodically dealt with bumper crops of cats even they couldn't tolerate was to loose crates of them in the dark on the ferry dock in Crisfield.

Maybe it finally came down to an issue of freedom, the single word I heard most when I asked islanders what they valued about living here. There is a telling scene in Katherine Paterson's Newbery Award winner, *Jacob Have I Loved*,* about teenagers growing up on a fictional island that seems obviously derived from the author's travels to Smith and Tangier. Two youngsters in the story are shocked by an elder's cussing as they round up stray cats. Such language is "against the commandments," the old captain is admonished.

*(New York: Harper & Row, 1980).

"I know those blasted commandments," he replies, "and there is not one word in them about how to speak to tomcats."

"You're right!" [Louise] screeched through her laughter. . . . "I bet there's not one word in the whole blasted Bible on how to speak to cats." And as they all rolled with mirth, she thought: *why was it so funny? Was it because it was so wonderful to discover something on this island that was free—something unproscribed by God, Moses or the Methodist Conference? We could talk to cats any way we pleased.*

In a place where the all-encompassing, salty regime of the Chesapeake permitted little diversity in either plant life or people's careers, cats were true indulgences: roaming and reproducing unfettered, "lilies of the field," toiling precious little, to judge from the equally ample populations of mice and rats.

Of all catdom in Tylerton, the centerpiece was the school cats, a tribe some forty strong. Every morning Miss Alice, the principal, would arrive by boat from Ewell and head to the store, emerging with a gallon or so of fresh milk and an armload of canned Huff-N-Puff, a grayish, foul-smelling catfood of the bargain variety. Since dawn her beloved charges ("my babies") would be gathering on the wooden planked deck that served as the town basketball court outside the last one-room public school in Maryland. They would feed, greedily, just outside the school door until classes began, at which point it seemed as if several would always make it inside to lounge happily through the lessons.

It pains me that it was the schoolyard that became the killing ground and source of so much bitterness, because it was the school, and Miss Alice, that had drawn us to the island. We had considered a move to Maryland's Eastern Shore for years, but Tyler had needed special schooling for a severe learning disability since he was three. After years in Baltimore's best learning disabled facilities, he had begun to blossom; but performing in the larger, more impersonal atmosphere of a mainstream school, which was all the rural Shore offered, seemed daunting and too much of a gamble.

Then, on a trip to the public elementary school in Tylerton, we fell in love with the bright, cheery little structure, its library (and the town's) a retired Book-Mobile set up above the level of high tides on concrete blocks outside. Inside, Miss Alice taught grades one through six on one side of the room, while Miss Evelyn, her assistant, taught pre-K and kindergarten on the other side. Perhaps it was no fast track to Harvard, but Alice's great spirit and motherly caring, and Evelyn's serene competence, lavished on a grand total of thirteen children, made the education that went on there extraordinary.

Some whole grades were empty, because no one was born in Tylerton those years. One day I heard two island mothers sketching, with a precision that mainland education planners would envy, the enrollment for each grade for the next decade. Only two new babies had been born in the last few years; so-and-so might have one more, but all other women, as they ran down the list, either had no more family plans or had gotten "fixed" (or their husbands had). "And so that's it, that'll be the last child, the last class," I heard them say.

In the short run, things were somewhat brighter. At the time of our visit, a "huge group" of four year olds, five in all, was due to hit pre-K, we were told. They were the bumper yield from the big freeze-up that had hit the Chesapeake in the winter of 1982, when the watermen, locked out of tonging oysters up the bay around Annapolis, had been home with time on their hands. Alice said the island's declining birthrate seemed always to have the county speculating whether it should close the little school in Tylerton. Our two kids would be more than welcome—they were *needed*, both teachers said.

And the situation looked ideal for Tyler, his learning disability by now upgraded to "mild/moderate" by intensive early intervention. In the Tylerton school, individual differences in how kids learned seemed more than catered to; it was expected, natural as breathing. A particularly difficult student might indeed seem "peculiar," the teachers would say (no P.C. jargon like "special" or "challenged" had yet invaded the island); but peculiar only if you didn't know his father and grandfather, who had been just the same; and of course, everyone not only knowing the student's forebears but most probably sharing some kinship with them, it would have seemed peculiar only if the kid had been an academic ball of fire.

And in fact, our own peculiar little boy flourished with the individual attention he got as one of only seven kids in six grades. Did he have problems writing as fast as the others? Miss Alice found an electric typewriter for him. Was he a bit disorganized? No problem. Kristy and Craig, the rest of the fourth grade, would make sure he was straight on the lessons. Did he get flustered at night about exactly what was expected the next day? He would just ring up Miss Alice that evening for a calming chat. That winter Tyler made the county honor roll, and later that year scored above average on standardized national testing. Abby, a superior student whose own test scores just might have qualified her for a fast track to Harvard, was also kept interested by helping Miss Evelyn with the two island boys in her class. One day I picked up the *Baltimore Sun* to find a front-page story, "Learning the Little Red Schoolhouse Way." A creative teacher had opened a one-room school in the metropolitan suburbs. It would accommodate fifteen students and was hailed as "the latest innovation in education."

It did not, I suspect, have school cats. Cheri had spotted this as a potential source of conflict early on. Everywhere we go, even for a day trip, she is alert to whether or not there are going to be cats. She is severely allergic to them, and Tyler, along with gorgeous, big round eyes and attractive legs, has inherited all his momma's feline antipathy and then some. Worse, the cat allergy sometimes triggered his chronic asthma, which was a serious concern on a remote island that lost its only doctor a few months after our arrival. Three times during our stay on the island, his choking became so bad at night we could not control it, and I would make a high-speed, twelve-mile run to the mainland hospital, steering with one hand, picking out channel marks and crab pot buoys with a searchlight in the other.

No one could have been more sympathetic to Tyler's need for a cat-free environment than Miss Alice, who was known to teach occasionally while holding her favorite, an orange tabby called Murn, on her lap. All children would be alerted, no school cats inside. It was actually against state and county school policy anyhow, she allowed.

I believe she really meant it. I do not think now, though I did once, that she cared more for a cat than she did for my son's health; but I also think, having observed numerous cat lovers, that there is a fine line between affection and addiction. The first school year was one of skirmishes. Tyler, who loved cats, would come home snuffling and wheezing and, under questioning, concede that yes, one or more cats had spent the afternoon near his desk. "But, Dad, they are the pride and joy of our school," he would remind me.

Alice would agree that the cats must be kept outside. She did not know how that one had managed to sneak in. They would shoot through a crack in the door before you knew it. I suggested more than once that perhaps moving their feeding area from within a foot or two of the school door might help control entry. Why, yes, that it might, Alice would reply, and that was where we usually left it. That we had a real problem began to dawn on me that spring, when during a polite exchange about the extreme difficulty of keeping cats out, she asked whether Tyler might ever outgrow his asthma. I said that often happened, and we lived with that hope. Oh, she said, a beatific look on her face, I long for the day when that little boy can pick up a cat and bury his face in its fur. And so the first school year ended.

We decided the next fall to strike early and firmly. We presented Alice with doctors' notes stating, in essence, that to expose Tyler to cats was to risk bringing on a life-threatening medical condition. That worked—for about three weeks. My "doomsday" weapon was to send a detailed account of the whole sorry struggle, along with doctors' notes and records of Tyler's asthma, to the county school board's lawyer, clearly implying I would hold them responsible in the event of his death. I never really intended to do this, because it might get Alice fired, and no one in town, least of all our own children, wanted that.

Then came the day that Tyler came home early, with an allergic reaction that lapsed into one of his worst-ever asthma attacks. Cats inside? I asked curtly. Yes, but they were put out immediately on being discovered, Tyler said . . . well, after their naps they were put out. I decided then on direct action, a bold strike at the school cats in the heart of their territory. For a few weeks, I talked the idea around to several islanders, including some of the leading cat fanciers, such as Roy Orbison's owner. I found what seemed like a fair amount of support, given Tyler's circumstances, and even a couple of ladies who said they, too, were fed up with cats, and would help any way they could.

Suggestions on how I should proceed ran the gamut. " 'Coy 'em [decoy them] in with catfood just like black ducks on corn," advised an old market hunter. When the feeding cats had formed in a tight cluster, he said, I should fire my 12-gauge once, then hesitate just a fraction of a second to let the survivors' heads come up, and then "cut 'im down like wheat" with the remaining rounds. A friend who is a trapper recommended purchase of a small pistol that fired small-caliber rounds with low velocity and minimal noise, but deadly force. Just begin strolling by the school at nights, perhaps throwing out food, and pop off a couple at a time. Others said to "bushel 'em up," capture them in crab baskets and usher them to that long-favored resting place for so much of the island's un-wanted things—the "60-foot channel," as they called the deep water running up Tangier Sound a few miles east.

None of this set well with the rest of my family. I compromised. We would bait them in, early one morning before the school boat brought Miss Alice. With help from Denny, a waterman friend, and the two island ladies who promised to contribute cats from their own herds, I would bushel them up, load them aboard my own boat, ferry them to Crisfield, load them in a borrowed truck, and take them to the only animal pound in a hundred miles that had returned my phone calls when I mentioned the magic words, "Smith Island cats." And the pound would make sure to find good homes for each of the kitties, the kids asked. They will do their very best, I hedged.

It was a cool, windy morning, big orangy sun rising over the marsh, when we moved in, armed with dozens of baskets and gobs of slimy, gray Huff-N-Puff. How many cats can you fit in a bushel basket? I had figured on four; but as soon as we would open the lid to shove in another yowling, scratching cap-tive, the first occupant would shoot like a furry meteor through the crack. We soon had to send for more bushels.

One huge black tom, muscles rippling, claws extended lethally, I backed into a corner, where Denny came up from behind and clapped a basket over him. *Pow!* A sinewy black arm crashed a hole through the basket. *Wham!* Denny over-laid it with a second. The tom had almost splintered his double-walled prison when we added a third basket, and tied the whole affair with stout crab buoy line.

I had added to our arsenal a bank trap, a rectangular wire mesh affair mea-suring about five feet by three feet, with access through a funnel in its side. The islanders sunk them near the marsh edges to trap fish and crabs, which entered through the funnel's large end, but once inside couldn't reenter the small end they had just pushed through. Slathered on the inside with the contents of a few cans of Huff-N-Puff, it had successfully caught six cats. They were threatening to punch out one of the trap's end panels. As I went to secure it, a small tabby scaled the wire side and bit down hard on my finger.

I wasn't the only one cursing. By now the remaining school cats were getting wise. Every cat we trapped was an effort. I heard expressions from my crew that morning I didn't dream the good women of the island knew.

From Rhodes Point we could hear the school boat coming. In minutes Miss Alice, arms full of milk and catfood, would be upon the scene of the crime. I had my boat running at the launch ramp near the school. As the school boat docked in Tylerton, I was planed off for Crisfield, roaring through a back-channel shortcut in the marsh, pitiful howls and mewing, along with great quantities of cat urine, issuing from nearly three dozen bushels on the rear deck. It was a rough ride over; the 12-gauge, I thought, might have been more merciful.

The pound, of course, had no happy home for thirty-seven stray cats. What it had was a gas chamber, into which the attendant expertly unbusheled and placed each cat, one at a time. She then injected CO_2 gas, freezing their lungs in half a minute or so, bringing quick death. The carcasses we deposited in a nearby furnace, each one giving out a little *foof!* as it vaporized up the chimney. The black tom she wisely elected to place in the chamber bushels and all. Only one occupant escaped, a cat that unexpectedly gouged the chamber operator with its claws. The last I saw of it was an orangy blur, streaking for the city limits of nearby Snow Hill.

I RETURNED to the island victorious, but surely no hero. Alice had been too tearful to even talk in school that day, and when she returned to Ewell, she took with her the remnants of the school cats. Like fine dust from a windstorm that takes forever to settle and pervades every crevice, the incident had stirred up a cloud of what the islanders called "nomini," a word they used for bitter backbiting of the sort that can wrack a community. The cat roundup was the first time I had abandoned all pretense of being a neutral observer and taken an action that directly affected the island. Until you jostle a portion of it, you can't imagine how intricate and pervasive is the web of connections amid such a place.

There were pro- and anti-cat factions, muddled further by pro- and anti-Horton factions and pro- and anti-Alice factions; and of course just about everyone in every faction bore some kinship to one another. The nomini grew very intense. The PTA for a time looked as if it might dissolve over the incident, just before its big fundraiser. "Beloved Murn, Rest in Peace," read the message hung in the school beneath a cut-out picture of a cat. Murn, you see, was supposed to have been saved, but a top-secret message to Miss Evelyn to keep him penned up the night before the roundup never got through.

My own son solemnly informed me, just in case I had forgotten, that it was after all "the pride and joy of the whole school" I had done away with. To atone, I paid an exorbitant sum to take three survivors of the massacre, who had been penned the night before, to the vets in Princess Anne and have them spayed (not a moment too soon, as all three proved pregnant with sizable litters). For a time some of the watermen would joke, "Hey Tomcat," when I passed; but they soon recognized it was not a joking matter.

As summer neared, and crabbing pulled the island into its frenzied orbit of round-the-clock work, the nomini seemed to be fading. I was in Baltimore, visiting friends who used to live in the bay islands. Famished, I ordered a large pizza, a rare treat for the water-locked. Something distracted me for a few minutes, long enough for a trio of pet cats to nearly devour the whole pizza. They were hardly housebroken, my friend apologized. He had just brought them up a few days before from Tangier island. I have no doubt, even if it is separated by six miles of water from Smith, that those cats were avenging their Smith Island kin.

JUNE HAS COME; graduation night for the Tylerton Elementary School, and we're all packed inside, standing-room only, given the wide nets of kinship cast by even so small a group of students. Alice is there, acting her old self, arranging kids in gowns, handing out mimeographed sheet music. The PTA, united once again, has supplied plenty of "noogs" (sweets) and other eats. Miss Evelyn is a "crippled sud'ly" (sick duck), subdued by a bladder infection, but has struggled out to watch anyhow.

No one wants to miss these events. Every year now it gets more emotional, what with the population shrinking and no one being born here much any more. Just to see all that remains of the town's youth assembled, and realizing that this could be it, brings tears to people's eyes nowadays. But tonight is a celebration, of the students—of America. Miss Alice has arranged nearly two hours of patriotic songs and recitations, and festooned the building with red, white, and blue. Murn's picture, I notice, is down.

Recounting the school year, Miss Alice, rumored widely to be a Democrat, notes that the school voted for Dukakis 12–3, which causes a few Republican murmurs to the effect that "she led 'em to do that." But Bush, once elected, she soothes the murmurers, "became our man."

This is the last year of two in the Tylerton Elementary School for Tyler and Abby, and Miss Alice lavishes praise on the both of them. And when she and others say they will be missed, you look around that little room, which contains almost all that is and will be of Tylerton, and you know they will be missed to a degree almost impossible in the rest of growing, sprawling, mobile America.

We all sang "Yankee Doodle Dandy," "God Bless America," and shoveled down the noogs. I forgot to look to see whether any cats had gotten in.

The Line

$\mathcal{T}$*HE BOUNDARY* separating Maryland from Virginia, where it crosses Chesapeake Bay, has been adjusted several times since the original charter from England's king to the Lord Baltimore in 1632. Each new tangent has reapportioned the rich seafood grounds lying between Smith Island and its Virginia neighbor, Tangier Island. In 1877, a bi-state arbitration officially settled the line "for all time"—a wishful thought then, and now.

Immutable lines are antithetical to the very nature of the Chesapeake. It is a place where the ocean pushing inland perennially tussles for dominance with the freshwater flowing seaward from forty-odd rivers that collect rainfall from a sixth of the Atlantic seaboard. Daily, Atlantic tides surge the 180-mile length of this indentation of the North American coast. Seasonally, heavy rainfall may strengthen the rivers' hand, hurling the ocean back and turning large sections of the bay favorable to life that likes its water fresh or brackish. Conversely, in dry spells the ocean's advance can extend the range of sea-loving creatures far up into the lands of the drainage basin. This inherent dynamism operates even through the millennia. Several Chesapeake Bays have withered and flowered, as Ice Ages and warmer epochs alternately bind up the seas in polar ice and then release them to flood the continental fringes.

Overlaying, and attuned to, the estuary's comings and goings are the great migrations to and from the bay of fish and crabs, eels and waterfowl, their routes and cycles worked richly into the Chesapeake fabric. In and out, up and down, here and gone—with the tides and the weather and the ages; for the bay, the only constant is flux. And among the islanders, whose very existence resonates with a fluid environment and the quixotic cycling of the estuary, static lines seem dangerously confining.

THE CRABBERS REMEMBER

✦ Once it was Maryland waters nearly five miles south of our towns, all the way down Tyler's Creek from Tylerton to Herring Island [the Maryland-Virginia Compact of 1785]. That has not been so for more than a hundred years. Now the line is drawed right to our back door, and even where you live, you cannot work the water the way you ought. I can look out my window and there are the line markers. It has been a thorn ever since I was a boy, and it makes you hard.

We had a boy shot down there on the line. His name was John T. Evans and he was the youngest son of Mitchell Evans. He was three months short of fifteen, and he had only four or five crabs in his box. He was planning to quit early that day to go a'gall'in [courting] in Crisfield, and he had his good clothes folded under the bow.

The Virginia police boat come up with Captain Buck Savage in command, and commenced to shootin' and struck the boy in the back of the head as he tried to sail back into Maryland. They hauled him layin' in the floor of his crab skiff all the way to Tangier, and when they put him out on the dock there, he was still a'floppin' around like a chicken. The policeman put his boot on the boy's neck to stop him, until a woman of the island come down with a pillow and put his head on that. The cop, they say, lost his mind later, and people said he deserved it.

The next morning was Sunday, the first day of Smith Island's annual Camp Meeting, and it was a sad day. Usually there were visitors from Tangier, but that day there were none. The boy's family was too poor to go to law, and nothing further was ever done about the case, which was murder clear. Years later at a prayer meeting, old Capn' Will remembers turning to the boy's dad, Capn' Mitchell, and saying: "Mitch, you had a hard thing to forgive, have ye done it?" Old Mitch started cryin' and said, "That's the hardest thing I've ever done; forgive a man for killin' my boy over a crab."

When did it happen? Oh, no one alive would be old enough to have seen it. But they still tell it in the store, and if you were to walk in, being from off here, you might think it had just happened. I know there's some don't think it ever happened; like Colonel Wilson—he's the expert on the history of this county. Says it was never in the *Crisfield Times,* and he would know if it happened. Well, that's like Crisfield, to think if it happened on Smith Island, it wasn't important. But you can see the boy's grave where he's buried in the churchyard in Tylerton.

That was not the first time we got into it over the line, and surely to Christ it weren't the last. Around the end of the [First] World War Virginia put a 40-footer, all decked over with cabin, patrolling down there. She was the *Marguerite,* and Tommy Anderton was her captain. There's men here still a'livin' have had Capn' Tommy shoot around 'em with his big old rifle when they crossed below the line, burst water close enough it'd wet 'em. Romey says he went aboard of 'im once and complained he had come mighty close to shooting him. "Go on," Capn' Tommy told him. "If I wanted to hit ye, I'd done it with every shot." And Romey reckons he was right. He was a right good shot, Capn' Tommy.

Anyhow, there come a time when it got pretty hot between the Smith Islanders and the Tangiermen over who was goin' to catch the swimmer crabs which in those days would rise up on the flood tide and come up Tyler's Creek from Virginia through our island. The Tangiermen, if you let 'em, would follow 'em up with their dip nets and catch most of 'em before they could reach into Maryland. Our men would come down across the line and row with 'em. After a few weeks of cussin' and shootin' and fightin' over who would take charge of the creek, Capn' Tommy brought the *Marguerite* up around Horse Hammock, a mile and a half below the line. She was one of the first diesels around here, and she carried a lot of black smoke. You could see her comin' a long way off. I guess he knew he was in for a hard day because at the mouth of the creek there was a sign our men had put out with a black hand painted on it, and the words: "WE ARE GOING TO CATCH SWIMMERS OR DIE."

Some of our crabbers had set up a sort of fort behind a heavy bank of water bushes along the side of the creek. Capn' Tommy fired his cannon at 'em, and they returned the fire with rifles—Krags and Winchesters. Now Capn' Tommy was always a'hollerin' that the state of Virginia was stingy with supplies, and this day we run him out of ammunition. Our men's fire put several holes through his cabin and broke out most of the windowlights. Eulice Thomas, a Tangierman, was aboard the *Marguerite* and later that summer one of our men, Donald Marshall, caught up with him in Crisfield and knocked him cold with one blow. You can talk to Donald's great-nephew, Bill, today, and he can show you just how it happened, Donald putting one hand on Eulice's shoulder, turning him half around and . . . *POW!* After that day in the creek, Capn' Tommy put in a request to the state for a machine gun.

I am only telling you a little bit of all that has gone on over the state line across the bay. It has been fought at various times from the Potomac on the western shore to the Pocomoke on the Eastern Shore. I have heard more than fifty men, Marylanders and Virginians, policemen and watermen, have died over it. ✦

ON THE LINE—SEPTEMBER 1990

May to October is high harvest time for the soft crab in the Chesapeake, which supplies more than 75 percent of the nation's softshells. I met Dave Laird at 4:30 A.M. in his shanty, a weathered plywood and tin-roofed affair, situated close enough to the bay's passage through the island that the tide often rises through the planked floor, forcing him to wear knee boots as he tends his crabs.

Dave is of moderate build, with the sinewy forearms that come from constantly pulling in the heavy metal "scrapes" or dredges that soft crabbers drag in pairs behind their boats. He has lost 20 pounds since scraping began—about average for him between winter and summer, he says. He is considered one of the best crabbers on the island.

His shanty on the outside is unremarkable; but inside it is papered with posters from environmental and animal rights groups to which he belongs. "Farewell the Spotted Owl?" reads an article pinned above the door. "Studying the Diamondback Terrapin," reads another. A classical music magazine, well worn, lies open on a table. "NO HUNTING," reads a big sign on one wall.

He gets kidding, he says, about his outspoken anti-hunting stance in a place where fur trapping and gunning for waterfowl is part of the culture. "But the more I have read and watched public TV, I see what's happenin' to the animals all over the world, and I can't bear it."

The eastern sky is turning the color of a dark bruise as he fires up *Scotty Boy*'s little diesel and eases out onto "main street." The channel is busy at 5:00 A.M., the velvety, warm darkness studded with red and green running lights. Soft crabbers head one way, for the island's grassy, shallow creeks; hard crabbers head the other, out into the main bay. The water is "slick, slatey c'am," waterman's jargon for smooth as glass.

Dave is a good acquaintance, but this is the first time I have asked him to take me out. He confesses he was reluctant. "I seldom want anyone aboard when I am crabbin' because it is something I give my full attention to. When I come aboard here, it's like I take on a different personality. I'm Dr. Jekyll on land, and here I'm Mr. Hyde."

It is half an hour's run to the crabbing grounds in the southern reaches of the island. The sky now is dully luminous with pewters and pearls. Greens, tipped with the merest hint of gold, are beginning to bleed from the dark lines of distant marsh. Sheens of rose and mauve tint the dark, slick water. To the north, the island's three towns are white specks amid the overwhelming horizontality. To the south, the faint blink of a radio tower marks Tangier. The mainland is a smudge in the east, and the western shore is invisible in the summer haze. "Just crossed the line," Dave says, gesturing toward an undistinguished point of marsh. It is very hard to accept the notion that a legal boundary scores this remote and wild scene.

Dave is already rigging a bushel basket to a stout cord. He attaches the other end to a colored cork. This will mark the basket when it is filled with crabs and sunk in the water, safe from inspection by the law. "Just in case," he says cryptically.

As the day unfolded, Dave talked about life with the line:

◆ I am fifty-five and have been crabbing right here for more than forty years. This boat is nearly the same age. Leon Marsh's dad built her for Delmas Tyler in 1937 and my dad took her over a few years after that. Dad would take me out even when I was just a little boy. I never paid no attention to crabs then. I took a big stack of books and read up in that little forepeak. It's hard to remember when I was small enough to fit up there. When Dad had a heart attack in 1957, I took the boat over. She is still good for the job. If you were to put me in a new boat, I don't think I would even know how to crab.

It's nearly always been a war down here on the line. You would think the two states and the two islands mighta worked things out, but in three hundred-some years, they have not. Sometimes I think a waterman just hates a line. Watermen is a good name for us because we aren't just oystermen, or fishermen, or crabbers. We follow the water; we say we're in the water business. We catch whatever we can make a livin' on . . . fish, crabs, terrapins, clams, oysters—ducks, too, before the law got so tight on that.

The bay don't go by lines nor rules that government sets. The last time this line was fixed, it was for oysters. Back then [1877] they wasn't even a'-thinkin' of crabbin'. They say there was a thousand oyster dredge boats in these waters then—big schooners, sail and steam-powered—and they took 20 million bushels out of this bay in a single year; and outta the whole bay there weren't any better rocks [oyster reefs] than right around here.

Oysters, they say, is the reason that line is so jaggedy crossin' the bay and shoots up into our backyards on the island. It looks odd, don't it, how the line turns them sharp corners out in the middle of the water; but it was the bottom that druv it, fightin' over which state got the best oyster rocks. Now the oyster is in bad shape. Last year I don't imagine half a million bushels came out of the whole bay, and very few of them from around here. Disease has done it, and pollution—men's greed has done it, too.

It's the soft crab that's tops around here now, and there's no better place on earth for the crab to shed his shell than these bottoms right here to our island, the places which was give no thought at all by Maryland when it let Virginia have most of it. It was only a little worthless marsh, they thought, and water so shoal [shallow] it wouldn't no more'n float a skiff.

You can run for miles from here to Tangier and see bottom right under your keel near every foot of the way. But that shoal water's what favors the grasses a'growin' on the bottom, and the grass is what the crab seeks for matin' and sheddin' his shell. It don't look like much down here if you only see the water, but that grassy bottom's right full of life.

A crab, o'course, he don't care nary bit for a line. Knowin' the crab as we do, you know you can't say nothin' about what he will do next. You want to be able to move around after him. I very seldom, almost never go crab-bin' up in Holland Straits, which is several miles north of here; but if there was to be a law said I couldn't, well I'd want to overthrow that law so I could go if I ever needed. Around 1978, the pollution from up the bay got so bad we began to lose our grassy bottom here. It was worse than we ever remembered. Clear down to South Point at the end of our island, which was two miles into Virginia, crabbin' was worthless. We had to go further toward Tangier to make a livin'. We wasn't trying to bust no line. We was just trying to crab.

That was when the hell started all up again. That was when Virginia put that crab cop, Juney Crockett, up here to sit all day in his little speedboat and enforce the line. Juney is a Tangierman, but I'll say this about him, that in all these years I've never really disliked him. He's got a good way about him. He'll kick you one day and you'll like 'im the next. If he went into politics, I believe he'd been governor of Virginia. For a while I believe he did the best he could for us. He sorta had his own version of the state line; wasn't on any maps. He'd let us crab to around the end of the island, below the real line; and when he caught you over, lots of times he'd just run you back up, maybe make you dump overboard what you had caught in Virginia.

We spent two years tryin' to get Maryland and Virginia to work out a special crabbing area that would let all of us, Smith Islanders and Tangiermen, share the good bottom. Neither state would hear us. The line was the line, they said. It was like the 55-mile-an-hour speed limit, Juney's bosses in Richmond said; and that meant 55, not 55 and a half, and he was not to allow a Maryland crabber to come a foot over the line. That's when we hired a lawyer and went to federal court, and in 1981 we busted that line, busted it for the first time in 350 years. I was one of the names on the suit. The judge, he was a Virginian, said that crabs moved all around, and watermen must be able to chase 'em. He didn't open it up the same for oysters, though; he said they stayed put and you couldn't cross a line after them.

Well, we thought that would be an end to it. We bought our Virginia licenses just like the Tangiermen and went to crabbin' either side of them poles in the creek that mark the line. You know a lot of the line is marked by buoys, and they used to say there were the strongest tides on earth around here, that could drag those line buoys a mile or more south, or back north, overnight—with a little assist, y'know.

Well, the judge had spoke on the line, but you could just feel them Virginians a'growlin' to themselves down there about us comin' across. And it wasn't long before Virginia put the jimmy crab law on us, and the main reason, no matter what all they may say, was revenge.

Smith Islanders and Tangiermen both are out here mainly to catch the soft crab and the peeler crab, which is a crab that soon will shed his shell and become soft. But Smith Islanders always has saved the big hard crabs they catch in their scrapes. These are mostly jimmies [males]. Bringing the jimmies to our wives to pick is a very important part of our income. Last summer, I don't think without it we would have made it at all. The Tangiermen never has depended on this. Their women don't pick much. I can't say why. But they knew the best way to make it hard on us in Virginia was to outlaw savin' jimmy crabs.

These bottoms between Smith and Tangier seem like the greatest place in the world for the male and female crabs to come together to mate in the summertime. The Tangiermen say if you throw the jimmy back, he will find another wife and fertilize her, and that will mean plenty crabs in the future. Smith Islanders say we have been savin' jimmies for many a year and still there is plenty crabs. And a'course, that same jimmy crab Virginia thinks is too valuable to catch in our scrapes is perfectly legal to catch in all the Virginia crab pots set not 200 yards away from where we are scrapin'. The main purpose of the jimmy law is to keep us from crossin' that line.

Look!

There goes Johnny Carroll, all wrung up [boat moving at high speed], a'headin' back into Maryland to put his jimmy crabs up in the marsh. He may'a caught 'em legal in Maryland earlier this mornin', or maybe not; but now he's below the line, and if ole Juney comes up in his speedboat, he's had it. It cuts into your work somethin' terrible to have to stop and run up to Maryland like that.

Hey!

There goes Don all wrung up for the line. That's his jimmy crabs, them two bushels on the stern, and . . . Dast! There comes Juney, 'shootin' outta Fishing Crick in that speedboat like a little, pesky mosquito. He's closin' fast on Don. Don's not goin' to make Maryland with his jimmies. Jeesu! There he had to dump a whole mornin's work; and there's Juney, turnin' off from the chase. 'Nother half a minute and Don woulda made it. I will say this for Juney, if he sees you dump 'em, he'll let it go at that. But it is aggravatin' that the state of Virginia puts a cop, sometimes two, all day long to sit here in the middle of Chesapeake Bay to spy on a few dozen Maryland crabbers. On top of that, last week they began flyin' the line in a little police plane. One day a bunch of our crabbers climbed atop their engine boxes and dropped trousers and mooned him.

It looks as if Juney's goin' to stay with us awhile today. That'll cost us plenty of jimmy crabs. Last week I hid mine in a bushel I sunk in the water with just a little cork attached by a string to mark her. Damn' if Juney didn't spy it and dump the whole lot. I think where we sunk 'em today will be safe, just above the mouth of Fishin' Crick, where the line runs. So I think I am safe this time . . . now, what the hell? There he goes a'sniffin' around right along the line. He's checkin' every cork he comes to, to see if it's a crab pot or a hid bushel. I know I sunk mine above the line, unless that tide has drug it across. Swagger it ain't been drug!

Weell, if that ain't the champ. That son of a bitch. He has got my jim-mies again!

POSTGAME ANALYSIS

The next day on the marine radio, channel 78, the frequency used by Smith Island crabbers, several voices crackle across the speaker:

What'd Juney do, pull a sneak attack on Dave yesterday?

He wouldn't bother 'em if they were mine. I'd feed him to the damn prop.

Takes your jimmies when you left 'em in Maryland. Naahhh, that's baseball bat time.

I'm crabbin' up north today. Felt like I just wanted to get outta . . . you know, outta the line's jaws for a day or two.

Hey, if them old-time islanders was to come back, Juney'd have water from their rifles bustin' in his face . . . he'd have a shower every day.

Hey, he don't win 'em all. Last week I was a'comin' up the crick around Smith Gut Point and Juney come near, but the tide was a'fallin' and he couldn't float where I could. Oh, he could see three bushels of jimmy crabs lined up across my stern, and it like to drove 'im wild. You could hear his big Merc outboard a'strainin' to push through the mud. Eeeeeeer, Eeeeeeer . . . you could hear her goin' and I hollered, "You ain't a'goin' to make me throw these jimmies over today, old Juney!"

JUNEY CROCKETT, CRAB COP

✦ My name is Peter H. Crockett, Jr., but all the Smith Islanders call me Juney. I was born and raised on Tangier Island. Crocketts have lived there as long as people have been on the island. I ain't a'boastin', but I have been in a little bit of law in my career—fifteen years as policeman for Tangier, inspector, Virginia Marine Resources Commission, deputy sheriff Accomack County, and Virginia Special Game Warden. My one son is sheriff of this county. Another's principal of the Tangier High School. A third is a waterman, like most of my family and neighbors.

I've wrote tickets for my first cousin, for my four brothers; I've wrote tickets for 'em all. If you can't do that, you might just as well forget this kind of work. There are two ways you can be the law in a place that don't always put a lot of store by law, especially when it comes to the water business. My mate, when we are home, he almost never goes out. But I go up to the restaurant, get a sandwich . . . I ain't gonna let anyone keep me in my house. You let it get started and it only gets worse. I told 'em at the restaurant once, damn if you bunch of crabbers feeds Juney. If I want a mess of crabs or oysters to eat, I'll buy 'em. I won't take gifts. One thing I did have to give up that I enjoyed was huntin' ducks. It would be too easy for someone to bait my blind [a hunting law violation] and make trouble.

I have to say we have had a little problem with them jimmy crabs around the line with the Smith Islanders. Did you ever know James Marsh up there before he had a heart attack? Boy, I miss him. He'd change, sort'r, with the full moon. One day he'd be friendly as all get out, and the next day he'd have a little hell in 'im. He had it in his mind that the true line run down to Herrin' Island, which it did from 1785 to 1877, and so he had a lot of run-ins over that.

One day he picked up a propeller shaft and beat the hell outta the side of a police boat. One of his brothers once threatened to chop an inspector's fingers off with a hatchet as he tried to board. Another time I had come alongside to check James, and he was legal, but he reached down anyway for a big mop handle and I commenced talkin' real slow to him. "Now, James," I said, "you know that's the last thing we want, ain't it?" I have a .38 special, but it would be the God's job to pull it. I never have. Finally, James set his stick down.

Now there come a day when I was a'chasin' him, and with that big Merc, I got right up on his stern, runnin' 5,000 [rpm], and him tryin' to make for a shallow ditch in the marsh where my boat couldn't go. There was ten or twelve Smith Islanders a'watchin' it all, and I told my mate, if we don't stop him, we might as well tear up our badges. Right then, James he made a mistake. I was a'circlin' to come up on his port side when he turned right across me, and my bow knocked his motor clean off'n his skiff.

The night before the trial, James called me and said, Juney, can I get a ride to court with ye? I said sure, James, and I told him I didn't mean to knock his motor off. I'll give it to 'im, he wouldn't lie on a witness stand. He said guilty to all counts. He was a good man, and I miss 'im.

That witness stand, there's been more lies told there than anyplace in the world. We caught this young Smith Islander nettin' doublers [mating crabs] while he was on break from some college where he went. Well, he showed up in court dressed up all like a lawyer, suit and sunglasses and carrying this briefcase. Weren't nothin' in the briefcase 'cept the summons we had give him. He told the judge he was just a college boy visitin' home who had gone down to get him a mess of crabs for dinner. Well, it was some mess he had—fifty-seven doubler crabs and twenty or twenty-one soft crabs and two thirds of a bushel of jimmies. 'Course, his daddy always was one of the best crabbers around. We knew it was all over for us when the judge looked at his hands. They were soft and white as a guy's that types all the time, and he was let off clean.

It was 1979 when I was sent up to enforce the state line on crabbin'. I'd sit there and stay right with 'em 'til the last one quit. Early on I was met by eight of those Smith Islanders in their boats. They had me in a diamond shape, big workboats all around my 17-footer, comin' closer and closer. I guess they thought they were gonna run me out of the crick. I told 'em the only way they would do that is to kill me. I called in more inspectors on the radio, and we arrested all eight.

As long as I was able to let 'em go down to the end of their island, chase 'em up sometimes, things was tolerable. But the Tangiermen wanted the line enforced right to the foot. I told 'em the Smith Islanders were goin' to sue, but they'd just cuss me, so I said, let 'er go. I don't believe they ever would have busted the line in court if everybody had let me give 'em a little leeway.

Since 1985, it is outlawin' the jimmy crabs that everybody is hot over. See, if the soft crabbers don't leave enough jimmies there in that grass, the females that are a'comin' there to shed their shells and mate will leave and go somewhere else in the bay. You needn't doubt it. Hell, if you took all the women off these islands, I'd leave, wouldn't you?

My mate gets discouraged about the watermen always gettin' pissed off at us, but I say, hell, if it was yourself, you wouldn't be in a good mood either. Nobody likes to get a ticket. I got no complaints about 'em. They got their job and I got mine, and tryin' to catch 'em is always excitin'.

There's Disco Bill. He can hide jimmy crabs in that little scrape boat so's he can't hardly find 'em hisself. That Denny, boy, he wouldn't save a small [undersized] crab, would he? There's Bobby . . . he's a slick one and you seldom know what he's been up to. Usually, though, I can tell when a man's hidin' crabs. They can't keep still. They talk too much.

I'm sixty-four now, and I hope to do this 'til they tote me off on a stretcher. One thing I dream about is that I would get me an air boat, like they use in Florida, and all them Smith Islanders would be down on the Knoll a'nettin' doublers, thinkin' the tide is so low my speedboat can't get near 'em, and here I would come, skimmin' right across the mud. That wouldn't be no fun. ✦

They found Juney Crockett, dead from a heart attack, in the bottom of his patrol boat on a Sunday in September 1992. He had just busted a Maryland waterman for taking illegal crabs across the state line in Virginia, and was kneeling to steady his hand—the water was choppy—to write out the citation. He was sixty-five. Many crabbers from Smith, Tangier, and Crisfield came to his funeral. He had probably ticketed every one of them.

JUSTIFIABLE HOMICIDE

Coroner's inquest into the death of John T. Evans, the island boy shot on the state line so long ago. The document was found, somewhat deteriorated, in a metal box holding the records of the August 1900 session of the Circuit Court of Accomack County, Virginia.

"In an inquisition held at Tangier before me . . . over the body of John T. Evans, a non-resident there lying dead, the ff: sworn evidence was taken":

"George W. T. Savage of the police boat *Pocomoke:*

"There was frequent rows among the Virginia and Maryland crabbers and some fights. I have tried several times to catch them but couldn't, so on Friday night I went over on the crabbing flats toin [sic] a small batteau with one of my men so as to be there among the crabbers at day break, and I believe I could have captured some of them *had not the Virginia crabbers commenced hollering at them, that gave them warning and they all started to run.**

"By the time they got there [sic] sails up I was tolerably close to them and told to heave to but they would not, so I commenced shooting at them.

"They got flat in their boats and could outsail me so the last one of them I got the nearest to I told him to heave to or I would shoot him. We struck his sail and boat five times. When he saw he was going away from me he said 'shoot, you damned sons of bitches,' and a ball struck him from one of our guns and we went alongside and found him wounded. It was impossible for me to catch him without shooting him as he was in a much better sailing boat and under similar circumstances I would do this same again."

Ruling:
"We, the jury of inquest . . . believe that it was justifiable homicide according to the evidence in the case and done in the line of duty."
[signed] Hanson L. Crockett
L. H. Thomas
Joshua T. Pruitt
T. A. Crockett
Henry W. Crockett
Elisha Crockett

---

*Emphasis mine—the Tangiermen apparently disliked the law even more than their competitive neighbors, the Smith Islanders.

Waterworks

JENNINGS EVANS, RELUCTANT WATER CZAR

◆ It's hard for us to be like the mainland. We know things work over there, and are good and all; but they just don't come out the same way over here. It's interestin' that all the trouble with the government started over our drinking water, because we're about as proud of that as anything. It ended up with the island deciding to vote, for the first time in history, on whether to have our own government. It was something, I guess, that had to be tried, but I wish it had never happened.

We didn't always have such good water. We used to have these little sand wells, just people on their own diggin' far as they could go. You'd bring a bucket home and wait for the sand to settle out. The first artesian well I can remember was 1938. She went clear down to the Magothy aquifer, more'n 900 feet. It is water that fell on mountains to the west of us and seeps down beneath the bay. It was a marvel at the time, an endless flow comin' from a pipe, and was it good! Crabbers for years used to take jugs of it to the mainland when they unloaded their catch, for a little present to the packers there. Our schoolkids today, some of 'em, when they travel overnight, will take water from home, 'cause they can't stand the taste of other places'.

Lora Whitelock, after the war, was the first to hook up his house to the new well. Plumbing just came to him natural. He had a shop, and he could make anything. Others would pay him to hook them up, and some would go together and drill their own wells. That is how Smith Island, which has got less than five hundred people now, come to have eight different water-works. Just a pumphouse and a 1 horsepower electric pump, and two-inch plastic pipe is all they are. It's nothin' fancy; and when something breaks, those on that particular system does whatever it takes to get it going. I have seen 'em hold the whole works together with a roll of duct tape at times. Other times, when there is a leak somewhere, they will tell neighbors, hold off on waterin' your tomatoes, other people need to get their shower. My water bill—every waterworks sets its own charges—used to be a dollar a month, but lately, like everything else, it has gone up, to nearly $25 a year. Most people pay their share, but you've always got a few that you've got to go get it from. If we know somebody can't pay, then we just give 'em the water free. I remember a hot meeting about one old man, whether he couldn't pay, or he just wouldn't pay. They decided he wouldn't, even if he could, but that he probably couldn't, and that was the end of it.

We had all been going along pretty good for about fifty years that way when the EPA and the state health department around 1989 decided we needed help. We began to get these letters about the Safe Drinking Water Act, and about new standards for benzene and chlorine and vinyl chloride, and how our monitoring was inadequate and our system was marginal, and they were talking about fines and lawsuits if we didn't come into line. It don't make you feel good when you see yourself named in letters like that as "respondent," and all you are is the one that volunteers to check the water pump from time to time.

It seemed like it bothered the health people most that they didn't have someone official to deal with. One time they came down, nice people too, and asked who was in charge, was the waterworks incorporated, what was their rate structure, and all that. I explained the situation, and the eight companies:

There was Allen's restaurant, where he brings the tourists off his big boat, that's one waterworks just by itself. The town of Tylerton is 108 people, and being off alone, separated by water from Ewell and Rhodes Point, has got its own pump. The Methodist church there handles the costs when they collect for the community fund once a year. Rhodes Point is another eighty-eight people, and it is divided into two waterworks, upper and lower. Where the dividin' line is, I told 'em they would have to check in Rhodes Point. Ewell, which has got 244 customers, has got five water companies. There's Ewell waterworks, the biggest; Hill waterworks is around what they call "Over the Hill." You can't really see the hill; it is just a little ridge around the church, and when the tide comes up high, it is about the last spot of land to get covered. Now the Capital waterworks—you know sometimes we joke that Ewell is the capital city of Smith Island—is down by Junior Evans's and has only got five more people than the minimum size the drinking water laws cover. At one of the meetings we had, somebody said it might be easier if the people on Capital just shot five of themselves so they could get on with their business. Then there is the Field, which is the area they call "Down the Field" here; and finally, I told the health people, there's Dicky and Otis and them, and if they got a name for their company, I couldn't remember it.

What it come down to, the state proposed a modern system to serve each of the three towns. It would cost $3 million, which is about $7,000 for every man, woman, and child on here. They would help us get grants to pay for it. They said there was no reason the island had to be any different from the rest of the country. They said once it was installed, it would be a "fifty-year" solution. We told 'em the way this island's washin' away in places, it didn't seem like there'd be many here to enjoy a water system in fifty years. A letter was sent by islanders to the *Crisfield Times* that said: "We feel like the man adrift on the ocean for many days without water, who said, 'water, water everywhere, but not a drop to drink,' except Smith Islanders are saying, 'water and money everywhere, but not a dime to keep our island from shrinking.'"

It didn't help a bit that we had already been down the same road with our sewer system. The state and federal government in the 1970s spent about $1.5 million to build us two fine new sewage treatment plants. At the time, a lot of septic systems weren't working too good, and many people thought it was a good idea. What the government didn't figure on is what saltwater and high tides do to equipment out here. And what we didn't know is that they figure on the number of people growing to keep the rates down. We've probably lost two hundred people since those plants was built. And now we've got the highest sewer rates in this county.

Well, the government wrangled every way to get us to do a new water system, and we wrangled every way to get out of it. It looked like it was either gonna be we do something ourselves, or have it rammed down our throats by the county, which was then being ordered around by the state to take action. Nobody wanted to give up control of our water. It would be a lot easier, the state said, if we would get incorporated. It seemed like the rest of the world could deal with us a lot easier that way. Meantime, we had formed the Committee for Smith Island Affairs, which was nine of us men from the three towns. Nearly all were steady members of the church, which is about as close as we got here to government. We held a meeting and drew up a ballot, sent to every home on the island. This was in August 1990.

We asked two questions: Should the island incorporate, with elected officials, or be left the way it is? And should we have a government-operated water system, complying with all rules and regulations of the Maryland Department of Environment, or be left the way it is?

The way the vote went, it weren't a complete whitewash. Some people figured a new system would mean swimming pools and a golf course and enough pressure to put showers in on the second story. But "leave it like it is" won, 230 votes to 3. It was the first vote on government in our history, and I imagine it'll be the last. I think the idea of one citizen telling another what to do after all these years was just too much.

The Committee on Smith Island Affairs still exists, but it is near 'bout dead since the water vote. We did work it out where Sally, one of our crabbers' wives, does some monitoring of the wells every month. Our rates on my water system has gone up to $40 a year to pay for that. A couple of the water companies already has dropped out of it, and so far the government has not come against 'em. A few months ago I got a letter from the EPA. It was announcing new monitoring requirements under federal Phase II and Phase V regulations of the drinking water laws for sixty-two organic and inorganic chemical compounds. ✦

Christian Outlaws

ROMEY SMITH

✦ In my grandfather's time and before, the foundations of this island were the oyster rocks of Tangier Sound. It was one of the greatest oyster places in all the world, I would guess. But by this century, big dredge boats from as far off as New England had destroyed a lot of those rocks—and part of what was left had been give to Virginia when they redrew the state line [in 1877]. It meant us islanders had to forage for a living, wintertimes, throughout the bay.

When I was a young man, in the 1930s, about the only place we could make a livin' oysterin' was in the Potomac, which lies—the mouth—almost twenty miles run from here. Once there was oysters in that river nearly up to Washington, D.C. Even in my youth I believe that river had more oyster bars than the rest of the whole Chesapeake Bay. Oh, just the names of 'em take me back: Kettlebottom, Swan Point, Roses Creek, Machodak, Under the Guns, Nomini Lumps, Chiseltine . . . I could go on a while.

There was a period when neither the Maryland nor Virginia cops was too serious about stopping us from dredgin' there under engine power. The laws that governed the Potomac, and a lot of the other bay rivers, said you were limited to taking oysters with a pair of hand tongs, which is the same gear the wild Indians were usin' when white people come to this place. Out here on this island, you couldn't afford to run that far for no more'n what you could get with tongin'. So we would dredge, and the cops would sorta tell us, we'll be comin' out there about such-and-such a time, and we'd finish up by then, and it worked all right.

But it didn't last, and in the 1940s, with the price of oysters soarin', and both states disputin' one another over the river, there come a fierce crack-down on dredges in the Potomac. That's when us islanders shifted to workin' at night, just like the black ducks done with their feedin' habits once people got to hunting 'em so hard. We'd pull out of here about the edge of dark and run an hour or two to where the rocks was at. Sometimes there'd be ten or twelve boats workin' all night right together.

We'd rig a ten-quart bucket, upside down, with a light bulb screwed up inside it, and run to a wire off the engine battery. It would give just enough light to cull the oysters, but a police boat couldn't see nothing unless he was right alongside. We would all carry a big, sharp knife to cut our dredge rope in case the police caught us. Without the evidence, they couldn't do much. One night, they came up to one of the island men and got a gun on him before he could cut his line. All the other boats ran away, but we circled them once and the police—see, he wasn't sure what we might do, and he let 'em go.

Another time, the police come up and threw their grapple hooks onto the same fellow's boat. Well, he went to cut their grapple line, but this time they had chain. A lot of us carried rifles aboard, and he bent down, like he was a'reachin' for something under his washboard. The police boat's mate saw that and hit him smack in the face with a big bucket of ice-cold water. It was a good thing for the mate the man didn't have a gun aboard that night.

When I got shot was in the 1960s, and it was during night dredging up a river off the Tangier Sound. The cops put a light on me and got a man on the bow and began shootin', both of us runnin' full speed. What he was trying to do was to shoot my engine out. I wasn't about to let that happen, and I got between the cop and my engine, to protect it. That's when he got me in the shoulder. It wasn't 'til they threw us in jail in Princess Anne that night that I think they got a little scared and decided to take me to the hospital up to Salisbury.

That was one of the last years of dredging at night. The state finally broke it up. They took boats away from people and shot at us; put us in jail and hit us with big fines. They were determined, and they beat us. The scientists say oysters is nearly gone now from the Potomac, but I know better. I guarantee we could find 'em again if they would let us dredge; but the law will never allow it.

I consider myself a Christian, but I never felt bad about breakin' any law that forbids you to make a living. The Bible says abide by the laws of the land as far as within you lie. Now, I take that passage to mean that, if it is unbearable, and takes away your ability to make a living, it's not so wrong to do what you have to do to survive. So many of these laws that have kept Smith Islanders from crossing state and county lines for more'n a century, we have found out in recent years, when we went to court, was unconstitutional all along. Most of my life, we had the greatest time, just makin' a living. ✦

Peanut Man

BAIN BRADSHAW AND LUCY, HIS WIFE

✦ Lucy: Smith Island has always been gettin' in trouble over ducks, and I don't know why, because nobody ever did waste none over here, which would be a crime.

Now Bain, he thinks everybody born was naturally honest and square, and he would invite a rattlesnake in for dinner. And one day he comes home from Crisfield with this man who is lookin' for a place to room, a salesman sellin' peanuts, he said.

I had an old coil refrigerator back then and I was cleanin' it, and I had been workin' in crabs and had my old crabby dress on, barefoot. And I said, I'm not runnin' no boardin' house and you're not a'stayin' here. Oh, I thought even then he had a sneaky-peeky look to 'im.

But noooo. Come right on in, says ole Bain. Well, we put 'im up, and Bain and Francis, our son-in-law, they took him out on the bayside fishin'— on the Sabbath, which we never done—and they loaded him up with rock-fish long as your arm.

And eat! Why he went for them rockfish and dumplin's I made that night same as a hog; boy, that bastard could wad it in. Well, before long he says, hey, is there some way we can get some ducks—claimed he wanted 'em for a friend in the hospital in Cambridge. I said, listen, Bain, don't you get him ducks. We got no ducks, we don't catch no ducks, we don't tangle with ducks.

Oh, why sure, says Bain, we can get a mess down t'Tylerton; and him and Francis went down and got a mess from Billy Smith, who was a'catchin' 'em. Bain never even saw them ducks, but he went along. Francis paid $7 for them.

Well, when it come time for him to leave, Bain wouldn't charge that peanut man a brownie. Our little girl wanted a transistor radio, and he give her $20 and said that's for that radio for Christmas. We put it in the Bible to keep.

And we saw 'im no more that winter. Then in April, Bain was just back from oysterin' up the bay, and right around daybreak—it was rainin' and a'blowin'—come a knock, two men at the door with guns all strop around their hips.

I was a'swellin' up, mad, 'cause I knew they wasn't here for no good, but oh, yes indeed, come on in, come right in, says Bain. Well, they just set there and wouldn't say nothin' straight, and finally I said, "Stop a'yarnin', what are ye here for?"

And then he hands Bain this summons. It was a paper he couldn't understand, but I looked at it and said, "My dear God, the name on here ain't the same, but this is that peanut man." Noooo, says Bain. But it was.

Bain: They carried us to Salisbury—we had to tow them actually, 'cause it had breezed up too much for their little boat to cross. The states attorney there advised us to get a lawyer. Charged with sellin' ducks, we were.

Well, Millard Tawes from Crisfield was gov'ner of Maryland then, and we growed up together, drank whiskey together, you know, and he lined us up with his campaign manager, this big-shot lawyer in Balt'mer, Herbert R. O'Conor. Take 'im a box of soft crabs, Millard said, and that's what we done.

We got up there to the [arraignment], in the federal courthouse in Balt'mer, me and Francis, and this is what I told that judge: Your honor, I always been taught to treat everybody alike and help those come to me in trouble, but if that peanut man come to my home like he did this past fall, I'd give 'im these five bones right in the eyes. We fed 'im, cooked for 'im, took 'im fishin', and give 'im the best bed in the house, and this is how he's treated us.

Asbury Tyler, lives down the road, he was there, and he said Billy Graham couldn't told a better story than I told on that stand; but I weren't scared up there one item in the world. I mean, I went aboard of that thing; I said, Judge, do you believe there's a just God? He said, why? I said if there is, he'd kill that peanut man a'settin' right there.

That ole judge, he said, I can't find these boys guilty, and we thought that was all there was to it. But them feds got a new judge and a new trial, and they told our lawyer if we'd plead guilty, they'd go light on us. Francis, he pled guilty. I said I wouldn't do that for every son of a bitch in Balt'mer City. Before it ended we were both out 100 bucks apiece.

It was maybe the next year after that and Lucy was here, and I brought a man by, it was Eddie Smith from North End, and Lucy knew him, but she didn't recognize him, and she said, he's not a'comin' in, and she wouldn't let him in. Well, that's what that peanut man did to us. ✦

CHURCH

Church

"And it came to pass . . . the whole Peninsula was the garden of the Lord."

—*JOHN LEDNUM, A History of the Rise of Methodism in America* (1859)

"by Thursday, you can feel Sunday coming on."   —*AN ISLAND TEENAGER*

THE CIRCLE'S CENTER

IN THE LATE 1730s, across the southwest of England, John Wesley, in open fields, graveyards—wherever crowds could assemble—began preaching the new theology known as Methodism to an enthusiastic working class. From this place and time and social group came families who would settle Smith Island; and it is at least possible some had a glimpse of the religion that would define the island as much as its seafood and marshy isolation. Nearly three centuries later, John Wesley might recognize here, more than any place, practices of the faith he launched.

Wesley sent missionaries like Francis Asbury to America a few years before our War for Independence in 1776. It was a time when no more than 5 or 10 percent of Americans belonged to any church; a time of widespread bawdiness, drinking, and lawlessness in regions like the rural Delmarva Peninsula and the Chesapeake islands off its mainland. In those days, "unchurched" meant more than lapsed attendance, as a Methodist missionary discerned in 1778, on his way into the county encompassing Smith Island. He asked a settler: did he know Jesus Christ? The man replied that he was familiar with neither the name nor where the man might live. At that time, the arrival of the first Bible on Tangier Island was a recent memory; and the first copy had yet to make its way to neighboring Smith.

Arguably, Methodism caused more of a revolution than the Revolution itself on the isolated peninsula. The establishment religion of the period, Anglicanism, was tepidly ritualistic, catering to the gentry, with a clergy often indulgent in drink and gambling. Methodism was a fresh wind sweeping through the region's farms, pine forests, and marshes. Its ministers often were as unrefined as most of their audience. They preached with such vigor they were labeled "enthusiasts" by critics. Their Methodism opposed drinking and the sale of liquor, as paths to economic and spiritual ruin. The new religion's emphasis on hard work, frugal living, material sharing, and community support appealed to the pioneer masses; especially to women (white ones at least), who were allowed liberal participation in the church's heavy weekly schedule of services and duties. Another strong tenet of early Peninsula Methodism was its belief that local citizens, through their faith, could do a far better job than government in running their lives ("Amen!" I can hear modern-day islanders saying to all the above).

Neither did early Methodism mince words about heaven and hell. A telling comparison to the Anglican message comes from William H. William's *The Garden of American Methodism—The Delmarva Peninsula, 1769–1820.** An Anglican rector, debating the afterlife with an itinerant Methodist circuit rider, said he had "hope, as all Christian people had, of being saved, and that was all any of us had." The Methodists preached no such weak-flavored "hope," no purgatory to be prayed out of; rather, unadulterated, eternal, salvation—or damnation. When death came, or the end of the world, you were either shipping out for paradise or sinking into sulfurous, bottomless hellfire.

Not surprisingly, the Methodists placed a great deal of emphasis on converting souls. Also on "class meetings," personal testimony of the most soul-baring nature; and on revivals, especially the great "camp meetings" that began in Kentucky around 1800 and rapidly spread back east to Delmarva and its islands. Unlike the "once elect, always elect" doctrine of the equally fire-and-brimstone Calvinists, Methodism saw life as an unending struggle for earthly perfection, with a constant need to prevent backsliding and revive the spirit in those fallen from grace.

That all this struck a special chord on Delmarva is clear: within a couple decades of the Revolutionary War, Methodists on the sparsely populated peninsula had risen from near zero to 10,000; and in 1784, it was reckoned that one in every three Methodists in America lived on the Delmarva Peninsula. Truly, the seeds had been planted that would make the region Methodism's "garden."

Nearing the twenty-first century, Methodism remains a dominant religion there, albeit evolved to suit the lifestyles of a more comfortably suburban flock. Long gone are the class meetings and camp meetings. The opposition to alcohol is much softened, as is the evangelical style of preaching and emphasis on conversion and healing. Methodism on the island, however, has retained more of its original vigor and flavor. Even the early circuit riders who carried the faith are preserved, symbolically, in the preacher who travels each Sunday by boat

*(Wilmington, Del.: Scholarly Resources, Inc., 1984).

among the island's three towns and their congregations. Methodism remains Smith Island's only religion; but it is uncommon to see an islander move off and join a mainland Methodist parish. They are more at home in the evangelical churches that have proliferated in recent decades across the adjacent mainland.

Churches dominate the island physically, and have influenced its human geography. They are the tallest buildings, erected upon the highest ground. Their white steeples, catching the light, often are the first sights of habitation seen by visitors as they cross from the mainland. A fateful decision was made in the 1890s not to build a central church, but to have one in each of the three communities. Perhaps the island's three islands of people eventually would have coalesced, had they chosen to anchor themselves spiritually in one place. As modern-day Smith struggles to retain people and maintain its infrastructure, a centralized populace would, in hindsight, have been more viable, though perhaps not so rich in character.

On their inside, island churches are exceedingly well cared for. They seem even more of a sanctuary, a refuge, than mainland houses of worship. Perhaps it is the contrast between a place so roughly exposed to sun and tide, weather and insects, and the warm polished woods, red carpeting, flower-bedecked altars, and high, airy interiors illuminated through stained glass. Central air conditioning helps, too.

It is difficult to speak of church on Smith Island as something separate or discrete. Emotionally, socially, economically, and governmentally—through most any lens you might use—church is too tightly interwoven with the rest of local existence to unravel. It is the center of a place that by virtue of its watery surrounds, is inherently centered—the innermost point of a tight circle, including and enveloping—also radiating a security and constancy that seem particularly comforting in a place so dependent on nature's vicissitudes.

The church in Tylerton where we lived was funeral home and wedding chapel, social hall and meeting and feasting place. Santa Claus knew his way to the church basement meeting hall at Christmas, and Cupid on Valentine's Day. Locally produced plays and pageants and musical reviews filled the place with reverence at times, hilarity and rambunctiousness at others. There was not a soul in town who had not eaten their weight in crabmeat many times over at annual watermen's banquets and other dinners there.

Cheri and I had never been in a church where the people so freely and simply stood and spoke to God, or wrestled, in front of us all, with understanding His word. In the course of their lives, the place became as personal and familiar as their own home. Often we would accompany guests to the church, and an islander would get up and say something about them, and how glad they were to have them visit. It sounds a small thing to write it, but there was an earnestness and openness, a caring in this simple act that never failed to touch strangers deeply. This gentle goodness of the islanders often formed an odd contrast with the services based on the Book of Revelation and other apocalyptic themes, which they also loved.

The church gloried in its children, bringing them all down front each Sunday for a special, brief service. Just the sight of what represented virtually the entire future of Tylerton, arrayed across the altar, never failed to touch our hearts. During the rest of the service, kids were allowed considerable latitude to squirm and scribble and otherwise fend off boredom, as long as they remained fairly quiet. A steady diet of candies and Life Savers, pushed into little mouths, seemed the universal pacifier.

The religious schedule occupied up to six days a week, only Mondays being generally exempt (and no guarantee of that). Sunday was testimony, followed by Sunday School, church, and evening church. Bible study, men's and women's prayer groups, evening services, and choir practice rounded out the week.

All this is not to say every islander was absorbed in churchgoing. The island had its complement of Easter and Christmas attendees, and non-attendees. It grappled, like most churches, with ways to interest its youth. There was also a less obvious but potentially destructive tension between the main body of parishioners and a hard-core minority who would have the church disavow worldly ways with even more fervor. A few years before we arrived, a thoughtless preacher had caused this to erupt, seriously fragmenting island society—all over Santa Claus.

Christmas on Smith Island is not just a major holiday and religious observance. It is also a homecoming, perhaps dating from the great era of oyster dredging, when men who had been gone for weeks returned. For as long as anyone can remember, a high point of the holiday has been the gala of Christmas songs and speeches put on by the children of the island in the church basements. People who never set foot in church all year attend. One Christmas in Tylerton, jammed shoulder to shoulder with islanders, I estimated that all but three of the town's residents were there—everyone who could walk, literally, and a couple that couldn't. The capstone of the evening was always the entrance of Santa Claus, with presents for the kids.

The preacher at the time, actually a student preacher, had declared that it was irreligious to allow the secular presence of Santa in the church building. Furthermore, Santa was a lie, and kids should not be deceived. To this upsetting revelation, the majority of churchgoers quietly (and a few not so quietly) said no thank you; but some of the more devout seized on the opportunity, and managed to evict Santa and the Christmas event to another site. Far worse, some of the children in Tylerton, told by their parents that Santa was a big lie, promptly passed the message on to every child in the school. They were devastated, and parents were outraged. Family was set against family, and Christmas lost some of its luster. It took several years, and the preacher's unlamented departure, before the split healed somewhat and Santa once more made his way to the church basement.

But no matter what your views or your attendance record, you could not exist on Smith Island in isolation from the church. The funerals, the weddings, the good food, discussions of the island's future—somehow, someday, all islanders knew they would be drawn into the center of the circle, if only through burial in one of the three churchyards, where every grave is laid out east-west, to align with Jesus' Second Coming.

"You are starting out, sitting way up there in the back," I heard an island woman tell the teenagers of Tylerton as she led a service one evening. As they grew older, she said, they would take their places as adults and then elders, occupying pews progressively closer to the front. "And the day will come," she intoned, slapping the altar rail, "when you'll move right up here, laid out in your coffin before all your neighbors." It gave pause to the chattering teenagers, and seemed not such a bad way to measure one's passage through life.

PASTORS

✦ I couldn't say there has been great competition within our Methodist Conference for the job of Smith Island preacher, what with the low salary and the isolation and lack of so many opportunities taken for granted on the mainland. One minister came with his fiancée a few weeks before he was to begin, and nearly as soon as they regained the mainland, she broke the engagement. It can be hard on ministers' wives in such a small place that looks to the church for everything from its spiritual needs to its street lighting. But for me, it was always a love affair with this island, and I think most who have preached here have felt that.

The people really do feel closer to God, they not having any industry except the crabbing and the oysters and the fish; and working always just a slip of the foot or a loose bottom plank away from disaster, or death. They trust utterly in God to give them the abundance of the sea, and to protect them in the storm. "Steady reap, never sow": you will hear them say that a lot, and it is a basis for faith. They see themselves like farmers who never plant, just harvest; harvest seafood in cycles of glut and scarcity they have no control over. It makes them humble, makes them sure there's got to be a bigger scheme of things than they can see.

When you think about it, everything they do to survive—pull up crab pots, pull up oyster tongs, pull in nets and scrapes—what will they catch; each pull is a little act of faith, repeated a hundred times a day, all their lives.

A very good experience for islanders in the church continues to be the class meeting, testimony held early Sunday mornings before church and Sunday School. It is where they give their experience of what God has done for them, and how much they love and depend upon their neighbors. Some people who see it for the first time say it is like an encounter group, or therapy. It is as old as the Methodist Church and was begun by John Wesley himself. It comes from what Jesus said. *"Confess me before men and I will confess before the Father in Heaven; but if you do not confess me before men, I will deny you before the angels in Heaven. . . . "* They still take that seriously here.

Class meeting can start early, around sunup sometimes, when the soft crabs are shedding heavy and people must go to fish them up. Originally, they were for men only, and it is still men who mostly attend, though women are welcome. It's a time when they can express emotions, cry, show feelings they wouldn't usually show to others in the rest of their lives. You will have one or two leaders of the meeting, watermen, who will walk up and down the aisles of the church, speaking softly:

Am I worthy of leading; Lord knows, I don't feel like a leader,

And one will set out a theme; and it could be anything, the simplest things:

Gnats and skeeters and scarce crabs . . . got to be a better world beyond this; somebody speak on't.

And then a waterman will rise and praise God, and tell how he tore himself away from the only good crabbing he found all week, to help a neighbor whose boat had gone aground. It ended his workday, but lucky it did, because when he got home he found a float [holding tank] full of prime crabs had got its drain stopped up and was about to overflow, and all the crabs would have escaped.

Then one of the leaders will come back in:

Some mornin's you pull your pots and got thirty to forty doublers in the first one; other times your pots are all empty, drug way down the bay by ships that caught on 'em. Well, you praise the Lord just the same both mornin's.

And there will be a rumble of "amens" and "uh-uhs" and "tell it, brothers."

Give the Lord the praise he deserves ALL the time.

As the bay's oysters have declined, you may hear a tonger stand, just anguished:

I am going back up the bay tonight, but I really don't know why. What's to become of us if the winters get any worse?

Or a crabber will get up, hesitating, and a leader will go to him, and listen close, 'cause he's speaking real soft and low, his voice trembling:

I got catherized [sic] to Salisbury last week. It was the hurtin'est thing I ever had done. I can stand the pain, but . . . four in my family died of heart attacks already.

Pray for me.

And another:

You all know how scarce crabs has been. I needed to buy some medicine for my sugar [diabetes] and an inhaler for my asthma last week, and I kept two bushels that wasn't legal.

It was wrong, but I felt like I had to do it. The law give me a ticket. Now I'm goin' to court next week, and I'm about to lose my mind worrying.

You did what you had to. Amen.

And each testimony ends with the leaders clasping the witnesser's hands, placing their own hands on his shoulder, and others around him will come over to offer handshakes, or sometimes a hug.

Bless you.

Pray for me.

It is very reinforcing, and one of the most touching things you will ever see, these strong, tough watermen reaching out to one another.

Sometimes the prayers can get right to the point. Once, they prayed over moss. The crab potters had a kind of algae, a moss they called it, that was clogging their pots and making the crabs shy away. A couple days after the prayers, you could hear them talking on their CB radios; the moss had gone away.

If testimony is slow, someone will spontaneously break into a hymn. Sometimes a man will just get wound up, talking, and you know, they don't have all day. They say an old captain, Lacey Wes, told such a long story in class meeting about going to the western shore and coming back across the bay to Tylerton with a load of wood that finally, to shut him up, they just began a hymn—"sung 'im down," they call it when they do that. Cap'n Lacey said later he didn't mind, but he wished they had at least let him get back to the head of Tyler's Creek.

They back their faith here with their money, hard-earned every penny. It would amaze you the sums that go through the churches in this little place. It amazed even the islanders when several years ago a most unfortunate oc-currence tested their faith and forced them to take stock of their finances. Let me explain first how the money comes in.

Besides the church upkeep and our normal contributions to missions and to the Conference, there is a lot goes to what government might do in other places—water systems, street lights, doctor's house, the needs of residents who are having a hard time. The church has even lent money to the fire depart-ment. This form of "taxation" is getting to be a problem now that we have so many outsiders taking up houses here. Some give and many don't, and perhaps don't even realize that it is through church funds that a lot of com-munity services are maintained.

We take up offerings at most services, like other Methodist churches, but a lot of people here tithe, give a tenth of their incomes. In Ewell and Rhodes Point, money is also collected through "preacher's call," where youth volunteers call on every household for donations. My recollection during my time there is that only two homes didn't give something to that collection. It was not something I ever looked at, the list of who gave and who didn't. My charge was to minister freely to one and all, and I didn't want to know who was giving what. Money here ebbs and flows with the seafood. In summertime, when crabbing is big, preacher's call was every Sunday. In the winter, because oystering has fallen away so bad, it cuts back to every other Sunday.

In Tylerton, it was a source of some pride that they had never needed preacher's call to keep their church in the black, even though the population there, in recent years, has got down to a hundred folks or less. So it was a shock to them when they found one year they had to borrow to pay bills. Some of the leaders there had a suspicion for a few years that something was not quite right. "That ole devil's workin' against us . . . we know people are giving, but we can't seem to get ahead," they would say. Maybe they even suspected what was happening, but could not bring themselves to point fingers.

It got so bad it finally forced an examination of the church's books. Accounting had been handled fairly casually up until then. Later, folks would say they felt so stupid for being so trusting. That was a sad thing to hear. One of their own, a church member in a position of great trust, had been diverting money from the church's accounts—everything from the remodeling fund to seafood dinner proceeds to the memorial fund for a drowned teenager, nothing had not been raided. When they began to add up the losses, I think it astounded them all: as much as $40,000 had disappeared in one year alone, a good year for crabbing, some recalled. All told, it looked like $100,000 or more was gone in just a few years' time. So much involved cash, no one will ever be certain of the true amount. The church decided not to bring the matter to the courts. It was not a unanimous decision; maybe not even a popular one. It probably played a role in at least one family moving off. A portion of the theft was made good, but most is gone forever, and no evidence of where or how it was ever spent. The guilty one still lives here, and someday maybe will talk about it.

Some of the emotional scars from that dark deed may never heal, but financially, people dug right in. Within a year, the Tylerton church had paid off its debts, lent money to the bigger church in Ewell, and showed a checking account balance of $38,000. They said the church took in close to $90,000 in that year.

So you can see that church is not just a weekend thing on Smith Island. Even when the island must deal with the mainland, which seems to be more and more, it has usually been leaders in the church who are chosen to represent us. They will be called "the Committee for Smith Island," or something appropriately secular; but they are churchmen. I think this has been mostly good, but it has had the effect of cutting people out of the political process if they were not involved in the church.

Of course the preacher in such a place has always had a good deal of power. When I first served the island, there was a fellow who was selling beer on the island to young people. I kept complaining about it, and one Sunday in the church, one of the old heads said, "Well, you're the boss. You call a meeting and we'll do whatever you say." So I did, and the trustees listened and said, let's go see the man and tell him he has got two weeks to stop it or he'll have to get off the island. And so, we went to him, and in two weeks he was gone. But I don't think you could get the backing to do that now.

So much has changed in the last twenty to thirty years. People were shocked around 1978 when one of the youth died from huffing PAM in a plastic bag; and it was around then that I am told marijuana was first brought to Tylerton. People didn't even know how it smelled before then. Now you have got some kids and young people here with cocaine nosebleeds. It is not as bad as the mainland, but it is not like it used to be, either. The main drug here is just what it always was, alcohol, but it is so much more open and widespread now. And all the church people want to get rid of these problems, and it is all right if the minister preaches on it, and gets them fired up on it a little bit, but then they go down to the store and talk about it for a few days, and then it dies out. The courage to take a real stand doesn't seem to be there. I think it is partly because so many people here are related, and to take stern measures against liquor nowadays might put almost anyone up against someone in his family.

What a sermon on the abuses of liquor the island might hear if Joshua Thomas were to come back and see it now! He was the greatest Methodist among all the bay islands, present at the first meeting of the new religion ever held here. That was in 1808 in the home of "King" Richard Evans, at Fog Point. From that time nearly until his death in 1853, he would sail the length and breadth of Tangier Sound, preaching and ferrying other preachers. At the sight of the twin sails of his log canoe, the *Methodist*, the Sons of Temperance here would unfurl their flag from the church steeple, and a crowd would gather no matter what the time of week. He grew up on Tangier Island, knowing well the devastation alcohol can work on a family. His stepfather's drunkenness and neglect kept the family in poverty. The man would force his young sons to help him steal fish at night from neighbors' lines. He eventually drowned.

Joshua attended his first Methodist meeting on the mainland in 1807, and you can imagine how he must have been drawn to its strong support of temperance and industry. He was also struck by the joyful singing, which is still so big a part of the Methodist Church.

He was a simple man, the stories say; not much of a reader, nor possessed of the booming voice much prized in those days of preaching to crowds along the shores or under a great tent. In everyday conversation he was a stammerer. But no man ever had more fun in the pulpit than Joshua Thomas. He was a mover and a shaker, literally, a fine dancer and an exhorter who is said to have often "shouted himself happy." And as an excellent waterman himself, he was great for mixing fishing and sailing and everyday experiences at home and work in with his preaching. He'd be received well on Smith Island even now.

His role in the British assault that failed to take Baltimore in 1814 is not nearly so well known as the song by Francis Scott Key that the fight inspired ["The Star-Spangled Banner"]; but for Joshua's sermon to the British before the battle, I wonder whether Key would have had such a proud tune to write. Their forces had been camped on the beach at Tangier, and Joshua was commanded to give them a farewell blessing. He stood there and told that mighty force, "Thou shalt not kill"; that "you will never take Baltimore." It was not just brave talk, either. He was aware that thousands of Methodists in Baltimore were praying hard against the invaders. I believe his words came from a deep faith; and delivered by such a man, had a great effect on those soldiers.

You will still hear Joshua Thomas stories in the islands. An older man told me how Joshua was able to walk across a mudflat with white socks on and not get either one soiled—that one even beat walking on the water, the old fellow thought. Then there was the sick man whose doctor said he needed to have a good fish to get well; but the whole Sound was frozen over, and no fish likely until spring. Joshua told him, come on, we'll go down and catch you one, and he punched a hole in the ice and right off pulled in a big rock [striped bass].

The main way Joshua Thomas's spirit lives on is through what we call the Camp Meeting, which began as a sort of tent revival. It was at such a meeting near Pungoteague, Virginia, that he found Methodism in 1807; and a year later he began a meeting on Tangier, and worked to spread them throughout this region. That period was when a lot of the names of places you see on old charts of Tangier Sound changed: Devils Island became Deals, Damned Quarter became Dames Quarter; and our own Rhodes Point went from being Rogues Point.

The Camp Meeting by 1857 was fading from mainland Methodism, but it still occupies a full week here in late July and early August, and it is the high point of the island's religious year. It is a combination of spiritual revival, entertainment, feasting, and the whole island coming together in a way it seldom does any more. It is a pretty sight, of a summer morning or evening, to see the marsh creeks humming with little skiffs and workboats carrying families, all dressed for church, to and from the tabernacle in Ewell.

The tabernacle will seat more than the population of the island, for a lot attend from the mainland, including politicians from all around the state. It is used just for Camp Meeting, nothing else, and for over a century has been located in a grove of pines and oaks between the graveyard and the ballfield. The original burned on an October Sunday in 1937, in the great fire that also destroyed the church. It is cool and restful inside, with a high roof and screens all around. The floor is sawdust, and some of the old people recall a time when they strewed it with wild grass cuttings, which they say smelled so good. Originally, people spent the whole week in tents gathered around the campground. That gave way to permanent wooden cabins and sleeping aboard boats. A wooden picket fence used to surround the whole place, and there would be ice cream and lemonade stands, even a barber and shoeshine stand, set up to accommodate the people. Nowadays, with modern transportation, the camping part is gone, and it's just the tabernacle there; but it is still a scene to behold.

A committee spends most of the year planning the meeting, which can include some big-name evangelists—the island people love ones who can sing. Recent ones included Dan Betzer, of Revivaltime, and Donnie Summer, who was a personal aide and co-performer with Elvis Presley and became addicted to drugs before he found Jesus. Also they have had people like local black choirs from the mainland, and Connie Cohen and the singing Cohen children from Jews for Jesus.

Camp Meeting is a time to clean house, get yards in shape, get out the best china and linens and silverware. Lots of people in Ewell have family and friends from the rest of the island stay over for dinner in between services. And they do eat. I can give you every item of a Camp Meeting Sunday meal I was served, though it was a while ago:

Eye of roast beef, ham, fried chicken, crab casserole, soft crabs, fresh string beans, baked corn pudding, candied sweet potatoes, sliced tomatoes and fresh pickled beets, iced tea and coffee, homemade strawberry ice cream, German chocolate cake, pecan pie, Jell-O salad, and baked yeast rolls. Oh, my.

All week long there is preaching and Bible school for the children, and testimony. It is no longer the "shouting" meeting of Joshua Thomas's time, but there is still a heavy emphasis on conversion of souls at the altar, and there is no telling how many have walked down that sawdust aisle to salvation. What they say is so true: Smith Islanders without camp meetings would be like a ship without a rudder. •

Drinking

LIQUOR ON A DRY ISLAND

LATE ONE hot summer's night, a few months after we had settled in Tylerton, two watermen in their thirties eased their scrape boat into the pool of light where I was fishing from our dock. It was a Saturday, and they had been drinking fairly steadily since they came in from crabbing around midmorning. Did I want to go with them to North End to B......'s shanty, where there was bound to be some partying going on? I jumped aboard, a cold Bud pressed into my hand as we pulled into the dark channel that wound some two miles between the two towns.

The boat's owner had been standoffish up until now. The invitation marked a new level of acceptance; also, I quickly learned, a bit of an initiation. "Take 'er," the captain said, and walked forward, leaving me straining to navigate the mostly unlit channel markers, set on foot-thick concrete and steel poles. Get too close and you courted disaster; but stray more than a dozen yards from the channel edge they marked, and you risked running aground, only slightly less damaging to your reputation than a crackup.

Though other crab boats and small, high-speed skiffs were about in the dark, many lacked legal running lights. Aboard ours, one of the watermen lit a cigarette, which periodically he would suck on hard, and wave the glowing ash in a small arc to warn off any fast-approaching vessels. After ten minutes that seemed like half an hour, the captain took back the controls as we headed into Ewell. I took my first sip of beer.

As advertised, the party shanty blazed light and music. The occupants, in loud conversation, did not even hear us dock. Our entry to the smoky interior triggered a reflex so common on the island that Reuben, our resident artist, once constructed a marvelous drawing around it: all drinks automatically and smoothly were lowered and, with a practiced curl of the wrist, placed behind the drinker, or cradled partly out of sight by the hand and forearm.

Though the two Tylerton crabbers were quickly recognized as drinking buddies, my presence was enough to ruin the evening. "Late for dinner"; "got to help the old lady steam some crabs"; "things to do." The shanty emptied out, music and lights still going, several of the beers left where they had been "hidden." The excuses might have seemed more plausible if it hadn't been nearly midnight.

Drinking is a very private affair on Smith Island. The island is in a wet state and a wet county, and since it has no local government, cannot be said to be dry in any legal or technical sense. But that reckons without the Methodist Church here, whose pastor in 1910 expressed sentiments that could as well ring from the pulpit now, with little dissent from the congregation: "There has never been a liquor saloon or licensed hotel . . . if such should ever be built, by a mutual understanding of the people it shall immediately be burnt to the ground."

In 1933, when the nation repealed Prohibition, Smith Island voted for its continuance, 165 to 4. References in old diaries of islanders dating back into the mid-1800s make it clear that for a long time the island, officially, has been dead set against alcohol. What I also came to feel is that at the same time, there has been a fairly high tolerance of drinking, so long as it does not directly confront the surface image of a dry community.

One had only to sit in the island stores on slow winter mornings and listen to the old people banter with the younger ones about drinking to realize this. There were tales of those who imbibed hair tonic, various homebrews usually named after their creator, even Aqua Velva—"that H., he didn't have no good breath, did he?" It was, the islanders would agree, "part of growing up," and a good many who are now staunch church supporters would admit that it was part of their own growing up (this tolerance, even expectation, seemed to apply mostly to men).

One day the conversation turned to marijuana, which hit the island's younger watermen full force during the 1970s, and is still enjoyed by many today. A number of the older men acknowledged that, yes, had drugs been around in their own youths, they probably would have tried them too.

Even in Tylerton, the town most uniformly and ardently opposed to strong drink, a local was known for more than a decade to be bootlegging whiskey from the mainland out of his house. It was a real thorn in the community's side, but the strongest action it took was to "pray against him." (He did eventually move away.)

The curious accommodation between official Smith Island and Smith Island in its shanties and crab boats on weekend nights seemed to work. No tourist place or rooming house served anything stronger than black coffee and iced tea. Crab feasts, almost synonymous with cold beer in Maryland, featured huge pitchers of tepid Pepsi. Even the biggest of drinkers among the locals were seldom seen publicly with liquor in hand. Even the increasing numbers of mainland second-home owners generally followed suit and kept it indoors. Alcohol-induced fights, which did not occur often, were usually confined to shanties and other out-of-the-way spots.

There were less fortunate effects. Most islanders never developed much concept of social drinking, of having a beer or two after work, or one drink at a party. Once drinking started, it usually progressed to the point of drunkenness. Some watermen, because they would lay off drinking entirely during the grueling workweek when crabbing was in full swing, or in some cases for virtually the whole crabbing season, felt they "could handle it"; but in fact they followed a classic pattern of binge drinking.

Problem drinking seemed worse in some parts of the island. A medical person who served the island several years ago felt that a significant percentage of people from Rhodes Point were alcoholics. Heavy drinking there and in other parts of the island was often followed by panic attacks. It got to the point, the island medic said, where he had to raise rates for house calls on Saturday nights, to cut down on late-night summonses concerning drunks.

From all this, some observers have cast the islanders as a hypocritical lot, concerned more about presenting a quaint image to the outside world, keeping the reality under wraps. But the truth lies closer to how small islands must deal with a whole range of contradictions if they are to survive.

For example, Carolyn Ellis, a professor at the University of South Florida, lived on Smith Island in the 1980s as part of her Ph.D. work in sociology, later published as *Fisher Folk*. She concluded:

> Maintaining the appearance of a "moral" community was very important . . . open confrontation and avoidance were difficult in a community where people had to participate in organizations with others, serve on church committees together, confess in public prayer meetings, or assist people in disasters.

In sum, it is one of the geniuses of Smith Island that it has simply existed for nearly three hundred years in a small space with an astoundingly low level of violence—murders are virtually unknown, as far back as island history is recorded. The way the island handles liquor is a small insight into how it copes. The reflexive lowering of drinkers' beers in the shanties seems more a ritual genuflection to the governing order than actually hiding anything from anyone.

Increasingly, nowadays, the liquor issue threatens to override local coping mechanisms. Liquor that used to be brought over discreetly is now openly carried on the island ferries. Some outsiders have moved on the island in recent years who either don't know or don't care about the strictures on public drinking. Beer cans have begun to pile up visibly under one crab shanty in Tylerton in the last few years, an affront to many who must walk by it every day.

And recently, the church received the most public challenge to its authority in the history of the island. Let D . . . . . . , a waterman who had mixed feelings on the subject, tell the story of the great beer hearing:

✦ I am forty-five now, and I can't remember a time when it weren't easy to get liquor on this island. They used to have an old boat to Rhodes Point, called the *Dew Drop,* would bring it over and you could see 'em icin' it down aboard her on a weekend. When we were teenagers—we'd call it a rum run—we'd pool our money and jump in a skiff Saturday afternoon and haul it by the case back from Crisfield.

They say everybody on the island's a Methodist, and I guess we're all on the church's books; but there's always been, you know, the Christians and the sinners. Drinkin' was one of the ways they divided up. I guess I'd be a sinner, but I always give part of my crabbin' money to the church, and I support it; and there's a lot of the Christians used to drink, as far as that goes. From what I've heard the old people say, used to be it wasn't nothin' to get up on Sunday morning and see two or three drunks layin' outside. I think they always drunk pretty heavy here.

Now with the ferry service seven days a week like they have had since I was a young man, all you gotta do is pick up the phone and order a case put aboard in Crisfield and have it delivered right to your front door. Now it's expensive—Heineken is $18 a case in Salisbury and $27.25 by the time you get it here, with freight and all. And if you forget to order enough and run out durin' a party, well, you are just outta luck until the first ferry runs back across the next afternoon.

So a lot of us liked it when Charlie began bringing over beer in quantity and sellin' it outta the back of his store to North End. Everybody knew about it, and o'course the church people didn't like it, but if you didn't want to see it, you knew to not use the back door. And it seemed like that worked all right 'til the tax people up in the state [Annapolis] caught Charlie for buyin' alcohol without a proper license.

Well, a lot of us told Charlie, hell, go ahead and try to get a license to sell beer and wine, we'll support you. Enough of us asked, he decided to put in for it. No one had ever done that before, and it caused the greatest row. I guess it was right to try, to bring it out in the open; but sometimes I don't know. It was hard on the island.

The hearin' was set for the end of May [1988], in the courthouse to Princess Anne. The petitions was a'flyin' thick and fast between the sinners supportin' Charlie and the Christians sayin' it was a damnation on our community. The preacher was the head spokesman, and he tried everything to make sure the community turned out against a license. He figured the one thing everybody here would hate is more law; so he started sayin' that if a liquor license was to be granted, the island would need a full-time police station to handle all the drunk and disorderlies.

Oh, it got tense. Charlie's wife was the head teacher at the school down in Tylerton, which has got more holy rollers than the other two towns put together. And they loved her down there, but it was hard for them to abide what her husband was standin' for.

None of the ferry captains, Otis Ray who's got the *Island Belle,* and Larry and Terry Laird, who run the *Captain Jasons,* really liked being the beer deliverymen. Otis, he backed Charlie, though. Terry's more of a Christian these days, and Larry, well, his wife and in-laws is big against the evils of drink, so he went against.

Well, on the evenin' of the hearing—it was to the county courthouse to Princess Anne—they run two special ferries, Christians aboard the *Jason,* and Charlie and the sinners aboard Otis Ray. We turned it into a party, win or lose. No beer going across, but coming back, beer for everybody. So there we went, side by side across the Sound, Christians and sinners a'pointin' and a'hollerin' and jokin' at one another.

It went about like you'd expect. There was about twenty of us, and moren' a hundred of them. One of the Christian ladies from Rhodes Point got settled in the booze section by mistake, and she jumped up from there like a scalded cat just before the hearing began. It had hardly got under way when they told one of our side, who was hollerin' and wouldn't shut up, that he would have to leave. Some claimed he had showed up drunk, but he was just being aggravatin'.

Then one of the Christians hollered at Charlie about how could he ask for a liquor license when everybody knowed his own brother-in-law had drunk himself to death. Our side come back with how the ferries were already deliverin' maybe eighty cases of beer a week to the island. But you could tell we weren't goin' to get it; and when they denied the license that night, it was like the whole room was standin' up clapping and praising the Lord and singing hymns.

We had a few beers on the way back, wavin' at the Christian ferry. They told Charlie he had the right to appeal, but he said he'd had enough. ◆

(In April 1995, Charlie was charged by State Police with selling alcohol without a license. Police seized sixty-three cases of beer and twelve one-liter bottles of vodka.)

WE HAD SPUNK

Of all the names opposed to a liquor license on Smith Island, one had checked the "opposed" box twice. She was an older lady named Audrey Brimer, and she told the story of a stand against alcohol she made nearly sixty years ago:

◆ Self brag, half scandal, they used to say; but I will tell this one anyway. I was twenty, with a three-year-old son. The only beer on Drum Point then was what they could sneak. The word was out one day that my husband and my brother and some of the other men had an order of beer coming. I went to some of the other young women and said, girls, let's get together and put a stop to this.

We knew where they was a'going to drink it. We met near the edge of night and hid beneath Capn' Johnny's store porch, which is all gone now, but it was high enough you could crouch underneath it. I brought a hatchet, and we all prayed about what was to come. By'n by, here they come. They got to this shed that belonged to Capn' Woods, and we heard 'em go inside and wrap twine around a nail to hold the door shut.

Girls, let's go, I said, and we hit that door and snapped the twine. Capn' Woods put his beer down and *BAM!*, I smashed it with my hatchet. It's a wonder he didn't smack me, but we had the element of surprise. I yelled at 'em, "None of you don't scare me a bit. I got the Lord on my side," and I hatcheted my husband's beer. They all just stared. Then they ran.

We came out from that place all foamy and soaked from the beer that was splattered around, and Mary Tull, she had the devil in her anyhow, said, hey, let's pretend we are drunk. We locked arms and pretended to stagger down the street, singin' "Sweeeeet Aaadooooooline." We told the men in the store what we had done and they took to callin' me Carrie Nation.

My husband was sore at me for a week. Audrey, you oughtn't to done it, he said. But we had spunk, and we had the Lord and the community on our side. My grandfather, Willie Evans, told me I had done a great deed; and it was a long time before the beer came back to Drum Point. ✦

ISLAND LIFE

Islands Within Islands

Rhodes Point, a very religious man from Tylerton once said, is next to hell itself. That it is, a Rhodes Pointer replied—right next to Tylerton.

THIS BOOK is about all of Smith Island; but readers should understand that it was written by a resident of Tylerton, and would inevitably have been somewhat different had the author settled in Rhodes Point; and slanted yet another way had I taken a house in Ewell—this despite all three towns being within view of one another, and none more than a few minutes apart.

Smith Island looks homogenous when viewed from the outside, and compared to the mainland, it is. The gap between richest and poorest here is far less than on the mainland. All citizens shop and socialize and worship in roughly the same circumstances. The webs of community and heritage, blood kinship and water work, likewise sponsor an unrivaled commonality.

And yet, with the possible exception of preachers, who come and go, I could not name a soul here that one might call a true citizen of the island. One is a "cheese eater," which is to say a Rhodes Pointer; or a "herring huckster," the old-time nickname for Tylertonians; or a "bean snucker," meaning from Ewell.

Well into their third century of settlement, the three communities retain distinct identities, even to subtle differences in their speech. I heard a man mention that a neighbor's cat must have swum over from Rhodes Point. He knew, because when it mewed, it came out "meow-*uh.*" This was lost on me, but had islanders rolling on the dock, laughing about the unrefined manner of speech just down the channel.

On the ferry, I once heard a vigorous debate between Ewell and Tylerton ladies on how best to pick a crab, and one could imagine their great-grandmothers going on the same a century before. There is of course no true hostility among the towns, whose families are quite related, and less different from one another than from any place else.

Physically, each town has quite a different feel. Rhodes Point is relatively treeless, laid out in a long, thin, westward-facing line, hard by the island's fast-eroding bayshore. A narrow, mile-long roadway extending east across open marsh connects it to Ewell.

Tylerton is literally on an island by itself, most of its homes in a compact, cozy village cluster with fine shade and fruit trees.

Ewell is the only one of the three large enough to feel as if it has different facets, which include restaurants, a tourist shop, gas pumps, visitors' museum, and the big tabernacle that is the center of the island's summer religious revival.

In nearly three years on the island, I got to the other two towns less frequently than I had planned. Some of it had to do with travel by water. Several boats at my disposal, including a large diesel workboat with a cabin, still were far less convenient than roads and automobiles. Wind, darkness, low tides, ice, bugs, fog—they are simply not large factors in car travel; in boats, they very much are.

There was more to it than that, though. I would not be long in Ewell before the noise and traffic of the dozen or so cars active at any one time would begin to grate on me. Rhodes Point often seemed a bit depressing, both store and post office closed, church peeling paint, and about half its fifty-odd homes owned by off-islanders. I enjoyed friendships in both towns, not to mention the world's most hospitable crab shanty at Olden Bradshaw's in Rhodes Point, and the best cheesesteak sub under heaven at Ruke's in Ewell. Still, I was always glad to get back home to Tylerton.

Islanders, while generally presenting a united face to the mainland, knew where they were really from:

✦ Tylerton is where I married and where I raised my family and probably where I will die; but I still call Ewell "up home." I guess there was two or three years after I left there I had nightmares and crying fits, even though I could see it right across the marsh ten times a day.

Now, I think it's Tylerton I like best. It's quieter, and the people here are open and forthright. Ewell, there was always a little more keeping up with the Joneses; you always had to figure out where some were really coming from. But it's still home.

I married up to Ewell from Tylerton. I got used to it. I guess it took eight, maybe nine years. The noise there seemed terrible. Also, it is just different ways in the people. It seemed like they were closer down home, or maybe I was just so used to being around them.

Down by Tylerton's still where I crab most days, and it's where I still love to go sit and talk in the store. My skiff knows the way by itself.

Isle of Patmos is what I call Tylerton—so isolated; religious in the old-timey way. Patmos was the rocky old island [a Roman penal colony] in the Bible where John got the Revelations. I believe it means nowhere.

Growing up in Ewell, Tylerton was as much a mystery to me as Baltimore. We considered ourselves very cosmopolitan by comparison.

Move to Ewell? From Tylerton? No, my God! Now, we have had lots of our people marry up there, and their people marry and come down here, but there's always been a difference in the people there and the people here, and always will be.

I think they always thought they were about like New York compared to us. I can also tell you me and my brother used to lease oyster bottom up there, and just as fast as they grew big, some of them North Enders [Ewell residents] would catch 'em.

When I was in the fifth grade, Dad took me and some other boys from Tylerton up to Rhodes Point. He let us out at the end nearest home, where the boat haul-out is, and said he would be back for us in an hour. We never left the boat place. It seemed like a strange land.

I never really had a bad thought about Ewell or Rhodes Point, but I always knew I didn't ever want to live there. I am so glad, looking back, that I grew up in Tylerton.

I'd be in good heart if I drowned and washed up in Tylerton [a Rhodes Pointer].

At one time, there was talk about the state building a bridge to connect Tylerton to the other two towns. Some say it was just talk; but we didn't want it to happen. Why? Well, there was for years a skiff on a rope that you could pull yourself back and forth across the channel into Tylerton and walk on up to Ewell, and when our children would be little, we'd go to look for 'em and they'd be all the way up there, into who knows what.

We have always been afraid, too, that with a bridge we'd wind up with one church, one school, and one store—and you know where they'd all be: up to the "capital city," Ewell.

When I told Ma I was getting married, she said, "Oh, my, you will be movin' from North End to Rhodes Point," like she was grievin' for my soul.

The morning after my wedding night, I was sittin' at his mama's table with her and him. I was so excited, I couldn't keep my eyes off him, and I wasn't even noticing that she was melting cheese into his coffee. Ain't that going to make you sick? I finally said; but it's what they do here. Cheese eaters they are.

Now, Tylerton talks a lot closer to Tangier than either Ewell or Rhodes Point. *"I'll hiyte you"* for I'll hate you; *"howse"* for house; *"schuyl"* for school.

Oh, North End—you ought to hear 'em say "outhouse": *eyete hise*. It's comical. I believe they even talk different there between the ones live in the part of town they call Over the Hill, and the ones live where they call Down the Field.

Rhodes Point's different, too. It's like they got a kind of a long drag to their talking. I don't know that Tylerton really has any accent at all.

You can be called by your nickname down home, but by your real name when you are in the other two towns.

One thing I know all three towns would agree, Rhodes Point always has stewed the best chicken. ✦

To Be an Islander

✦ I'm committee-pissed-off right now. I have been to one meeting about a new government water system for the island, and to another about a tourist museum the state is putting here. It seems to me when we were all just a bunch of wild horses over here, there wasn't much anybody could do with us; but now, with all these committees, they got us corralled down to where they can push us whichever way they want.

This museum bunch is making a movie of Smith Island for the tourists to see. It's not like I'm against entertainment. I spent $600 of my own money to bring Root Boy Slim and The Sex Change band over here. I set them up on the county dock, hooked their amplifiers into Terry's crab shanty; even got a flyover by the county mosquito control plane. But I don't think anyone's shown the real Smith Island. Really, it'd be hard to do that in a movie.

The movie I'd make would start with about twenty minutes of a Smith Island sunset—you could play just that part on rainy days, and for people here who can't get out any more. It'd show how the men fight the heat and flies and sea nettles all day long, and still sometimes get no more than a hot dog and chips from their wives when they get home. But I'd also want to show how so many men here, if their wife was to die, would just be ruined—seems to me around here they go right from mother to wife, which is basically the same person.

You'd want to show how well people know each other here. You know just how to avoid an argument, and you know just how to start one when you get bored and need a little entertainment. I really do believe it's passed down in our genes to not hurt each other for real, because we know we all got to live here. All the real shit got settled way back. I told a new preacher that came here: Half of this crowd is going to love you, and half's going to hate you; and if you're here long, the two halves'l switch, so don't sweat it. He said later it was the best advice he ever got.

You'd have to show what a pain in the ass it is just to go to Salisbury and back; how you get that sinking, awful feeling when you just miss the 12:30 ferry back over here and know you got about three hours to kill in Crisfield. And have a scene where you get your mouth set for spaghetti and clam sauce for dinner one afternoon; but you have to wait until tomorrow to get a nice bottle of Chardonnay on the ferry to go with it, 'cause the Christians won't allow liquor sales here.

My movie—how long is it getting now, a couple days?—it would have lots on people just talking. They relish that here. Right now, they are talking a lot about ghosts. Barry says he has had one in his house for several months. Dixie says she saw Mary Evans, who just died, three nights in a row in her dreams, all dressed up in a wedding gown. They say the day after Elmer passed away, the back door to Charlie's store swung open, but no one was there. It was the way he always came in, and about the time of day when he always did it. Ma Willy says she's seen her husband, who's been dead around twenty years. "Seen 'im in your dreams," they say to her. "Wasn't even to bed yet," she says back. Harry Reed says he's noticed people see ghosts more in winter, when they're not so busy with crabbing. But someone like Mary dying just lets all these emotions out.

One more thing that gets overlooked in the movies on this place is cats. I got twenty-eight outdoor ones, three inside ones. Watchin' new kittens play is better'n TV. I figure, take care of animals, and you'll be taken care of. And you know, all these cats over here, breeding all the time, maybe they are getting to be a breed of their own, worth some money, don't you think? Maybe we could tell that to *Cat Fancy,* or one of those magazines; you know, descendants of cats come from England three hundred years ago. Well, some of 'em came from the humane shelter in Salisbury, but we don't have to emphasize that.

I think rock 'n' roll has a lot to say about the island, too. A lot of the watermen like Pink Floyd, like where they sing about rabbits runnin' to dig one hole after the other. What they are sayin' is, about the time you pay off one $18,000 diesel in your crab boat, you'll be needin' another. I believe, too, there's a lot of reality to life here, like Dark Side of the Moon sings; what you touch and see bein' all your life's ever gonna be.

The Beatles had just come on the radio when I left here for the first time. It was 1964 and I was fourteen. I went to Washington, to work in a seafood business owned by an island family. It was the devil's playground, that city. I was there ten years. I got into drugs and alcohol, went to all the peace demonstrations, came back down here with some powder, some dope, a load of hits and other stuff, and sold 'em to islanders, including some of the big Christians. I didn't appreciate the island in those days. I finally got all Quaaluded up one night and backed my car through a store window in Salisbury. I was loading my trunk with stereo gear when the cops came. I told 'em I was doing it for love, for two friends who loved music. I did six months and six days in the Salisbury jail. Ten years later I went back to my old job in Washington for a few months, but the old recklessness came back. Now, I don't think I will ever leave this island again.

I do a little bit of it all to make it here. I crab a little, sell crabs out of the back of a truck on the mainland. I have managed an oyster-shucking house and worked with the electric company; had an ice cream cart and a little museum and soft-crab-shedding operation I charged tourists to see. I've sold Indian arrowheads, old and new, and painted rocks for the tour boat captain's gift shop. The grocery store's been good to me in the winter with credit, and I know my poor man's rights well enough to keep the electric turned on until spring.

I am sort of phased out of it now, but for a while I handled local real estate. This place is too hard to get to and the prices mostly too low for agents on the mainland to fool with. I helped one person here sell his house, and the word just spread. I would take out ads in the *New York Times* and the *Washington Post*. I wouldn't sell to anybody; like one time a woman called and I said, do you know anything about Smith Island, and she said, "Sir, if I did, I wouldn't be talking to you." Well, to hell with her. I've had what I call Perfect Posture People—you know, everything's got to be just so. They'd give me a deposit check and I wouldn't even tell the owner of the house, just send it back, 'cause I know they'd be miserable here. If they want night life and beaches, I warn 'em off. It's island people make this island, and if you'd get along with them, then maybe a house here is just the ticket. It's all changing, I know, and you can't stop it, but maybe you can control it a little bit.

I have sold a lot of places to Cancers—maybe it's all the crabs attracting their brothers. You're a Cancer, aren't you? I thought so. I've got the whole place down by astrological sign. I don't take it as Bible, but if it's foggy and damp and dreary, it shows on the Cancers. There's a bunch of Geminis all the same—they go along and they're fine, and then, *pow!*, they get pissed off, friendly to fickle like a thumb snap. The Libras can't give you a straight answer at first. Virgos, they're tight, like C___, she's even got her spice cabinet in alphabetical order. Clyde, who used to captain the *Lorraine Rose*, dredging oysters—I call him Ole Blue Eyes. He looks to me like Frank Sinatra; same eyes, both Sagittarius. Taurus is me: down to earth, stubborn, overweight. It's all entertainment to me; cheaper'n calling those 900 numbers.

I think it's easier to be poor here than on the mainland. People got more sympathy for it here. We've got our leading families here, too. I call them Cartwrights, after that old show, *Bonanza*. And we've got lots of Christians. They're not shy about letting you know who they are. It may sound neat to the outside, about how we have no government but the church, but if you aren't one of the Christians, then it's almost like you're denied the vote sometimes. To tell you the truth, I don't trust anyone who is really comfortable in church. It's like, I know everybody here so well; and I hear what they say on Sunday, and I know how they are, and I can't swallow the difference. But we get along, we all do.

We've also got our own sort of underclass, people from a couple families we call Fotneys. My ex-wife was a Fotney, and my son gets teased about being half-Fotney. It's something you got to work through, like the back-handed compliments: "They're such nice people, I don't care if they are Fotneys," shit like that. I think they got some of the nicest families there are. Some of them don't want to be called Fotney—you might as well say "nigger" to 'em; others, they don't care. It's the ones don't care I like most.

I think there's a lot of godly messages in rock 'n' roll. If I was more edu-cated, I'd make a rock 'n' roll Bible for this place. I think ideally the main-land could just forget about us and we forget about them, but it ain't that way—we gotta be more civilized now. Ain't that hell? ◆

MISSY, THIRTY-THREE

Often, as your ferry winds through the island's channels, you will see a young woman astride the bow of a skiff, expertly netting soft crabs from the grass; or drifting down the channel, rod bent double, horsing a big ray to the surface; or windsurfing far out on the grass flats; or jockeying her outboard around the marsh guts to pull peeler pots, with a flair any waterman would envy. Usually, it is Missy, happier to be home than anyone I have ever known.

◆ On the island, I was free; and now I'm in a building without windows, stuck to a cord, like a child to its mother: *"Beep";* "What number, please?"; *"Beep."* People think working for the phone company is the world's greatest job. It's security, they say; and it is, some. It's good benefits, and I got a new truck, and it means I can take care of Mom and Dad someday. But I hate going to work. Why, I never even liked to talk on the phone. I have put in for outside work, as a lineman, which would suit me more.

On the island, I grew up playing with guys. I never wanted a doll, I wanted a boat. Daddy found me one when I was seven and had just learned to swim. *Little White,* we called her. She was a rowboat with a pointed bow, and I could shove her the whole length of the town by pushing off from one dock to another. I've been in boats long as I can remember. When I go home, and get in one and hear the water slapping the sides, it's like a great big re-lease of energy: ahhhh, I'm back.

I always thought I'd never leave. Dad didn't have any boys, so I fished pots, traps, went scraping with him. I've done it all, and I can do it well as many a waterman. I never really talked with Dad about a career on the water. Mom knew what I was thinking. She'd say, girl, you don't want to do that. When she married Dad, she helped fish pots and went out to fish channel traps, and she saw what it was doing to her, and she felt it wasn't for a woman to do. Dad would always say, try it; it's going to be hard, but it didn't bother me. Mom, I think, did everything in her power to make me Miss Feminine, but it was a failure.

I believe if my grandfather had not died, I might have still been there. He was so much fun, but serious about crabbing. I saw him every day of life. If I didn't like what Mom had to eat, I'd walk to Ma Ginnie's and Pa John's and they'd fix me something. My sister and I used to walk down to the end of the county wharf and call to him to come get us—his crab shanty was across the channel. He'd be asleep in his rocking chair on the shanty porch, and he'd wake up and come across and take us back with him. I'd sit with him and watch the little shanty birds [barn swallows]. Sit still, he'd say; sit still, watch; and they'd fly right up on his chair and he'd talk to 'em and they'd twist their little heads around and listen right to what he was saying.

He died of prostate cancer one month after I graduated from high school. I had a lot of feelings for him. All my life he was always there. For a while I would work at this job or that up in Salisbury in the winter, and move back home when crab season started. I finally went off to school because everybody kept saying I should—that's really the main reason I did. I think college really hurt Smith Island, the lure of it, once girls began to move off to go. Everybody tries to talk young people out of being a waterman, and I think that's wrong. You got to find something else, they tell you, because people are moving away, the island's going down. Well, it *will* if people let it.

It would be devastating to me to see a time when the people have all left. I feel some guilt for being one of those that moved. You can't imagine the fun of growing up there, jumping ditches in the marsh, finding otter and muskrat, going old-bottlin'—that's taking your fishing rod and poking in the mud along the shore 'til you strike an antique bottle. There was so much to occupy your mind. We'd round up wild billy goats, fish and hunt and swim and hunt for wild asparagus; in the winter we'd play tickly bender, which is racing across the ice when a thaw has made it limber. I remember when Dad would come home from oystering, we'd plunder around in the cabin of his boat—that musty old smell of workboat cabins, we thought that was perfume; and hot coffee never tasted so good as aboard the boat in the cold winter.

If I could only put into words how I feel about home; it's like a religion, I guess. Up where I work, where they say I have made something of my life, I feel so useless somedays. Down here, I feel like I belong. Sometimes, when I get back, I run the skiff out by Smith Gut Point and drift there in the sunset, waves slappin' at the sides, cool breeze comin' off the bay, I just want to give a big holler—*People, can't you see what you got here?* ✦

CHRIS PARKS, THIRTY-SEVEN

◆ I'm at ebb tide now. I grew up in the most wonderful way, in a place bounded only by my imagination; also realizing it was not my future. I left the island in search of a world I knew only through television, books, and magazines; a world where possibility was waiting around every corner. In the years since, I have found only scattered fragments, nothing that has become a meaningful whole. Growing up on Smith Island, you get used to completeness and order. The world beyond my native home is anything but meaningful. I think often of a quote by the farmer and writer Wendell Berry:

> There is no "there." We can only wait here, where we are, in the world, obedient to its processes, patient in its taking away, faithful to its returns. And as much as we may know, and all that we deserve, of earthly paradise will come to us.

I have moved back, and am living in my mother's house, baiting pots in the summer as a crabber's mate, and trying to write a novel so great it will outlast the human race; or at least make people understand what a special place this was. Sometimes, I feel like a ghost, haunting an ancestral home. For me, there is no "there" any longer, only here; but I fear we are a vanishing people, dying in small pieces so as to prolong the agony.

Childhood was so special, maybe everything else was bound to suffer by comparison. What seems confining later on is just secure and free when you are a kid. The island seemed big as the world, and there were no Charles Mansons or serial killers to worry about; not any strangers at all, or enough traffic that you could get run over. I remember a county road crew that came to repair potholes, and I must have looked so nervous to those outsiders; one finally turned to me and said, "Boo!", and I ran and ran.

I was among the island's first television generation, and after we saw *The Great Escape* with Steve McQueen, we spent weeks trying to make escape tunnels. Of course, every hole we dug, when we got down a few feet, it would fill up with water.

The hummocks of old trees growing out on the marsh were mystical, enchanted places. I remember going there in new hip boots, which kids would get in the fall. There were old foundations of early settlers, huge, old spreading trees, perfect for climbing and building treehouses; also ghosts, or so we'd be told. Out there you could be a hunter, or Magellan exploring the wide world, or an astronaut. Some places had wild goats that we'd round up, or try to. I remember in the spring, watching eagles come down and snatch young goats not long after they were born.

Kids also had a full schedule built around the church—Good News Club, where they'd show movies like Laurel and Hardy; Wednesday night services,

Sunday night and Sunday morning service; Bible School with Camp Meeting in the summers. Personally I avoided church as much as possible. The local dump was more fun. Landfills are better for the environment, but not half as entertaining. We would play dress-up with what people had thrown away. Spring and fall cleaning were good times for that, and right after somebody died. People ask me now, how did you manage without movie theaters and restaurants and shopping malls, and I just shake my head.

Some of our play, I see now, was learning things you might need to survive. One of the old men fixed us up with a box of mousetraps, and he would show us how to stake them down out in the marsh where we saw muskrat tracks, to play at being trappers. We would crawl into duck blinds to go gunnin' for sparrows and sea gulls with our beebee guns; and of course everyone had a skiff, and we would shove them all around, learning the guts, and how to dip doublers out of the grass beds. The first time I ever shoved across the deep channel through town, I guess I was ten, and I didn't understand about current. I thought the water stood still out there. Well, that tide grabbed me, and I thought I would shortly be out to sea, and I began to scream. Dad was watching all the time, and he let it go on for a little bit, before another waterman came and rescued me. It was the last time I ever hollered for help, though.

We were taught the value of money. Always have some put away, for hard times *will* come; *"you'll come to want,"* is how the old people would say it, if they saw you spending it fast as you got it. From first grade on, many boys were required to put crab pots together. We'd get a quarter a pot, and that was our spending money. Before you were old enough to make whole pots, you might get a few cents for making the funnels that went in them. We sat in the store and listened to the men tell yarns, and looking back, I can see that some of it was like instruction. They would talk about so-and-so taking off in his boat, and his bow line was overboard, and floated back and got all tangled in his propeller and cost him a day's work; also the money to get hauled at the railway. Don't ever have your bow line longer than the length of your boat, they'd say. That way it can't get tangled; and they would tell stuff like that over and over. So much was being passed down, I wish now I'd listened to it more.

The best times of all without a doubt, was, and is, Christmas. You got a big white cotton sock of your dad's and carried it around, and at every house, people filled it with quarters and nickels and dimes. I still remember my Christmas speech from the big evening when all us kids would put on a play: *Christmas is for children, they say, with trees and candy and toys to play.* Everyone goes back to the island for Christmas, even the gay kids. If you are from the island, there is just no place else to be at Christmas.

I'm not sure just when it was I began to think about living beyond the island. I remember one of my first times away, a trip to Washington, D.C. It was so big, so white, like Olympus. The Washington Monument made our church steeple, the tallest thing in our world, seem like a matchstick. Around eighth grade, I realized I was smart—it sounds terrible to say it like that, but that was the age when so many of us were dropping out to work, or thinking hard about it. I always loved to read. I'd go around to people's houses and grab up their magazines: *Life* and the *Grit,* which is sort of a *Reader's Digest* for old people, was mostly it, with a *National Geographic* every once in a while. Around that time I wrote a story for a class, for Patriots Day. I wrote about a pilot who got shot down, and I described bullets whizzing by, and the blood, and my teacher said it was so good, she read it aloud to everyone. Well, I was never a strong person physically, and I was not as good as many boys in boats; and now, here was something I could do better than the rest. Mom just about busted with pride, and it gave me a lot of satisfaction.

There were eight boys from the island in my class when I began high school, and by graduation, I was the only one left. My group was the last of the islanders who spent high school boarding in Crisfield. We got daily school boat runs to and from the island my senior year. In Crisfield, I roomed with other kids in a lady's home, and she did the best she could; but we were always sneaking out, cutting class, getting into booze and drugs—that was the 1970s, but the way Crisfield runs five or ten years behind the world, it was really the sixties just hitting there then. High school was where I lost that special innocence you have growing up on Smith Island. I was made to feel not quite as good as the Crisfield whites, but not as bad as the blacks. It was the first time I'd encountered the notion of judging people by the way they look. Not knowing everybody else—that was new to me; it makes a big difference in how people get along.

After high school, I tonged oysters and crabbed for seven years. Becoming a waterman was not something that was ever stressed to me. You aren't taught it like subjects in school. Your father will tell you things, but you've got to learn a lot just by watching him and others, and you've got to have enough drive to pick it up on your own, or you'll never be any good. I think parents know how hard a life it is, so they don't oversell it to their kids. Dad loved crabbing, and he was good at it; but I never was. When I was twenty, I decided to take my SATs and apply for college, but the week I was to take the exam was the start of the big freeze-up, and I never did get off to take the test that year. I knew by then, though, I couldn't stay. There were too many days when I hated what I was doing.

Crabbing for a living did have its virtues—mostly, I thought, in the spring, when crabs were scarce and the air was clear and you could see all the way to the western shore and see ships passing up and down the bay's deep channel. There was a peace and satisfaction I never felt on the mainland, when you would finish your week's work on a Saturday, and feel a cool breeze washing across the island just before a squall came across the bay. In the fall, when the haze cleared again, watching the clouds while you worked out on the water, seeing the sun come up; that is where I first began to feel part of something bigger than myself. It all seemed uncomplicated then.

But oh, the summers. They were hell. I remember a scene from a Sally Field movie, *Places in the Heart*. She's picking cotton to keep the farm, and it's cutting her fingers, and she's sweating in that hot, Texas summer. That's how it was, but worse. I would be so tired by Saturdays that I couldn't even go out on the weekend. Every day was get up at 3:30 A.M., crab all day, drag myself home, shower, eat, and crawl into bed, so beat I couldn't read—even that small pleasure, crabbing took from me. One real hot July day I had fallen behind Dad, who was pulling the pots. I had a whole washtub of crabs to sort. The washtub was half full of sea nettles and sooks, which have got a vicious bite; also lots of little crabs, which are fast, and are mean sons of bitches. One of them flipped a piece of nettle in my eye, like driving a red-hot nail into the center of your brain. I looked at the bait that was left—that's how you measure time—and we still had several boxes, about two hundred pots, to go. I was so damn tired. It was only Tuesday. I hit my head on something. Then, I just began to cry. Summertime is when you make the money crabbing, but it will separate the real crabbers from the rest.

I went to college when I was twenty-five. If I hadn't gotten away, I think I'd be crazy now, maybe even killed myself. But I never thought I would not come back. My idea was to study premed, then become a physician's assistant, because the island is more often than not in need of medical personnel. I still have a lot of guilt about not doing that, but in college I got off into history, literature, philosophy. I wanted to be a writer, a scholar, a thinker. Instead, after I graduated, I ended up manager of a convenience store, and also started a newspaper, which did not last long.

Now that I am back, I see the island in ways I never could have before. It is still home, and I am welcomed, and appreciate the place even more than in the happiest days of my childhood. But it is never the same again. I am aware of this curious duality people there have—a feeling of inferiority deep down that makes them way too easily impressed by someone who speaks "proper" and can talk easily in public, and has traveled widely or gotten an advanced degree. On the other hand, they have this quick, stubborn pride; if they even suspect you are putting them down, or making fun of them, or trying to put something by them, they will just cut you off, even if it might pay them to listen and learn.

Wendell Berry was right; "there is no 'there';" but our "here" is changing fast. We are losing more than our oysters. Crabbing fills most of our year now, and time that was always cyclical, seasonal, is becoming linear, a change in the very rhythms of our lives. My generation, and those who followed, demand more convenience, more leisure time, more things. We operate on the notion that with just a little more, we could have everything the rest of the world has, and keep all we hold dear. People in state government talk about replacing the "inefficient" waterman, out there harvesting crabs and oysters in the wild, with modern aquaculture. But I don't see how a crab farmer could possess the same bond with the bay. After years of trying to come to an analytical understanding of the bay, listening to the scientists and the environmentalists, I have concluded the only real understanding comes from sharing the bay's fate, which requires patience, self-reliance—a certain reverence. Share the bay's fate. Maybe that is what people here have always done best. ♦

JESSIE MARSH, THIRTY

♦ Don't we look proud in that picture? It ran on the cover of the Baltimore Sun Sunday Magazine in May of 1974. The student body standing in front of Tylerton's brand-new elementary school. There are nine of us boys in the picture. Seven have left.

David still follows the water, but from the mainland. Don and Jim took jobs guarding at the new prison in Princess Anne. Duke went to college, and he's a Nationwide agent in Crisfield. Mark works at a seafood plant, and Vince does something or other in Ocean City. Willard's still here and married, but he and Becky both got their applications in to the prison.

Back then, I never had a doubt what I would do. I love the water and I love living in Tylerton. I quit school in the eighth grade—I was a big, strong kid for my age—and started in the water business. You could still anticipate making some money then, which was around 1980. Still, it was not easy to become a waterman.

Dad's heart got bad around then, so he was not there to show me a lot. What I inherited from him was independence, go my own direction. I watched the older watermen close and learned. I would not say anyone took me under their wing; not a bit. I don't know if anyone really wanted to see you fail, but it seemed to me they enjoyed once in a while seeing somebody not make it. I am not bitter about that, because I think that's just the way it always has been. I made it, and I did it on my own. I was about twenty-one or twenty-two before I began to get ahead a little financially.

That was about the last winter you could oyster the whole bay, before the diseases started bringing catches down, to where watermen from Baltimore to the Virginia line were all corralled into working the spots where oysters had survived long enough to grow legal. And of course that wasn't great on the oysters, all that pressure. Since then, we have gone here on the island from looking forward to winter to worrying about it. Summers, we ain't human any more. We're like machines, driving so hard to make enough crabbing to get through the winter. I'm sitting here this spring, praying a lot of freshwater, which kills back the oyster disease, comes into the bay. If it does, then my hopes for next year is high. If it is dry, then I've lost my hope. If we ever get to where we depend totally on crabs, then we're ruined, because there's been at least two summers in Dad's life when the crabs failed and he had to go off to get work.

There was a time, around 1990, when I began to think about leaving. I had passed the test for my professional captain's license, which everyone says is a hard exam. I applied for a bunch of jobs off the island, running boats and other things like that.

There were three or four of us young watermen looking at moving off then. My friend interviewed for the State Police, and they asked whether he had ever smoked marijuana. He said a lot of young people had tried it, but he hadn't smoked for a couple years. They told him he was perfect except for that. I guess they'd rather had a liar.

Several places called me for interviews, but I canceled them all. I had thought it over, and decided money wasn't the most important thing for me, and I would stay a waterman here as long as I could. I look at people I know who finished high school and college. Some are making more money than I am, but they're all working under somebody. I don't consider that necessarily doing better than me.

I'm willing to make the sacrifices to stay. I am thirty and I still live at home with my mom, in the house where I was born. Every summer when the money's coming in, I tell myself to remember how hard the winter's going to be. I've had to cut back on my crab pot rig. My outboard went up and I miss it like hell, but I won't replace it this year. If I do right by putting aside enough money for expenses, and for the years when I can't work this hard, it means I can't get married. I've got a girl who comes down to see me from up the bay. She's a nurse and I think she would like to get married; but she's got twelve years in already toward retirement, and I'm not going to drag her away from that. What would she do down here with her training? Learn to pick crabs? It wouldn't be right.

I don't get lonesome easy. Some of us here, we're to this marsh like an otter. I can hunt ducks and progue around this island the rest of my life and be quite happy. There's places around here no one even owns, no fences, where you can go and just collect your thoughts. There ought to be more places like that in this world. I just hate what's going on in the rest of the world. Watching the news in Baltimore scares the hell out of me, all the shootings. If it keeps up, public pressure's going to take away something I love, my guns. I'm no fanatic. I wouldn't even care if they took the assault weapons away; but I've got fifteen or sixteen guns, and they are a lot of fun.

I do worry. I've got no health insurance. I'm feeling pain in both elbows. Oystering's working on the left one and crabbing's working on the right. I worry about becoming like some of the old bachelors here. I'd like a little kid, a boy. I'll miss that if I never have it. But I love it on the water. I love to wonder what's next tomorrow, and next season. I love to catch stuff you can't see with your naked eye. Another few years and I will have my boat paid off. If I can keep doing like I've been doing the rest of my life, I'll be content. ✦

Six months after this interview, with crabbing poor and oysters forecast for another down winter, Jessie took a job as captain/educator with the Chesapeake Bay Foundation.

The Artist

Anyone who survives long out here has to be creative.   —*Reuben Becker*

Reuben lives in the white, gabled house at the end of the lane, by the willow tree, where the town stops and the marsh rolls on to the horizons. The three-story frame home is typical turn-of-the-century island architecture; but enter—and leave the island like Alice tumbling down the rabbit hole. Inside is a pure statement of the artist's life, a temple to frugality and whimsy. Odors of wood smoke, tobacco, incense, and last night's white clam sauce suffuse the interior, along with southern light that filters softly through panels of castaway plastic, joined with putty and painted to look like leaded, stained glass. Old, mellow wood is everywhere exposed—beams, floors, tables, walls. Heat flows through the floor-to-roof, open architecture from twin 50-gallon oil drums. A short pipe joins them, one atop the other, to efficiently burn and reburn the scavenged wood Reuben stockpiles year round. An old hot-water heater has been converted to burn anything from bacon grease to the used oil watermen drain from their boat engines. Decorative planters and light shades, formerly bushel baskets cast up in the marsh, hang from ceiling and walls. An elegant room-dividing screen turns out to be crab basket bottoms glued together, carved and lacquered.

The bathroom, also a combination greenhouse and solar collector, has a glass outside wall. It encloses a small wetland, alive with minnows, fiddler crabs, and marsh grasses. A ceiling is swirled fantastically with hues of closeout-priced duck decoy paint. An antique brick wall across the back of the kitchen, on close inspection is Styrofoam packing. A single brick made it. Reuben used it to impress a pattern in the foam, then ground it into a brick paste which he spread across the panels.

Virtually every surface and nook, every chair and lamp and decoration throughout the old house is artifice and invention—all scavenged, recycled, retrieved from islanders' trash and the bay's flotsam. Total cost of the whole interior and furnishings is about $500. Utilities run around $400 a year, this mostly to run lights and the big Bose speakers that thunder Shostakovich and other classical music while Reuben paints. A single, small tube of propane suffices for a year's cooking, since only top burners, never the oven, are used. The house takes several visits to comprehend, and seems to change and grow like something organic.

Reuben keeps late hours, and because he has no phone, does not mind unannounced visitors, who are even more welcome if they bear a bottle or two of wine. Then he ushers you into his living room, fashions a smoke from the can of Roll-Rich loose tobacco that seems never out of his reach, and regales you with stories of his twenty years amid the islanders. He is, to my knowledge, the only outsider, other than a few women marrying here, who can be said to have stuck permanently. If a visitor is lucky, the artist invites them to his second-floor loft, where a painting has progressed far enough that he feels comfortable showing it. He works exclusively in oils, which he applies thickly, preferring application knives to brushes. He loves the paint for its physical, textural self, and has nothing good to say about watercolors. His works tend to be large, some close to the size of doors—literally. He has an attic full of interior doors, thrown out from a public housing project in Crisfield during renovations. They are cheaper than canvas, sturdy enough to withstand knocks coming and going aboard the ferries; and he likes the way they take the paint. Once he has framed one of these, employing whatever lumber is at hand, it is all a proud purchaser can do to lug one home. "Two-nailers," he will say, in advising how to mount them.

Always, a visit to the loft is a new experience. Reuben's skills and range of expression run the gamut. He can do portraits and landscapes; impressionism and near-photographic realism; also abstract—I believe if he never had to make another dollar, he might compose nothing the rest of his life but door after door of pure color. At the other end of the spectrum he can, if finances are perilous enough, churn out lovely, trite renditions of abandoned crab shanties and old skiffs in the marsh, such as most tourists seem to want to remember the island by. I once heard a local waterman cajoling him to "do my workboat . . . make it about yea-long, 'cause my wife says she needs it to run across the back of the living-room sofa." It is a mighty ugly boat, her keel badly hogged, Reuben told him. Check back this winter. If he is starving, he may have to do it.

Because he refuses to deal with art galleries, or exhibit his paintings, or otherwise market himself, he accepts what the drop-by, word-of-mouth market pays—from a few hundred to a thousand dollars for his large oils, less for his small studies and drawings. Each painting is all that usually stands between him and tomorrow's living expenses, and what is on his easel is normally all he has in stock. If you like a piece, you learn to speak for it immediately or it may be gone. And having tired of a subject, or a particular palette of colors, he may abruptly depart and never, or not for years, revisit it, even if patrons plead. In fact, the surest way not to get a particular painting is to tell Reuben exactly what you want. He prefers to get to know you, and come up with what he deems suitable.

My personal favorites were his huge, impressionistic marsh- and waterscapes, in which the island became Reuben's wilder, tidal version of Giverny, the French country home whose tended gardens and lily ponds Claude Monet immortalized. At some point it dawned on me that Reuben's paintings, each works of art in their own right, represented, collectively, an extraordinary portrait of the island. Into his studio, into his consciousness for nearly two decades, the best and worst of island and islanders had flowed like tide; and flowed back out, transformed into art.

The dying of an old Rhodes Pointer, and a way of life, were commemorated in his oil of a decaying house and skiff, intricately shadowed by a ghostly tree whose interlocking branches symbolized the tight community. Once in Baltimore, quite by accident, I came up a stairwell in a house I was visiting and gasped: before me, painted in dark, crab-shell tones, was a large work that so evoked the grinding drudgery of traveling half your life on ferries to get on and off the island, I knew without hesitation it was a Reuben. A surrealistic vision, a storm over the Methodist church, graves in the nearby cemetery all open, recalled a time when he felt the island's always exuberant religious bent had become oppressive.

Another, titled *The Color of Money,* was a vast representation of water on which the island appeared as little more than a long, green smudge. It hangs now in my living room, and a film crew, interviewing me in front of it, exclaimed that on their video monitors it looked uncannily like the Chesapeake Bay that lay behind me. A lot of people, Reuben said, would consider that waterscape an empty painting, but not people who made their living from the bay. In hundreds of ways, he has preserved the beauty and joy, the sadness and hypocrisy, the gossip and humor of a people and place—neither of which may prove as permanent as his oils. He has catalogued nothing of this, and since he doesn't own a camera, has rarely photographed a piece before he sold it. He still knows, he says, where many paintings reside, but each year they become more scattered.

This bothers Reuben not half so much as it does me. As always, he has his own agenda, this man who spent years managing a Baltimore dental laboratory, but so distrusts dentists that, one by one, he is pulling his own teeth as they rot; who came here married for the second time, but in love with another—a man. He eventually stood up in one of Methodism's most conservative churches and announced his homosexuality, which he never practiced here, having vowed on moving to become celibate. His balls, he would later say, had always taken so much energy away from his art. One day he handed me these lines from the introduction to a book about Joseph Conrad—"the way I feel about myself here":

*I gave up my own world to share what I knew with your people. It takes a radical to
so destroy his own life, yes? . . . to exile himself among people who feel uncomfortable in*

his presence, who fear his most deeply held values as treason, and who are not interested in what he had to say in the first place.

One could argue Reuben was fitted to flourish among the islanders, who have, after all, a keen sympathy for cussed independence.

REUBEN BECKER, FIFTY-EIGHT

✦ I came here from Baltimore in 1972, when I was thirty-six. I was struggling with my art and my sexuality. I think now what I sought was a certain freedom of expression. Freedom to be themselves seems to me the main reason the islanders are here. I knew I would be alienated, and that is what I wanted. I knew *how* to paint. I had to work out the *why,* free of anyone's opinions. This was a place where nobody had even known a painter, nor would they be overly interested in one. Ultimately, the island helped me discover my reason for painting. I believe it is about the same reason cavemen did it. They just had an urge to decorate. People here already sense what scientists, using computers, are just getting to with their Chaos theories—that the meaning of life is . . . it's just a damn mess. Express yourself, as a painter, as a crabber; and trust in the Lord. We are all Christian anarchists out here.

Apart from the intellectual isolation I knew I would find, I did romanticize the island before I came. Most people do attach a mystique to islands. How do you think an awful show like *Gilligan's Island* stays in reruns? But you couldn't live here long and do that, because it's just not that romantic except maybe for the closeness to nature, and even that's not romantic; it's just real. But how could I be disappointed? Reality is what I was looking for. Art that doesn't begin with it is just mannerism.

There is a beauty and an eloquence to the reality of their lives. Watermen, maybe because what they do is mostly just boring, reflect on things like beauty in the marsh or the water more than most people think. Here, it influences your whole day whether the wind's blowing or the sun's out. When you hear an old dredger captain talk about his sailing vessel, there's an edge of love there, almost poetry; yet, objectively, life aboard those old boats in the winter had to be the hardest, coldest, riskiest, meanest existence—just a bitch—and yet those old guys get tears in their eyes talking about it. I'm a back door ecologist; I believe a lot of what makes a human is the earth, and here they're right involved with the process. Their lives must find a harmony with the environment to make a living here, and in that respect they can be artful. Anyone who survives long out here has to be creative.

I have drawn deeply on the people here. There's a wisdom, an intelligence among them—I don't know how you would measure it; the way a top crabber factors in a hundred subtle things that lets him find the soft crabs day after day. Good painting is intimate like that. The wisdom is beyond simple connection to nature. "We live here among a cloud of witnesses"—it is a biblical expression they often use. They mean it as the need for Christians to act rightly and in the best interests of the community; but to me it goes further, implies almost subliminal connections that bind people.

I'll explain it this way. By the time you are a teenager here, there's almost nothing you don't know about everybody. You know how they think, what they look like naked, how they're likely to react. A person an outsider might think is strange; here you think, well, they're like their grandfather; and probably they are like their great-great grandfather, who is probably your great-great grandfather too. If I lived to be a hundred in Baltimore, I would never have understood how some people could stab me in the back. There's people here who will stab you in the back, too; but it's all known, you are never surprised. Charlie, one winter, who owns the only grocery in town, cut off my credit after an argument he had that didn't involve me directly, but involved some people close to me. Now, a lot of people knew about it, and you could just see 'em factoring that into all their knowledge of Charlie; and somehow that made me feel good. It is part of why a fairly high percentage of people out here know who they are. I have heard so many of them say of their lives, which were genuinely hard, "I was content."

In the strictest sense, the island's faith is not my faith. I am spiritual and Christian, but in my twenties I converted to Catholicism. I've sat in on their Methodist testifying, and the Lord, I'm afraid, just snickered. But I know I've experienced more miraculous things here than any other place. It is a miracle most weeks that I eat, and keep a roof over my head. I'm a lily of the field. Part of what drew me here was that it seemed a place where I could slough off lots of things like money, cars, insurance to just paint, and I did; but if I were to project my life a week ahead, most times I'd be starving to death.

One of the lowest points I hit here, during a particularly bleak winter, I decided to go off and get a real job, but an islander said to me, no, don't worry, we're always still here when spring comes, and of course we were. I get what I need, somehow, and it has been like that for years. Just when I ran out of wood to heat, in one of the coldest winters of the decade, the biggest ice storm of the century came and broke half the trees here, enough to last for years. When I was struggling to turn this gutted old shell of a house into something habitable, here came a fool outsider who tore off a perfectly good porch, which paneled my home. When I wanted a solar rig to help heat the house, it seemed like everybody in town wanted Anderson windows, and I got stacks and stacks of old glass.

I think that in the natural state, man is religious because he experiences things that seem miraculous, and they aren't at all the Hollywood-type miracles, heavens opening and so forth; it's getting your daily bread. The most hardened waterman here will say, "The Lord took care of me today." They think that's a miracle, or at least cause for thanks. Maybe one reason watermen don't believe everything scientists say about the bay is it would drive them crazy, projecting those gloomy trends on out for months and years; better for your sanity to take it day by day and trust in the unknown. An outsider might think that is unreasonable, but what's reasonable about faith? I think it is probably an ongoing miracle that this place exists, persists.

I rarely leave the island, and then usually in the little sailboat I "bought" for doing four paintings of the tourist type I hate to do. Outsiders often ask if it doesn't wear on me, spending my life in such a small place. In fact it is far less provincial than Hanover, Pennsylvania, where I grew up. Here, I was able to stand up in the church and admit to people that I was gay. I did not do it to shock them. I felt it was important that I explain. I didn't feel like being a second-class citizen. I had been through the in-the-closet phase, and then through the "I'm gay and I'm proud" bit, swishing down Howard Street in Baltimore. Now, I just wanted to be me. There was very little reaction. They are more liberal, more capable of acceptance here than outsiders might dream—more so as individuals than as a church or a community. I don't mean to say I am considered one of them. That is something I never expected or even wanted. After I had been here some twenty years, I nearly died from a rare fungus that invaded my whole system. I was hospitalized for forty days at Johns Hopkins. Given my background, and the fact I had low T-cell counts and other symptoms similar to AIDS patients, of course I was tested for the HIV virus a dozen times or more. I am the most certified HIV-free person on Smith Island, but I guess at least half of them will tell you—tell you sadly, I'm proud to say—that poor Reuben seems to have got the AIDS.

This was not the first time I made the local news for having a little different lifestyle. The great dope raid of 1980 came in late winter, when it always gets craziest around the island. The preacher then will get on a drug and alcohol kick, and people are in between oysters and crabs, home a lot and not so busy, and have too much time to worry about their kids and their community going to the devil. Anyhow, a plainclothes state trooper began showing up around town, passing himself off as a "novelist." Back then, I was in a phase of being sort of a hippie guru to some of the young men and older teenagers around here, who would gather at my house. One of them brought this sport along, and I offered him a pipe of marijuana, which according to the report he would write later, he "simulated" smoking. Hah!

The raid came at 5:00 A.M. Apparently the "novelist" had concluded, on God knows what evidence, that Smith Island was a major transshipment point for drugs coming into the country; and my house was the alleged nerve

center of the operation. The police staged a regular battlefield pincers movement, with boats and helicopters coming at the island from Deal Island to
the north and Crisfield to the east. I was painting when they came pound-
ing up my back stairway and through the front door, shotguns drawn. They
ripped the place half apart looking for bales of dope, and found about an
ounce of homegrown and the one little, four-leaf plant I had on the window
sill. Fortunately they did not find the pound of homegrown I kept in my old
organ. The lid to the keyboard was stuck, and the trooper was afraid it was
an antique and did not want to force it open. I think they felt foolish about
failing to crack the nerve center of east coast drug distribution that night.

They took me off that night with a few co-conspirators, most of us in cuffs,
bouncing in big head seas all the way to Deal Island. I got three years pro-
bation and $3,000 in fines, an impossible sum by my standards. I finally paid
off $1,500, and told the preacher I was going to jail rather than come up with
the rest. He raised the balance from people on the island and paid off my
fine. The painting I started that night is still on the island, in one of my fellow drug lord's houses. It is the one with the colors of the American flag all
knotted and contorted, a memento of the evening.

I also came close to drowning just off the bayside of the island. I was just
slipping away, remembering my childhood, when they rescued me. Another
time, before I knew the waters here, a few of us sank in a small boat just inside the Tangier Sound entrance to the island. The boat turned over, and
with great effort we managed to get atop her bottom and straddle it, and there
we sat, cold and shivering, and worried sick it would tip and drown us all.
Finally, a waterman came close in his workboat and motioned to us. No one
moved. Then finally one of us said, "Let's swim for it, boys," and we jumped
off, into water that for acres and acres all around was about two to three feet
deep.

Although I came here because I thought it might free me to paint, I never
came here to paint the island. The subjects are not so important. Expression
is important. The paint is important. But I have always been attracted to
water, and I do find peace in the marsh. I could be very happy to just do
painting after painting of a single view out my window, showing the way the
light changes on the marsh and water, changes the way the paint goes on.
Monet did that with haystacks, you know.

I think there is a rough parallel between the art of painting and the lives
of islanders, the subtleties and richness of culture derived from such a spare,
demanding environment. You only have three primary colors, blue, red, and
yellow, and all others are the addition of shade and light, and it's in that
tremendous limitation that painting gains its tremendous power—suggest-
ing colors that really don't exist. Painting water, which is truly colorless, is
all about that, and I do think I paint nice water. I find beauty, too, in the

impermanence of the solid, static structures: the spidery, rickety docks and poles and shanties, set against the permanence of the fluid environment that surrounds them.

I can't imagine leaving here now. There is a sense of place that has captured me completely, and draws me back so strongly whenever I do leave for even a bit. And I care deeply for people here. Have I captured the island in my art? Perhaps the whole body of my work might help explain it a little. I know this; science and fact will never be adequate to explain the island. It will take art. ✦

Island Doctor

ERIC SOHR

◆ The day in 1983 I first went to see the island, the captain bringing me over asked, did I need help getting aboard. Before I could answer, he said, "Because if you do, doc, we don't need you here." The accents there were very strange, and I remember thinking how dirty the place seemed—at the time there was an open dump, and half a mile of rusted cars lining the one main road. So many of the docks and shanties seemed just patched together, and the waterfront was full of junk.

I was recently separated, a single father of two boys, four and seven, and looking to get off the treadmill of a family practice in Montana. I had three choices: a fellowship at the University of Missouri; moving to Saudi Arabia and making an enormous amount of money; and Smith Island, where I was not sure I could survive financially. Years before, I practiced in a town on the Eastern Shore mainland. I didn't like the town, but I became absolutely addicted to crabbing. The day I first visited the island, I listened to the men in Tylerton's church, talking about all the ways there were to catch a crab. I was impressed. The job would include a house, rent-free, and my utilities paid. For making house calls I acquired a skiff and a bicycle. I arranged to work a weekly, twenty-four-hour emergency room shift in Crisfield's little hospital to make ends meet, and that was how I became the island's first doctor in fourteen years. When there was slow time in the E.R., I sometimes passed it by weaving crab nets as the islanders taught me.

The island was a good place to be a single parent. The boys were always in a crowd of kids. I felt like I had a hundred sets of grandparents. The people were so affectionate and polite. There was just a gentleness to them. In nearly four years there, I got very little business from fights. The islanders were very good at not taking offense. They have worked out non-violent ways of living better than most.

It seemed resident doctors had served the island, periodically, for at least a century. Other times, there had been nurses; also, in modern times, a number of dentists and doctors and nurses from the western shore—including the National Institutes of Health, Johns Hopkins, and Georgetown University—had volunteered time there. Most recently, several of the local volunteer firemen and women have trained as Emergency Medical Technicians.

I was struck by how motivated to work the islanders were. If injured, their first question was always how they might get back to work in spite of it. Both men and women were that way. I don't think I have ever seen such a strong work ethic except among cowboys I treated in the West. Islanders had a heritage of taking care of problems on their own. They would talk about old-timers like the man who got blood poisoning after a crab bit him. With red streaks shooting up his arm, he decided to "walk it off." For two days and nights, in agony, he paced back and forth in his house, sometimes putting a jacket or blanket over his head to try and blot out the pain. A young woman with no health insurance said she had treated herself for what must have been quite severe burns from a kitchen accident that scalded all over her thighs. It was not unusual for men to do minor surgery on themselves—for infection around fingernails, for example; and I recall a housewife setting her own dislocated elbow.

I was very impressed by the physical strength of the men, from pulling scrapes and pots and tongs all their lives. One crab scraper in his late seventies came to me with a bicep muscle that had ripped completely loose on one end. Soon after, he was back on the water, pulling in scrapes that, moving through the water, were like lifting 100-pound weights.

For all that, I would not say islanders were an unusually healthy population. Diabetes and heart disease seemed to run in some families with extraordinary frequency, and there was more obesity than on the mainland. Some of it was lifestyle and diet. I gained ten pounds a year, every year I lived there. They ate lots of seafood, but mostly deep fried; and they put sugar in everything, even lasagna. Also, though they worked hard, aerobic activity in such a confined place was easily avoided. Smoking was rampant, especially among men. It is that way on the whole Delmarva Peninsula, which has one of the nation's highest rates of lung cancer deaths.

Some of their problems likely were genetic. A western shore doctor to whom I showed photos from the island remarked that just from some of the faces, he could tell there was inbreeding. He acted as if he had already decided they were somehow inferior. To my knowledge, no one has ever done a careful study of the island's genetic situation. On Tangier Island, a similar population to Smith, a study in the 1960s identified a rare genetic abnormality that causes elevated cholesterol, enlarged liver, spleen, and tonsils. It is known as Tangier Disease, and only a few dozen cases have been documented worldwide.

Of course the gene pool is less diverse for Smith Island than most of mainland America. On the other hand, it is scarcely as if people are going around marrying their first cousins. This stuff about the islanders all being descended from the same families who founded the place a few centuries ago is overstated. You find out, when you start talking to them, that quite a few people, in just the last few generations, came from other places, often through marriage. Several of the kids there, some of them now grown and married, were adopted from the mainland. There is a branch of the Smiths that is unrelated to the other Smiths. The family was established on the island around the turn of the century when a Smith from Manhattan, to get away from an abusive home situation, found work on an oyster dredge boat and settled here. It's said there were some marriages that brought Native American blood over here several decades back. At any rate, you quickly grow to see through the faces; and what you see are some of the most interesting and beautiful people you will ever meet.

Other medical conditions are what you would expect from people in the occupations they follow there: bone spurs from standing so much on boat decks; eye trauma and precancerous skin growths from constant exposure to the sun's glare. A gynecologist on the mainland said it was not uncommon to see women with hernias and other problems aggravated by the heavy lifting they do, horsing bushels and boxes of seafood on and off boats and into crab steamers.

I never expected my practice would be a normal one. My first emergency house call I set off on a bike, down a wet, slick road, with my emergency defibrillator dangling from the handlebars. I had not been there a month when a woman came over from church with asthma. I was working on her when the State Police Medevac helicopter landed, and this trooper comes running in with an emergency medical pack and a gun in his shoulder holster. We tried, but she kept arresting and died in the office. Afterward an islander remarked it was a shame she couldn't have gone en route, on the 'copter. I asked why. Been a little closer to the Home Office, he said.

Three days a week, I made house calls, a day for each town. For Tylerton, I went down in my little skiff. A third of the population there was over sixty, and medically, the most important place to see older people is in the home. I would find a reason to peek in the refrigerator, to see if they were eating right; use the bathroom, to look in the medicine cabinet to make sure they were taking their medications—with so many same last names on the island, it could be a problem making sure the right person got a prescription.

The island can be a hard place to stay when you get old; but I have never seen a place where it is harder on old people to have to leave. "They throb with this island, like the bay with tide," a former preacher said. I don't think it is strange that all three churches say special prayers every Sunday for "all those in the nursing homes."

They valued a doctor, and were good about paying their bills—the most honest people I ever treated as far as expecting to pay for services and not expecting to get anything for free. They didn't have enormous expectations;

just expected you to be straight with them. A far bigger concern for me was tourists in the summer. You became an E.R. for strangers, and that made me nervous, because unlike the islanders, they could be litigious. I don't think I ever made more than $20,000 a year from the island practice. The mainland E.R. shift and some small savings allowed me to survive.

I have a personal interest in alcoholism, so I was attuned to alcohol abuse on the island. Even so, it seemed of major proportions. At least five young men in a decade had died, essentially, from drinking, even if that was not what the death certificate usually said. Some of it may have been genetic. One part of the island called me out so much on Saturday nights with alcohol-induced panic attacks that I doubled my usual fee of $20 a visit in those cases, and after that the calls stopped.

Maybe the drinking also had to do with the fact that people were seeing their whole culture implode, their way of life dwindle as the seafood declined and the population dropped. They have gone from subsistence to consumerism on the island awfully fast, in little more than a generation. People's time wasn't as free any more, they said.

I had guaranteed to stay a year, and I stayed almost four. I moved because my oldest was getting near the age when he would leave the island every day for school on the mainland—not a school that impressed me, either. I still miss the nature of the place, the way the reality of work was so apparent. You saw your dad and mom working right around you; watched your whole community harvesting a living as you rode across the Sound to school. Your surroundings were so connected to your whole being. And I remember the people, how beautiful their voices were—they loved to sing. And of course the crabbing, which I came for, was just superb. ❖

Technology

PHONE MAN

I HAD BEEN meaning to get a new phone installed, and as luck would have it, while skiffing down the main channel I saw Henry sitting in the sun on his shanty dock, fixing a crab pot. I put in my work order:

"Hey, Hen! Hook me up a phone down to Paul and Mable's house?"

Paul and Mable had been dead a while; but before I and some friends bought it for a vacation home (for after I moved to the mainland), it was their home for forty years, and before that Mable's dad's, and before that, probably her grandad's. Also, Henry's mother-in-law, Lil, lives two houses away, and grew up with Paul and Mable. So we still call it Paul and Mable's, and will for a while.

Henry is the Chesapeake & Potomac Telephone Company's sole representative on the island, which got phones connected to the mainland in the early 1950s. Like most aspects of life here, phone service always has marched to its own tune. Once I asked Hen whether C&P could do something about the big old red cedar whose limbs were pressing perilously on the phone and power lines in front of my house. " 'Deed they could," Henry said, disappearing inside his shanty. He returned with a murderous-looking pole saw, about 15 feet in length, which he put in my skiff. Keep it as long as I needed, he said, "and watch out for the limb when she falls."

We had few frills. Touch tone service was simply not an option; nor was direct-dial long distance. Crisfield, the mainland port of a couple thousand people, was the only non-toll call. Still, the system had its funky charms. It was ancient enough to be mechanically switched, which meant that often, Henry could solve a problem in the line by walking outside to the little phone building beside his house and jiggering the switches until you were restored. And of course, getting a new hookup was as simple and as friendly as my hollering across the channel to the phone man.

But something was wrong. Henry was flagging me down, trying to explain that we could not have these intimate conservations any more; could not go on meeting like this. I must go through the C&P computer with orders now, he said, looking a little embarrassed. But who would hook my phone in at Paul and Mabel's? Oh, he would, same as always, Henry said; but until the computer told him what I wanted and where I lived, he couldn't make a move.

I called the computer. A lady at C&P answered; very nice, very sympathetic, very patient. She had, I suspect, a Ph.D. in placating smartasses. She would need the address of my house to enter in the computer, the lady explained. But I had no address. No one on the island used addresses. The little lanes that passed for streets had no names for the most part. It was a small place where everyone knew everyone.

Tell the computer to tell Henry to come to Paul and Mabel's house, I told the lady, adding that his mother-in-law, Lil, lived just two houses down. Perhaps I could give the address of the house directly adjacent, the lady suggested. Well, that'd be Marsha and Brov's; but I didn't know how to spell Brov. Come to think of it, that wasn't his real name anyhow. Come on, lady. That computer is not going to install my phone. Henry is, and he doesn't need a print-out to find the place.

Round one ended in a draw. The next day, the computer lady called me back with good news. We had an address. Seems that Civil Defense in Somerset County had numbered every house and named every lane on the island the year before as part of the new statewide 911 system. It meant that the ambulance or the police could find you quickly, she explained. I didn't mention to her that in three hundred years, the island has had no police force; nor is there a street in Tylerton wide enough for an ambulance to even turn around.

Meekly, I received my address from the lady. I now live on Marshall Street. That seemed fair, since five of the seven families living on the street for most of this century were named Marshall, including Lil, Henry's mother-in-law. My house number had five digits, which seemed a waste, since there aren't much more than fifty inhabited houses in the whole town. She sent me a copy of the street names, and I was relieved to see they hadn't gone too cutesy in naming thoroughfares—not any "Singing Swan Courts" or "Feisty Crab Lanes." Tylerton's main paths were Center Street, Back Road, Shore Road, and Cemetery Road. Ewell favored Oyster House Road, Shell Road #1 and Shell Road #2. Rhodes Point was most straightforward: Marsh Road ran roughly east-west, and Smith Island Road ran north, and that was it.

As for my new phone, Henry was duly dispatched by the computer, and he found Paul and Mabel's, he said, with no trouble; even visited Lil while he was down. The computer dispatch proved just the tip of the iceberg. Since then we have gotten digital switching and something called "memory administration" that runs the whole show out of Baltimore. We even got touch tone.

Islanders are upgrading their phone exchanges, trading in their old 425's for 968 [Crisfield] exchanges, which lets them call toll-free all the way to Salisbury. It is getting to where, for the first time, you can tell by the phone exchange who's watching their pennies (425) and who's got a little extra (968).

One lady has even put a two-line model with conference capability in her crab shanty. Every morning in summer, about 3:00 A.M., she dials up friends in two other shanties and pushes the conference call and speaker phone buttons. They stay connected all through the morning, talking occasionally; other times just listening to the sounds of their friends smacking and cracking hard crabs over the speakers.

COMPUTER MAN

The island has now got a resident computer expert. He is so smart, some of the islanders say, they do not even know how to talk to him. At a community supper held to thank him for donating a computer to the Tylerton Elementary School, I was asked to sit next to him, as a sort of buffer between the locals and his unintelligible intelligence. I found him quite a pleasant fellow, though RAM and ROM and even more esoteric terms so peppered his conversation that I had to work hard to stay afloat in the digital torrent.

He had contracts with the Pentagon for software development, he said, implying it had something to do with the "Star Wars" anti-missile development program, launched a few years before by President Reagan.

Like Star Wars, the computer man was, at least superficially, very technologically impressive. He had wired the old frame house he rented for a serious array of electronics and communications. Somehow he had gotten a Washington phone exchange, which gave him toll-free calling capability that I envied. His kitchen was dominated with a state-of-the-art Jennaire, the kind for which "stove" is not sufficient description.

He had acquired a 24-foot Fiberglas boat, with a monster Mercury outboard. In it he could make a beeline from the island, across the bay, up the Potomac, to Washington in less time than you could take the ferry off and drive. It was loaded with electronic navigational devices, but its owner seemed neither to know or care much about tides and weather, or just how Godalmighty rough the bay between here and the Potomac's mouth can get.

I asked him how he came to set up shop here. He said he did a computer search for the best community in the United States to settle his family and business. Many of us thought this odd, since he had settled in Rhodes Point, which has its loyal supporters, but which, if you took a vote here, might not even come in first as the best community on Smith Island, never mind the whole United States.

I wished the computer man and his family well, but I feared they would turn out to be yet another example of what I have come to call the "Big fish in a small pond" syndrome. Smith Island is like a flytrap for a variety of dreamers and schemers. It is a charming place, and cheap to buy into. It is small enough that it seems an individual could make a difference. The islanders are friendly, and tend to be overly impressed by a bit of education, or the appearance of wealth; and they never tell anyone they are a fool, even if they think it.

And so, for reasons both noble and selfish, harebrained and considered, every year or so a few outsiders are seduced: the retired Navy man who would restart the oyster industry here, never mind that intractable diseases are killing oysters baywide; middle-aged men with not a callus on their hands who think they can adapt to the life of the watermen; artists who trust that someway, somehow, they will find a way to support themselves; people who make an initial show of wealth, only to leave suddenly, owing money; developers who see luxury waterfront condos, but not the sea nettles. Almost none ever stick; and the computer man was no exception.

He began to lose luster when he decided to erect a tower in his backyard to enhance his multiple communications capabilities. He had some software he claimed could tell him precisely how much concrete he would need to anchor it. His neighbors thought he was light on concrete by about half, maybe more. The west winds blow hard against Rhodes Point, and the soil there, one said, "is a darn sight marshier than anything that computer's ever seen, swagger it ain't."

The tower went up according to computer specifications; but before long it began to lean, and lean some more. It was great sport to watch its downward progress. I took to using it in my education programs, riding kids by in the boat, giving a little homily on local wisdom versus science. Perhaps it was an omen. Before it had completed its slow- motion, months-long crash into the marsh, its builder and his family were gone, owing many months rent, abandoning the Jennaire as too large to move. The boat and big Mercury were for sale, but the motor's lower drive unit was shot, islanders said. The computer man had run her aground once too often, and tied her up wrong and let her sink in a storm at least once. And now the marsh vegetation has grown over the antenna to where you cannot even see it.

Trash

My personal impression of a day I spent walking the island was disgust at
all the trash along the walkways and spare ground. Everything was there from beer
cans to rusted out engines to broken down cars. I noticed many people kept
their own places very neat, but obviously did not care about the big picture which
was presented.

—PAPER BY A STUDENT AT THE UNIVERSITY OF MARYLAND

MY PROFESSOR friend is upset. He sent a student here to do a paper he thought
would explore the island's sturdy values and delights. She was less politic than
most in her comments; but in truth, for all the spotlessly maintained interiors
of its homes, and the charm of approaching its villages through the marsh, this
island up close can be shockingly unaesthetic.

Every higher-than-normal tide brings forth a harvest of plastic motor oil containers, Pepsi bottles, and aluminum cans from the marsh. Not all of it is locally generated, but much of it is. More than once I have brought a boatload
of Bay Foundation kids back into town from crabbing down Tyler's Creek, following a trail of Budweiser cans that stretch, on the ebb tide, for nearly a mile
from a watermen's shanty party. There aren't many days when an oil slick does-
n't float by our dock from one of the workboat harbors. Just outside town is
"Refrigerator Gut," a winding little marsh creek, so dubbed by my assistant for
all the rusting appliances disposed of there.

The throw-it-overboard mentality is strong here. An islander told me about
the time he got a job, taking a dead man's relatives out on the bay to scatter his
ashes. "A good breeze came along, and I held the tin box of ashes out there and
let 'em blow. Next thing I knew, they were all hollerin' at me . . . well, I didn't
think they'd have use for an empty tin, so I had flung it overboard, too."

I gave considerable thought to the irony of a place both uniquely connected
with nature and treating it trashily. Almost every group of schoolkids I got asked
about it. It took the bloom off an otherwise inspirational environmental experience.

There is no wholly satisfactory explanation, but there are some partial ones:

—Erosion constantly preys on islanders' minds. The big stuff that goes overboard, the engine blocks, crankshafts, diesel batteries, and such, is seen as shoreline protection, not just dumping.

—This is working waterfront, not a yacht club, which is what dominates more and more of our shoreline in suburbanizing states like Maryland. No one here gets paid to paint pilings white and make sure ropes are all coiled neatly clockwise, or store all the equipment at 5:00 P.M. quitting time.

—There is somewhat of an "in your face" reaction to the modern environmental era, which embraces the kinds of regulatory coercions islanders detest in their very bones. I have seen more than one of them finish a Coke on the ferry, make sure I'm looking, and toss the can. "Might be a baby oyster catch on that and grow," one said.

—The historical explanation: people have been overboarding their trash here for a while, as evidenced by the fine collections of eighteenth- and nineteenth-century bottles many crabbers have scraped up. Many came from British warships that plied the bay during the American Revolution and the War of 1812.

—This has become, in recent decades, a community in decline. When the towns were more populated and vibrant, and the economy better, "we used to keep our waterfront up," the older women say. It would have been considered a disgrace to allow the litter that now clogs the shallows.

Mostly, it is just harder to get rid of trash here than on the mainland. Islands, for better or worse, make you confront many aspects of the human condition that can be put out of sight or moved away from on the mainland.

Consider the route taken by a bag of household trash, or for that matter a discarded stove or fallen tree limb, upon leaving a home in Tylerton. We carry it away by hand or by cart. You put it on the county dock to await the trash boat, which comes twice weekly, unless there is ice, or a holiday, or it is hauled for repairs. Several days of sun can turn the contents of those piles of black plastic trash bags into a fragrant stew; and despite our efforts to enclose the trash with plywood and chicken wire, the intrepid island cats usually find a way to get at it.

The trash boat carries everything to Ewell, where it is then loaded onto the dock, loaded into a truck, and taken halfway to Rhodes Point to an incinerator. Metal and other non-burnable scrap is impounded at the incinerator and periodically loaded back on a truck, taken back to Ewell, then boated to Crisfield, loaded on another truck, and taken to wherever the mainland puts such stuff.

Casual observation tells me the mainland doesn't do a much better job than Smith Island; but they usually do it well out of most people's sight and smell. That is the luxury of being connected by pavement to the rest of the North American continent. Here, we are not, and with our trash, it shows.

Perhaps the tide is turning, even here. The schoolkids have begun to embrace recycling aluminum. There is mild interest in the Bay Foundation's compost pile; and at least one waterman has installed an oil-recycling device in his crab boat.

Meanwhile, when you come to Tylerton, you won't be greeted any longer by the stench of garbage on the county dock at the entrance to town. No indeed. We have learned from the mainland. We have moved it around to the county boat ramp on the backside of town.

The Wedding

THE TYLERTON United Methodist Church is lovely, and full of eager antici-
pation as I've ever seen it. We've had too many funerals and too few christen-
ings; and now, for the first time in nearly three years, there is to be a wedding.

A cool nor'wester is beginning to blow in, brooming out the last of summer's
torpor, winding up the soft-crabbing treadmill everyone's been on for nearly
six months. The church is decorated with a pristine elegance, unlike the great,
bright splashes of flower baskets that accompany deaths. A simple garland of
evergreen and baby's breath accents the rails of the altar and choir loft, and rows
of long, slender white candles and a couple baskets of white flowers complete
the effect.

The bride is tall, blond, willowy, radiant. The bridesmaids are chatty and
teary; the flower girls are adorable; and the ring bearer is rambunctious and antsy.
The groom and his ushers have that oddly powerful dignity that results when
men you are used to seeing in crabbers' cap and boots and workclothes suddenly
appear in beautiful tuxedos.

You are aware of the bride's struggle, even at such a young age, with medical problems, and the tough time the groom has had making a go of it on the
water. You know what the bride's mother has gone through since cancer took
her husband less than a year ago. And then there are her own health problems,
and the difficulty one of her sons has had with his girlfriend. You think how
much she deserves this happy day.

The soloist sounds wonderful, her very act of singing an affirmation. You
wondered if she ever would raise that voice in song again, after the tragic drowning of her son not long ago. When she sings a phrase, "gave your child to the
Lord," there is an almost audible sigh, and scarcely a dry eye in the church.

And then one of the town's oldest watermen—how many times has he been
called upon to settle disputes?—stands and gives the bride away, in a strong clear
voice, "Her mother and I, in memory of her dad"; and you know how much
he thought of her dad.

For music, the family has pulled out all the stops, bringing Clarence K down
on the ferry from Ewell. Of all the considerable number of pianists on the island, he, self-taught, is in a class by himself. No major event for many years has
been complete without his trademark flourishes that turn every song into something special. Only in the processional does he play it standard.

A duet follows, and you realize how much you miss the singers, husband and wife, since they moved off. Her voice is so extraordinary, the first time visitors would hear it, they would think she was lip-synching to a recording; and you see their daughter, a bridesmaid, tearing up, and you know she's still not over the young island waterman she left behind when they moved.

And helping with the register where guests sign is another beautiful, blond young woman, the last island girl to get married here; and you know how her mom doted on her, and how proud a day that was; also you know, in more detail than you wished, that it failed. What must be going through her head now?

And now the crystalline air moving in on the northwest breeze has produced a golden late afternoon, and slants of sun through the stained glass have caught an old lady's face, just so; and you suddenly see in her the image of a waterman, her distant kin, buried here last year, tragically young; so much potential wasted.

Such images can spring upon you at any time with the islanders, who while they are not inbred in any clinically meaningful sense, do share a shallower gene pool than most mainland folks. When you first move here, many look alike. After a bit, they seem very individual. Then the time comes when a certain angle of the light, a way they hold their head, or use their hands, or say certain phrases reminds you of whole families and of friends moved away or long dead.

The father of the groom is attracting more attention than you might expect. Many of us haven't seen him, except out in his crab boat, for a long time. He has not been anywhere. He lives about 150 yards from the main body of Tylerton, just off the main track along the town's waterfront. But it's been a year, maybe two, since he came this far into town. He looks quite distinguished, and at ease accepting congratulations; but after the ceremony, he'll pass up the reception and head back "Down Below" at a determined pace, and who knows if he will ever pass this way again?

At the reception, featuring five times as much as you can eat at the upstairs part of the Tylerton Volunteer Fire Department, a baby is squalling. You notice, even in the crowd and hubbub, because he is the only one born here in the last four or five years; and you know the whole town is wondering whether he won't be the last, unless the newlyweds, and maybe one or two other young couples here, come through with some more.

And all these are just the thoughts and connections and memories triggered by a simple, one-hour wedding in yourself, who have only been around this curious and close little island for a few years. You can only wonder, what must it be like for people imbued with generations and centuries of the place?

YARNIN'

Wordplay

"WELL, get me tied, Marsha, *get me tied."* The speaker was an elderly island lady known for her "old-timey" ways of speaking. I scribbled to record yet another colorful expression of a place where centuries of watery isolation have nurtured a unique dialect.

"Yeah," she continued, "get me a small box . . . that's right, *Tide."*

Many a slip and simplistic assumption have been made in attempts to categorize the Smith Island speech. The islanders themselves, though willing enough to help, will often put down as unique phrases like "smart aleck" and "fit to be tied"; and then express surprise that you are intrigued by their use of "cod" for penis, or "he ain't lookin' for knotty logs" (i.e., he's lazy).

Uncritical writers (among them, a younger me) frequently have declared the island to be a pocket of "Elizabethan English"—as if utterances from the time of Shakespeare had been preserved in amber through the centuries.

That almost certainly overstates the case although, as Stanley Ellis of Weeton, England, my wonderfully helpful consultant on dialect, says, "Who knows what the Elizabethans sounded like? They haven't been around for a while, you know."

The Smith Island way of speaking—*"yarnin',"* as locals describe their rich storytelling tradition—is assuredly like nothing encountered by the modern, mainland ear. The Bradshaws, Marshalls, Marshes, Evanses, Somerses, and Tylers of the island are of English and Welsh origin, and in the mid-Chesapeake region these names go back to the seventeenth century, when the colony of Maryland was established and Elizabethans like Captain John Smith roamed the Chesapeake.

I sent some tapes of Smith Islanders, along with lists of island vocabulary, to Stanley Ellis, who is secretary of the Yorkshire Dialect Society and a principal field worker for the survey of dialects published in 1976 as a *Linguistic Atlas of England.* Stanley, who also works as a voice identification expert for the courts in England, says it is in the vowel sounds of English that regionality and origin of the speaker may surface most clearly. He found in the Smith Island tapes vowels "beautifully similar" to some nineteenth-century dialect recorded in Devon, in the southwest of England—tapes made of aged countrymen during the 1950s.

Such dialect, he contends, had been fairly well unchanged for three centuries.

The island vocabulary also matched a number of words from the *English Dialect Dictionary* of 1893. In sum, it is all far less than definitive, nothing that would impress the academic linguistics community, but if one wants to mention Elizabethan English and Smith Island in the same sentence, Stanley says, there is nothing farfetched to the proposition.

Certainly the charm of the islanders' speech resides in their vowels, rich and yeasty with intonation. And it is easy to imagine, in their soft, full *arr*'s, the mellow west country burr of Raleigh. Sometimes, returning to the island for a visit, I harken to a conversation just to let the warm patterns of the islanders' brogue flow over me, embracing and invigorating. "You'd take their words and use them if you could," Barclay Sheaks, a Virginia poet and painter, writes of such bay watermen: "but you couldn't make them *yaw* like they did."

The Elizabethans, isolated by political disputes from the rest of Europe on Shakespeare's "sceptered isle," were in a passionate love affair with their language. They made more than 12,000 additions in about 70 years. Words for them were succulent treats, to be mixed and simmered and stewed; doughs to be kneaded and shaped in new and fantastic ways.

You could, in this new, unrestrained vocabulization, *happy* your friend; or *uncle me no uncles*. In the autumn, *leaves and swans* both might fall from the sky. Nearly four centuries later an island friend, seeing how my teen-aged son had grown, exclaimed: "Why, I can see the muscle a'swellin' under that young skin like yeast in the bakin' pan." Another told me she would like to get a computer, "just to progue around in them electronics."

Ladies arrive back from Christmas shopping "scuppers under" with packages, like boats in danger of sinking; and a waterman says if he could just see Disney World once, "Swagger [swear], I wouldn't crave the world." A young hunter says he has concealed his gunning skiff so well, "ducks didn't know it was in the world"; and an old hunter, told by the nurse in the hospital to close his fly, replies: "Don't you worry—what's there nowadays is soft as diddle [duckling] down."

It ain't Shakespeare; but it ain't bad.

Language is still, in a modest way, being made up here. A child a few years ago emerged one morning to see an extreme low tide had left thousands of acres of the bay bottom in front of his home dry. "All the overboard's done gone," he shrieked; and "overboard" has since become an expression for the tide, or the shallows around the island.

And a woman who knew she was getting a reputation for being pushy characterized herself: "Ain't I the boss tippet?" ("tippet" being an island word for vagina, or the genital area of a female crab; derived possibly from the old English expression, "arse over tip"). Once as I returned, badly seasick from a crabbing trip, a passer-by said I was "greengilled." Where did you get that word from, I asked, weakly. "From how ye look," came the reply.

All of the above is flavored further by frequent use of wry sarcasm and "backward talk." "She's ugly" means they think she's pretty; and if "there ain't no gnats," then you are certain to be chewed alive. "I'd do that" means no way, Jack; and "that's fair" means anything but fair—excepting, of course, if it is inflected just so, when it means just the opposite, the opposite of its backward meaning, that is. It ain't confusin' none, is it?

Sometimes this kind of talk can get quite delightfully dry, as in the following monotone exchange between two local duck hunters:

> Let's go huntin'.
> I am [not about to].
> C'mon, let's shoot some ducks.
> Yer a nice man [no way I'm going].
> Don't ye want to go?
> That's just what I want [how many ways do I have to say no?].

In the age of television and satellite communications, you might expect serious erosion of the Smith Island manner of speech. Indeed, when the younger islanders want to indulge you with "proper talk," they can carry it off with aplomb—even mocking your own accent with embarrassing accuracy if they choose.

But the old ways do persist. I had just returned from a fast and furious canoe paddle through the guts with Abby and some of her elementary school friends, laughing all the way. One of the little girls hollered to her mother:

"Ma, that was poor fun. Comin' back, we weren't a'headin' it none."

Tell It Like It Is—Life on Smith's Island

THE FOLLOWING vignettes are the author's invention, though derived from actual incidents or typical island life. They afford a taste of the unique local expressions, including "backward talk"; also some of about fifty different terms applied to crabs.

While it is unlikely a modern-day Smith Islander would cram so much of the local expression into so short a space, virtually any adult would comprehend everything here.

I WAS BORN in Ireland(1) in the worst winter the island had ever seen. It was a genuine fuzz cod(2) from nor'west, glass(3) a'fallin' like a striker(4). Warn't no wind that night.

Tide was druv so high, Dad could not fetch Granny Evans from Longbranch to help Ma with the birth. 'Board of a boat Dad warn't fear'd o'nothin'—scrape or drudge or tong with the best of 'em. Stickin' them great ole big poles to hold his pound nets out in the bay, he could shout 'em down(5) like that clay bottom was butter.

But now, all alone with Ma, and me a'comin', all he could do was pace the floor and say over and over, "What must I do?" Ma began to screechin', you could hear her holler to Warsaw.

"I'm in cod(6) now," Dad said, "swagger I am."

It was time. Ma squeezed his big, hard hand and looked 'im in the eye and said, "Bay or bull"(7).

He bent to help. "Goin' to Boggses,"(8) he sighed.

Growin' up, a dollar looked big as a bed sheet. No one had much, but our family was poorer'n Pern(1). To make ends meet, we kids would 'spargas(2) in

1. *Ireland:* a marsh hummock, origin of name unknown. 2. *fuzz cod:* gale. 3. *glass:* barometer. 4. *striker:* tern, a bird that dives for fish. 5. *shout 'em down:* drive into the bottom, by attaching a cross piece to each pole and jumping on it. 6. *in cod:* in a jam. 7. *bay or bull:* fish or cut bait—when semi-wild cattle ran on the island, people would get caught between facing a bull or swimming to safety. 8. *goin' to Boggses;* here goes nothing—reference to the burial place of a black family, far outside the white churchyards. Black residents have been rare throughout the island's history

1. *Pern:* name of a Tangierman, legendary for his poverty. 2. *'spargas:* hunt wild asparagus..

the spring and nipper(3) in the fall. Summers, we'd progue in the marsh for pennywinkles(4).

One winter, come a freeze-up so hard Pa and the other drudgers all had to quit oysterin'. We warn't hungry none—we ate pheasant and sudleys(5) one whole week. When the ice broke, we went tarp'nin(6). We got three bushels and sold 'em for three dollars. Swagger die if that warn't the champ(7).

When spring finally came, it put us in heart(1). The first ladder of diddles(2) come off more'n I ever saw, and the figs and pears was a'swellin' on every limb. The peeler crab run seemed like ever' one rank(3), not a snot(4) among 'em.

There were nine of us kids—Ma was all the time leveled off(5), seemed like. One evening Pa gave us all money to go to the store in Ewell for noogs(6). That was poor fun(7).

We was leavin' when a big boy cussed me for fishing his crab pots. We nearly went to clinkin'(8). I mean, we was down to temple locks flared off(9). I could smell his ole breath, bitter as owl gravy. He had me backed spang against a float full of jimmies and sooks, all doubled up a'matin'.

Quicker'n a eel I reached back and snatched me a big jimmy and flung 'im, jest a'snappin' and a'clackin', right at that yarny(10) and his buddies. A jimmy took away from his wife like that, now he wouldn't harm ye none. That was a tender(11) crab. Ye'd think a bum(12) had fell among 'em, way them boys scattered.

The big boy, he moved fast, but the big jimmy, he was faster. He cotched one earlobe in his right pinchers, which has got them square biters like your own back teeth, for crushin' and a'squeezin'.

The big boy was in cod now, screechin' and bleedin' and a'shakin' his head like a broad-billed oyster toad(13); and all that jimmy crab did was swing up and grab the other ear in his left pinchers, which has them sharp, pointy biters, for sawin' and cuttin'.

We left jimmy and his new wife, just waltzin' and whoopin' it up on the dock. We never laughed 'til we landed home; then we never laughed none(14).

---

3. *nipper:* pick up individual oysters in the clear shallows with miniature tongs. 4. *pennywinkles:* periwinkles. 5. *pheasant* and *sudleys:* merganser and old squaw, both poor-eating, fishy-tasting waterfowl. 6. *tarp'nin:* catching terrapin. 7. *swagger die . . . champ:* swear to die if that wasn't the greatest thing.

1. *in heart (out of heart):* feeling good (depressed). 2. *ladder of diddles:* hatch of ducklings. 3–4. *rank:* best kind of peeler, ready to become a soft-crab *snot;* earliest stage of peeler, many never turn soft. 5. *leveled off:* pregnant; full, as leveled off with flu. 6. *noogs:* dessert, sweets. 7. *poor fun:* great fun. 8. *clinking:* fighting. 9. *temple locks . . . :* red-faced, nose to nose. 10. *yarny:* Tangierman; or general derision, like bozo. 11. *tender:* mean. 12. *bum:* bomb. 13. *broad-billed oyster toad:* ugly fish with bulldog head and jaws. 14. *never laughed . . . never laughed none:* mixture of straight and backward talk; they didn't laugh . . . they laughed a lot.

By the summer I turned fifteen I was gorged on school. I went to scrapin'
and tongin' in Pa's old bateau, and many a mornin' my back felt kofered(1) as
the planks in that boat. But it was good to be on my own, even if Ma still packed
my bail(2) every night and told me not to forget my oilskins les't it rain.

My little shanty became the takeup place for the other young men, where
we would gather to pass the evening, making pots, griping about the skrags(3),
and just watching the tide run and the stars come out.

One week crabbin' had got bad as ever I knowed it. Everything in the scrapes
was buckramy(4); the pots was right sooky(5), and when the breeze died, there
wouldn't be neither gnat.

You'd spend more on gas than you'd catch in crabs; so there we was one
mornin', middle of the crabbing day, boats rafted up in Hog Neck Bottom,
passin' 'round a joint of killer weed. Nobody did much more crabbin' that day.

In the store that night, I heer'd the older crabbers talkin' worried like:

"I fear the young men of the island has got plumb out o' heart with these
scarce crabs. Today I see'd 'em all pull over together just to share one little bit
of a cigarette."

Even if you never went to church, you never missed going there for the Christmas pageant, which had been a'goin' for moren'n a hundred years.

The champ'n'est one there ever was was the year they asked Severn to play
lead angel. It was the talk of the town, 'cause he had not set foot inside a church
since they kicked him outta Bible School.

But I'ma die(1) if he didn't take it to heart; even announced he would be
givin' up drinkin' until after the pageant, and commenced to practicin' "proper
talk," like a mainlander.

Christmas week him and me was a'tongin' on scarce arsters up to Terrapin
Sands, when here come the arster police.

Now Severn may 'o been workin' overtime to obey the laws of God; but the
laws of man, 'specially the ones 'gainst keepin' small arsters; well, even the holi-
est roller from Drum Point(2) would see that as a separate thing.

So the cop zooms up in his speedboat, just as Severn dumps three bushels of
little ones in the Tangier Sound and scrapes the last of the evidence off his washboards.

1. Koferred: warped, bent. 2. *bail:* meal, lunch. 3. *skrag:* inept waterman who horns in on your good
fishing spot. 4. *buckramy:* stiff, cardboardy shell of crab turning from soft back to hard; meat of a buck-
ram is still poor. 5. *sooky:* full of sooks, mature females that fetch a low price and won't ever turn soft
again.

1. *I'ma die:* I hope to die. 2. *Drum Point:* modern-day Tylerton, reputed to have the island's hardest-
core religion.

Well, the cop seen it all, but he didn't have no evidence; but then he did a dirty thing.

"Severn," he says, "I know ye are a truthful man, and I'm goin' to ask you straight, did you tong them little arsters down there?"

Well, Severn, for all his bad habits, never liked to lie, and this month especially, it woulda kilt 'im. Cop looks 'im in the eye. Severn looks at the cop, like he'd love to wrap his killet(3) 'round his scrawny neck.

Then he asks the cop, who's got kin on the island: does he know about the Christmas pageant?

That he does, says the cop. It is the most inspirin' service he was ever to, though it's been a while; and he just goes on and on about that pageant and Christmas on the island and all.

"Well, then," says Severn. "I don't guess ye'd want to be the man that give the Angel Gabriel a ticket for small arsters."

Dast if he didn't have 'im there. Swagger die, if that warn't the word with the wool on it(4).

---

3. *killet:* from killick, or small anchor; heavy weight used by oystermen to keep boats positioned.
4. *the word with the wool on it:* the last word, final thought.

Jennings Evans

IT IS NOT by their work nor by their homes that one will discover the diversity and personality of Smith Island watermen. They harvest the same crops in the same fields, from boats uniformly and similarly functional, down to the color of the anti-fouling paint on their bottoms. They return, all at about the same time of day, to white bungalows and two-story frame houses that are exceedingly well kept but generally of unremarkable architecture.

If you were to really know a waterman here, chances are it would be through time passed in shanties or outhouses (a term applied generally to outbuildings). Were he to live in a castle, with a yacht docked in front, a man here who did not possess a shanty or an outhouse, and preferably both, could not be considered a full-functioning citizen of the island.

Shanties are the crabber's office and personal space, where he docks his boat, sheds his soft crabs, and takes his ease, especially in the summer. Until recent years, shanties were placed of necessity on poles along the island's boat channels or on the marshy edges of its harbors. There the shedding crabs, confined in floating wooden pens, would receive a constant supply of well-oxygenated, clean water. Shanties placed thus are the defining architecture of the island communities. An endless repetition of photographs and paintings focus on the shanties from outside; but the real essence of island life lies within.

Electric pumps and PVC plumbing now allow the "floats" to be built to the landward side of a shanty where access is more convenient. Theoretically, crab shedding could be done now just as well in a waterman's backyard—even in a garage on the mainland; circulating water and a metering device to add salt is basically all that is required. This has resulted in the slow abandonment of more isolated shanties across the channels from the towns; but no one here can imagine moving them far inland. Rude little structures that they are, they offer million-dollar views of sunrise and sunset, and breathtaking views of summer squalls and autumn cold fronts moving like the curtains of a celestial stage across the twenty-mile broad bay. Even on the most airless days, they catch a delicious bit of cool from the spray of water pumped across the shedding crabs, and from the Chesapeake sliding by, ebbing and flooding, bottle green, beneath their gapped floorboards. Among the poles that underpin shanties, encrusted by barnacles and small oysters, wild ducks forage and huge, old eels lurk, growing fat and "tame as house cats" from a regular diet of discarded crab scraps.

Some shanties are family places, where three or four generations gather in the cool of the evening to steam crabs for picking, fish up the shedding softies before they turn hard again, angle for stripers, and tell stories. A few others, favored by the younger set, are the dry island's unofficial party places, where on Friday nights the empty Budweiser cans emanate in strings bobbing for miles on the tide. On summer nights and early mornings, when the crabs are shedding extra-heavy, the shanties blaze like little cruise ships passing through town, with their strings of bare electric bulbs that illuminate the floats for fishing up. From a distance it lends a carnival air to what is in fact a time of work intense as the wheat harvest in Kansas.

Less noticeable than the island's shanties are its outhouses—plywood, tin-roofed structures, usually located in backyards close by the waterman's house. When I first came to the island, and thought the term meant a lack of indoor plumbing, I was intrigued to hear a crabber boasting about his new outhouse of 400 square feet. Finally, he would have enough room, he said. I remember thinking: how much room do you need?

Outhouses, maybe even more than shanties, are places where a waterman's individuality and character are most clearly displayed. There was one next door to me in Tylerton that, like its owner, was always locked and shuttered, a place you just didn't go near. Sometimes late at night there would be comings and goings, and lights on inside briefly. I learned later he was one of the last active illegal duck trappers.

Another outhouse belonged to an old bachelor, who as far as I could tell had little in his life but his cats and his crabbing. Cancer of the jaw made his speech difficult to understand, so we never talked much. But in his outhouse, he had made shelves of scrape boats, roundsterns, skipjacks—some of the most beautiful and detailed wooden boat models I have ever seen. He never displayed them, never would sell them, though they would have brought a huge price in Annapolis or Baltimore. It was just something he did for himself.

One of the top watermen on the island was revealed, inside his outhouse-shanty (the two can run together), to be a fierce anti-hunter and protector of animals. Posters from Greenpeace, anti-handgun groups, humane societies, and articles on the spotted owl papered his walls, along with his membership in the Titanic Historical Society. There were outhouses of waterfowl decoy carvers, storytellers, and "junkmen," who could magically rummage up the glass settling bowl for an old kerosene tank, or the fitting for a toilet's flush tank, long out of stock in mainland stores.

One of the highest evolutions of such places on the island is reached at Jen's, which is how they call Jennings Evans, a crab potter in Ewell, and quite literally the voice of the island. At first visit his outhouse was unremarkable, which is to say it contained Jen's collection of miniature NFL helmets, a couple freezers, refrigerator, furnace, dartboard, TV, comfy, padded old rockers, a fine model skipjack, the *Bernice J.,* done by his dad; also tools, a sack of potatoes, and a Tangier Sound Watermens Association poster; also bales of wire mesh and coils of framing wire for making crab pots during the winter.

But, ah, the characters who file through Jen's outhouse would amaze you. They range from high state officials to Disharoon, the insurance salesman; also the cantankerous and litigious Smut Tagger, and the pretentious and doltish Herkimer Highbrow. Skipjack races in which the local favorite, the *Ruby G. Ford,* wins again, set sail from Jen's outhouse, as does the ill-fated voyage of the *Lead Bottom* and the *Wormwood,* piloted by island captains who gab with one another on the CB radio as their boats leave from opposite shores of the bay— and crash head on, captains talking right up until the frantic moment of collision ("Hard Down,* Sherman! *HARD DOWN!!*).

It's all there, and much more, on eight-track tape cartridges, created by Jen during slow hours in his outhouse over the years. Some of it is fanciful, but much is embellished from real life, with Jen playing all the characters. Then there are the poems, done in his own resonant voice, punctuated with that infectious laugh— *"Scarce Oysters," "The Hazards of Crabbing," "The Good Old Days—"* and the radio shows he has created around island life, like *Culture Time.* "It got to where the skits on the salesmen, I'd played 'em for people here and they'd near about die laughing," he says, "and then the salesman would come back through and start his pitch and the islander would just crack up, and he would-n't know what was happening."

THE MORE you go back to Jen's outhouse, the more you discover. One Saturday, after a long, hot week of crabbing that has driven the whole island at a furious and debilitating pace, you approach the outhouse and hear the excited chatter of men playing a game. Not poker; not even the ubiquitous dominos. They are playing at crabbing, with a board game of Jen's invention.

Jen came up with the crabbing game one winter when the oystering was slow and he was laying up aboard his boat at Solomons across the bay. Now, using his homegrown, illustrated board, "outhouse crabbers" from their rocking chairs roll dice to traverse a cardboard Chesapeake Bay in little paper boats, hoping to land on good crabbing spots, and picking up cards along the way that contain every piece of fortune, good and ill, that can strike a waterman. Spinning a dial before each round sets one's gas and bait expenses; also sets the price Crisfield packers are paying that day for your catch. It is as elaborate as Monopoly, and much closer to real life. Play a few rounds, and you will *know* what it's like to be a crabber—even understand how an otherwise moral man could be tempted to keep more or smaller crabs than the law allows somedays:

*I.e., reverse engines.

My turn t'roll. One, two, three . . . oh, I've landed into 'em . . . load four baskets aboard my boat here.

Gas is high, market's low today. I've got to move around here fast.

No, no. See, if ye move too fast, ye'll miss a lot of crabbin' . . . just like your real pots. Want to fish as much water as ye can. . . .

I hit a Trouble card. Lessee. "Bent [propeller] shaft! Go directly to Marsh's railway [the boat repair yard]. Pay $200."

Ow! Figure me up, what I've caught. I may have t'borrow money to get 'er off the railway. Oh, dear.

You need to borrow $60? Well, see, the least y' can borrow is a hunnert, with interest. We'll take it out'n your crabs tomorrow. . . .

Jeeezu! Here's a break. Card says, "Pull a speedboat off a shoal. He's so grateful he tips you $30." . . .

I'm headin' in, leveled off with crabs.

Yeah, but the card says the packers are layin' crabbers off. Got all the crabs they can handle already. . . .

Roll 'em. . . .

Jen's voice and presence fill the outhouse. He is a barrel-chested man of medium height, striking blue eyes set in a ruddy, strong-boned face. He wears a blue, satiny jacket emblazoned with "Crisfield Crabbers," as the mainland high school's teams are known. A Baltimore Orioles cap sits atop his coal black pompadour. A pair of checked slacks and a pink-on-pink patterned shirt and Nikes complete the outfit.

Scarcely an island event occurs that he is not called upon to emcee it, or produce original entertainment. Stacks of dusty notebooks hold, inscribed in his careful block printing, his scripts for womanless fashion shows, beauty pageants, dedications of new firefighting equipment, testimonials for retired schoolteachers, odes to old-time outhouses (outdoor toilets, that is):

> . . . our thanks to Ruth Bradshaw for the fine flower arrangements that adds to the beauty of our young ladies prom gown pageant . . . and to William Tyler for bringing the P.A. system, without which nobody would be able to hear one word . . . he's been bringing it for years, at no cost what so ever. . . . And what would we do without Bev, Reba, and Elsie, who get the building clean and ready, set up the chairs, wash 'em down, and go door to door collecting wigs, clothes, and furniture . . . and now: It's Show Time! . . .

> . . . now the tissue paper was a little bit coarse
> You used Sears, and Spiegel, and Montgomery Wards

The newspapers you used were far from smooth
But there was no better way to use the news. . . .

. . . then in January of '58, the Ewell Fire Department received its charter:

Of Course, that was to be only the Starter
A lot of work remained to be done
And Elmer was appointed chief, to get the job done. . . .

. . . welcome to this important event in the lives of two of our community's highly esteemed friends . . . the fiftieth wedding anniversary of Elmer and Lillian Harrison Evans, who were married September 21st, 1938, by the Rev. Elmer L. Bennett at the Home of Mr. and Mrs. Harley Corbin, which used to be on the site where Mark and Anita's trailer is now. The attending couple at the wedding were Mary Jane Evans and John T. Tyler, Jr., better known as Johnny Nig . . . we're sure his thoughts are with us tonight

Fifty years ago
When love was young and new
Elmer L. Evans and Lillian Harrison
Said to each other, "I do." . . .

Jen's filing system is nonexistent, he concedes, rummaging for the tape he made, based on a famous skipjack race. "I had that song, 'Ebb Tide,' playin' as the background . . . but you know, I think the silverfish may have eat that one up."

◆ I never studied to get into this sort of occupation. I only went one year of high school at Crisfield. That was back in '44. After that, Dad was buyin' oysters and it's just natural when you're living on the island, you start doin' whatever your father did. Now, a few didn't. My uncle William, he went on to be a doctor of education in Montgomery County next to Washington, D.C. He was actually the superintendent, and he only come back one time, to help his dad shed crabs; and I think he just come back to remind himself that he didn't want to come back.

Now Dad was, I'd say, progressive. He always took the *Baltimore Sun,* and there's very few here, maybe just one or two others, took it. It's nice readin', that paper. And it was either the summer of '45 or '46, Dad was one of the first ones to start crab pottin' . . . crabs pots, well, there's a million of 'em in the bay now, they say, but they were invented by a guy down in Virginia and they were the newest thing then. You got your fish to bait the pots from the western shore then, and by the time the bait man'd get here, they'd be smelly . . . you'd have to shovel 'em out of the hold and then shovel 'em in your boat; and then you'd take 'em out to your shanty and salt 'em in those big sugar barrels. Every time you wanted bait, every mornin', you'd dip 'em out with a crab net. And after five or six days, they'd near'bout turn to chaff, maggots and everything, but still, that's all you had. And you'd reach in the basket to bait your pot and my, that was stenchy.

So I was a crab potter. But I had a teacher in the sixth grade, Lora Whitelock's wife. I wasn't real smart, I don't think, but she saw something in my voice, when I'd read, it was pretty clear. She asked me to be valedictorian for sixth-grade graduation, and she give me a paper to read. She'd say, "Slow down, put expression in your voice" [his notebooks to this day are filled with margin notes: "read slowly," "slow, slow"]. Anyhow, the paper came out good, I thought, and I never forgot that.

Well, later on the community would get up variety shows and had a womanless fashion show. Some asked me to be the emcee . . . it was out to the church basement. I put on a red wig and described all my latest fashions. After that I kinda saw a need to have one of them about once a year. It seemed I didn't want to have skits that were done by outside people. I liked to give it a local angle. And it just went on from there. Sometimes things'd come to me when I was makin' crab pots; other times when I was laid up to Solomons and it was too stormy or froze to get out oysterin'.

You know, it doesn't look like we have much over here, and in a lot of ways we don't; but we've got a closeness. Things like I do, I feel they help that sense of community. A lot of times I feel like Kermit the Frog, just trying to hold things together. ✦

THE NIGHT FLIGHT OF THE GREAT KITE

At the annual banquet of the Tangier Sound Watermens Association, Jen was holding forth on "The Good Old Days":

> . . . we never had no electric lights
> In the good old days
>
> A bunch of us boys flew a kite one night
> And on the end of the tail, we tied a big flash lite
> It caused nine or ten people to nearly die from fright
> In those good old days. . . .

Dallas Bradshaw leaned over and nudged me. "Ask 'im about that kite; there's more to it you ought to hear." Jennings said:

✦ It happened in 1945, when I was fifteen. We were back from Baltimore, where Dad moved us that time the crabs got scarcer'n anyone could remember. I was always a fancier of kites, and I weren't able to fly 'em in Baltimore. When I got back, I said, I'm gonna try to make the biggest kite I ever made in my life.

I went out and cut some water bushes for the frame. They go plenty tall. I think my main struts was four and a half foot. It could have been five, but I don't want to say too much because I don't have no way of provin' how tall it was, but it was between four and a half and five foot tall by about three foot wide, I imagine.

I didn't even know if she would fly. But one Sunday night, about twilight, there come a heavy southeaster, blowin' 25, maybe 30 knots o' wind. It was in the fall, and they used to hold revivals down on the other part, in Tylerton, back then, and what people was goin' had already gone down on the boat.

Well, Henry Guy and me and two boys that don't live here no more was walkin' around, no church to go to in Ewell that night, and we said, let's do something, let's try to get that big kite up. We got her out between where the pop house and the old school used to be, and threw her up—she hadn't never been tried. She went to swirlin' and swirlin' and down she went. I said, she don't have enough tail. It was darker by now; only the western part of the sky weren't real dark.

Anyhow, Hen says, "Dad's got a pair of overalls he's just done away with this week. If they're still in the outhouse, we can cut them up and I guarantee that'll be enough tail for her." So we ripped 'em up and ripped 'em up and good golly, we had a tail—I bet it was 25 feet long. It was all one guy could do to string it out, that's how long it was.

So we threw her up again, and she still wanted to lean to one side, that's how bad it was blowin'. And she wouldn't go up, she acted like she wanted to dive again. Now, by that time it was getting real dark. So I said, tell you what, we'll try one more thing. If she don't do it then, we'll take the daggone thing home cuz it's blowin' too hard.

So I pulled out Ma's flashlight—I had brought it along to see the kite when she got airborne, there in the dark and all. In them days we had no electric lights on the island. Well, we hooked that light to her tail, and she lifted right up and she just soared right in the air like a bird. That flashlight give her just enough balance to soar just right.

I said, "Boys, there she goes," and we kept payin' out the line and payin' out the line. She didn't go far, but she went high. I said, "Gee whiz, that's a pretty sight." We couldn't see the kite. All we could see was that light. She was playin' right over Willy's store. The light was kind of swayin' and we tied her up—I'll never forget—we tied her around a little brick, you know how they would stagger the bricks for the air to get under the school.

Well, that kite would sort of tug from one area to another, and this big beam o'light would flash on a store and then dart across the road and then play on the parsonage, and it was right spooky-lookin'. We were gonna try to get under the beam, see if it would pick us up, when all of a sudden we heard somebody talkin' out in that yard where Terry lives now.

It was Mr. Calvin and Wilroy, the one who used to own the fuel dock. He was living there with his dad and all of 'em were out there, their wives and Wilroy's daughter and the other guy's granddaughter, and she was cryin'—the little girl—and they're goin', "Now, now, now, don't cry." And by and by the grandfather says, "I'm afraid it's somethin' Russia sent over." You know we were having a little Cold War problems with Russia right after the war.

He said, "Yeah, I think it's something Russia sent over," and we was just lookin' at each other. Then Wilroy says, "What's got me is it's a'rattlin'. That rattlin's what's got me." And we're just lookin' at each other—we didn't want to say anything cuz we didn't know if we'd done something bad or not. I said to Henry, "I guess if we start pullin' her down, they'll follow the light and they'll find us." Hen said, "Let's go home and get a bottle of pop." So we're cuttin' through right around where Mark and Naylor's got their trailer—there was a home there then, and this man and his wife were standin' out there and she was going:

"Honey, I'm horribly afraid it's the end of time." Well, Henry, he got to laughing at that, and she said: "You needn't laugh, Mr. Henry. The end of time, that means the end of everythin'."

Hen, he says, "They're thinkin' this is something awful," and I said, yeah, guess it is. We come to Hen's house and he says, let's have a little fun with this. He calls out, "Ma! Come here quick!" She had a whole load of people who used to visit in them days. She had about ten head in there. We got 'em all out on the porch, lookin' at that light, swirlin' and tuggin'. You know, they believed in tokens an' everything in those days, indications of death and things like that, and they all stood out there, and there was some Biblin', and one of 'em said, "Let's go out there and see if we can see it." And Bertie said, "No, no; I'm not going nowhere near that until this is explained."

Well, that's the way it'd become. Then from Tylerton, the ones coming up on the boat, coming up from revival, they saw the light . . . Preacher George Townsend and the whole bunch of 'em. They came up all Biblin', and they didn't know whether it was a sign or the world had come to an end or what. You know, the Bible speaks of funny things happenin' at the end.

It was gettin' late then and our joke had about run out, and I said, "Hen, we got to get her down." But by now people all over town were lookin' at it—the power of light! It was ten o'clock by then, and we were supposed to be in. "Hen," I said, "we soon got to make a move." And while we were talkin', that thing broke loose. And she fell. That was the eeriest-lookin' thing, that light a'twistin' and turnin'.

I woke up the next mornin' and I thought, well, I'm still alive. Along about ten that mornin' word come that Buz—he was one of those fellows that like to go ride in the marshes and progue, just see what he can see, you know— that he had found a big kite across the creek with a light on it. I asked, ca-sual-like, what had he done with it? He had it home, they said. Well, about ten minutes later, Ma had gone to look for somethin' in the closets, which was dark in them days; and she said, "Jennings, have you seen anything of my flashlight?" "No, no, I ain't seen nothing of it."

But one thing led to another, word of mouth got around about the light and the kite, and she knew I'd been workin' on kites, and she put two and two together. She put it to me and I had to confess to it and I hated to do that. Well, she said, you go right over there and get that light; and I said, "I can't do it, Ma, to save my life, I can't face that man." So she went and got it. And about that time Hen's brother, Gene, found out Hen was in on it and he got him by the collar and took him into Bernice and said, "Ma, here's your little Einstein."

So the great hoax was over, but the thing of it was, it weren't nothing to terrify nobody. It just turned out it was a once in a lifetime event. Kids tried it every year for a long time, but never, ever were able to get the kite up. ◆

VHF

THE MARINE RADIO consists of several dozen VHF (very high frequency) channels, licensed by the Federal Communications Commission and regulated by the U.S. Coast Guard to pass essential information in terse and proscribed formats. Think of it, compared to normal conversation, as a military bugle is to popular music. But in the crab boats, kitchens, and shanties of islanders, the VHF is a non-stop jam session, a giant party line, open to anyone with a radio, which out here is absolutely everyone. Across the ether of mid-Chesapeake flows a quixotic, rambunctious stream of consciousness, blends of earthy humor, religion, everybody's and nobody's business, to a background of sea gulls mewing and diesel engines rumbling.

In the predawn black, first boats heading out, the VHF begins to stir with the islanders' mellow brogue:

> Hayee, John.
> Hayee, Charruls . . . fair maarnin', I swagger.

Suddenly, this is shattered by a young crabber pressing his mike against the commercial radio, subjecting all to the ribald patter of the Greaseman, a shock jock coming at you from up the Potomac in D.C.

Later on, come these important medical bulletins:

Edward?, calls out the wife of an elderly crabber on 66, the channel the scrapers use.

> Yeah Ella Marie.
> Take your pills?
> Yeah Ella Marie.
> Got your jacket on?
> Yeah Ella Marie.

One of the ferry captains radios his wife. *Tell C. she left a little brown paper bag aboard;* and he proceeds, to the titillation of all Tangier Sound, to tell us what was in it: *birth control pills.*

Other times, the VHF proves its real worth. A thunderstorm hits, with 50-knot gusts and lightning. The electricity goes out, and crabbers frantically radio wives to run to their shanties and fire up the "air-cooled," the gasoline-powered backup pumps that will keep lifegiving water circulating over the soft crabs.

Sometimes, action on the radio slows and phrases are trolled across the airwaves, inviting anyone to bite:

"*Guiding Light*"... "*Orioles game*"... "*derned gnats*"... "*Tanjermun* [*Tangier Island men*]."...

The VHF is also a forum in which islanders talk most like themselves, with no thought of "proper talk" they might use when meeting outsiders. What follows are unretouched conversations among the island crabbing fleet, with anywhere from two to half a dozen crabbers joining in. It was taped from the VHF during a few days in the summers of 1990 and 1991.

> *Sun's 93 million miles away, they say on TV.*
>
> *Lord have mercy.*
>
> *Swagger it hain't.*
>
> *Like to know how they measured that.*
>
> *93 million miles. Boy, that ain't nowheres away.*
>
> *Was it sun or moon they said? 'Cause if it's moon, them astronauts didn't go nowhere.*
>
> *Ain't no room up there in space, is there?*
>
> *Yeeah, ye'd need a LORAN t' find yer corks [crab pot markers] up there.*
>
> . . .
>
> *Wind.*
>
> *Little southeast to it.*
>
> *Little south to it.*
>
> *Speaks of breezin' up.*
>
> *Comin' sou'west, seems like to me.*
>
> *No wind where I'm crabbin' a'tall. But I'll take everybody else's word for it.*
>
> . . .
>
> *Mean crabs this summer.*
>
> *You'd better b'lieve it.*
>
> *Been some pretty jimmies come outn' Hollands Straits.*
>
> *How 'bout that Julie on* The World Turns?
>
> *Think she wouldn't slip next door?*
>
> *Yeah, uh, her husband found out, I think.*

I made nearly a fifteen-minute lick [drag of the scrape] for one crab.

That April's hotter'n a fryin' pan.

Ain't that the champ.

Who's April?

Don't know no April.

Never see'd meaner crabs.

Channel 16 she's on.

Guidin' Light?

Made two licks and got four . . . ain't no good place t' crab [it's a bad place].

She said she done it 'cause it made 'er feel she'as wanted.

Yeeah, and she was wanted all the time, ye needn't doubt it.

April?

Julie?

Hey. Juney [the local crab cop] busted Dave yesterday down t' Shankses.

Dickhead.

That Allen on Guiding Light, *boy, I love him 'bout as much as I do Juney.*

Thirty-ought six'd shoot his ass. [Juney's? Allen's? Both?]

(long silence)

That Juan Valdez, he ain't picked nary a coffee bean.

(long silence)

. . .

Hey, Jukey.

Hey, Woosie.

Ole B—— come by me just now, he didn't have no balls!

Mooned ye?

Mooned me front and center. I ain't gonna get 'im back. I'm gonna strip down stark nekkid and go to him in a minute.

What'd he look like, Woos? That billy goat 'a Nicey's?

Turkey gins!

He wouldn't moon ye, B—— wouldn't.

He got no nuts.

Noo, he got no nuts.

They big nuts?

Put a bushel of jimmies in his bag. Got them wreckin' balls.

Dast!

Woos, were you eatin when he done it?

I was pullin' my scrape, had to let her go.

. . .

Jonathan? [young waterman's mother calling him]

Up one, Ma [go to another channel, not monitored by the majority of crabbers]

. . .

Nightmare on Elm Street.

John's been a'dreamin' again?

Says he ain't caught no crabs.

I swagger he ain't caught nary one when he goes to dreamin' about 'im.

Noo, ye ain't caught nary one when ye dream about 'em, when ye close yer eyes and see 'em.

He told us, that was a pretty dream he had. Well, I thought he dreamt somebody died. Dern, he said he dreamt he couldn't find his crab net.

Johnny Kruger, ain't he. No, he ain't catchin' no crabs.

. . .

Saw that TV reporter had Ed on.

Said he's enjoyed every moment, all them years crabbin'.

I'd like to ask him about that marnin' up to Sedgy Point—cold, rough, him overboard in his oilskins with a boat hook, trying to get a crabpot off his wheel [propeller].

Moments to remember.

. . .

My heels a'hurtin', elbows a'hurtin'; I've done a good job today.

Ye gotta stay out 'til ye get them twinges in yer chest.

Put two on the scoreboard yesterday [two striped bass, illegal to catch].

Blue Jays is a'closin' on the Bosox.

That April, she had a mini skirt on, it just was a'coverin'.

BOATS

Boats

FOR TELLING time in Tylerton, we have no town clock chiming the hour, but we have our boats:

> 4:00 A.M.—Crabbers and tongers head out.
>
> After a while, even half-asleep, you can recognize diesels from gas engines, wet from dry exhausts; individuals—the blatting of Dwight's Detroit diesel backing from the slip; the new model, four-cylinder Cummins in another crabber's boat; Merle's old roundstern.
>
> 6:30 A.M.—The school boat, *Betty Jo Tyler,* arrives from Rhodes Point, taking on students for Crisfield.
>
> 7:00 A.M.—The 42-foot ferry, *Captain Jason,* leaves for Crisfield.
>
> 7:15 A.M.—Mail skiff comes from Ewell to pick up.
>
> 10:00 A.M.—The old *Eleanor White,* North America's only wooden gas boat, comes sedately down from Ewell to fuel watermen's boats when they return from work.
>
> 11:00 A.M.—*Darrell Dale,* the trash boat, pulls into the harbor behind town to haul our garbage to the incinerator in Ewell.
>
> 1:30 P.M.—*Captain Jason* returns from Crisfield.
>
> 2:00–3:00 P.M.—Crabbers returning.
>
> 2:15 P.M.—U.S. Mail skiff comes from Ewell to deliver and pick up.
>
> 3:00 P.M.—*Eleanor White* leaves.
>
> *Jason* leaves for second run to Crisfield.
>
> 3:30 P.M.—*Betty Jo Tyler* returns.
>
> 6:00 P.M.—*Jason* returns for the night.

This regular traffic is interspersed with the buzzing of flat-bottomed, 14- to 18-foot outboard skiffs that, on weekends, may continue until past midnight. It is a rare hour when boats are not threading the island's channels. Even within town, it is sometimes more convenient to make short trips by skiff than by walking or bicycle.

With no airstrip here, everything depends absolutely on boats. They bring the daily newspaper and groceries, shingles for the roof and the repairmen for washing machines and air conditioners; also fresh tomatoes in summer and shrimp for feasting on New Year's Eve, wood for the fireplace, and dump trucks loaded with gravel for occasional county roadwork.

Boats take off the dead for embalming, and bring flowers and caskets for their funerals. They transport ball teams and choirs and politicians and the sick, including cats needing a vet; also take off the harvests of soft crabs and hard clams, and return with cloth bags full of cash and checks, and boxes of frozen bait for the crabbers' pots; also liquor, still often discreetly disguised, in deference to the Methodist Church's anti-drinking stance.

Islanders have been born in boats, courted in boats, and doubtless conceived in boats, which are one of the few places young people can go for space and privacy, whether to drink or just contemplate the sunset. Once, years ago, I was invited out to a party at "Club Pruitt," which turned out to be the 10- by 8-foot cabin of a young waterman's old crab boat, the *E. C. Pruitt*. Fitted out with soft red lights and stereo, the "club" for a time was *the* place to socialize and partake of various contraband.

Boats here get you to work and to church and to school; break ice; take you hunting for ducks and muskrats and Indian arrowheads, and the occasional shark. With few exceptions, they are not yachty or large, ranging from 12-foot skiffs to a couple that exceed 60 feet. Most watermen's workboats are from 27 to 42 feet, of traditional Chesapeake design: a sharp, shallow V-shape to the hull at the bow, flattening rapidly to almost horizontal by the stern. Topsides, the pattern repeats, with a bow that rises sharply, followed by a modest cabin, then descends gracefully to a long, low, open workspace. The design has evolved from a combination of what was simple to build and what works best to provide a stable platform for oystering and crabbing in the sharp chop that characterizes the Chesapeake. Also, the hulls must be shallow draft in a bay whose seafood often comes from waters a few feet deep.

Perhaps it is coincidence, but there is a striking similarity to the shape of bay workboat hulls and the underside of a great blue heron in flight, its breastbone jutting in a classic deadrise V, flattening rapidly along its underbody toward its trailing, horizontal legs.

Boats have a status here just short of family member; close to what a cowboy's horse was in the Old West. They are rarely lent to others, though the owner might be willing to take you anywhere you had to go. When their working life was done, an islander's boat would be stripped of engine and all usable equipment, and floated on a high tide into some shallow nook of the marsh "to die," as they would say. But death, even for a half-rotten wooden craft, could take decades. For all practical purposes, a waterman might spend his life surrounded by the corpses of his own and his family's boats.

Boats were a large reason I moved to Smith Island. I always knew I could never personally afford all the craft I needed to explore the bay. Here, at the end of my dock, I had canoes, a sea kayak, a crabbing skiff, a husky 21-foot outboard, and a 35-foot diesel workboat; also a fast 24-footer with small sleep-aboard cabin that served as my mobile headquarters as I enjoyed for nearly two years the world's greatest commute to work.

I managed education centers at Smith and two other bay islands, a triangular journey of some twenty miles—if you ran in a straight line, which I often did not. I would follow the winding marsh channels, follow the sea gulls to see whether they were diving on rockfish and bluefish; stop sometimes and just drift, watching thunderstorms move across the bay like a giant stage curtain being pulled. After the storms, double rainbows were common, and even triples. Once I saw a quadruple.

I commuted through sunrises and sunsets that were simply impossible on land. One day I ran for half an hour through one of the most intense lightning storms I have ever seen—wrapped all the while in a thick fog. I commuted in the company of wintering swans and geese and old squaw, through summer blooms of bright corks, marking crab pots; across grassy shallows where, for miles at a time, my hull was never more than a foot from bottom, and you could spot individual crabs and oysters at 20 knots; and through night waters coolly brilliant with phosphorescence and bioluminescent algae.

The absolute best times were the dawns when mine was the first boat of the morning to issue from the island eastward into Tangier Sound. The water signaled the day before the land. Every gut you passed was a stab of gleaming color, deep into the heart of the still-dark marsh. The satin surface of the Sound lay virginal in the still, clear air, a perfect slate, bidding you inscribe the day's first passage. Such mornings were times to essay exuberantly, carving great, sweeping S's and circles, your wake tinged with all the colors and textures of the kindling sky, routing flocks of waterfowl from their night's rest.

The water then would sometimes hold the impression of your wake for a long time; and for miles you could look back at your dawn pean. Perhaps a farmer feels such joyful renewal plowing his first dark furrows of the spring into lush green winter rye; maybe a painter, first touching color to canvas. In our palimpsestic water world, one left nothing so substantial behind; but every single morning held possible a fresh and lovely beginning.

In such conditions, I logged around twenty thousand of my life's best miles.

That is not to say the boating life was without its drawbacks. One morning, to make a late-afternoon meeting in New York, I arose at 4:00 A.M., my shoulder burning with bursitis, and broke ice for two hours with a heavy pole to reach the lone boat on the island that could get me to the mainland.

And once we attended a zoning hearing, on a matter vital to Smith Island. The county held it on a week night, and declined all requests to have a hearing on the island. "People can get to [the county seat] at night from every place else," said the county attorney. He did not see why Smith Islanders should be any different.

I thought about what he said all the way back—running into big, cold seas for nearly ten miles, at 11:00 P.M. in an open outboard. I thought about it each time a wave broke against my oilskins; thought about it when it became too rough to sit, and I had to wrap the anchor line around my waist to keep my footing. In my dreams I make that run again, with that smartass lawyer strapped to the bow.

Ferry Captains

THE *ISLAND BELLE*

✦ She was built in 1917, two years before I was born. Since I was a small boy, it was always my dream to run her on the route to Crisfield, which she completed, once a day, every day but Sunday without fail. Captain White-lock, whose family built her and ran her for so long, said he never did look at the glass [the barometer] to see what the next day's weather would be, 'cause he knew he was going, no matter what. Only if he was to take a day off to go gunning or fishing would he pay close attention to weather. People were so proud of that boat, they would write little tributes:

> How we eagerly look for her,
> Just as the clock strikes three;
> For I know she soon will be coming
> With the U.S. Mail for me
>
> He has been decked with flags
> She has been drenched with the icy blows and storms
>
> For eight long years she has been going,
> And may she ever go on still. . . .

A woman wrote that in 1925, and that old boat did go on a little while—for another fifty-three years she was this island's main connection to the rest of the world. I don't know how you could ever put into words the part the *Island Belle* played here—the hub of the wheel, you could say. When she was built, she was considered one of the big boats on the bay. Fifty-three feet long, 14-foot beam, a cabin that would seat fifteen and storage below decks. She was heavy-built, only the very best lumber, cedar topsides, oak timbers, and her bottom planked all lengthwise with Georgia heart pine. She ran her whole sixty-one years on that same bottom. One time the boatyard here decided to renail her bottom, and they almost wished they hadn't. They said it was like driving nails into concrete.

Her hull was built upside down in a local apple orchard. Old-timers today remember getting paid, as kids, to plug all the nailholes in her bottom. She rose from that orchard big as a whale, they said. The whole town of Ewell gathered to turn her right side up and watch her rumble down the oyster-shell street on beams attached to wooden spoke wheels. When she was launched, some worried whether she could even get in and out of the channel to Ewell, though she only drew three feet. The channels within the island were not wide and deep as they are now; just little creeks. Before the federal digging in 1931, there were no navigation markers, just stakes put down by the watermen, and on low tides it was easy to go around. A compass was all you had then in the fog—no radar or LORAN. The captains then used a heavy piece of lead on a line, with a concave place on its bottom. They would put tallow or wax in that hollow spot, and drop her down. By the depth and the type of mud that stuck to the wax, they had a pretty good idea where they were.

The *Island Belle*'s engine was a a 24 hp Lathrope that burned kerosene. Later she went to a 36 hp Palmer, and in the forties, she got the first diesel ever was on the island. Her top speed in the early days was about 7–8 mph, fast for those times. She would leave Ewell in the morning about 8:00 A.M., call in Tylerton, and get to Crisfield about 10:00. Passengers had about two hours to get their business done before she headed back at 12:30. If they had to go anywhere much outside of Crisfield, they would have to make arrangements to spend the night. There was no such thing as day trips over here for mainlanders, because the *Island Belle* did not run again until the next morning. And that was pretty much the way it would stay, nearly until she quit in 1978.

For sixty-one years, life here revolved around her. As she hit Cooney Island going into Tylerton, she blew her horn, and that was the signal to get to the post office, get your crabs straight for shipping, get down to the dock. She would blow again as she entered Ewell, time for people to get their mail and groceries, to gather and visit. On her way to the dock, she would stop at each crab shanty up and down the channels to pick up the soft crabs and unload ice. I guess it doesn't seem like such a big deal now, that faithful old boat a'comin every day, but it was.

Passenger fares were originally 15 cents one way, a quarter for round trip. She was allowed by the Coast Guard to carry around twenty-two head; but we would have as high as seventy hanging all over her somedays, like at Camp Meeting time in July and August. Freight was 10 cents on a sack of corn, 50 cents on a drum of oil. As late as 1972 we were still only charging 50 cents round trip for passengers to Crisfield.

She was an able craft, but she would roll right smart in a heavy sea. I recall her loaded deep with coal one Christmastime, and a full load of passengers and presents, and every time she would plunge into the waves, water would just run right through her, cabin and all, until everyone and everything aboard was sob wet.

It surprises people from off here, but several of our people, mostly women, are scared of the water. Every trip on the *Belle,* especially in rough weather, was a great trial to some. I've had people fall down, fainting by my feet; had 'em begging me to turn back. I've seen some move off because of the ferry ride. People had their different ways of getting through a hard crossing. One, when we neared open water and she heard the *clink, clink* of the brass handle that turned the *Belle*'s gears, she knew that meant she was gonna roll that day. She'd alert people around her, "Don't panic, but I'm going to jump up and holler, I can't hold it in"; and she'd commence: "Oh my Jesus! Oh my blessed!" Every pound of the hull: "Jesus! Oh!," 'til we was through the worst of it.

Sometimes the old watermen—oh, they could be birds—they would lean over to some passenger they knew would catch like gas and whisper something like, "If we go down, there's no life jackets aboard today." Once they got a woman to crying and screaming, and her boy was hollerin', "Ma, shut up, you are embarrassing me"; and a girl next to her was cryin', "We're all gonna die." It was something to behold.

One woman to this day, when it gets rough, will get down in the floor of the ferry on her knees, like she is praying. She says it just keeps her from getting seasick to stay down like that, and I think it does, and I think she prays a little too. After one rough time, a man put his hand on her shoulder and said, most grateful, "Lady, your prayers were answered."

I began cutting school in 1929, when I was ten, to help out aboard the *Island Belle*. It was a dream come true when many years later, I finally became her captain, and later on, her co-owner. It was the finest experience of my life to walk of a mornin', early, from home in Ewell to Rhodes Point to pick up the mail sack, and be comin' back across that mile of marsh to the *Island Belle*, sun comin' up in front of me.

I suppose it was my travelin' so much to all three parts of the island on account of the *Island Belle* that gave me my start as the local political man. I got my big boost in 1936, when Millard Tawes, in Crisfield, ran for clerk of the Circuit Court of Somerset County against Harry Phoebus, who was favored to win. Tawes gave me a quarter—he always said it was 50 cents, but it was a quarter—to hand out his literature and get the vote out around Smith Island. There was no phone in those days, so the ballot box on the morning after the election was sent over on the *Island Belle* to be counted. Phoebus had beat Tawes by 42 votes, until we docked in Crisfield. The island put Tawes the victor by 142. He said later if he had lost that race, it would have wound him up. He went on to become governor of Maryland, and I was his boy after that.

The *Belle* by the late 1960s was beginning to show her age. Even with a 671 diesel, she was hardly the fastest boat around. She took about an hour and twenty minutes to Crisfield then.

That hard winter of 1977, I headed by the beacon at Fowlers, just before you hit the open water of the Sound. There was fog and wind and heavy ice, and I turned around and tied her up, and never ran in her again until the next March. She was playin' out. The drydock man said it must take a lot of nerve to go in her. It got me to thinkin'. She had done her job. In sixty-one years, she had missed only very few days, though there were a few I thought I'd lose her. She always delivered the mail, though once we got the Tangier mail by mistake. She never lost a passenger. One old waterman did fall off the back of her, and he couldn't swim a lick; but his overcoat caught air and floated him 'til we could come about. The spring of 1978 she made her last trip. I tell you the truth, by then, I was glad to get in something made of Fiberglas.

What happened after that was a shame. She sat around in Rhodes Point. The state was going to buy her for a museum, but never did. She was bought by a man from Tylerton and towed there, where she sank. She was put on the National Register of Historic Places, and there was talk of making a monument out of her in Ewell. She was floated and towed there, where she sunk again. There she rests to this day, stern rotted right out of her, nearly sunk from sight in the mud of the harbor. It's there she was born, and it's there she's died.

What can you say? She done her job. ✦

THE *CAPTAIN JASONS*

✦ No one believed we could do it. I think now, nearly twenty years later, it was as big a change for Smith Island as when Methodism came in, or the oysters dwindlin' away. All we had set out to do was to better serve the people of Tylerton. It was 1977, and anybody could see the *Island Belle* was on her last legs. Her one trip a day was fine for hauling freight and mail, but it did not give people much ability to get off the island, or for outsiders to visit it.

We told our plan at a meeting in the store. Two of us were going to throw in and buy a 42-foot Bruno & Stillman, a heavy-built, Fiberglas, lobster-boat type of hull, from New Hampshire. With a big diesel, she would cruise at 18–20 knots and make the trip in half the old ferry's time. And we would run twice each day, Sundays too—leave the island at 7:30 and return by 1:30; back to Crisfield at 3:30 and leave for the island again at 5:00.

The people, I'd say 70 percent of them, said they were for it. On the strength of that meeting, we took a $125,000 loan and went into the ferry business. We called her the *Captain Jason,* after my boy.

June 14 was her first trip. We were going up against an established and powerful competition. The *Island Belle* had the mail contract sewn up, and her owners also had the freight business and the school boat contract. They said we'd be crabbin' out of our boat for a living before that summer was up.

Somebody wrote the PSC [Maryland's Public Service Commission] saying there was no proven need for another ferry service. We hadn't even known we were supposed to file with the PSC. They held a meeting in the church, and the preacher and the island nurse spoke up in our favor.

So did a lot of other people, who said they'd like some competition for a change. The community here is very strong, and there is a big emphasis on everybody helping everybody out, and abiding by not working Sundays, and not crabbing a lot earlier or later than the rest. This kind of head-to-head competition was a new thing—a good thing, I believe.

We kept running. We offered reduced rates on soft crabs and store freight and we would ship crabs twice a day. That was about the time the Save the Bayers [the Chesapeake Bay Foundation] set up a center here to bring schoolkids over. They figured to try and please everybody, and said they would split their business equally between the two ferries. My partner, who lived next to their house, told them pretty strong that it was their business, but he would hate them a long time if they did not give it all to the *Captain Jason;* and they did.

In July 1978, we took delivery on a second 42-footer, the *Captain Jason II.* Both are still running. By 1979, the owners of the old *Island Belle* had also bought a modern Fiberglas boat and were running the same schedule.

Just the two of us were running those boats twice a day, seven days a week, 365 days a year. Some days, with special runs for the phone and electric companies, dredging companies and hunters, we'd make as many as six round trips a day. Only very heavy ice, the kind you'd not see for several winters at a stretch, kept the *Jasons* at the dock. We would take any wind the bay could throw at us. We ran once in 80 knots. We had a passenger that day in a wheelchair.

That second daily trip may have changed life more for Smith Island than anything in my lifetime. Suddenly, ladies could travel up the road to Salisbury and shop, or see the pediatrician with a sick kid and still get back by suppertime. The doctor could commute and do emergency room work in Crisfield to help out his income. If the Meatland sent the wrong grocery order for your dinner on the first ferry, or the wrong part came for repairing your boat or for your emergency plumbing job, you could call and get it corrected on the second run. There was just a different feeling to the island, more relaxed, a feeling of less confinement and restraint.

Some people did say it started more "keeping up with the Joneses," more shopping, bigger presents at Christmas, more people keeping cars on the mainland. Outsiders began to visit more, and to buy homes on the island, now they could get off on a Sunday and catch a late-afternoon ride over on Friday. It changed the way islanders saw themselves, and the way outsiders saw the island.

For all the improvement, you mustn't think it is easy, depending on ferries for your link to the rest of the world. It wears you down. Somebody once called the trip over a "forty-five-minute elevator ride." These are not pleasure yachts. The motors are loud, people sit on wooden bench seats. They are not air-conditioned, and it is impossible to regulate the heat in the cabins in wintertime. It is not a pleasant time when a woman has got to carry a kid over, in rough weather, throwing up with flu, and half the people in the cabin smoking cigarettes, and water sloshing off the roof down your neck if you try to walk out for fresh air. There is no bathroom aboard.

Old people suffer the most. Some must come and go to get chemotherapy or radiation in Salisbury. At low tide, a lot of them, especially if they are heavy, or a woman wearing a dress, really cannot step on and off the ferries from the dock here. I have seen them come out, take a look, and just turn around and go home on low tides. And to bring anything here requires more handling than you would believe. Say you put shingles on your roof. You are talking about lifting tons of shingles. You must load them on a truck, unload them on the dock at Crisfield; load them aboard the ferry, unload them on the dock at Smith Island; load them onto a cart, unload them by your house. You can see why we don't have many brick homes over there.

After eight or nine years, it wore me out, and my partner soon after—just the stress. I was going to either have a heart attack or a nervous breakdown. Fuel prices had gone up, and fares had to rise—up to $5 each way when I quit. Since then they have gone to $7, or $14 round trip, which is a lot if you are carrying your family on and off. With oysterin' so down, there wasn't as much money in the winter, and it seemed like every year there was more and more complaint that prices were too high, or service wasn't what it should be. It just was not fun, and we sold out to some other islanders. But we had a good run of it. I think we started something important, that people wanted, and there'll be no going back. ◆

TOUR BOATS

ALAN TYLER, SIXTY

◆ What would I do with more than $2 million? That's what I was offered for my boat business. But what do I really need? I buy about two pair of pants a year from Sears. I never wanted a vacation, and I have never taken a day off. People here treat me good, the way they have treated me all my life. My house, which is built over my restaurant, is fairly cool in the summer and warm in the winter, and I love to sit there evenings and watch the sun set on the bay. I think the biggest difference between the richest people on here and the poorest ever lived here is the rich ones work every day. I hope I work one day and die the next. It's how I want to go.

I only went to the eighth grade. I just didn't care to go further. My father had a little workboat and we hand-scraped oysters out of her. Dad never owned a car, and when I was growing up I'd see one, and think, wouldn't that be great to drive one of those and get paid for it. A taxi driver is what I always wanted to be.

I got married young, and worked on an oyster dredge boat, which I hated, but we had to eat. Then I went into the grocery store business in Rhodes Point, but it was never a going proposition. People wanted to shop in the big town, Ewell; isn't that the way it always is? So me and a friend scraped together $8,500 and bought a big scow, which we hired out to the state to transplant oyster shell and seed around the bay; and some weeks we actually made money at that. The next year I bought out my partner's half—I had to give him $8,000 for it by then.

Then one night I got this call from the Whitelocks, that owned the *Island Belle*. They wanted to sell me their freight business, the school run, and the mail contract. My wife said, if you get into that, I am leaving. I came back that night and said, you better be packing. She did leave finally, but it was years later.

Around 1973, the state offered me a contract to buy a modern school boat that could take the island kids to Crisfield daily, instead of them boardin' there all week. That was the biggest deal I ever made, close to $150,000 for the new boat, which I named the *Betty Jo Tyler,* after my little daughter. Smith Island had never seen a boat like her—50 foot, solid aluminum, cabin almost the whole length of her with shag carpet and red vinyl seats inside just like on a school bus; and air-conditioned, too. I figured that was a plus, because I could run tourists to the island on her in the summers.

For three years, that's what I did, tried to build a tourism business. Wouldn't you know it? With that big air-conditioned cabin on the *Betty Jo,* what did all the tourists want? To stand outside. That's when I decided to build the *Captain Tyler.* She is a 65-footer, double decker, a pure tourist boat. Meanwhile, I kept running the shell boats and the freight boat; and somewhere in there, I bought out the oil company, too.

It was a write-up in the *Baltimore Sun* that really made our tour business take off. I made my old store in Rhodes Point into a family-style restaurant, and we would give a package deal: boat ride over to the island, a big seafood dinner, and a quick tour of the island in a school bus. Next, I opened a little tourist shop—I couldn't believe how many people just wanted to buy anything that had "Smith Island" printed on it.

One day I got a call from a tour broker in New York. He wanted to know, could I take out a hundred people for the president of the *New York Times* for a big party and seafood dinner—and could I do it in New York Harbor? They were rededicating the Statue of Liberty. Well, we sent the ladies who would cook up in cars, and a couple of us took the *Captain Tyler* through Delaware Bay and up the ocean coast—left here Sunday night and ran straight through 'til Tuesday. And we gave them a lunch and a dinner: soft crabs, potato salad, macaroni salad, cold slaw, shrimp salad, crab salad, crab-cakes, string beans, the works, just like we serve in the restaurant. It was some party, only we got a bad check for half of the $50,000 they promised us; it wasn't the *New York Times,* it was a crooked broker.

But the tour business kept on building. I put up a motel in Crisfield, and bought a restaurant there, and I made one of my old oyster scows—oysters are dyin' in the bay—into another tour boat. Nowadays I run from both sides of the bay, Crisfield and Point Lookout, over on the Potomac. They say there is 7 million people living within two and a half hours drive of Point Look-out—that's big, isn't it?

My daughter runs the restaurant and the business side, and my son keeps the boats running. I'm the taxi driver. Seven days a week all summer I leave the western shore with a load of tourists at 10:00 A.M., get to the island about noon, and go back to Point Lookout by 2:00. Often I'll just stay over and sleep aboard the boat, or maybe come home, get back about 7:00 P.M.

The rest of the year, I drive the school boat over and back to Crisfield, and drive the school bus between Ewell and Rhodes Point each morning and afternoon. Afterward, I'll usually go to the oil dock before I come home. Sometimes I tow the oil barge over to take on gas and oil. I'll tell you, you could have a lot worse jobs than those.

The tourists will come here more and more. The state says soon, count-ing all that comes on the ferries and tour boats, there will be more than thirty thousand a year. Liquor will come here, no matter that the church is against it, because the tourists will demand it. The state is developing a tourism plan for the island now. They want to increase it on account of how the seafood economy is struggling; but they are worried about how to do that without overrunning the place with visitors. Already, you see watermen have put up "Keep Off" signs to keep somebody from coming down their old docks and maybe falling through a rotten board and suing them.

I think after a few hours here, most of the tourists have had a good time, but they are ready to leave. I get asked a lot, "How can you stand to live your whole life here?"; "How do you keep from getting bored?"; "What do peo-ple do here for excitement?" I tell 'em, we're no more bored here than you are wherever you are at. It's not the island, it's the people. See, you got to have help to live here, you got to help each other, whether it's your boat sink-ing or a refrigerator you got to move off the dock, or getting to the doctor when you are sick. All my life I thought I'd like to go places and buy things and get new clothes; but once I got money enough I could, the thrill of it was gone, and if somebody doesn't like me in the old clothes I got on, well, I really don't give a damn. ✦

FUNERAL BOAT—THE KING TUT

BOB BRADSHAW

✦ Since 1885, whenever an islander has died, my family has undertaken their funeral. The word, you know, "undertaker," came from how you used to undertake it all, from getting the grave dug to even preaching at the funeral. On Smith Island, a death is still quite an undertaking, I can assure you.

My great-grandfather was a lay leader in the island church, also a farmer who supplied islanders with milk, and an unofficial judge who held court in his store. As the story was told to me, his first wife died of childbirth complications, and he could not get any help with the body—maybe the men were away dredging. He shoved in his skiff all the way from Pitchcroft, his farm in Ewell, to Rhodes Point to get lumber for her coffin. He dug her own grave, too. I guess that worked on him, because he made the statement no one else on the island would ever have to go through that, and he began to build coffins and undertake funerals.

They would make them of chestnut, which was a most rot-resistant wood and easily worked. They were wide at the shoulders, narrow at the feet, covered with black broadcloth, held by nails with decorative heads. He tried to keep at least one built in advance at all times.

He would go with his horse and cart to the house where someone died; clean the body up, comb the hair out, dress them, and tack the coffin liner in. Wintertime, they would leave the windows open, and in summer, they would put the body on some ice, to keep 'til they went to the church. Some coffins back then even had an ice compartment in them. Even if it was in the middle of the night, when someone died, they would go immediately to the church and toll the bell, one toll for each year of life.

His son, my grandfather, took over the coffin business and promised he would stay on the island so long as the old man was alive. After he died in 1921, my grandfather moved to Crisfield and established the funeral home that we run today. He had studied at the Eckles College of Embalming in Philadelphia. Embalming was starting to become common in the 1920s; but it was 1952 before the islanders stopped insisting that we come over there to embalm the dead. They just did not like their dead to leave those islands. Even after that, a funeral on Smith Island was still a three-day affair. One day to go over and bring the body to Crisfield for embalming; a second to take it back, along with all the flowers, and arrange them around the coffin in the church; and a third day to assist with the funeral and take back all the paraphernalia.

Around 1935, we decided we needed our own boat. One of the island's best builders had finished a 37-foot roundstern in Rhodes Point. We put an 18 horsepower Palmer in her, and a cabin most of her length, a little galley and beds. She had special pull-out tables and some of this region's first battery-powered electric lanterns—all so we could do the embalming work right there aboard of her. Gaslight was not bright enough for the job. We named her the *King Tut*, after Tutankhamun's tomb. Islanders called her "the hearse boat."

With the *King Tut*, we could go over any time of day or night, haul the caskets, embalm bodies, and carry flowers; also sleep aboard of her, which was a real convenience sometimes. Watermen tonging or crabbing out in the Sound would see her crossing to Smith or Tangier, and they'd know somebody had died—although sometimes it was just my dad taking her out gunning ducks.

Only once can I recall we had trouble getting there. It was a fall morning, very hazy, and we were carrying a steel casket, which was a new thing at the time. We always had used wood. I didn't realize it, but all that metal had pulled my compass off 20 or 30 degrees, and I ended up south, halfway to Tangier Island.

They hold a great regard for their dead on the islands—most places do, of course, but there, it's special. Children all gather at the dock to carry flowers to the church. Watermen stop work to attend the funeral. The church is usually pretty full. Funerals when I was younger used to go on for an hour and a half or more. It was common for anyone who felt moved to stand up and say something about the deceased. They don't do it as much now, but you still get the feeling that whoever died was just so well known.

We sold the *King Tut* in 1972, to a local crab potter. The last we heard of her, she was up the Nanticoke River with a set of patent [oyster] tongs on her. Now the ferries carry the dead off and back over. They don't charge freight for the body; but they do charge on the caskets. I would say Smith Island spends a little higher than the national average on their funerals—certainly they go above average on their caskets. They are very conscious of having models certified air- and watertight. They want to keep that bay out of them.

They do not believe in cremation, though they may have to think of it, with the little cemeteries running out of space. In Tylerton and Rhodes Point, with the population shrinking, it'll be a close race whether they run out of islanders or grave sites first. It costs about $850 extra for a burial on the island, but very few want to be buried on the mainland, and many who have moved away want to be buried back there. They don't call it the island, they say "home." ✦

EDUCATION BY BOAT

THE HIGH SCHOOL TEACHER

✦ Over the years, many students who came to school in Crisfield from Smith Island have distinguished themselves. Islanders have gone on to the U.S. Naval Academy, to be college professors and school administrators, executive secretary to a U.S. Secretary of Agriculture, and a state treasury official.

Even now, it is not as easy to get your education as if you live on the mainland; and it used to be you really had to be determined. They tell of a young man home from college, visiting his folks on the island in the great winter of 1918. The bay was frozen from Smith Island to Crisfield; but he must get back to study for exams, the boy said.

His dad hired two strong young men from Ewell to haul him off. About 4:00 A.M. they showed up with an old wooden gunning skiff. They had nailed metal to her bottom like runners, and they put him in it and set off for Crisfield, twelve miles away. Coming out of the Big Thoroughfare into Tangier Sound, snow threatening, they came on a wild goose with a broken wing, which they chased down and put in the skiff. Walking on ice is a hard thing, even if you are not towing a skiff, and it was getting late in the afternoon when they came to the Puppy Hole, where the water is nearly 100 feet deep and the currents in the Sound run the strongest. There was a streak of open water, tide just boiling through it.

Right there, the two men gave their passenger a little pep talk: Sit very still in that little skiff while they ferried across the water. One bad move, and we're all dead men. They made it after dark, with snow beginning to fall. Tired and nearly starved, they met a local doctor who saw the bird and made them an offer—all they could eat at the restaurant in trade for the fowl. Think they ate some?

Getting to school was not usually that hard, even in the old days, but it was hard enough. Schools on the island never have gone beyond eighth grade. For high school, kids had to board all week, at their family's expense, with people in Crisfield. This, of course, was one reason many islanders just dropped out of school at that point; but a lot made real sacrifices to keep up with their education. Many island families moved their whole household to Crisfield for several years so their children could go to high school without hardship.

Other kids used to cross over Monday mornings on the old *Island Belle,* arriving late in the morning and often pretty green if it was rough. If the ferry was loaded with passengers, the schoolkids would have to ride down in the hold with the freight. Then on Fridays, they would get out too late to catch the *Island Belle* back, and would have to catch whatever ride home they could. Crab potters unloading their catch in Crisfield of an afternoon would come back to their boats and find the cabin full of schoolkids. That situation did not get any better until 1959, when the state began paying for the old *Island Star* to make Monday and Friday school runs. The state also allowed families $50 a month toward room and board for each child. Boarding was difficult for some kids at first, but I think a lot of them kind of enjoyed it. The seafood economy was still booming here then, and Crisfield had a moviehouse, a soda fountain, sweet shops, stores open in the evenings, dances; and Smith Island kids, for the most part, were treated well by the people here.

If you lived in Tylerton, your commute started after sixth grade, when you began riding an old, leaky wooden workboat to Ewell for middle school. The old captain always said not to worry, the boat would last as long as he did; and it is a fact that not long after he died, she went right to pieces and was hauled up a gut to die.

The biggest change in getting to school from the island came in 1974 with the *Betty Jo Tyler,* a fast, aluminum-hulled boat that could make the run across Tangier Sound daily. At that time, kids also got the option of beginning to school in Crisfield in seventh grade. It is still quite different than mainland schoolkids ever experience. The boat takes about an hour each way, and you can't stay after school for sports or other activities or you'll miss the boat; and then there is the weather—it is probably the only school system that allows a certain number of days off for high winds.

There has also been a change in the last twenty years in the attitudes toward education among islanders. I remember a conversation in my classroom years ago with an island boy, about sixteen. I was trying to motivate him, and he asked me: How much you make in a year? I told him, and he said, I make that in a good summer on the water. How many boats you got? he asked. I said one, a little fishing skiff. He had two, one a big one; and on and on he went. I told him, look, the bay's not gonna always be there for you. He is still out there, doing all right, I think. But most of them coming up in school now, they know they probably can't make it on the water.

It's not just pollution, or overfishing, either; it's expectations. They are the first generation of islanders that expect to start out living like the rest of America, and that means mortgages, big boat payments, big car payments; and yet, I don't think people who harvest seafood are getting paid much more for it than they were fifteen or twenty years ago.

The boys, at least some of them, want to try and stick there—more than the girls. A few of them you see, you think might just be able to do it. I had two like that graduated a few years ago, both really committed to working the water, best friends almost since they were born. Graduation weekend, they collided in their boats at night, and the one drowned. Soon after, the other sold his crabbing boat. As small as that community over there's getting to be, it seemed like it was more than the death of just one teenager.

The school boat is a big decision point for families. I have seen preachers, teachers, doctors, and some native islanders move off when their children reached the age they would begin that commute. Sometimes it has been that a child got so seasick they could not manage the trip. Up to that point, I think everyone agrees that the island is a paradise for kids growing up.

A long time ago, an old man from Tylerton told me this about education. He said it would be the death of Smith Island. I guess I looked shocked, because he said, no, he didn't think education was bad; but it was like a roller skate, he said; it wasn't a bad thing to have once you'd learned how to use it, but you couldn't ever put it to use unless you got away from the island, with its little dirt and shell paths. Educated people wouldn't want to be plain old Smith Islanders as much, he thought. ✦

JOURNALS

SPRING

*M*ARCH is a time of transition and muddlement.

The oyster bars are exhausted, and the crabs remain buried in the cold muds of the bottoms. Income taxes are looming, and simultaneously, bank loans must be negotiated to afford gearing up for the summer.

"Nine more weeks 'til crabbing," reads a sign in the store; and another sign: "Absolutely no more credit." A sheet tacked to the telephone pole near the church that serves as Tylerton's bulletin board touts a "CHEAP community supper" by the Ladies Auxiliary—"chips and hot dogs, 50 cents apiece."

Things are so slow that starting of the town oil truck, which has stood dormant around by the harbor all winter, attracts a goodly crowd. To get heating oil and kerosene here, the island school boat, the *Betty Jo,* tows a small barge, the *Little Swan,* to Crisfield. Once it returns, loaded, to Ewell, it transfers fuel to the *Eleanor White,* the nation's only wooden gas boat, complete with pumps just like your mainland filling station. The old *Eleanor,* which the Coast Guard won't allow to travel outside the island's protected channels, steams down to Tylerton, where it transfers its load to a 1960s vintage truck that will squeeze its way through the village's narrow paths to fill tanks against next winter's needs. "These domehead sixes start every time," the oil man proclaims, and so it does. The crowd disperses in search of other action.

In the stores, men nurse cups of coffee half the morning, buying nothing but essentials. There is plenty of time to talk nowadays, but nothing new to talk about. "Jeezu, they've gone to quotin' Scripture," exclaims a young waterman, emerging to eat his cheesesteak sub elsewhere. Inside, an elder statesman is explaining the plight of oysters, bringing to bear everything from the books of Timothy to the nation's rising divorce rate.

This is the time of year the region's newspapers usually dispatch correspondents to interview watermen about the upcoming crab season. March interviews are uniformly marked by discouragement: "This old bay's about had it, and watermen too," and variations thereof. Come back in August or September, and the tune will have changed: "Plenty crabs. We would be fine if the scientists would just quit worrying and leave us to work."

THE DAYS do march on, though. We are not long past a blizzard that drifted snow five feet deep against the houses, but mornings are beginning to look like spring. The length and angle of the light have been increasing since December 21, the shortest day of the year and the winter solstice. On March 21, the vernal equinox, day will reach parity with the darkness. On sunny mornings, the men are beginning to assemble in the warm lee of the shanties, tarring pots, building crab-shedding floats, rigging net bags. New iron scrape frames arrive daily on the ferries from the blacksmith in Crisfield.

My neighbor, Dwight, paces like a caged lion. His 36-foot workboat, the *Miss Marshall,* is hauled on the railway at Rhodes Point to be scraped and painted and otherwise readied for crabbing. Ed Harrison, a soft crabber from Ewell, is on the railway too, and has just heard his boat won't get off for another day. He looks agitated almost to panic. They are like cowboys who have lost their horses.

AS MARCH creeps into April, the panoply of summer birddom has begun to reassemble. The island is a magnet for breeding shorebirds and colonial waders, attracted by the miles of wetland feeding areas and isolated breeding spots. There are the herons—great blue, tri-colored, black and yellow crowned, little blue, and little green; the egrets, snowy, American, and cattle; also glossy ibis, oyster catchers, osprey, dunlin, yellowlegs, terns of several varieties, pelicans, skimmers, and the ubiquitous gulls.

Sometimes, Maryland's chilly early spring gives you a perfect day—one fit for sky dancing. The temperature hit 78° F, and in T-shirts we took to our canoes. The sun on our backs made the cool edge to the breeze feel delicious. The afternoon marsh stretched goldenly, veined with sparkling tidal creeks.

An osprey swooped to pluck a torporous eel basking on the surface, still semicomatose from a winter buried in the cold bottom. Brandishing its wriggling prize, the fish hawk soared in a ritual of courtship and bonding with its mate known as sky dancing. It flew so high we could scarcely locate it but for its piercing peeps, and glints of light on the eel and the bird's wings as it hovered, flapping furiously. To his lady, and to the whole of Chesapeake Bay, the osprey proclaimed: Look at me! I can provide eels without end to feed our chicks; and I am beautiful to behold!

The sky dance we had figured on; but not what happened next. A magnificent marsh hawk, working the salt meadows for rodents, glided across the gut just ahead of us. From out of nowhere, a fist-sized projectile raked the hawk's back. The silent peregrine moved so fast it seemed barely to graze the larger bird. It appeared a gust of wind had ruffled the hawk's feathers. But it dropped as if poleaxed, very nearly submerging in front of our canoe. Struggling mightily, streaming gouts of water, the hawk regained the air, only to have the falcon descend on it again. The hawk dived unceremoniously into a pine thicket, where it huddled, refusing to budge, as the deadly little falcon fluttered and screamed at the transgression of its nesting territory.

UNTIL October comes, May is the finest time to be here. The days are concerts—flute-bright mornings, afternoons mellow as a viola, sunsets soft and sweet and pure as a French horn.

All over town you can hear the glad sussurus of rushing water—the "overboard" has been turned back on. The sound comes as saltwater, circulated by pumps through the shallow soft crab holding tanks in each waterman's shanty, overflows and spills back into the bay. It is soothing to the ear; also the sound of money finally being made again. Until October, it will be our unceasing background music.

A NEIGHBOR leaves off a few dozen tiny, silken soft crabs, just shed out—the season's first. They are the size of large garden spiders, tender as grapes. Sautéed in sweet butter and popped into the mouth hot, we eat them like popcorn. They are smaller than legal market size, neither the first nor the last illicit fish and fowl to enter our diet here.

One of the first meals I ever had, the spring I arrived, was fresh, out-of-season rockfish and fresh, out-of-season black duck. It was one of the best meals I have ever had. Also, in retrospect, a sort of statement: "Welcome to our island. This is how we do things here, and you'll manage just fine if you can accept it."

I would have found it hard to look the other way at excessive fish and game violations for commercial purposes; but that era had pretty much vanished from the island. It was also, I had decided before moving, their culture, not mine. I would try to set an example, but I did not intend to be a reformer.

Unfortunately, it was an islander, Allen Smith, who ended up making the first compromise. He offered to take me gill-netting my first spring there. He had nets set for white perch up the Sound. White perch were few and far between, but the last net held a fine, fat rockfish of about ten pounds. There is not much an islander would rather have for Sunday dinner, and I quickly told Allen to regard me as a good neighbor, not as a representative of the Bay Foundation, which had lobbied hard to put a moratorium on the rockfish to halt its decline. But he was already slinging the big rock overboard. "I wouldn't a' kept it anyhow," he insisted; and for a deeply religious man, he did a better job of fibbing than I would have thought possible.

My last spring on the island, I returned from a trip, and Cheri offered me the remains of some large trout filets Allen had brought her while I was away. She had, she declared, never eaten better trout. She still hadn't, I said. It was rockfish, and it tasted just fine.

A BIG OLD Brobdingnag of a blue crab latched onto one of our education kids' fingers as we sorted our catch today. It broke the skin right through a thick rubber glove. It could have been a whole lot worse, said Newman Marshall, one of our neighbors, and he told this story:

+ I still got the mark. It was one of them big he crabs, eight or nine inches long from tip to tip, across the back of his shell—so big he wouldn't come outta my pot. I reached in to get 'im and just like that—he had me.

His big old pinchers went right through my thumb on top and bottom, until they met in the center. Sweat was pourin' off me, and I thought I was goin' to faint. I held 'im over the side. When they sense the water close, most crabs will let go. I put him right down in the water. The more I done, the more he was a'bitin', like it was makin' him madder.

By'n by, I pulled him 'til his claw broke off, still in my thumb. I got a pair of pliers and crushed that claw, and all the time, he was still a'puttin' the bite on me—that claw just quiverin'; just killin' me. Well, I got so sick I had to lay down in the bottom of my boat. For about an hour I thought I was goin' to die. That's what a crab'll do if he gets ye. +

SUMMER

We are moving into brown fly time, which means it is two months past no-see-ums, a month past greenheads, and a month before the heart of mosquito season. We have become more sophisticated then anyone should wish with the ecology and qualities of biting insects. We can debate their relative afflictions as ranchers might discuss the merits of cattle breeds.

Worst bite, no contest, goes to the greenheads. You can see the tiny pit they excavate in your hide, as blood wells up in it. They are good flyers, too, able to buck a head wind and greet incoming boats several hundred yards offshore. They tormented one islander so badly, he caught a "symbolic" greenhead and, careful to keep it alive, uncrimped the end of a 12-gauge shotgun shell, inserted the victim and, *blam!*

On the plus side, greenheads are slow to bite and easy to swat before they do—assuming you have nothing to occupy you but swatting greenheads.

melted butter in which to immerse the meat, and eight-layer chocolate cake to complete the savory descent into cholesterol hell.

As you might expect, people here have refined tastes for crabmeat. They disdain to eat softshells with the claws, flippers, or back shell left on, as they are served almost universally in restaurants and mainland homes. Islanders eat only the twin packets of backfin from the softies; tantamount, in my humble opinion, to butchering whole steers and discarding all but the filet mignon.

As for hard crabs, many swear that no potted crab is the equal of a scrape-caught crab, on the theory that the former, while waiting to be removed from the crab pot, has been chowing down on the decomposing menhaden in the pot's bait chamber. Scrape crabs, by contrast, are sort of free-range chickens, taken while gamboling through the grass beds, foraging as nature intended.

However, you don't hear any complaints about pot crabs now that scraping has ended. Mary Ada, one of the best pickers, announced the other day that even after a long, hot summer's immersion in crabs, "I get solid excited" at the big jimmies her husband is bringing her to pick now from pots he has set over by the Potomac. Fatter crabs or prettier meat she cannot recall.

Jimmy crabs generally seem accorded a higher status than sooks and she crabs, though not to the extent they are in mainland crab houses, where most patrons will pay a gigantic premium to be served the males. Here, it is mostly that the males, because of slight differences in their internal cartilage, are easier to pick.

But in autumn, the deep bay channels surrounding the island become sook highways, and potters increasingly load up with mature females, swimming by the millions for Virginia and the bay's mouth as water temperatures cool. There, in the high-salinity ocean water they must have for successful spawning, sooks from all over the bay will hibernate in the mud, emerging to release their fertile eggs the following summer.

The sooks we have had this fall, never mind the twin strikes—pot-caught and female—against them, are sweet and fat beyond compare; backfin fairly bursting free at the picker's touch, firm and white as soap. Every available recess in the shells is packed with orangy-yellow fat, so rich and dense it spreads on a chip like creamy peanut butter.

It is a tasty season for man and beast. Great energies are reaching an apex. Out in the bay and Sound, thousands of acres dimple with schooling "peanut," or juvenile menhaden. Their fatty, oil-rich flesh makes each a silvery, bite-sized packet of pure nutrition. Everything from striped bass and bluefish to sea trout and migrating loons is greedily slurping the peanuts. We fishermen are in turn loading coolers with the fattened gamefish. A single, savory filet on one's plate represents a lavish distillation of energy up through the food web: trillions of BTU's of sunlight falling on the bay, brewing millions of tons of plankton in its warm shallows and fecund marshes. This mammoth biotic production is in turn grazed by thousands of tons of anchovies and menhaden, concentrated fur-

The brown flies tend to swarm you, and can deliver more bites per minute than greenheads. They are wonderfully adept at sticking to the sides of even the fastest boat, to resume their attack once you slow. Like the greenheads, however, they usually vanish with the onset of evening.

The night belongs to the mosquitos, which is not to say they cannot make the day fairly miserable on occasion. To stand on the edge of a marsh as dusk approaches, listening to the loudening whine as cloud upon cloud of mosquitos billow aloft, is to know a dread that probably inspired prehistoric humans and saber tooths to seek shelter.

They tell of an itinerant artist who came here for solitude, and shoved an old skiff one summer day over to a hummock of trees by the bayside, where he planned to camp and think for a couple weeks. Two nights later he returned, not saying much. Asked how it had gone, he replied:

"If it's reasonable to assume I got bit by a mosquito every two minutes all the time I was there, then I was gone for ten thousand years."

The prize for unrelieved aggravation, however, goes to the tiny gnats known as no-see-ums, which the islanders say come in late spring, "along with soft crabs and strawberries." I would always seem to first encounter them while doing something messy with my hands, like cleaning trout out on the dock. Your scalp begins to itch slightly, and you twist your neck to rub the spot with a shoulder or upper arm; but it gets worse, itching furiously, burning, until you are shaking your head and rubbing it against a dock post, frantically trying to finish scaling and gutting your trout. You see nothing. To an observer onshore, you would seem possessed.

Normal mesh window screens do not stop the gnats a bit; and screens fine enough to bar them block even the breeze. It was as captives of the gnats that Cheri and I spent our first—and nearly one of our last—nights in the old house we had rented.

The move from Baltimore had frayed our nerves considerably. Everything we owned had to be put on the dock at Crisfield, transferred to the ferry, offloaded on our dock at the island, and carried by cart to the house, which had only a cramped and twisting back staircase leading upstairs. Our box spring would neither pass up the staircase nor through an upstairs window, and had to be taken back to Baltimore. Even the mattress, a queen size, had to be dragged across the porch roof, folded in half with a tearing and popping of springs, and bludgeoned through the bedroom window. We could not afford air conditioning upstairs that first year, but there was almost always a good breeze, I had assured my wife.

But I had not told her about gnats and screens. There we lay, on what was left of our bed, alternately opening the window and scratching, then closing it and soaking the sheets with sweat, neither wanting to talk about the horrible mistake we had made.

All these horror stories are true, but not the whole truth. The fact is, the buggy reputation of marshy places like Smith Island is much overdrawn. It is the difference between visiting and living in a place. One fly-bitten excursion will stick in memory forever. In residence, you come to realize that bugs, like the rest of nature, have their good years and bad years, their peak seasons within each year, and even peak hours within a given day or night.

And you learn to adapt your schedule accordingly, to do your outdoor business when there is a breeze, or in hours when experience tells you there is usually a lull to whatever biters are in season. You keep the favored local repellent, Skin-So-Soft, available from Christine, the local Avon lady, stocked just as you would milk or butter. I seldom used even that. I just wore socks, long pants, and long-sleeved shirts underlain by a T-shirt, and a cap. In our bedroom, we discovered that placing a dim lamp in the corner farthest from the bed cut the gnat problem to a minimum on all but peak nights (and yes, the second summer we scrounged an air conditioner).

The island's marshes had so much natural tidal flushing, they actually bred fewer mosquitos than much of the bay's dammed and impounded mainland wetlands. Also, the island is virtually without ticks, probably because it lacks enough wild mammals to support and distribute them.

As for bees, we were certified free of them by the U.S. Department of Agriculture. That came about when the department's honeybee lab in Baton Rouge began casting about for places to propagate a promising new variety of bee without contamination from existing varieties. The island turned out to have the perfect genetic isolation: too far from the mainland for native bees to fly over; also too shallow for large freighters, on which Africanized "killer bees" often hitchike, to get within flying distance.

So it has come to pass that we have actually gone to great lengths to bring more stinging creatures here. Hives are going up out in the marsh. Some islanders were at first skittish of importing more biters and stingers—coals to Newcastle and all that. But others said their gardens had never done so well.

AUGUST is solid crabs here. Soft and hard, scraped and netted and potted and banktrapped and trotlined—all the ways they know to catch a crab are working to the max, all at once; and the softies are shedding so fast they must be tended—fished up or transferred from one holding tank to the next—nearly round the clock. The women bathe several times a day and still complain they reek of crab. The air is redolent with crabs steaming in the picking shanties.

Our neighbors, even those closest to us, have no time or energy for us. They look like zombies some days. The wave of wishing for crabbing to begin, which swelled anxiously in March and April, broke blessedly in May and June, has receded. The islanders, even as they know they must wring every cent they can

out of this season, have begun to long for the fall, when things will begin to wind down.

SOMETIMES the competition for crabs in August can lead to warfare. Everywhere there are fat, brownish juvenile herring gulls floating in the channels and on the grass flats, just fledged and now learning how to fend for themselves. Every year there seem to be more. "Bay buzzards" and "winged rats," some watermen have taken to calling them.

Occasionally, a few, looking for easy pickings, will take to lighting on the edge of a crabber's shedding tanks to feed on the softies therein. That is like plucking dollar bills—rather hard-earned ones—from the waterman's pocket.

One day I was bringing twenty junior high kids up the channel into town in the Bay Foundation's workboat, the *Wood Duck.* I had been hitting on a favorite theme: how the islanders were unique in their close relationship to nature. As we neared a particular shanty, my charges began shouting excitedly:

Mr. Horton, Mr. Horton! Look at the sea gulls diving! All ran toward the bow to get a better look. Then, as we drew closer, the cries changed to shrieks:

Oh, Mr. Horton! They can't get up . . . they're all bloody!

About the same time, I noticed Don on his shanty porch, 12-gauge in hand, daring another crab marauder to come within range. He already had half a dozen down and dead, or fast bleeding to death. Seeing us chugging into the line of fire, he doffed his barrel and waved to the kids, pleased, I think, that his marksmanship had not eroded since waterfowling season.

Back at the house, I tried to explain that people who make their living in nature sometimes behave, well, more naturally than we might wish.

FALL

The season has changed with the flick of a switch—literally. For the first time since early May, the rush and plash of water from electric pumps, flowing across the soft crabs and falling back into the bay, has ceased. Islanders sometimes call this the "overboard," and for months we have been as intimate with its sound as our own breathing.

October also brings a return of social life. Worn nearly to the nub from round-the-clock soft crabbing, islanders breathe a sigh of relief, even as they regret the decline of income, and the whole place seems to relax as the men contemplate a shift to oystering and hard crabbing. We begin to get invites once again to neighbors' homes for steamed hard crabs and potato chips, washed down with quarts of Pepsi and sugary iced tea. Often there are bowls of war

ther in the firm flesh of baitfish-slurping rockfish, and then in us—one's fork, poised above a choice filet hesitates, a whole summer of Chesapeake sunlight hefted on its tines. Ummmmm.

OVERNIGHT, on the trailing edge of a roaring northwest cold front, we have had a swanfall. The rising November sun this morning lit them up, the bay's largest waterfowl, white as snowdrifts clumped along the golden rim of marsh down Tyler's Creek. *Wow-HOWoo, Wow-HOWoo.* The island has regained its winter voice. Issued from a looping, four-foot windpipe, it is the lonesomest sound I know. Yelping, baying, whooping, yodeling, halloooing, the pure notes of swansound, French horns in a higher, wilder key, will flavor our air from now until March. Wild geese seem shrill by contrast. Perhaps only a wolf howling in the deep woods, or a loon call floating from the mists of a northern lake, are as able to inject the landscape for miles around with such a timeless and thrilling quality.

On seven-foot wings, the tundra swans come to the bay from Arctic nesting grounds as far off as Alaska's North Slope. On the final leg of their journey the great birds, which weigh as much as Christmas turkeys, remain airborne up to twenty-four hours, covering more than a thousand miles. Their final descent to the welcoming Chesapeake shallows and marshes, from up to a mile in altitude, is a balletic triumph—gliding, spiraling, careering, spilling air, carving lines of elegant poetry across the sky, sculpting the wind. A British friend who comes here often, who has devoted his life to the study of birds, says his countrymen have a term for this glorious return and descent—*swanfall*—and he thinks it should be celebrated with festivals and poetry, appreciated as much as the turning of autumn leaves.

One day, usually in late March, the swans will erupt in a final flourish before lifting off en masse to catch the brief summer nesting season back on the tundra. Their great wings will beat the water to a froth, with a clopping sound like hard wave chop spanking the marsh bank; then, gaining altitude, the sound changes to a whistling of wind winnowed through their pinions like the jingling of bells from on high; and a few faint *Wow-HOWoo's;* and silence. The birds of summer will already have been setting up shop in great and interesting variety; but nothing to replace the sound of swans.

WINTER

It is February, one of those mornings when you know why the human race long ago mostly chose cars over boats. Abby has been up since 1:00 A.M. with earache and nausea. At 7:30, we bundle her up and board the *Jason* for Crisfield.

Every roll and pitch threatens to throw us from the hard wooden benches that pass for seats; then slams us back just as hard against the sides of the cabin, down which cold water is drizzling through the window caulking.

The cabin is packed today. It is far too cold and rough, and our little girl too sick, to go out on deck, and the cabin fills with smoke from watermen's cigarettes. Women fan themselves and sip colas to ward off seasickness. Abigail is a pathetic lump, pale and hollow-eyed. At 8:30 we dock in Crisfield, but the pediatrician can't see us until 10:20. A lady who knows my mother from their college days kindly takes us in.

It is the flu, the doctor says, and prescribes medicine. She promises to call the pharmacy. We can pick it up just before the ferry returns to the island at 12:30. Except someone screws up, and it is 12:25 and there is no prescription waiting, and we go back across in as much pain and suffering as we came. The medicine will come on the next ferry—five very long hours later.

For three days and nights of January the north wind has played like a hellish great, bow arm across the island, moaning and blasting unrelenting against our old house. A strip of tin wrenched from a nearby shanty roof flaps and shrieks incessantly. The bay is whipped to a riot of white and gray, and the harder gusts pummel the marsh nearly flat in places, like some invisible beast is treading the island. We're heating with everything we've got to stay in the low 60s—propane, kerosene, electric baseboard, and portable oil-filled radiators.

The plastic I stapled to our inside windows has exploded from the pressure of air sieving around the frames, despite a double layer of plastic on the outside. The thick, dry-rotted wool carpet rises and falls on the living-room floor from wind swooshing through the foundation. After a couple days we feel physically assaulted by the battering. Cheri says that growing up in the West she read how, after a hard winter, they used to carry pioneer women, catatonic, from their sod huts on the wind-blasted prairie. She does not think it will take her nearly a whole winter.

Then it is done; late the third night the wind moves on, and a great mass of Arctic air floods silently across the bay. Temperatures plummet to the single digits, and the next night dip below zero. You can literally see ice making up, solidifying by the minute. The island descends into an eerie, profound quiet— not a boat can move, no bilge pumps piss in the harbor; from the bayside there is not a murmur of surf, no lap of wavelets in the channel. Even the piercing, winter obbligatos of geese and swans have faded, as the fowl abandon the frozen marshes and shallows for open bay. In the frozen night sky you can almost hear the hard sparkle of starlight.

A warming trend is forecast not far off, but for the meantime we are imprisoned. The islanders drift between the two stores like fowl trading between patches of open water; and in the cheery warmth, over coffee and doughnuts, the stories of ice-ups past begin to flow.

It was a bad freeze some fifty years ago that made his most memorable Christmas, Dallas Bradshaw says. Ice had forced his dad and other island men to beach their dredge boats where they were oystering across the bay on the Potomac. There would be no familiar Christmas-week sight of the skipjacks' tall, raked masts returning home to Smith, "that made you know Santa Claus was a'-comin'." Mayor Jackson of Baltimore sent a bus to bring the stranded watermen around the head of the bay and down the Delmarva Peninsula to Crisfield. From there, with ice making up fast in Tangier Sound, they boarded the *Island Belle*. Trailed by another boat carrying supplies, she made it to within sight of Tylerton, where both stalled in the snowy dusk, about two miles short of town.

The dredgers walked home across marsh and ice. Come with him up the channel the next morning and help unload grub and supplies he had left aboard, Dallas's dad told him. "I was twelve," Dal says, "and before it was even light we headed straight up the channel in my grandfather's sleigh—that's how thick she was froze. When we reached the boat, Dad said to climb up on top of her pilot house; there's a sack of potatoes and something else. Well, it was a second-hand bike. I never had a bike in my life. She had cost five dollars, which was a lot of money then.

"You talk about happy! I weren't proud that morning. I laid that sack of potatoes across her basket and handlebars, and I rode that bike right down the middle of the channel—come clean into town like that."

OCCASIONALLY, ice in the old days brought tragedy to the island. I had found in the files of the *Baltimore Sun* a striking picture from a freeze-up winter in the 1930s: island men surrounding the *Island Belle*, sawing a path for her through ice that looked to be a foot thick or more. I was showing it around one of the stores when a woman came up and said she was pretty sure she knew what was going on in that photograph.

Inside, her grandmother was in labor. The birth was not going well, and the *Belle* was struggling to get her to Crisfield. But the ice proved too thick. Mother and child died. One of the old people who was there said the cries and the moaning haunted him for a long time afterward. Nowadays, we can have a state of Maryland Medevac chopper here from Salisbury in ten minutes flat.

Phenomena

SHANKSES

After more than a year in residence, I finally paid my first visit to Shanks Island. Seldom had a month gone by when some islander did not mention "Shankses." Though it is no more than a fifteen-minute skiff ride south from Tylerton, across the Virginia line, it is not a much-visited place any more. Always, I had heard it referred to as something separate, a place of almost mythical qualities.

"Oh, we aren't from here, my family's from Shankses," old islanders would say, as if speaking of a distant country. They spoke of a place with broad beaches and huge old trees; pretty anchorages in its Soundside coves, meadows and yards dotted with fruit trees and heavy-laden fig bushes. There were yarns about pirates landing there, and a British admiral during the War of 1812 who demanded the residents feed his troops—in an act of quiet defiance, he was secretly served sea gull. "Uncle William," an islander not long deceased, spent much of his life searching down on Shankses for buried treasure.

Shankses is part of Smith's past and maybe—the way global sea-level rise is proceeding—indicative of its future. All that is left today of this garden spot is an eroding splinter of white sand and emerald tide marsh. It is a few hundred yards long and in places no more than 50 feet wide—even less on a high tide. Few people ever visit, and on the blazing summer day I went, you could see why. Though shallowness is one of Chesapeake Bay's dominant characteristics—average depth about 21 feet—Shankses goes to extremes. For thousands of feet around it, the depths range from a couple feet to a couple inches. Even in a canoe you must disembark and walk in the last couple hundred feet, across a bottom that turns nearly to quicksand the closer you get. Stinging sea nettles seek any chinks of bare skin between bluejeans and sock tops; and lusty greenhead flies welcome fresh, sweating flesh as a rare treat.

Yet, life seems drawn to Shankses as strongly as in the days when the earlier settlers favored it. You walk in across swan wallows: big, shallow depressions excavated from the bottom by the winter flocks that feed here on tubers of aquatic vegetation from November until March. The beach is littered with the desiccated carcasses of horseshoe crabs, which heaved ashore here in late May to deposit their eggs—a ritual they have performed on such sandy beaches for some 400 million springs. The leathery little shells of terrapin eggs indicate that another crop of diamondbacks has hatched successfully from the beach, probably in June.

And all this is mere prelude to Shankses late-summer extravaganza of nesting birds. As we draw close to the island, a third of its beach erupts in royal terns. Gyreing, blizzarding, screeching like hard chalk on a thousand blackboards, the adults fill the air. Their rapier wings, in swirling, close formation, lattice the blue sky, compartmenting it into diamonds, triangles, ellipses. On the ground their flightless chicks, perhaps a thousand of them, trot along in the same manner, so that the beach seems to writhe with eddies and whorls of terns. The whole effect is confusing to the eye, grating on the ear, and probably an ingrained and effective defense against predators.

Now we are approaching the main attraction—the bay's first colony of brown pelicans, and the northernmost nesters of their species in the East. Just last summer they took up residence here. They command your rapt attention: big, regal birds, seldom uttering a sound, even when alarmed. Beautiful to watch, whether in repose, in flight, or fishing, they have a force of character, an individuality shared by only a few other fowl, like the bald eagle and the great blue heron. It is small wonder that Audubon, in his classic *Birds of America,* gave them more pages than all but a couple other species.

Why it is the pelicans chose to grace a single, 100-foot stretch of little Shankses from among the bay's estimated 9,000 miles of shoreline is a mystery. The fishing is no doubt as good for pelicans as for island crabbers in the great, grassy surrounds of the shallows here; and the remoteness and inaccessibility of the place keep predators and human traffic to a minimum. There must be more to it than that, but only the taciturn pelicans know. That they chose well is not in doubt, because some fifty chicks, nearly as large as the adults and covered in creamy down, huddle together against our intrusion, maintaining even at that tender age a certain dignity.

Departing, you notice that further down the island, cormorants, gulls, oyster catchers, and skimmers are all rearing young. Scarcely a square inch of sand is not tracked by birdlife. You think of Uncle William, who, they say frittered away half his life down here seeking pirate gold. Maybe he found other reward in Shankses which, even in retreat before the waves, radiates a magical and outsize attraction to life.

TIDE

Santa's sleigh is perilously awash, the swirling bay waters nearly up to the old boy's butt, as his reindeer climb skyward in a belated attempt to thwart disaster. Fortunately, Santa is only made of plywood, a lifesize Christmas display in an islander's front yard. The watery tableau, though striking in effect, was never intended.

It is 7:00 A.M., and something lovely and ominous, regular as clockwork and quite unpredictable, is happening this late-autumn day.

The tide is rising.

Usually, that's no big deal. Especially in this water-riven marshscape, where the heave and sigh of baywater is omnipresent and regular as breathing. More regular actually.

Twice every 24.8 hours the pull of moon and sun, and earth's rotation, knead and mound the oceans into great, elongated waves that break on the coasts, not as surf but as tide. So lengthy is the travel time of such waves up the 180-mile Chesapeake that by the time one crests at Havre de Grace, Maryland, at bay's head, another crest, or high tide, is occurring around the mouth near Norfolk, Virginia. Smith Island, nearly halfway in between, lies in the trough, experiencing low tide when either end of the estuary is having a high. Conversely, when it is low at head and mouth, the tidal wave is humping highest around the island.

The timing of tides, hitched directly to the cosmic clockwork, is so predictable that it can be published for Smith Island or any place else on earth to the minute, years in advance, or calculated by computer; and so we have known for a while, with wonderful certainty, that the tide this particular day at Smith Island will be at its fullest around noon. The *when* of a high tide is easy. But what we couldn't predict, couldn't even suspect until yesterday, and won't know for certain until noon comes, is *how* high.

The previous high tide, last Saturday night, was a tad bigger than normal, but nothing remarkable. But by 7:00 A.M. today it is already well above that, and rising fast—with nearly five hours more until the crest.

By 10:00 A.M., our yard is covered, which has not happened for more than two years. In the street, a tabby cat crouches on a tuft of high ground and flips minnows from the water. The marsh is beginning to blossom with colorful bits of red and blue, yellow and white—plastic trash being dislodged from places where it has accumulated, undisturbed, for years. Herons seize the moment, stalking the infrequently flooded ecotone, where high marsh and uplands merge, as the rising water flushes fiddler crabs and small rodents from cover. The islanders have all begun eyeing their personal "marks," a planter in one's front yard, a notch in another's fence post, gauging whether this tide will be a nuisance, or something more.

And still two hours left to rise.

It is the bay's extreme shallowness, combined with the caprice of the winds, that make the *how* high (or low) of tides here so difficult to forecast. Easterly winds like the one that just passed through blow up from the bay's mouth, force-feeding extra ocean water to the estuary, and blocking it from flowing out before another tidal wave enters the mouth. Northwest winds have the opposite effect, causing extreme low tides. In April of 1975, after nearly four days of nor'westers, the low tides got so low as to stop fully loaded ships from leaving the Port of Baltimore.

The wind blowing across the bay's surface also routinely sets up what oceanographers call "seiching" (French for sloshing), so that the whole surface, between western shore and Eastern Shore, is in effect tilted, depressed on one side and elevated on the other. Because the bay is so "thin" (average depth about 21 feet), it doesn't take much wind to get it sloshing pretty good; and this can further amplify (or dampen) the extent of a given tide.

Now it is 11:00 A.M. The island kids are out in force, commandeering canoes and big chunks of Styrofoam floated from the marsh, paddling down streets and through the flooded yards. High tides are their equivalent of the mainland's occasional big snowstorms, which they seldom get because of the bay's moderating effect on temperatures. Sunday School and church have been canceled—too wet for the old people to get down their walks; nearly thigh-deep, too, between the parsonage in Ewell and the boat dock from where the preacher leaves to come here. People are busy moving freezers in their crab shanties up on blocks, and jacking up the under-house floor furnaces many still use.

And another hour still to rise.

The actual rise of water, even on days like this, is gentle compared with the 20-foot and greater tidal ranges that are routine along coasts in Alaska and parts of Canada. The difference between mean low water and mean high water on the Chesapeake is seldom more than a few feet—tame even by comparison to Long Island Sound or New Jersey's sea coast. Even the highest tide at Baltimore in nearly 150 years of record keeping—on August 23, 1933—was just eight feet above normal.

But a few feet of vertical rise can translate into hundreds, even thousands of feet of horizontal flooding around the Chesapeake's broad, flat edges. And the island is the flattest of the flat among all Maryland's inhabited lands. The highest elevation in Somerset County is 46 feet above sea level; and here on Smith, unless you count a few mounds artificially raised by pumping up silt dredged from the channels, the average elevation is just two feet, with no point in any of the three towns exceeding five. Many of the neatly mown yards, on close inspection, contain enough tidal wetland plants that cutting them probably technically violates federal environmental statutes. The same August 1933 tide that hit Baltimore caused a disaster here, floating away livestock, shanties, and flooding virtually every building but the church.

It won't be that bad today. It is nearly noon, and the weather has turned calm and sunny—a good thing, because water now covers 80 percent of Tylerton; the big nor'wester that had been forecast could have caused real damage if it rolled waves through the streets atop this tide. People are relaxing now, joking about Santa Claus's sleigh needing anti-fouling paint, same as the crabbers' boats, "to keep the bar nackles [barnacles] off her runners."

Suddenly, a delightful afternoon for "gut running" lies before us. For the next several hours, miles of shallow, narrow tidal creeks and thousands of acres of marsh will be accessible by boat. We will skim through the tips of the spartina and the needlerush like airboats through the Everglades, flushing herons and black ducks and rails. From our skiffs, we can see on the eastern horizon with uncommon clarity Crisfield, Deal Island, and even clumps of trees some thirteen miles distant around the mouth of the Pocomoke River. It is as if they are afloat, suspended, in the monochrome merge of bay and sky. Actually, it is we who are floating a few feet higher than normal; and even small variations in one's angle of view transform our supremely horizontal world here. The marshes, even necklaced with trash, are of surpassing beauty, fat and sleek with tide, and enameled with reflections of blue sky and creamy billows of cloud.

All we lack is buffalo. A sculptor who came here was struck by the resemblance between the untrammeled midwestern prairies of yore and the sweep of the island's marsh. He proposed anchoring herds of lifesize bison, sculpted from Fiberglas and mounted on floats, to swing to and fro with the tides as if grazing on the Kansas plain. It seemed bizarre, and we kidded about adding Fiberglas Indians on Fiberglas ponies, giving chase; and perhaps a Fiberglas cavalry bringing up the rear. Maybe it is the balmy, perfect weather, but today it seems like that would be a sight to behold, the Wild West, raised on the bay's inhaled breath, gliding eerily across the horizon. The charge would be accompanied by the swans down Tyler's Creek, yelping and yipping like fierce warriors.

Even as we glide the guts, the bay at Norfolk is exhaling huge volumes of saltwater back into the ocean. Soon, we will all sink a few feet, back into our normal routines, dreams of ghost riders in the sky subsided.

"BEING THERE"

My friend Dave, one of the finest photographers of Chesapeake Bay, talks a lot about the value of "being there." Of course, to photograph anything, you have to be there; but what he means is there are so many variations on even the simplest scene. No matter how well you think you have captured it, you can bet that the second, or the tenth, or the hundredth time you revisit it, something unique or special will occur.

That is one of the reasons I moved here. The more I visited the island, the more the limitations of such short glances at the beauty of the place became apparent. I wanted a good, long look, a total immersion, a baptism perhaps—or maybe nothing so high-flown; just a good, long nature binge. At some point I realized I had to stop calling Dave in Baltimore to report every remarkable scene—"God, the sunset on the ice and the kids trying to tong oysters through a hole they've cut; you should be here right now." It was mental cruelty.

More than anything, "being there" meant feasting on color. The island, an austere landscape in most respects, spread itself wantonly to the light; and the light resonated continuously, and with infinite variety between immense, reflective sheets of marsh and bay and sky that embraced us above, below, and to the eye's limit on every horizon. Mists, moons, dawns, sunset afterglows, white noontime blazes, blue and golden late-autumn afternoons; the cirrusy calligraphy of winter skies—every hour and season, every atmospheric condition, was amplified, and seemed to have its distinctive signature. An outsider might wonder to hear Smith Island described as gorgeously flamboyant; but you just had to be there.

SACRED GROVES

In the hearts of the island, fleshy-leaved little violets and old daffodils bloom in winter; the grass is nearly always green, and living fossils gather around Valentine's Day to make croaking, clacking, howling love.

They are numinous places, where normal sound and weather seem arrested, like Auden's "gardens that time is forever outside"; and the full moon on wind-tossed nights, flooding down through the branches of giant old spreading hackberry trees, weaves the most fantastic patterns.

None are larger than a few dozen acres, but all save the tiniest have names—The Pines, Ireland, Hog Neck, Old Man Dan's, and such. Many have no owner, or at least no one claims them. They are essentially communally shared; places to hunt, gather wild asparagus, smoke dope, play pirate, to seek solitude, or a cedar tree for Christmas. Island kids have gone there in search of Bigfoot, or "Captain Charlie's horse," or whatever creature thrills and terrifies their generation. If Smith Islanders were ancient Greeks, these would be their sacred groves.

To reach these inner sanctums, you must usually cross water, then marsh, and after that a ring of ditch banks dug by settlers a century or more ago; and finally, bull your way through a breastwork of thick and scratchy shrubs before attaining the open understory within.

Islanders say that wherever you see such hummocks of trees today, there was someone living "way back." Many contain the mossy bricks of old foundations, rusted farm implements, and plantings of daffodils, arranged to cheer some long-gone walkway. The ditching and diking that surrounds most of the hummocks probably is responsible for their having survived salt flooding in our modern era of rapidly rising sea level. The dominant trees are mostly hackberries and red cedar, with some persimmon, locust, and loblolly pine. The hackberries, slow growers, are huge, undoubtedly in their second century of growth, and perhaps their third. From the air in summertime, they stud the tawny marsh like soft green oases.

In modern times the groves, devoid of human settlement, have become vast Bird Babels, rookeries that by late spring are raucous with the nesting chatter of more than a dozen varieties of herons, ibis, egret, grackles, crows, and assorted songbirds. By deep summer, these cool, quiet gardens of winter are carpeted by pokeweed, reeking of excrement and fishy vomit ejaculated by the heron and egret nestlings. At such times, they are perhaps best viewed from outside, their greenery festooned with the plumage of the nesters.

There is no debate about the dominant spirit of the groves. It is the largest and earliest arrival, the great blue heron. The first of these, winging nocturnally from southern winter quarters, begin circling the rookeries as early as mid-February. I saw spring's first pair once in a driving sleet storm. The close coincidence of their nesting arrival in Maryland with Valentine's Day has moved some ornithologists to dub these pterodactylous creatures, little changed in 67 million years of fossil record, "the love birds."

Lovers they must be, after a fashion, but to canoe quietly near the groves of the island, in the early still of a chill March day, is to experience such a moaning and keening and croaking and whooping as does not belong to our era. At such moments, with sunrise or sunset limning the ancient, stilted herons, courting amid the stark hackberry branches, the very dawn of time seems again at hand.

It is often tempting to speak of the groves'—and the island's—"timeless quality," but that is misleading. The landscape here has changed dramatically in just a few centuries. Historical accounts indicate the place was heavily forested as recently as the 1600s, and higher ground than one would imagine today.

Duck hunting one afternoon on the island's bayside, we began wresting some gnarled old logs eroding from the beach to construct a makeshift blind. My partner began idly whittling at one of the barnacled surfaces. "Look here"; he gave a low whistle. We had built a whole duck blind of finest black walnut, rotted not a whit by decades, or centuries, of immersion in salt and muck. There was no land within two miles of us that presently would be high and well drained enough to grow walnut trees.

Huge stumps of other species, mostly cedars and pines, seem to underlie most of the island's marsh. Erosion is always exposing them, as are cuts the islanders have dug and dynamited to make time-saving passageways for their boats. That big changes occurred rather rapidly seems obvious; but what was the scenario? Was there timbering in Colonial days, accompanied by a risen sea level that made regrowth impossible? Are the underlying stumps much more ancient than that? Do they date from the end of the last Ice Age some fifteen thousand years ago?

That is when the glaciers began to melt and the oceans rose to fill the old gorge of the Susquehanna River. The present-day Chesapeake reached its present extent around three thousand years ago.

Some islanders said they thought that cutting trees was what started the island eroding—the root masses that held things together were destroyed, and a process begun that eventually will destroy the place. Scientists would bet on an acceleration in the rate of sea-level rise as a more likely culprit; but there is no doubt that trees are seen by islanders as helping hold their homeland together. They hate it when watermen from treeless Tangier Island to the south come up to cut a boatload of shrubs to camouflage their duck blinds. It is a visceral thing, an innate appreciation for anything that stands upright and enduring against the elements out here.

Thus, it was a poor omen one spring night when we lost the oldest tree on the island. It was the wind-flagged cedar that clung to the eastern side of the thoroughfare between Tylerton and Easter's Point. Decade after decade of prevailing southwest wind had caused the old tree to branch in the shape of a flag, aflap in the breeze. Growing had been tough there on the edge of the marsh, and the cedar was not much more than a foot in diameter, or 20 feet in height; but it had been a landmark, unchanging, a reference point visible from every crabbing ground around the island, throughout the lives of even the oldest watermen. They said a man who died a few years ago, who was in his nineties, had observed that the cedar was unchanged since he was a child. We tried to count the rings later on, and they were so close together in places we had to estimate. Not counting a three-inch diameter rotten spot toward the trunk's center, we got around 175 years.

The tragedy was it didn't have to die. A skiffload of drunk teenagers took a chainsaw to the old tree one Saturday night. Just sliced down in a few seconds something that had endured and beaconed islanders since perhaps the War of 1812. I think what bothered people most was the lack of respect for something so rooted.

I'm not superstitious, but I've wondered since, at times when the island's future has seemed in doubt, whether cutting that old tree didn't signify some profound unraveling.

NOCTILUCA

No one here has ever seen the like. The bay for miles around is abloom every night with a strange, cold fire. Gary Tull, crossing the Sound for Crisfield at 3:30 A.M., swears he read his Bible in the glow of wavelets. Crabbers traveling westward toward their pots on the Potomac saw shoals of migrating bluefish streaking below like luminous torpedos; and watched ducks, startled by their boats' passing, flail lustrous gouts across the smooth, dark surface of the bay.

Everyone, of course, is familiar with the phosphorescence one often sees on dark nights, when jellyfish and other marine organisms are churned in their propeller's wake; but this is different. In places where the flow of water through deep spots draws foamy tidelines along the channel edges, the strange glow lies windrowed "thick as paint," stretching away like a line of breakers where no shoals exist, one waterman says. Plunge a crab pot hook into it and it lit up like a fluorescent bulb, he added.

Gary had scooped some of the stuff into a soft-drink bottle and we turned the lights off in the store to watch it. The glow had lost a lot of its punch after nearly twenty-four hours, but every time you shook the bottle, it still erupted in a thousand sparkles. Dwight, who is thoughtful and reads more widely than most down here, figured it was linked to the Navy's recent experiments across the bay at Solomons with electromagnetic radiation.

The Navy has been trying for years to get permission to moor near Smith Island a barge, with a generator that can create pulses the size of junior lightning bolts. It is a larger version of one they've already got at Solomons, and it would be used in tests to "harden" U.S. ships' electronic gear to withstand the electromagnetic pulses from nuclear bombs exploding in the atmosphere in time of war (seemed like that would be the least of our problems if it came to nuclear bombs exploding overhead, one waterman observed).

I told them that from what I knew about the Navy's experiments, it didn't seem like it could make the bay light up night after night. I was pretty sure what was causing the strangely beautiful state of the water, and said I'd check it out. The next night was moonless, sky ablaze with stars unblinking in the crystal fall air, and not a breath of air to mar the water's surface—perfect conditions for a night canoe with the group of eighth-grade science students we had in residence at the time. We would see about these weird goings-on.

Even the strongest phosphorescence usually is not very bright until one's eyes are adjusted to darkness, so we turned our backs to the lights of Tylerton and paddled out to a little marsh creek where banks of tall spartina grasses on either side blocked off even the faint glow of light from the island's homes and street lights.

I have paddled that creek a hundred times, but never before or since as it was that night. The sky, dense with stars, lay repeated seamlessly on the dark surface. And now, with every stroke, blue and gold and silver of the strangely luminescent waters streamed from our oar tips and jetted from our hulls. Canoes no longer, we were starships blazing through the constellations, suspended between two heavens in fiery silence.

A great blue heron swept above us, flight path visible by the stars he blotted out. From a tide pond a duck sprang, dripping liquid light among the dark, wet roots of the marsh. *Whack!* I hit the water, beaverlike, with the flat of my paddle, shattering the black surface into a million shimmering shards. *Whack! Whack!* Everyone joined in, 'til the whole creek crackled with light. For more than an hour we slipped through the magical night, scattering stardust and bayfire, before reluctantly turning for home.

The next day, I took samples from the creek's water to a well-known university expert on the algae of Chesapeake Bay, who confirmed my suspicions. Back in Tylerton, I told a few watermen that the cause of their wonderment was *Noctiluca miliaris,* a tiny algal plant invisible to the naked eye. It was unusual to see it this time of year, and highly unusual in such concentrations. When agitated, the noctiluca—literally, "night light"—produced bursts of short, bluish light, emitted by an enzyme called luciferase acting upon a complex protein, luciferin. The light was called bioluminescence, and it was quite literally cold fire, dissipating only 1 percent of its energy in heat compared to 90 percent in a conventional flame. I had a lot more stuff for them to read if they wanted, about noctiluca's circadian rhythms, divalent ion transport, dinoflagellate form, and so forth.

The men seemed interested, but they asked did the scientists know *why* it made that cold fire, and why it happened to be out there just now thicker than any living man could ever remember it? And how could something that small light up half the bay like that? Good questions, I said. No one has the slightest idea why bioluminescence exists or whether it does noctiluca the slightest good. They all thanked me for checking into it.

By then, the glow in the nighttime bay had begun to fade, and the talk at the store was turning to the prospects for oystering after Christmas, and nothing more was heard of the strange, bright water. Every year or so since then it comes up at the store, about how nobody ever saw its like before or since; and usually they will add how it must have been those Navy tests caused it.

BETWEEN HOLLAND
AND TANGIER

The Island's Future—and Ours

OUR APPROACH to the island sends wild swans, baying like lost souls, rising through a winter mist from the empty surface of the cove. A hundred boats of watermen once harbored snugly there. Of the once-bustling town beyond it, a lone, wind-blasted structure remains, housing occasional duck hunters. Often, I ferried schoolkids here from the environmental education center I ran at Smith Island, half an hour's run south. I would dub this "the mystery island," and turn them loose for half a day to explore and discover its harsh secret.

It wouldn't take long before someone would push through the thicket of high tide bush to the old cemetery, encircled by an ornate fence of heavy wrought iron; others would uncover brick foundations, and casket vaults beginning to protrude from the marsh. Beachcombers would return bearing fragments of pottery, sometimes the entire handle of an elegant teapot, or pieces of glass-stoppered medicine bottles from Colonial apothecaries. Notice the quality of the china, and the finely carved tombstones, I'd tell the kids. This was no fishing camp, but a prosperous community—and from the dates in the graveyard, a long-lived one, going well back into the 1700s. But something ended it, and rather abruptly; after the twentieth century began, scarcely a new grave appears.

It was not a place whose residents would have abandoned it lightly. Known on mariners charts as Holland Island, it is said by wags to have taken its name from a bottle of Holland gin found washed up on the shore; but old deed transfers from a Holland Haynie, of Northumberland County, Virginia, indicate a more likely namesake. A century ago, Holland's captains, and its fleet of schooners, skipjacks, and bugeyes, were considered among the bay's best. Rich upland soils grew wheat, corn, asparagus, and both white and sweet potatoes. Six orchards flourished there, and an old Holland Islander once told a newspaper interviewer that his most vivid memory was the sweet smell of the place, the fragrance of its fruit blossoms that greeted returning sailors.

Old photos show a picturesque main street along what was called the Bayshore Ridge, facing west across the bay; a long row of three-story, gabled frame homes behind neat, whitewashed picket fences, shaded by mature hardwoods. There were seven stores, including a confectionery; a church, a community hall, and two ballfields—the Holland Island Eagles routinely mopped up the diamond with teams from Hoopers, Smith, Deal, and other island communities; at least, that is how Holland Islanders recalled the scores. I once interviewed a former resident who left the island for the first time to fight in World War I. Must have been quite a shock, I said. Indeed; on the mainland and in the Army were the first times in his life he ever saw anyone steal, or get arrested, he said.

A favorite Holland Island story, told to illustrate the self-reliance of the place, involves the captain of a state icebreaker approaching the island during a hard freeze-up of the bay early this century. Shooting around the island had been interpreted as signals of distress. He had soup aboard for those in need, the captain told island youth who skated out to meet him. Soup? they cried; why they soon would be feasting on the wild geese and ducks they had just shot.

But even then, island and islanders were inexorably bound for the mists of history. Beginning with some fierce storms in the late 1800s, Long Island, a barrier that buffered Holland against the waves on its bayside, had begun to "wash." By 1911, as the bay gnawed at the main island, the owner of the main grocery store and several homeowners pulled out. Islanders wrote of lying awake at night and shuddering at the *crack!* of chunks of their homeland literally breaking apart. Houses were disassembled, board by board, and later re-erected in Cambridge, a riverfront town farther up Maryland's Eastern Shore. By 1918, the island had lost its post office; and by the 1920s, it ceased to be a community, although several people returned to their old homes for many summers to crab and enjoy what was left of their society.

On this mild, hazy January afternoon, we are accompanied by I. T. Todd, a prominent Crisfield seafood dealer, and, to his knowledge, the last child born on Holland Island—in November 1917. His parents moved off the following January, but he returned often as a boy to summer at his grandmother's house. The bay, it is apparent, is beginning to make its final meal on the island now. There are wash-throughs to the Tangier Sound side in two places; the whole northern end is gone. Of a few thousand acres, maybe 150 acres remain. I.T. points to where the Bayshore Ridge ran: "about a quarter mile out there," he says, pointing to the bay.

The forces that caused this have, if anything, accelerated. Sea levels have risen globally since the last Ice Age waned; but in the last century the rate of that rise has increased sharply, to about seven hundredths of an inch a year. And in the Chesapeake, the rate has jumped even more dramatically—sea level rising twice as fast as globally; and as it does, the pace of shore erosion picks up, too. Subsidence of land around the bay's edges accounts for the extraordinary Chesapeake rise, though its causes are still mysterious.

What is certain is that if the trend continues for another century, many of the bay's islands and low-lying mainland communities will experience, at the least, severe flooding, and turn from upland to marsh. As for Smith Island, by the year 2100, it will be gone—perhaps a few marsh tumps still sticking up, and mudflats exposed on low tides. Long before that, its people likely will have followed the Holland Islanders into history.

The main graveyard on Holland is what I.T. wants to see—it may be his last time, he thinks. Soft, lush grass laps insistently at the base of the marble stones—no doubt about which will prevail; the grass is *Spartina patens,* a sure indicator that periodic inundation already is occurring. Many stones are those of infants who didn't make it. One catches my daughter, Abigail's, eye: *"God needed one more angel child"* inscribes the grave of Carol Parks, eleven, the same age as Abby. Two others mark little children belonging to a woman known as Missouri Parks. I.T. finds Missouri's grave, elaborately inscribed:

> We miss her, yes, constantly miss her
> We think we can now hear her cry.
> Come up here my husband and children.
> The people here nevermore die.

She was related on his mother's side, he says. "If I'd had a girl, I was going to name her Missouri—what a great name." And then I.T., who is seventy-six, grabs a corner of Missouri's 250-pound gravestone and begins tugging it loose from the encroaching marsh. With the rest of us staggering to hold up our share, sinking shin-deep with every step, we lug it a quarter of a mile back to the boat: "like the Marines coming out from Inchon, bringing the dead and wounded with them," I.T. says, laughing.

As we head back to Crisfield and slightly higher ground, the four of us and Missouri Parks, the swans silently swirl back out of the mist to reclaim the cove.

THE FOLLOWING JULY, our steel-hulled tour boat from Crisfield, carrying close to two hundred passengers, idles down a channel lined with shanties, where islanders tend to the soft crabs shedding in rows of shallow wooden tanks. We are soon joined by tour boats from Onancock on the Virginia Eastern Shore and Reedville on the western shore. The regular ferry from Crisfield pulls in, adding to a throng that soon fills the town's narrow main street. Overhead, small planes of a flying club from Washington—just down for a seafood lunch—begin descending to the runway along the bayside. Streetside stands and small gift shops hawk all the standard fare, from snow cones to T-shirts and coffee mugs. Half the homes on the main drag, it seems, advertise they sell soft crabs; a good-sized business is done packing softies for fly-in customers—gourmets and small entrepreneurs from the metropolitan areas. Most islanders not directly involved in sales seem to vanish inside their homes or out to their shanties until the press of visitors subsides in late afternoon. Many homes sell local recipes on an "honor system"—recipes in plastic ziplock baggies hang from fences. You detach whatever appeals—instructions for crab salad, for brownies, or coleslaw—and put your quarter in a can. If you tire of walking, there are bike rentals and small taxi-carts that will whisk you on a generally uninspired, twelve-minute guided tour for just a couple dollars. A travel writer recently concluded his mostly favorable piece on the island this way:

> . . . islanders have made a Faustian bargain with the outside world. As the sea provides, so too, do the tour boats. Clinging to the old ways, they efficiently process thousands of visitors whose seasonal presence inevitably erodes those old ways.

With the possible exception of Holland Island in its glory, no place more resembles Smith Island than here. Tangier Island, Virginia, lies about the same distance south of Smith as Holland is north of it. Both Smith and Tangier were settled some three centuries ago by folk originally from the southwest of England. They are the only two inhabited offshore islands in Chesapeake Bay, both dependent on harvesting their seafood. Both are tight-knit, highly religious, hardworking, Protestant communities. Both are low-lying and threatened by erosion, just as Holland.

But some vital differences pertain. Tangier faces the twenty-first century with an optimism not evident on Smith. The Virginia island bustles with life. Its stores are larger and better-stocked, its population is stable at around 725 people. A house for sale or rent is a rarity. The situation on Smith reflects a year-round population that has dropped in the last half century from more than 800 to 424 by the preacher's latest head count. The job of choice for its younger watermen nowadays seems to be guarding at the new prison on the adjacent mainland. The rarity there is the birth of a new baby.

Some reasons for the difference include Tangier's tourism income, which is greater than Smith's; and its airport enables some islanders to remain there and maintain good off-island jobs like captaining tugs. Winter incomes have held up better on the Virginia island than on Smith. Its men have historically turned in December to a lucrative dredge fishery for crabs in the mouth of the Chesapeake, while Smith's, like all Maryland watermen, have been dependent on the dwindling oyster fishery. The Virginia part of the bay as a whole is bigger, wilder water than Maryland's half; and Tangiermen seem to have bigger, better boats and are perhaps more aggressive, wide-ranging harvesters, on average, than the Smith Islanders.

Tangier kids never have to leave the island for their schooling, as Smith's must by their junior high years. Most fundamental is the difference in geography. The scarce, high ground on Tangier is more concentrated, and has been a centralizing force, perhaps the reason the island has long had elected local government, a single school, sewage treatment plant, public wharf, and other unified facilities. On Smith, by contrast, the high ground is so distributed as to divide the island into three communities, which increasingly seem ineffective for dealing with modern life, even as they lend a distinctive charm and character to the place.

The differences were never more clear than in how the two islands have faced crises of erosion. Tangier erected a permanent, 4,000-foot seawall at a cost of nearly $4 million. The island community, to prove its interest, committed to raising $200,000 of that. During several years, islanders held bake sales and fundraisers ranging from all-night volleyball tournaments to sales of artists' prints of the island. They hawked T-shirts, wrote fund-raising letters to every former resident of the island. Donation cans for the seawall cause were placed everywhere tourists went. And local property taxes were doubled, with scarcely a grumble, for five years. This spurred Virginia's congressional delegation to push through special federal funding that declared Tangier a "national resource," by-passing normal Army Corps of Engineers standards for determining cost-benefit ratios of such projects. The rural mainland county of Accomack, which includes Tangier, also contributed another $200,000, though it is scarcely a wealthy jurisdiction.

Smith Island foundered for a decade longer, unable to put together an effective push for a bulwark against the waves. Neither the island nor its county of Somerset ever seemed to think a local share of the cost, projected at $250,000, was remotely possible. A partial solution finally was reached. The Army Corps laid down an experimental, sand-filled, cloth "geotube" off the bayside, and pumped sand around it to form a barrier at almost no cost to locals. It was rightly considered a great plus for the island, but it begged the broader question—whether Smith can muster what might be described as Tangier's "will to live."

For the wider public, in Maryland and elsewhere, it is also worth considering what value lies in extending the help that unique, living cultures like Smith Island—and even Tangier—may ultimately need to retain body and soul into the next century.

In strictest economic terms, there is minimal justification for extraordinary measures. With modern boats, crabs and oysters can be harvested as efficiently from the mainland—maybe even farmed there, if the Chesapeake region's fledgling aquaculture comes into its own. I will always prefer my bay seafood seasoned with the knowledge it was caught by free-roving watermen from salty little bayside communities; but I don't expect grocers can charge much extra for such an intellectual condiment, compared to pond-reared rockfish, oysters raised in tanks, and soft crabs from recirculating, factory-style shedding operations that could as well be located in West Virginia.

The island does have a worth beyond economics, and not simply in the mystique and nostalgia we harried moderns attach to any anachronistic lifestyle in our stressed-out midst. The islanders in an important sense are not throwbacks at all; rather, harbingers of our own future. They must live exclusively from a public commons, the Chesapeake Bay, whose resources are emphatically finite and already stretched to the limit as growing numbers of sport fishermen and recreational crabbers add their demands to the commercial harvesters'. In a word, they are forced in the here and now to live *sustainably*, largely unable to expand their incomes beyond natural limits.

Everywhere, people are beginning to realize that the planet itself is an island, that all of us, eventually, must act as if its resources, and capacity to absorb pollution, are finite, and learn how to live within our means. "Sustainability" is the buzzword—even becoming the watchword—of environmentalists and governments. We are all, in a sense, islanders. We just draw, as yet, from a bigger pool than the bay, and mask our overdrafts for a time with technology, or by flushing pollution off to "somewhere else."

For all that, Smith Island is inevitably a simplistic model for the planet. The island's truest value to society may be more as a lily of the field, which at first seems an ironic symbol for such a no-nonsense and hardworking place. But consider: in purely botanical terms, one can think of the natural vegetation in a place as the full and free expression of whatever soils, climate, and other environmental attributes conspire there. From desert yuccas to rainforest giants, from the sundews and pitcher plants of pocket bogs to the tiny, rare wildflowers of montane shale barrens, this is Nature poetizing in all her tongues, trilling all her notes, a phenomenon that fills whole books under the rubric of biodiversity, but might be better appreciated if we comprehended it as a symphony.

Too often we forget humans can be part of the song, can dance with the music as well as drown it out. I believe, as Lawrence Durrell once wrote of France, that if you were to wipe it bare of life and start over again, in due course, Nature there would give you, once again, essential Frenchmen, surely as she would a good Bordeaux. Just so Smith Island, where the spirits of place are strong indeed. The islanders and their culture and heritage are as much an expression of marsh and water, of isolation and Chesapeake Bay, as are soft crabs and spartina grass.

The bay never essayed truer, nor flowered more gloriously, than in its creation of Smith Island and Smith Islanders. Far more than any Mariners Museum, or Mystic Seaport or Williamsburg, places like the island are art—made all the more artful for contriving nothing, for simply *being*.

Time and again I have felt this essential power of the island, have seen it deeply affect visitors and the youth in my education classes. Sometimes it casts its spell while you are floating through moonlit marshes on the breast of the tide; other times it comes amid the humble eloquence of testimony in the little island churches. It flows from the landscape, from the kind, gentle spirit of the people—almost as if the island were reaching out . . . for what?

What is our obligation to keep such places intact? We are more practiced at building Disney Worlds and historical exhibits to capitalize on or commemorate them. Living cultures are messier, even unappreciative of our efforts to help sometimes. At a minimum, we must continue to build aggressively on the real but incomplete progress begun in restoring the Chesapeake ecosystem to health and abundance. And we ought to acknowledge that the charm and wonder of the island, to us, is that it is *different*—and agree to treat it differently, make it a sort of estuarine enterprise zone, where tax credits and more flexible rules apply to those willing to make a go of it. Perhaps even some concepts of Native American rights might be applied—limited, exclusive franchises to fish and hunt and trap come to mind. Tourism, compatible with the island's character, should be encouraged in ways that most benefit all residents. As for predictions that the whole affair will be covered by the rising bay in a century or less, I think we must do as the islanders do when faced with dire scientific projections: trust in God and keep on crabbing. It would not hurt a bit, either, to support a global cap on the fossil-fuel combustion that is exacerbating planetary warming and sea-level rise.

None of this—no comeback of oysters or influx of tourists, no mighty seawall—will work if the outside world continues to beckon to young islanders. Perhaps it is our fate that we, wanting them to remain, to feed lacks in our own lives, will end up waving as they cross to the mainland, "craving the world," as they say, passing our tour boats on the way to Smith.

EPILOGUE

*I*T HAS BEEN a few years now since I moved off. In the darkness, unnoticed, I board the Friday night special run to the island. It is something new the captain is trying to accommodate weekend homeowners and renters who cannot make it down from the cities in time for the regular 5:00 P.M. run. In the cabin a few island women, back from shopping, chat. The engine obscures the words, so the rhythms and soft brogue of the dialect come through—pure balm to my ears, bespeaking home. Listening closer, I hear one talking about how a young man who went to college and moved off has invested in building a new store in Tylerton. It is a risky investment, but he just feels the need to put something back, the speaker says. The young man has speculated about foster care as a potential island industry—so much love for children is just going to waste out there now. Maybe things are looking up. The men say oysters were better this winter, the best in ten years. My, yes, but the men say crabbing's going terrible. Isn't that always the way?

The ferry has entered the island's dark, winding channels now. A couple tourists at the stern rail murmur appreciation at the beauty of the tiny towns, sparkling on the black of the marsh. But could you imagine anyone having to spend their whole life out here? one says.

It makes me think of something Janice Marshall once said:

✦ They look in at us from the outside, and all they can see is how confinin' it must be.

But look out at these sunset skies and that old bay stretchin' away; why, some days there don't seem any limits at all. ✦

Rise and Decline of Smith Island:
A Brief History and Demography

Responses of Smith Island children, asked to state "their dream" in the Tylerton Times *school newsletter, January 1992:*

> That someday, people will move to Tylerton, instead of moving away—*Jacqueline*

> One day, a big seafood company will come to our island, so there will be lots of jobs and people will make money without leaving—*Maria*

> My community will grow. . . . It would mean there would ALWAYS be Junior League in church and a Tylerton Elementary School—*Adam*

IT IS EMBLAZONED here on a state historical marker, without much basis, that the island was first populated in 1657 by a band of "dissenters" from the bay's western shore. It is also commonly stated, again with no proof, that the island was named by and for Captain John Smith, the English explorer and leader of the Jamestown Colony, who mapped the Chesapeake with remarkable accuracy during 1607–08.

There is a Smith Island named for the captain, but it lies off Virginia's ocean coast, just above the entrance to the Chesapeake. Throughout most of the seventeenth century, the island that is the subject of this book, and several others along the bay's eastern edge, were lumped together as the Russell Isles, named by Captain Smith in honor of his ship's doctor, Walter Russell. Smith may have been feeling kindly toward the doctor, who at the time had nursed him back to health after a nasty wound from a stingray.

It seems doubtful anyone will ever know the details of the island's initial settlement—even Native Americans had no permanent villages here. What is documented is that between the 1650s and 1680s, there was considerable activity with the assignment and transfers of land patents on present-day Smith and surrounding bay islands.

By the end of this period, a Captain Henry Smith, a prominent settler living on the Eastern Shore mainland of Maryland, held title to nearly half of the island, which he probably used to pasture livestock. Smith never moved there, but by the 1680s at least two families, named Evans and Tyler, were established, according to county land records. A baby named Thomas Tyler in 1688 might have been the first child born on what by then was beginning to be called Smith's Island.

Population grew slowly, from perhaps a couple dozen families at the time of the American Revolution, to more than 300 residents at the time of the Civil War. It peaked at around 800 persons in the early twentieth century, and slipped to some 650 by the 1960s; then to a present-day count of not much more than 400 year-round residents.

In 1980, the Chesapeake Bay Foundation, which had recently begun an education program in Tylerton, asked the late Eddie Marshall to compile statistics on the town. Here is his report, with subsequent updates.

POPULATION IN 1980		153	
Houses occupied most of the time		57	
Houses owned by outsiders		3	
Widows		14	
Widowers		2	

LAST NAMES			
Marshall	48	Tull	5
Bradshaw	26	Clayton	5
Tyler	18	Evans	5
Corbin	14	Schoffstall	3
Marsh	11	Bruce	3
Laird	7	Roach	1
Smith	7		

POPULATION IN 1987	124 (−19%)
Houses occupied most of the time	55
Houses owned by outsiders	5
Widows	14
Widowers	0
Deaths, 1980–87	10
Births, 1980–87	10
People moved here, 1980–87	6
People moved off, 1980–87	35

POPULATION IN 1994	90 (−27%)
Houses occupied most of the time	43
Houses owned by outsiders (+200%)	15
Widows	12
Widowers	0
Deaths, 1987–94	11
Births, 1987–94	2
People moved here, 1987–94	4
People moved off, 1987–94	29

During the period 1980–94, population declined 41 percent.